# HANDS OF LIGHT

# HANDS OF LIGHT

## A GUIDE TO HEALING
## THROUGH THE
## HUMAN ENERGY FIELD

by
**Barbara Ann Brennan**

**A New Paradigm for the Human Being in Health,
Relationship, and Disease**

PLEIADES BOOKS
New York

PLEASE NOTE THAT *HANDS OF LIGHT* IS DOCUMENTARY AND REFLECTS THE PERSONAL EXPERIENCE OF THE AUTHOR. THE BOOK IS NOT TO BE INTERPRETED AS AN INDEPENDENT GUIDE FOR SELF-HEALING. IF YOU INTEND TO FOLLOW ANY OF THE EXERCISES OR SUGGESTIONS OF THE BOOK, DO SO ONLY UNDER THE SUPERVISION OF A MEDICAL DOCTOR OR OTHER HEALTH CARE PROFESSIONAL.

ISBN: 0-9617646-0-0

Library of Congress Catalog No: 86-063133

Manufactured in the United States of America

Editorial and production services by Martin Cook Associates, New York.

This book is dedicated to all travels on the path homeward.

Love is the face and body of the Universe. It is the connective tissue of the universe, the stuff of which we are made. Love is the experience of being whole and connected to Universal Divinity.

All suffering is caused by the illusion of separateness, which generates fear and self-hatred, which eventually causes illness.

You are the master of your life. You can do much more than you thought you could, including cure yourself of a "terminal illness."

The only real "terminal illness" is simply being human. And being human is not "terminal" at all, because death is simply transition to another level of being.

I want to encourage you to step out of the normal "bounds" of your life and to begin seeing yourself differently. I want to encourage you to live your life at the cutting edge of time, allowing yourself to be born into a new life every minute.

I want to encourage you to allow your life experience to be lightly dusted with form.

# CONTENTS

## Part IV
# THE PERCEPTUAL TOOLS OF THE HEALER

## Part V
# SPIRITUAL HEALING

## Part VI
# SELF HEALING AND THE SPIRITUAL HEALER

# Illustrations

# List of Exercises to:

# FOREWORD

This is a new era and to paraphrase Shakespeare, "There are more things twixt Heaven and Earth unknown to man." This book addresses those who are looking for self-understanding of their physical and emotional processes beyond the framework of classic medicine. It is focused on the art of healing through physical and metaphysical methods. It opens up new dimensions for understanding the concepts of psychosomatic identity first presented to us by Wilhelm Reich, Walter Canon, Franz Alexander, Flanders Dunbar, Burr and Northrup, and many other investigators in the field of psychosomatics.

The contents deal with defining healing experiences and the history of scientific investigations of the human energy field and aura. The book is unique in connecting psychodynamics to the human energy field. It describes the variations of the energy field as it relates to personality functions.

The latter part of the book defines the causes of illness and these are based on metaphysical concepts which are then connected to the energy disturbances of the aura. The reader will, also, find here a description of the nature of spiritual healing as it relates to the healer and the subject.

The book is written from the subjective experiences of the author, who was scientifically trained as a physicist and as a psychotherapist. The combination of objective knowledge and subjective experiences forms a unique method of expanding the consciousness beyond the confines of objective knowledge.

For those who are open to such an approach, the book has extremely rich material from which to learn, to experience and with which to experiment. To those who have major objections, I would recommend opening their minds to the question, "Is there a possibility of the existence of this new perspective which goes beyond logic and objective scientific experimentation?"

I recommend this book very highly to those who are excited about the phenomenon of life on the physical and metaphysical levels. It is the work of many years of devoted effort and represents the evolution of the personality of the author and the development of her special gifts of healing. The reader will be entering a fascinating domain, full of wonders.

Ms. Brennan is to be commended for her courage in bringing her subjective and objective experiences to the world.

John Pierrakos, Md.
Institute of CORE Energetics
New York City

# ACKNOWLEDGMENTS

I wish to thank my teachers who are many, so I will list them in the order in which I studied with them. First there was Dr. Jim Cox and Ms. Ann Bowman, who trained me in bioenergetic bodywork along with many others. I spent many years training and working with Dr. John Pierrakos, whose work in Core Energetics built the foundation for my healing work that followed. He had a great influence on me in training me to connect the auric phenomena I was witnessing to the psycho-dynamic bodywork. Thank you, John. I am forever grateful to Ms. Eva Pierrakos, who initiated the particular spiritual path I practice, called the Pathwork. I wish also to thank my healing teachers the Rev. C.B., and the Rev. Rosalyn Bruyere. I would also like to thank all my students who, by coming to me to learn, have been my greatest teachers.

In the production of the book itself, I thank all those who helped with the manuscript, and particularly Ms. Marjorie Bair for her editorial comments; Dr. Jac Conaway for use of his computer and Maria Adeshian for typing. I would like to thank Bruce Austin for final word processing. I am deeply grateful to Ms. Marilee Talman for her invaluable help in text editing and guiding the entire production process of this book. I am grateful for the constant personal support given to me by Mr. Eli Wilner, my daughter Miss Celia Conaway, and my dear friend Ms. Moira Shaw, who, when I most needed it, would remind me of my value.

And most of all, I wish to thank my dear spiritual teachers who have guided me every step of the way and who have delivered most of the truth that lies in this book through me.

# ABOUT THE AUTHOR

Barbara Brennan is a practicing healer, psychotherapist and scientist. She was a research scientist for NASA at the Goddard Space Flight Center following the completion of her M.S. in Atmospheric Physics from the University of Wisconsin. For the past fifteen years she has been studying and working with the human energy field and has been involved in research projects with Drexel University and the Institute for the New Age. She was trained in Bioenergetic Therapy at the Institute for Psychophysical Synthesis, Community of the Whole Person, and in Core Energetics at the Institute for the New Age. She has studied with both American and Native American healers.

Barbara is currently teaching courses and giving workshops on the Human Energy Field, Healing and Channelling. She has given workshops in many areas of the United States, Canada and Europe. She conducts a private practice in New York City and East Hampton, New York. Barbara is a member of the Pathwork Community, Phoenicia, New York.

# ABOUT THE ARTIST

Joseph A. Smith has contributed illustrations to *Time*, *Newsweek* and *Harper's*. He illustrated the book *Witches* written by Erica Jong. A painter and sculptor, he is Professor of Fine Arts at Pratt Institute in New York.

# PART I

# LIVING ON A PLANET OF ENERGY

"I maintain that cosmic religious feeling is the strongest
and noblest incitement to scientific research."

Albert Einstein

# Chapter 1

# THE HEALING EXPERIENCE

During my years of practice as a healer, I have had the privilege of working with many delightful people. Here are a few of them, and their stories, who make the day in the life of a healer so fulfilling.

My first client on a day in October 1984 was a woman in her late twenties named Jenny. Jenny is a vivacious school teacher about 5'5" tall, with large blue eyes and dark hair. She is known to her friends as the lavender lady because she loves and wears lavender all the time. Jenny also has a part-time flower business and makes exquisite floral arrangements for weddings and other festive occasions. At that time, she had been married for several years to a successful advertising man. Jenny had had a miscarriage several months earlier and had not been able to get pregnant again. When Jenny went to her physician to see why she was unable to conceive, she received some bad news. After many tests and opinions from several other physicians, it was agreed that she should have a hysterectomy as soon as possible. There were abnormal cells in her uterus where the placenta had been attached. Jenny was frightened and distraught. She and her husband had waited to start their family until they were more financially sound. Now, there appeared to be no chance of that.

The first time Jenny came to me, in August of that year, she didn't tell me any of her medical history. She just said, "I need your help. Tell me what you see in my body. I need to make an important decision."

During the healing session, I scanned her energy field, or aura, using my "High Sense Perception" (HSP). I "saw" some abnormal cells inside the uterus on the lower left side. At the same time, I "saw" the circumstances around the miscarriage. The abnormal cells were located where the placenta had been attached. I also "heard" words that described Jenny's condition and what to do about it. What I heard was that Jenny needed to take a month off, go to the ocean, take specific vitamins, stay on a specific diet and meditate daily, spending at least two hours a day alone. Then after spending the month healing herself, she should return to the normal medical world and be tested again. I was told that the healing was completed and that she didn't need to return to me. During the healing I received information about her psychological attitude and how that was affecting her inability to heal herself. She blamed herself for the miscarriage. As a result, she was placing undue stress upon herself and was preventing her body from healing itself after the miscarriage. I was told (and this is the hard part for me) that she should not go to another physician for at least a month because the different diagnoses and pressures to have a hysterectomy were adding greatly to the stress. Her heart was breaking because she wanted a child so badly. She was somewhat relieved when she left my office and said she would think about everything that had happened in the healing session.

In October, when Jenny came again, the first thing she did was to give me a big hug and a sweet little poem thanking me. Her medical tests were normal. She had spent August taking care of friends' children on Fire Island. She kept to her diet, took her vitamins and spent a good deal of time alone practicing self-healing. She decided to wait a few more months and then try to get pregnant again. A year later I heard that Jenny gave birth to a healthy baby boy.

My second client that October day was Howard. He is the father of Mary, whom I treated some time ago. Mary had had a class-three Pap smear (precancerous condition) that cleared up in about six healings. She has had normal Pap smears for several years now. Mary, a nurse herself, founded and directs a nursing organization that gives updates of skills training to nurses and also supplies nurses to hospitals in the Philadelphia area. She became interested in my work and regularly refers clients to me.

Howard had been seeing me for several months. He was a blue-collar worker but had retired. He is a delightful person to work with. When he first came to me, he was gray and had constant heart pain. He had difficulty even walking across a room without getting tired. After the first healing, his complexion was rosy, and the pain went away. After two months of weekly healings, he was dancing again. Mary and I have worked together to combine healing by laying on of hands with herbal medications prescribed by a Naturopathic Physician to clear his arteries of plaque. On that day I continued to balance and strengthen his field. His improvement was obvious to his physicians and his friends.

Another client I saw that day was Ed. He first came to me because he had wrist problems. The joints in his arms and wrist were getting weaker and weaker. He also had pain when he had orgasm during intercourse. He had had a weak back for some time, and now the weakness had progressed so much that he could not carry anything, not even a few dishes. In the first healing I gave him, I "saw" from his auric field that his coccyx (tailbone) had been injured when he was about 12. At the time of the injury, he had a great deal of trouble dealing with the burgeoning sexual feelings he experienced at puberty. The accident diminished these, and he was better able to cope.

His coccyx was jammed to the left and could not move in its normal way to assist in pumping the cerebral spinal fluid through its normal pathway. This caused a great imbalance and debility in his whole energy system. The next step in this degenerating process was a weakening of the lower back, then the middle and then the upper back. Each time he would weaken from lack of energy flow in one part of his body, another part would try to compensate for this weakness. He started carrying a lot of tension in the joints of his arms, and finally they gave way and became weak. This entire weakening process took years.

Ed and I had a successful healing process over several months' time. First we worked with energy flow to unjam the coccyx, realign it, and then increase and balance the energy flow through his system. Little by little all his strength had come back. That afternoon the only symptom he had left was a little weakness in his left wrist. But before I attended to that, I again balanced and strengthened his whole energy field. Then I spent extra time allowing healing energy to flow into his wrist.

The last client I saw that day was Muriel, an artist and the wife of a well-known surgeon. This was her third appointment with me. Three weeks earlier she had appeared in my office with a greatly enlarged thyroid. In that first appointment, I again used my High Sense Perception (HSP) to gather information about Muriel's condition. I could see that the enlarged thyroid was not due to cancer and that with just two healings combined with the medication her doctors had prescribed for her, the enlargement would disappear. I saw that no surgery would be needed. She confirmed that she had already been to several physicians, who had given her medication to shrink the thyroid. They said the medication would reduce it some, but she would still need surgery, and that there was a chance it was cancer. Surgery was scheduled the week after our second appointment. I gave her the two healings a week apart. By the time she got to surgery, there was no need for the operation; the physicians were very surprised. She came back that day to make sure everything was restored to normal health. It was.

How do these seemingly miraculous events take place? What am I doing to help these people? The process I use is called *laying-on of hands, faith healing* or *spiritual healing*. It is not at all a mysterious process, but very straightforward, although many times very complicated. It is a procedure that involves rebalancing the energy field, which I call the Human Energy Field that exists around each of us. Everyone has an energy field or aura that surrounds and interpenetrates the physical body. This energy field is intimately associated with health. *High Sense Perception* is a way of perceiving things beyond the normal ranges of human senses. With it one can see, hear, smell, taste and touch things that cannot normally be perceived. High Sense Perception is a type of "seeing" in which you perceive a picture in your mind without the use of your normal vision. It is not imagination. It is sometimes referred to as clairvoyance. HSP reveals the dynamic world of fluid interacting life energy fields around and through all things. For most of my life I have been in a dance with the living sea of energy in which we exist. Through this dance I have discovered that this energy supports us, nourishes us, gives us life. We sense each other with it; we are of it; it is of us.

My clients and students ask me when I first saw the energy field around people. When did I first realize that it was a useful tool? What is it like to have the ability to perceive things beyond the normal ranges of human senses? Is there something special about me, or is it something that can be learned? If so, what can they do to broaden their own perception ranges, and of what value is it to their lives? To answer these questions well I must go back to the beginning.

My childhood was a very simple one. I grew up on a farm in Wisconsin. Since there were not a lot of playmates in my area, I spent a great deal of time alone. I would spend hours in the woods alone, sitting perfectly still and waiting for small animals to come up to me. I practiced blending in with my surroundings. It was not until much later that I began to understand the

significance of those times of silence and waiting. In those quiet moments in the woods I entered into an expanded state of consciousness in which I was able to perceive things beyond the normal human ranges of experience. I remember knowing where each small animal was without looking. I could sense its state. When I practiced walking blindfolded in the woods, I would feel the trees long before I could touch them with my hands. I realized that the trees were larger than they appeared to the visible eye. Trees have life energy fields around them, and I was sensing those fields. Later I learned to see the energy fields of trees and the small animals. I discovered that everything has an energy field around it that looks somewhat like the light from a candle. I also began to notice that everything was connected by these energy fields, that no space existed without an energy field. Everything, including me, was living in a sea of energy.

This was not an exciting discovery to me. It was simply my experience, as natural as seeing a squirrel eating an acorn on the branch of a tree. I never formulated these experiences into any theories about how the world worked. I accepted it all as perfectly natural, assumed everyone knew it, and then I forgot about it.

As I grew into adolescence, I stopped going to the woods. I began being interested in how things worked and why things are the way they are. I would question everything in a quest to find order and to understand the way the world worked. I went to college, received a Master of Science degree in atmospheric physics, and then worked for NASA doing research for a number of years. Later I trained and became a counselor. It wasn't until I was counseling for a number of years and I began seeing colors around people's heads that I remembered my childhood experiences in the woods. I realized, then, that those experiences were the beginnings of my High Sense Perception, or clairvoyant vision. Those delightful and secret childhood experiences ultimately led me to the diagnosing and healing of the critically ill.

As I look back, I can see the pattern of development of my abilities starting from birth. It is as if my life has been guided by some unseen hand that brought me to and led me through each experience in a step-by-step fashion, very much like going through school—the school we call life.

The experience in the woods helped broaden my senses. Then my university training helped develop my logical thinking mind. My counseling training opened my eyes and heart toward humanity. Finally, my spiritual training (which I will discuss later) gave enough credibility to my unordinary experiences to open my mind to accepting them as "real." I then began to create a framework with which to understand these experiences. Slowly, High Sense Perception and the Human Energy Field became integral parts of my life.

I firmly believe they can become part of anyone's life. To develop HSP, it is necessary to enter into an expanded state of consciousness. There are many methods for doing this. Meditating is fast becoming the most well-known. Meditation can be practiced in many forms; it is important to find the form that best suits you. I will offer some suggested meditations, from which you may want to choose, later in this book. I have also found that you can enter an expanded state of consciousness by jogging, walking, fishing, sitting on a sand dune and watching the waves roll in, or sitting in the woods, as I did as a child. How are you already doing it, whether you call it meditation or reverie or something else? The most important thing here is to give yourself time to listen in to yourself—time to silence the noisy mind that constantly talks about what you need to do, how you could have won that argument, what you should have done, what is wrong with you, etc., etc. When that incessant babble is turned off, a whole new world of sweet harmonious reality opens up to you. You begin to blend in with your surroundings, as I did in the woods. At the same time your individuality is not lost, but enhanced.

The process of blending in with our surroundings is another way to describe experiencing expanded awareness. For example, consider the candle and its flame again. We normally identify ourselves as a body (the wax and wick) with consciousness (the flame). When we enter a state of expanded consciousness, we perceive ourselves also as the light coming from the flame. Where does the light begin and where does the flame end? There seems to be a line there but where exactly is it when you look more closely? The flame is completely penetrated by the light. Does the light in the room that is not from the candle (sea of energy) penetrate the flame? It does. Where does the light in the room begin and the light from the candle end? According to physics, there is no boundary to a candle's light; it reaches out to infinity. Where, then, is our ultimate boundary? My experience of HSP, resulting from an expanded consciousness, is that there is no boundary. The more I expand my consciousness, the more my HSP expands, the more I am able to see a reality that already is there but was earlier outside my perception range. As my HSP expands, more of reality comes into my view. At first I was able to see only the coarser energy fields around things: it reached only about an inch or so beyond the skin. As I became more proficient, I could see that the field reached further out from the skin but was apparently of a finer substance or less intense light. Each time I thought I had found the boundary, I would, at a later date, perceive beyond that line. Where is the line? I have concluded that it would be easier to say that there are only layers: the layer of the flame, then the flame's light, then the light of the room. Each line is harder to distinguish. The perception of each outer layer requires a more expanded state of consciousness and a more finely tuned HSP. As your state of consciousness expands, the light you previously saw as dim brightens and becomes more sharply defined.

As I slowly developed High Sense Perception over the years, I compiled my observations. Most of these observations took place during my 15 years as a counselor. Having originally been trained in physics, I was rather skeptical when I first started "seeing" the energy phenomena around people's bodies. But since the phenomena persisted, even if I closed my eyes to make it go away or moved around the room, I began to observe it more closely. And so my personal journey began, taking me into worlds that I didn't know existed before, completely changing the way I experience reality, people, the universe and my relationship to it.

I saw that the energy field is intimately associated with a person's health and well-being. If a person is unhealthy, it will show in his energy field as an unbalanced flow of energy and/or stagnated energy that has ceased to flow and appears as darkened colors. In contrast, a healthy person shows bright colors that flow easily in a balanced field. These colors and forms are very specific to each illness. HSP is extremely valuable in medicine and psychological counseling. Using HSP, I have become proficient in diagnosing both physical and psychological problems and in finding ways to resolve those problems.

*With HSP, the mechanism of psychosomatic illness lies right before your eyes.* HSP reveals how most diseases are initiated in the energy fields and are then, through time and living habits, transmitted to the body, becoming a serious illness. Many times the source or initiating cause of this process is associated with psychological or physical trauma, or a combination of the two. Since HSP reveals how a disease is initiated, it also reveals how to reverse the disease process.

In the process of learning to see the field, I also learned to interact with it consciously, as with anything else I can see. I could manipulate my own field to interact with another person's field. Soon I learned to rebalance an unhealthy energy field so the person might be returned to a state of health. Moreover, I found myself receiving information about the source of a client's illness. This information seemed to be coming from what appeared to be an intelligence higher than myself or what I normally considered to be myself. This process of receiving information in this way is popularly called *channelling*. Channelled information would come in the form of words, concepts or symbolic pictures that would enter into my mind when I was rebalancing the client's energy field. I would always be in an altered state of consciousness when doing this. I

became proficient in receiving information in a combination of ways using HSP (i.e., channelling or seeing). I would correlate what I received in either a symbolic picture in my mind, a concept or a direct verbal message with what I saw in the energy field. For example, in one case I heard directly, "She has cancer," and I saw a black spot in her energy field. The black spot correlated in size, shape and location with results from a CAT scan taken later. This combination of receiving information with HSP has become very efficient, and I have a very high accuracy in any particular description of a client's condition. I also receive information as to what self-help actions the client should take during the course of the healing process. This process usually entails a series of healing sessions that last over several weeks or months, depending on the seriousness of the disease. The healing process includes rebalancing the field, changing the living habits and dealing with the initiating trauma.

It is essential that we deal with the deeper meaning of our illnesses. We need to ask, what does this illness mean to me? What can I learn from this illness? Illness can be seen as simply a message from your body to you that says, *Wait a minute; something is wrong. You are not listening to your whole self; you are ignoring something very important to you. What is it?* The source of the illness needs to be searched for in this way, either on the psychological or feeling level, on the level of understanding or simply by a change in one's state of being, which may not be conscious. A return to health requires much more personal work and change than simply taking pills prescribed by a doctor. Without personal change you will eventually create another problem to lead you back to the source that caused the disease in the first place. I have found that the source is the key. To deal with the source usually requires a life change that ultimately leads to a personal life more connected to the core of one's being. It leads us to that deeper part of ourselves that is sometimes called the high self or the spark of divinity within.

# Chapter 2

# HOW TO USE THIS BOOK

This book is written primarily for those who are interested in self-understanding and self-revelation and the new healing method that is sweeping across this country, the healing art of laying-on of hands. The work presents an in-depth study of the human aura and its relationship to the healing process, both psychological and physical. It presents a comprehensive view of a way of life towards health and growth. It is written for health care professionals, therapists, clergy, and all those who consider themselves aspirants to better physical, psychological and spiritual health.

If you wish to learn self-healing, this book will be a challenge, for as outlined here, self-healing means self-transformation. Any illness, whether it be psychological or physical, will lead you on a journey of self-exploration and discovery that will completely change your life from the inside out. This book is a handbook for that journey, both in self-healing and in the healing of others.

For professional healers, in whatever discipline of the health care field they practice, it is a reference book to be used throughout the course of years. For the student, it serves as a textbook to be used in classes with or under the supervision of an experienced healer. There are questions at the end of each chapter. I suggest that the student of healing answer them without looking back at the text. This means studying the text and doing the exercises that are included in the text. These exercises focus not only on healing and seeing techniques, but also on self-healing and self-discipline. They are focused on balancing your life and silencing the mind to broaden your perceptions. This book is not a substitute for classes in healing. It should be used with a class or in preparation for classes in healing. Do not underestimate the amount of work it takes to become proficient in perceiving the energy fields and learning to work with them. You will need direct hands-on experience and verification of those experiences by a qualified teacher-healer. Perceiving the Human Energy Field (HEF) not only takes study and practice, but also requires personal growth. It takes internal changes that increase your sensitivity so that you can learn to differentiate between internal noise and subtle incoming information that can only be perceived by silencing the mind.

If, on the other hand, you have already begun to perceive beyond the normal sense perceptual ranges, this book can be used as verification of those experiences. Although each person's experience is unique, there are general common experiences people have when going through the process of broadening perceptions, or opening their channel, as it is often called. These verifications will serve to encourage you along your way. No, you are not going crazy. Others are also hearing noises from "nowhere" and seeing lights that aren't there. It is all part of the beginning of some very wonderful changes taking place in your life in a perhaps unusual but most natural way.

There is abundant evidence that many human beings today are expanding the usual five senses into super-sensory levels. Most people have High Sense Perceptions to some degree, without necessarily realizing it. Most can develop them much further with earnest dedication and study. It is possible that there is already a transformation in consciousness taking place and that more people are developing a new sense in which information is received on a different and possibly higher frequency. I did. So can you. This development in myself was a slow, very organic process that led me into new worlds and changed my personal reality almost entirely. I believe that this process of developing *High Sense Perception is a natural evolutionary step for the human race, leading us into the next stage of development* where, because of our newly gained abilities, we will have to be deeply honest with others. Our feelings and private realities will no longer be hidden from others. They already are automatically communicated through our energy fields. As everyone learns to perceive this information, we will see and understand each other much more clearly than we do now.

For example, you may already know when someone is very angry. That is easy. With HSP, you will be able to see a red haze around the angry person. To find out what is happening with her on a deeper level, it is possible to focus on the cause of the anger, not only in the present, but also on how it relates to childhood experience and to her relationship with her parents. Under the red haze will appear a gray, thick, fluid-like substance that conveys a heavy sadness. By focusing in on the essence of the gray substance, you will probably even be able to see the childhood scene that caused the deeply rooted pain. You will also see how that anger is harming the physical body. You will see that the person habitually reacts in anger to certain situations, when perhaps crying is a more useful emotion to release in order to bring the situation to a solution. Using HSP you will be able to find the words that will help that person let down, connect to the deeper reality, and help her find a solution. In another situation, however, you may see that expression of anger is exactly what is needed to heal the situation.

Once we have come to this experience, nothing is ever again the same. Our lives begin to change in ways we never expected. We understand the relationship between cause and effect; we see that our thoughts affect our energy fields, which in turn affect our bodies and our health. We then find we can redirect our lives and our health. We find that we create our own experience of reality through this field. The HEF is the medium through which our creations take place. It can then be the key to finding how we help create our reality and how we can change that reality if we so choose. It becomes the medium through which we find ways to reach inside to our deepest being. It becomes the bridge to our soul, to our inner private life, to that spark of the divine within each of us.

I want to encourage you to change your personal "model" of who you are, as I lead you through the world of High Sense Perception into the world of the Human Energy Field. You will see how your actions and belief systems affect and help create your reality for better and for worse. Once you see this, you realize you have the power to change the things you don't like and enhance the things you do like about your life. That takes a lot of courage, personal search, work and honesty. It is not an easy path, but it is unquestionably a worthwhile one. This book will help show you that path, not only through a new paradigm for your relationship to your health, but also for your relationship to your entire life and the universe you find yourself in. Give yourself some regular private time to experience this new relationship. Allow yourself to be the light of that candle that expands into the Universe.

I have divided the book up into sections that focus primarily on an area of information about the Human Energy Field (HEF) and its relationship to you. As you have been reading, this first section deals with the place of the auric field in your life. What does this phenomenon that has been described by mystics for so long have to do with you? Where does it fit in your life? Of what, if any, use is it? Case histories have shown how knowledge of this phenomenon can change the face of our reality. Jenny, for example, realized that she needed to take significant healing time for herself before she could bear children. Jenny took her health and her life into her own hands (where it always was anyway) and changed a possibly unpleasant future into the much happier one that she preferred. This kind of knowledge can lead us all into a better world; one of love born out of deep understanding; one of sisterhood and brotherhood where those considered enemies become friends because of that understanding.

Part II deals more specifically with the energy field phenomena. It describes the phenomena from the point of view of history, theoretical science and experimental science. After these are dealt with thoroughly, I then proceed to describe the HEF from my own view, which is a mixture of observation and theory combined with those conclusions of others found in the literature. From this information is developed a model of the HEF to use for both psychological work and spiritual healing work.

Part III presents my findings on the relationship between the HEF and psychodynamics. Even though you may not have been interested in psychotherapy or personal process in the past, you will find this section very enlightening in terms of self-discovery. It will help you understand not only what makes you tick, but also how you tick. This information is very useful to those who want to go beyond the normal bounds of psychology and body psychotherapy into broader views of us as human beings and of our energetic and spiritual reality. These chapters give specific frames of reference for integrating the Human Energy Field phenomena into practical psychodynamics. Drawings of HEF changes during the counseling process are presented. For those interested in self-discovery this chapter will introduce you to a new realm where the reality of your energy-field interactions in daily life will take on new and deeper meaning. After you read the book, you can find practical ways to make use of energy-field dynamics in your relationships with loved ones, children and friends. It will help you understand more of what is going on in the office in interactions with those you work with. Parts of

this section are very technical, and the general reader may want to skip some of the material (Chapters 11, 12, 13). You may want to go back when you have more specific questions about the functioning of the HEF.

Part IV of this book deals with the whole issue of increasing our perceptual ranges—what that means on a personal level, on the practical level and on a broader level in terms of changing the society we live in. I give clear explanations of the areas in which perceptions can be broadened, of the experience of that broadening in each area and how to do it. I also give a theoretical framework in which to place these experiences and the broad-scale implications for humankind as we as a group move into these changes. These changes not only affect us as individuals, but they change the entire fabric of human life as we know it.

Part V deals with the process of spiritual healing. I call it spiritual healing because it is always linked to our innate spiritual nature. This part presents healing experiences and techniques in relationship to the HEF. It contains drawings of the auric field changes during healings. It clearly delineates techniques of healing on the different layers of the HEF. It combines the information on broadened perceptions, given in Part IV, with healing, to enable the healer very effectively to initiate the healing process in self and others.

Because most of these techniques are not simple to learn, you will probably have to study them in a class. Written explanations of something this specialized serve to help the student to become familiar with the subject material but do not claim to teach the techniques. You must have personal instruction from someone who knows how to do this healing before you will become proficient in it. Verification of your experience by a qualified healer is very important. To become a professional healer takes a lot of training in didactic, practical, and personal work. Everyone who really wishes can become proficient in healing and channelling. You need to study and practice to develop your skills as in any other profession. I am sure that someday in the not too distant future there will be certified training programs in laying-on-of-hands healing and channelling. If you wish to become a professional healer now, you must find one and become an apprentice.

Part VI gives a detailed case study of the healing of David, in which the client takes an active role in his own healing. It shows how client becomes healer. Part VI then focuses on practical self-healing methods and suggests the next steps for those who want to practice healing, showing how to reestablish health and balance in your life, and how to maintain it. The personal developmental stages of becoming a healer are described, which then lead to the questions: What is health? Who is the healer?

*Chapter 3*

# A NOTE ON TRAINING AND THE DEVELOPMENT OF GUIDANCE

I believe it is very important for the healer to have a lot of technical training: counseling methods, anatomy, physiology, pathology, and massage technique, as well as some knowledge of acupuncture, homeopathy and nutritional and herbal cures. These other counseling methods are almost always combined with the laying-on of hands, either by the healer or other health care professionals who are working on the case. The healer must have some knowledge of these methods to understand how they dovetail to make a healing a whole one, and to be able to communicate with the other people involved in the case. Various other health care methods may be indicated through the channel of the healer. The healer will need to know anatomy and physiology to help interpret the information she is receiving. Above all, the healer should be able to work with other medical professionals to help a client heal herself.

My training included a normal B.S. in physics and an M.S. degree in atmospheric physics from a state university. I did research with weather satellite instrumentation for NASA for five years. I completed two years of training in bioenergetic counseling, one year in massage therapy, two years of anatomy/physiology, two years of specialization in altered states of consciousness, specifically in deep relaxation techniques, one year of homeopathy, three years of Core Energetic training, five years of Pathwork Helpership Training and several years studying

with various healers around the country both privately and in workshops. I also practiced working with people and their energy fields privately and in groups for more than 15 years. Since I was already a practicing counselor, the means by which people could see me for healing was set up. People just made appointments with me. More and more people requested healing rather than therapy, and the counseling practice slowly became a healing practice. I finally had to leave the psychological counseling work to others who focused on that, and I began to accept people only for healing.

During these years, I was also involved in various experiments to measure the Human Energy Field. Only after all of that did I feel qualified to practice healing in New York City and to begin to teach classes and workshops myself.

To become a healer is no easy task, just as it is no easy task to do anything well. One needs spiritual as well as technical training. One must go through self-initiated tests that challenge the weak parts of one's personality and develop one's creative focus, longing, and intent. The healer may experience these tests as coming from the outside, but in reality that is not true. The healer creates them to see if she/he is ready and able to handle the energy, power, and clarity that she/he is developing in her/his own energy system as she/he grows as a healer. This energy and power must be used with integrity, honesty and love, for cause and effect are always at work in every action. You always get back what you put out. That is what is called karma. As the energy flowing through you as a healer increases, so does your power. If you put any of this power to a negative use, you will eventually experience that same negativity coming back at you.

As my life unfolded, the unseen hand that led me became more and more perceptible. At first I vaguely sensed it. Then I began seeing spiritual beings, as if in a vision. Then I began to hear them talking to me and feel them touch me. I now accept that I have a guide. I can see, hear, and feel him. "He" says he is not male or female. "He" says that in his world there is no splitting along sexual lines and that beings at his level of existence are whole. "He" says that his name is Heyoan, which means, "The Wind Whispering Truth Through the Centuries." His introduction to me was slow and organic. The nature of our relationship grows daily, as I am guided to new levels of understanding. You will see it build as we go through this adventure together. At times, I simply call it metaphor.

Throughout this book, I will share with you some of the more obvious examples of guidance and its power. Here I want to show you its simplicity and the way it works.

The simplest kind of guidance comes every day, and many times a day in the form of discomfort. Heyoan says that if we just listened to this guidance and followed it we would rarely get sick. In other words, attending to the discomfort you feel puts you back into balance and therefore health. This discomfort can be in your body in physical form, like physical discomfort or pain; it could be on any level of your being—emotional, mental, or spiritual. It could be in any area of your life.

*Heyoan asks, "Where is the discomfort in your body/life? How long have you known about it? What is it saying to you? What have you done about it?"*

If you answer those questions honestly, you will find how much you disregard the best tool you have to keep yourself healthy, happy and wise. Any discomfort anywhere in your body/life is a direct message to you about how you are out of alignment with your true self.

Following guidance on this simple level means to rest when you are tired, to eat when you are hungry, and to eat what your body needs when it needs it. It means to take care of or change a life circumstance that bothers you. How well have you been able to structure your life so that you can do these things? Not so easy, is it?

As you become more attentive to your personal needs by listening to internal messages that come to you in the form of discomfort, you will become more balanced and clear. This will bring more health to you. The practice of listening-in will also bring on the phenomena of direct or verbal guidance. You may start receiving very simple verbal directives from an "inner" voice—a voice that you hear inside yourself, but that you recognize as coming from beyond yourself. There are two important points about learning to follow guidance. The first is that you will need to practice receiving guidance for yourself before you are qualified to receive it for others. The second is that the information or directives that you get may be very simple and seem totally unimportant at first. In fact, it may seem like a complete waste of time to follow any of it. I have come to realize that there is a reason for this. Later, when channelling important information about another person's life or specific information about illness, a professional channeller will get information that doesn't make any sense or seems irrelevant or just plain wrong. It may be, but most of the time this is the rational mind at work. The information coming through a clear channel is often beyond what the rational mind of the channeller can understand. It is at those times when the channeller will need a lot of past experience to remember all the other times the information didn't make sense when it came through, yet later the information turned out to be very helpful and understandable when all the information was in. I find now that during the hour spent healing and channelling I will receive information in a nonlinear way that slowly over the hour creates an understandable picture that gives more information than was possible in just a rational or linear mode.

If you look, you will begin to recognize guidance throughout the greater patterns of your life. Why has one event followed another? What have you used from each? It is no accident that I was first trained as a physicist, then a counselor, and then became a healer. All this training has prepared me for my life's work. The training in physics gave me a background structure with which to examine the aura. The counseling training gave me the background to understand the psychodynamics related to energy flow in the auric field, and also gave me an opportunity to observe the auric fields of many people. I would not have been able to bring this material together without those trainings. I certainly wasn't aware of training to be a healer when I was at NASA. I had never heard of such a thing, nor was I interested in illness. What I was interested in was the way the world worked, what made it tick. I looked everywhere for answers. This thirst for understanding has been one of the most powerful agents guiding me throughout my life. What is your thirst? What is your longing? Whatever it is, it will carry you to what you need to do next to accomplish your work, even if you don't know what that work is yet. When a thing is easily presented to you, and it sounds wonderful to do and a great deal of fun, by all means do it. That is guidance. Let yourself flow free with the dance of your life. If you don't, you block guidance and your progress. There are times when my guidance is more obvious than other times. One particular time was so beautiful and profound that it has carried me through many a rough time since. At that point I was a counselor in Washington, D.C. During the sessions I was giving people, I began to see what might be termed *past lives*. I would see the individual I was working with in a completely different setting in a different time frame. Whatever the scene was, it was relevant in some way to what was going on in the person's life. For example, a woman who was afraid of the water had drowned in another lifetime. She also had difficulty in asking for help in this lifetime. In the lifetime when she drowned, nobody could hear her screams for help when she fell off a boat. This personality difficulty interfered with

her life now more than the fear of the water. However, I didn't know how to handle all this information properly. I began praying for guidance. I needed to find a reliable person, or group of people, who could handle this information in a professional way.

The answer came one evening when I was camping on the beach at Assateague Island, Maryland. It was a rainy night, so I had a translucent plastic tarp over my head and sleeping bag. In the middle of the night I heard someone calling my name and woke up. The voice was very clear. "No one is there," I thought, as I gazed at the overcast sky. Then suddenly, I realized that I was looking at the plastic tarp over my head. With a great sweep of my arm, I pushed it off and fell back in utter awe at the outstretched stars twinkling above me. I heard celestial music singing across the heavens from star to star. I took that experience as an answer to my prayers. Shortly after, I found the Phoenicia Pathwork Center, where I moved and got the training I needed to interpret past life and other super-sensory material over the next nine years of my life.

When it was time for me to have a counseling practice in New York City, I knew it, because the internal pull to do so was so strong. Office space was readily available, and I wanted a change in my life, so I consulted my guidance through writing. I received a clear yes, and I went ahead. I was guided slowly to turn that counseling practice into one of healing. It happened "automatically," as stated before, when people started coming to me and asking for healing. Then I received direct verbal guidance to stop that practice and focus on teaching and on writing this book to reach a larger audience. Following these changes is not so easy. Each new change challenges me. It seems that each time I have a "secure" life established, it is time to change—and therefore to grow. What is next, I really do not know, but I do know that I will be guided each step of the way.

There is within every human personality a child. Everyone can remember how it was to be a child, to feel the inner freedom of a child and to experience life in a simple way. This inner child is very wise. It feels connected to all life. It knows love without question. This inner child gets covered as we become adults and try to live by our rational minds only. This limits us. It is this inner child that must be uncovered to begin to follow guidance. You must return to the loving, trusting wisdom of your inner child to develop the ability to receive and follow guidance. We all long for freedom—it is through the child that it will be gained. After allowing this inner child of yours more freedom, you can then begin a dialogue between the adult and the child parts of your personality. The dialogue will integrate the free and loving part of your personality with the sophisticated adult.

Scattered throughout this book you will hear the child and the healer/counselor/physicist speaking. It will help loosen your fixed reality and broaden your experience. This dialogue is a doorway into wonder. Find it in yourself and nurture it.

We are all guided by spiritual teachers who speak to us in our dreams, through our intuition, and eventually, if we listen, they speak to us directly, perhaps through writing at first, then through sound, voice or concepts. These teachers are full of love and respect for us. At some point along the way, you, too, may be able to see them or directly communicate with them as I do. This will change your life, for you will find that you are fully and completely loved, as you are right now in this moment. You are deserving and worthy of this love. You deserve

health, happiness and fulfillment in your life. You can create it. You can learn, step by step, the process to change your life and make it full. There are many paths to this fullness. Ask for guidance as to where you need to go, or which path you need to follow now, and you will be guided. Whether you have a life-threatening illness, a marital difficulty, a problem of the will, depression—or whether you are struggling with difficult situations in your chosen area of work—you can start changing now, right in this moment. You can realign yourself with your deepest longing and the greatest good you have to offer yourself and others. Simply ask for help. Your requests will be answered.

## Chapter 3 Review

1. What kind of technical training does a healer need? And why?
2. What is the simplest form of guidance in your life?

### Food For Thought

3. What are some of the more profound experiences of guidance in your life, and what effect did they have on your life?
4. How well are you able to follow your guidance?
5. Do you consciously listen for or ask for guidance for yourself? How often?

# PART II

# THE HUMAN AURA

"Miracles do not happen in contradiction to nature,
but only in contradiction to that which is known
to us in nature."

St. Augustine

*Introduction*

# THE PERSONAL EXPERIENCE

As we allow ourselves to develop new sensitivities, we begin to see the whole world quite differently. We begin to pay more attention to aspects of experience that might have seemed peripheral before. We find ourselves using new language to communicate our new experiences. Terms like "bad vibes" or "the energy there was great" are becoming household phrases. We start noticing and giving more credence to experiences like meeting someone and instantly liking or disliking him without knowing anything about him. We like his "vibes." We can tell when someone is staring at us, and we look up to see who it is. We may have a feeling that something is going to happen, and then it does. We begin to listen to our intuition. We "know" things, but we don't always know how we know. We sense that a friend is feeling a certain way, or needs something, and when we reach out to fulfill that need, we find we are right. Sometimes during an argument with someone we may feel as if something is being pulled out of our solar plexus, or we may feel "stabbed." We may feel as if we have been punched in the stomach. Or it may feel like someone is pouring thick, gooey molasses on us. On the other hand, we sometimes feel surrounded by love, caressed by it, bathed in a sea of sweetness, blessings and light. All these experiences have a reality in the energy fields. Our old world of solid concrete objects is surrounded by and permeated with a fluid world of radiating energy, constantly moving, constantly changing like the sea.

In my observations throughout the years, I have seen the counterparts of these experiences as forms within the human aura, which consists of the observable and measurable components of the energy field that surrounds and interpenetrates the body. When someone has been "shafted" by a lover, the shaft is literally visible to the clairvoyant. When you feel as if something is being pulled out of your solar plexus, it usually is. It can be seen by the clairvoyant. I can see it. So can you, eventually, if you follow your intuition and develop your senses.

It helps in the development of this Higher Sense Perception to consider what modern scientists have already learned about the world of dynamic energy fields. It helps us remove the blocks from our brains that keep us from seeing that we, too, are subject to all the universal laws. Modern science tells us that the human organism is not just a physical structure made of molecules, but that, like everything else, we are also composed of energy fields. We are moving out of the world of static solid form into a world of dynamic energy fields. We, too, ebb and flow like the sea. We, too, are constantly changing. How do we, as human beings, deal with such information? We adapt to it. If such reality exists, we want to experience it. And scientists are learning to measure these subtle changes. They are developing instruments to detect these energy fields related to our bodies and to measure their frequencies. They measure electrical currents from the heart with the electrocardiogram

(ECG). They measure electrical currents from the brain with the electroencephalogram (EEG). The lie detector measures the electropotential of the skin. They can now even measure electromagnetic fields around the body with a sensitive device called the SQUID (the superconducting quantum interference device). This device does not even touch the body when measuring the magnetic fields around it. Dr. Samuel Williamson of New York University states that the SQUID offers more information about the state of brain functioning than a normal EEG.

As medicine relies more and more upon these sophisticated instruments that measure impulses from the body, health and disease, even life itself, are slowly being redefined in terms of energy impulses and patterns. As early as 1939, Drs. H. Burr and F. Northrop at Yale University found that by measuring the energy field of a plant seed (which they termed the L, or Life-field), they could tell how healthy the plant grown from that seed would be. They found that by measuring the field of a frog's eggs, they could discern the future location of the frog's nervous system. Another such measurement pinpointed the time of ovulation in women, suggesting a new birth control method.

In 1959, Dr. Leonard Ravitz at William and Mary University showed that the Human Energy Field fluctuates with a person's mental and psychological stability. He suggested that there is a field associated with the thought processes. He suggested that variation of this thought field caused psychosomatic symptoms.

In 1979, another scientist, Dr. Robert Becker of Upstate Medical School, Syracuse, New York, mapped a complex electrical field on the body which is shaped like the body and the central nervous system. He named this field the Direct Current Control System and found that it changes shape and strength with physiological and psychological changes. He also found parti-

cles moving through this field that are the size of electrons.

Dr. Victor Inyushin at Kazakh University in Russia has done extensive research with the Human Energy Field since the 1950s. Using the results of these experiments, he suggests the existence of a "bioplasmic" energy field composed of ions, free protons and free electrons. Since this is a state distinct from the four known states of matter—solids, liquids, gases and plasma—Inyushin suggests that the bioplasmic energy field is a fifth state of matter. His observations showed the bioplasmic particles are constantly renewed by chemical processes in the cells and are in constant motion. There appears to be a balance of positive and negative particles within the bioplasma that is relatively stable. If there is a severe shift in this balance, the health of the organism is affected. In spite of the normal stability of the bioplasma, Inyushin has found that a significant amount of this energy is radiated into space. Clouds of bioplasmic particles, which have broken away from the organism, can be measured moving through the air.

Thus, we have been plunged into a world of life energy fields, thought fields and bioplasmic forms moving about and streaming off the body. We have become vibrating, radiating bioplasma itself! But if we look into the literature, this is not new. People have known about the phenomenon since the dawning of time. It is just that in our time the phenomenon is being rediscovered. It was either unknown or rejected by the western general public for a time, during which scientists concentrated on our knowledge of the physical world. As this knowledge has developed, and Newtonian physics given way to relativity, electromagnetic and particle theories, we are more and more able to see the connections between scientific objective descriptions of our world and the world of subjective human experience.

*Chapter 4*

# PARALLELS BETWEEN HOW WE SEE OURSELVES AND REALITY AND WESTERN SCIENTIFIC VIEWS

More than we want to admit, we are products of our western scientific heritage. How we learned to think and many of our self-definitions are based on the same scientific models used by physicists to describe the physical universe. This section gives a short history that shows the changes in how scientists describe the physical world, and how those descriptions correspond to the changes in our self-definitions.

It is important to remember that the way the western scientific method works is to find agreement between both mathematical and experimental proof. If the agreement is not found, then the physicist will look for another theory until there exists both mathematical and experimental proof for the explanation of a set of phenomena. This is what makes the western scientific method so powerful a tool for practical use and leads to great inventions like the use of electricity and the utilization of subatomic phenomena in medicine like x-rays, CAT scanners, and lasers.

As our knowledge progresses, there is always the discovery of new phenomena. Many times, these new phenomena cannot be described by the theories held when they are explained. New, broader theories, usually based on all the knowledge that has gone before, are postulated; new experiments are designed and performed until agreement between experimen-

tation and the new mathematical proof is found. The new theories are accepted as physical laws. The process of finding new ways to describe new phenomena is always one that broadens our views, challenging our current limited thinking about the nature of physical reality. We then incorporate the new ideas into our daily lives and begin seeing ourselves differently.

This whole section shows that the scientific view of reality supports the idea that we are composed of energy fields and, in fact, goes far beyond that into realms that we are just beginning to experience, that is, a holographic view of the universe. In this universe, all things are interconnected, corresponding to a holistic experience of reality. But first let us review some of our history.

## Newtonian Physics

Until recently, when the eastern religions began to have a greater impact upon our culture, much of our self-definition (largely unconscious) was based on the physics of a few hundred years ago. What I am referring to here is our insistence on seeing ourselves as solid objects. This definition of the universe, as made up of solid objects, was held largely by Isaac Newton and his colleagues in the late 17th and early 18th centuries. Newtonian physics was extended in the 19th century to describe a universe composed of fundamental building blocks called atoms. These Newtonian atoms were thought of as composed of solid objects—a nucleus of protons and neutrons, with electrons revolving around the nucleus much like the earth traveling around the sun.

Newtonian mechanics successfully described the motions of the planets, mechanical machines, and fluids in continuous motion. The enormous success of the mechanistic model made physicists of the early 19th century believe that the universe was indeed a huge mechanical system running according to the Newtonian laws of motion. These laws were seen as the basic laws of nature, and Newtonian mechanics was considered to be the ultimate theory of natural phenomena. These laws held firm the ideas of absolute time and space and of physical phenomena as strictly causal in nature. Everything could be described objectively. All physical reactions were seen to have a physical cause, like balls colliding on a pool table. Energy-matter interactions, such as a radio playing music in response to invisible radiowaves, were not yet known. Nor did it occur to anyone that the experimenter himself affects the experimental results not only in psychological experiments but also in physical ones as well, as physicists have now proven.

This view was very comforting and still is to those of us who prefer to see the world as solid and largely unchanging, with very clear, definite sets of rules that govern its functioning. Much of our daily lives still run on Newtonian mechanics. Except for the electrical systems, our homes are largely Newtonian. We experience our bodies in a mechanical way. We define most of our experience in terms of absolute, three dimensional space and linear time. We all have clocks. We need them to continue our lives as we have structured them—mostly linearly.

As we rush about our daily lives, in an effort to be "on time," it is easy to see ourselves as mechanical and to lose sight of the deeper human experience within. Ask anyone what the universe is made of, and he or she will most likely describe the Newtonian model of the atom (electrons spinning around a nucleus of protons and neutrons). However, if taken to its literal extension, this theory puts us in the rather disconcerting position of thinking of ourselves as being composed of itsy-bitsy Ping Pong balls whirling around each other.

## Field Theory

In the early 19th century, new physical phenomena were discovered that could not be described by Newtonian physics. The discovery and investigation of electromagnetic phenomena led to the concept of a field. A field was defined as a condition in space which has the potential of producing a force. The old Newtonian mechanics interpreted the interaction between positively and negatively charged particles like protons and electrons simply by saying that the two particles attract each other like two masses. However, Michael Faraday and James Clerk Maxwell found it more appropriate to use a field concept and say that each charge creates a "disturbance" or a "condition" in the space around it, so that the other charge, when it is present, feels a force. Thus, the concept of a universe filled with fields that create forces that interact with each other was born. Finally, there was a scientific framework with which we could begin to explain our ability to affect each other at a distance through means other than speech and sight. We all have had the experience of picking up the phone and knowing who it is before any words are spoken. Mothers often know when their children are in trouble, no matter where they are. This can be explained in terms of field theory.

In the last 15 to 20 years (100 years behind the physicists), most of us have just been beginning to use such concepts in describing our personal interactions. We are just beginning to admit that we ourselves are composed of fields. We sense another presence in the room without seeing or hearing them (field interaction); we speak of good or bad vibes, of sending energy to others or of reading each other's thoughts. We immediately know whether or not we like someone, whether we will get along with him or clash. This "knowing" can be explained by the harmony or disharmony in our field interactions.

## Relativity

In 1905, Albert Einstein published his Special Theory of Relativity and shattered all the principal concepts of the Newtonian world view. According to relativity theory, space is not three-dimensional, and time is not a separate entity. Both are intimately connected and form a four-dimensional continuum, "space-time." Thus, we can never talk about space without time, and vice versa. Furthermore, there is no universal flow of time; i.e. time is not linear, nor is it absolute. Time is relative. That is, two observers will order events differently in time if they move with different velocities relative to the observed events. Therefore, all measurements involving space and time lose their absolute significance. Both time and space become merely elements to describe phenomena.

According to Einstein's theory of relativity, in certain conditions two observers can even see two events in reverse time; i.e., for observer 1, event A will occur before event B, while for observer 2, event B will occur before event A.

Time and space are so basic to our descriptions of natural phenomena and ourselves that their modification entails a modification of the whole framework that we use to describe nature and ourselves. We have not yet integrated this part of Einstein's relativity into our personal lives. For example, when we get a psychic flash of a friend in trouble, say about to fall down the stairs, we check the time and call the person as soon as we can to see if she is all right. We also want to know if such a thing happened in order to validate our insight. We call, and she has had no such experience. We conclude that it was our imagination playing tricks on us, and we invalidate our experience. This is Newtonian thinking.

We must see that we are experiencing a phenomenon that cannot be explained by Newtonian mechanics, but we are using Newtonian mechanics to validate our super-sensory experience. In other words, what we saw was a real experience. Since time is not linear, it may have already occurred. It may occur at the time we see it, and it may occur in the future. It may even be a probable occurrence that never manifests itself. Just because it didn't happen at the time we tried to correlate it, by no means proves that our insight about the possibility was wrong. If, however, within our insight about our friend, we also saw a calendar and a clock with Newtonian time on it, our insight would be such as to include that information about the space-time continuum of the event. It would be easier to validate in Newtonian physical reality.

It is time to stop invalidating experience that lies outside our Newtonian way of thinking and broaden our framework of reality. We all have had experiences of time speeding up or of losing track of time. If we become proficient in observing our moods, we can see that our personal time varies with the mood we are in and with the experiences we are having. For example, we see that time is relative when we experience a very long, frightening period just before our car crashes or barely misses another, oncoming car. This time, measured by the clock, is a few seconds; however, to us, time appears to have slowed down. Experienced time is not measurable by a clock because a clock is a Newtonian device designed to measure the linear time defined by Newtonian mechanics.

Our experience exists outside the Newtonian system. Many times, we have experienced meeting someone after several years separation; it is as if we had just seen them yesterday. In regressional therapy, many people have experienced childhood events as if they were occurring in the present. We also find our memory has ordered events in a different sequence from someone else who has also experienced those events. (Try comparing childhood memories with your siblings.)

The Native American culture, which didn't have clocks to create linear time, divided time into two aspects: the now and all other time. The Australian aborigines also have two kinds of time: the passing time and the Great Time. What occurs in the Great Time has sequence, but it cannot be dated.

Lawrence Le Shan, from his experience testing clairvoyants, has defined two times: the regular linear time and Clairvoyant Time. Clairvoyant Time is the quality of time experienced by clairvoyants when they are using their gifts. It is similar to the Great Time. What occurs has sequence but can only be seen from the point of view of being or experiencing that sequential flow. As soon as the clairvoyant actively tries to interfere with the sequence of events she is witnessing, she is immediately thrown back into linear time and will no longer be witnessing events outside the normal here-and-now framework. She must then refocus her attention to Clairvoyant Time. The rules that govern such movement from one time frame to another are not well understood. Most clairvoyants will be led to "read" a particular time frame of a person's life or past life according to the needs of the person. Some clairvoyants can simply focus on whatever time frame is requested.

Einstein's space-time continuum states that the apparent linearity of events depends on the observer. *We are all too ready to accept past lives as literal physical lives that have happened in the past in a physical setting like this one.* Our past lives may be happening right now in a different space-time continuum. Many of us have experienced "past lives" and feel their effects as if they were a short time ago. But we rarely speak of how our future lives are affecting the one we are experiencing right here and now. *As we live our life NOW, it becomes more likely that we are rewriting our personal history, both past and future.*

Another important consequence of Einstein's relativity is the realization that matter and energy are interchangeable. Mass is nothing but a form of energy. Matter is simply slowed down or crystallized energy. Our bodies are energy. That is what this whole book is about! I have introduced the concept of energy bodies in this book but have not stressed that our physical body is energy also.

## Paradox

In the 1920s, physics moved into the strange and unexpected reality of the subatomic world. Every time physicists asked nature a question in an experiment, nature answered with a paradox. The more they tried to clarify the situation, the stronger the paradoxes became. Finally, physicists realized that paradox is part of the intrinsic nature of the subatomic world upon which all of our physical reality exists.

For example, one can set up an experiment that proves light is a particle. A small change in this experiment will prove that light is a wave. Therefore, to describe the phenomenon of light, both the concept of a wave and a particle must be used. Thus, we now move into a universe based on the concept both/and. Physicists call this complementarity. That is, to describe a phenomenon (if we continue to think in such terms as particles and waves), one must use both types of descriptions. These types are complements of each other rather than opposites, according to the old concept of either/or.

For example, Max Planck discovered that the energy of heat radiation (like the radiator in your house) is not emitted continuously, but appears in the form of discrete "energy packets," called *quanta*. Einstein postulated that all forms of electromagnetic radiation can appear not only as waves, but also in the form of these quanta. These light quanta, or energy packets, have been accepted as bona fide particles. At this stage of the game, a particle, which is the closest definition of a "thing," is an energy packet!

As we penetrate deeper into matter, nature does not show us any isolated "basic building blocks" as Newtonian physics suggested. The search for the basic building blocks of matter had to be abandoned when physicists found so many elementary particles that they could hardly be called elementary. Through experiments in the past few decades, physicists found matter to be completely mutable, and on the subatomic level, matter does not exist with certainty in definite places, but rather shows "tendencies" to exist. All particles can be transmuted into other particles. They can be created from energy and can be transmuted into other particles. They can be created from energy and can vanish into energy. Where and when this happens we cannot determine exactly, but we do know it is continuously occurring.

On the personal level, as we move more into the world of modern psychology and spiritual development, we find the old forms of either/or also dissolving into the form of both/and. We are no longer bad or good; we no longer only hate or love someone. Within us, we find much broader abilities. We can feel both love and hate, and all the emotions in between, for the same person. We act responsibly. We find the old dualism of God/Devil dissolving into a whole in which we find the Goddess/God within merging with the God/Goddess without. Anything evil is not the opposite of Goddess/God, but resistance to the God/Goddess force. All is composed of the same energy. The Goddess/God force is both black and white, both masculine and feminine. It contains both, the white light and the velvet black void.

As the reader can see, we are still using concepts steeped in dualism, but it is a world of "apparent" opposites that complement each other, not "real" opposites. In this system, the dualism is being used to propel us forward into unity.

## Beyond Dualism—The Hologram

Physicists have found that particles can be waves at the same time because they are not real physical waves like sound or water waves, but rather they are probability waves. Probability waves do not represent probabilities of things, but rather probabilities of interconnections. This is a tough concept to understand, but essentially the physicists are saying there is no such thing as a "thing." What we used to call "things" are really "events" or paths that might become events.

Our old world of solid objects and the deterministic laws of nature is now dissolved into a world of wave-like patterns of interconnections. Concepts like "elementary particle," "material substance" or "isolated object" have lost their meaning. The whole universe appears as a dynamic web of inseparable energy patterns. The universe is thus defined as a dynamic inseparable whole which always includes the observer in an essential way.

If the universe is indeed composed of such a web, there is (logically) no such thing as a part. Thus we are not separated parts of a whole. We are a Whole.

Recently, physicist Dr. David Bohm said in his book *The Implicate Order* that primary physical laws cannot be discovered by a science that attempts to break the world into its parts. He has written of an "implicate enfolded order" which exists in an unmanifested state and is the foundation upon which all manifest reality rests. He calls this manifest reality "the explicate unfolded order." "Parts are seen to be in immediate connection, in which their dynamical relationships depend in an irreducible way on the state of the whole system. . . . Thus, one is led to a new notion of unbroken wholeness which denies the classical idea of analyzability of the world into separately and independently existent parts."

Dr. Bohm states that the holographic view of the universe is a jumping-off place to begin to understand the implicate enfolded and explicate unfolded orders. The hologram concept states that every piece is an exact representation of the whole and can be used to reconstruct the entire hologram.

In 1971, Dennis Gabor received a Nobel Prize for constructing the first hologram. It was a lensless photograph in which a wave field of light scattered by an object was recorded as an interference pattern on a plate. When the hologram or photograph recording is placed in a laser or coherent light beam, the original wave pattern is regenerated in a three-dimensional image. Every piece of the hologram is an exact representation of the whole and will reconstruct the entire image.

Dr. Karl Pribram, a renowned brain researcher, has accumulated evidence over a decade that the brain's deep structure is essentially holographic. He states that research from many laboratories by sophisticated analysis of temporal and/or spatial frequencies demonstrates that the brain structures sight, hearing, taste, smell and touch holographically. The information is distributed throughout the system, so that each fragment can produce the information of the whole. Dr. Pribram uses the hologram model to describe not only the brain, but the universe as well. He states that the brain employs a holographic process to abstract from a holographic domain that transcends time and space. Parapsychologists have searched for the energy that might transmit telepathy, psychokinesis and healing. From the point of view of the holographic universe, these events emerge from frequencies that transcend time and space; they don't have to be transmitted. They are potentially simultaneous and everywhere.

When we will speak of energy fields of the aura in this book, we will be using very archaic terms from the point of view of these physicists. The phenomenon of the aura is clearly both inside and outside linear time and three-dimensional space. As in the case studies I have already presented, I "saw" the events of Ed's puberty when he broke his coccyx because he carried that experience with him in his energy field. The "shaft" of the lover can be perceived in the present energy field, and the clairvoyant can apparently go back in time and witness the event as it happened. A great many of the experiences related in this book require more than three dimensions for explanation; many of them appear to be instantaneous. The ability to see inside the body at any level with a varying resolution could imply the use of additional dimensions. The ability to perceive events from the past by simply asking for that information, or to see a probable event and then to change that event by intervening through the healing process, could imply nonlinear time. The ability to see an event that will take place in the future goes beyond linear time.

In using the concept of the fields to describe the aura, we will be steeped in dualism; that is, we will separate the field from us and observe "it" as a phenomenon that exists as a "part" of us. We will use terms like "my field" and "her aura," etc. This is dualistic. I must apologize for this and say that frankly, at this point, I am quite unable to convey these experiences without using the old frameworks.

From the holographic framework of reality each piece of the aura not only represents, but also contains, the whole. Thus, we can only describe our experience with a phenomenon that

we both at the same time observe and create. Every observation creates an effect on the observed pattern. We are not just part of the pattern; we are the pattern. It is us and we are it, only the term "it" now needs to be abandoned and replaced with some other, more appropriate term to release the blocks we experience in our brains when we try to communicate.

Physicists have used the terms "probabilities of interconnections" or "dynamic web of inseparable energy patterns." When we begin to think in terms of a dynamic web of inseparable energy patterns, all the auric phenomena described in this book do not appear particularly unusual or strange.

All experience is interconnected. Therefore, if we become aware of this and allow that interconnectedness into our cognitive processes, we can be aware of all events independent of all time. But as soon as we say "we," we have fallen back into dualism. It is hard to experience this connectedness when our major experience of life is dualistic. *Holistic awareness will be outside linear time and three-dimensional space and therefore will not be easily recognized.* We must practice holistic experience to be able to recognize it.

Meditation is one way of transcending the limits of the linear mind and allows the connectedness of all things to become an experiential reality. This reality is very hard to communicate in words, because we use words in a linear fashion. We need to develop vocabulary by which we can lead each other into these experiences. In Japanese Zen meditation, the masters give students a short phrase to concentrate on. The phrase, called a *koan*, is designed to help students transcend linear thought. Here is one of my favorites:

What is the sound of one hand clapping?

My reaction to this well-known koan is to find myself stretching out into the universe on a pattern of unheard sound that seems to flow on forever.

## Superluminal Connectedness

Scientists are now finding evidence for a universal, immediate connectedness within the framework of science, both mathematically and experimentally.

In 1964, physicist J. S. Bell published a mathematical proof called Bell's theorem. Bell's theorem mathematically supports the concept that subatomic "particles" are connected in some way that transcends space and time, so that anything that happens to one particle affects other particles. This effect is immediate and does not need "time" to be transmitted. Einstein's relativity theory stated that it is impossible for a particle to travel faster than the speed of light. In Bell's theorem, effects can be "superluminal," or faster than the speed of light. Bell's theorem has now been supported by experimentation. We are now talking about a phenomenon that stands outside Einstein's theory of relativity. We are trying to go beyond the wave/particle duality.

So once again, as the state of the art of scientific equipment advances, allowing us to probe deeper into matter with more sensitivity, we find phenomena that cannot be explained by the current theory. When this kind of probing happened in the late 1800s, the discovery of electricity revolutionized the world and made us think even more deeply about who we are. When it happened again in the 1940s, atomic power revolutionized the world. It appears that we are now headed into another period of tremendous change. If physicists learn how this instantaneous connectedness works, we could conceivably learn to be consciously aware of our instantaneous connections with the world and each other. This would obviously revolutionize communication. It would also drastically change how we interact with each other. This instantaneous connection may provide us with the ability to read each others' minds whenever we want to. We could know what is going on in each other and truly understand each other deeply. We may also see more clearly how our thoughts, feelings (energy fields) and actions affect the world much more than we previously thought.

## Morphogenetic Fields

Rupert Sheldrake in his book, *A New Science of*

*Life*, proposes that all systems are regulated not only by known energy and material factors but also by invisible organizing fields. These fields are causative because they serve as blueprints for form and behavior. These fields have no energy in the normal sense of the word because their effect reaches across the time and space barriers normally applied to energy. That is, their effect is just as strong at a distance as it is at close range.

According to this hypothesis, whenever one member of a species learns a new behavior, the causative field for the species is changed, however slightly. If the behavior is repeated for long enough, its "morphic resonance" affects the entire species. Sheldrake called this invisible matrix a "morphogenetic field," from *morph*, "form," and *genesis*, "coming into being." The action of this field involves "action at a distance" in both space and time. Rather than form being determined by physical laws outside of time, it depends on morphic resonance across time. This means that morphic fields can propagate across space and time and that past events could influence other events everywhere else. An example of this is shown by Lyall Watson in his book, *Lifetide: The Biology of Consciousness*, in which he describes what is now popularly called the Hundredth Monkey Principle. Watson found that after a group of monkeys learned a new behavior, suddenly other monkeys on other islands with no possible "normal" means of communication learned that behavior, too.

Dr. David Bohm in the journal *Revisions* states that the same thing is true for quantum physics. He says the Einstein-Podolsky-Rosen experiment showed that there would be nonlocal connections, or subtle connections of distant particles. So there would be a wholeness about the system such that the formative field could not be attributed to that particle alone. It could only be attributed to the whole. Thus something happening to distant particles can affect the formative field of other particles. Bohm goes on to state that "the notion of timeless laws that govern the universe doesn't seem to hold up, because time itself is part of the necessity that developed."

In the same article, Rupert Sheldrake concludes: "So the creative process, which gives rise to new thought, through which new wholes are realized, is similar in that sense to the creative reality which gives rise to new wholes in the evolutionary process. The creative process could be seen as a successive development of more complex and higher-level wholes, through previously separate things being connected together."

## Multi-Dimensional Reality

Jack Sarfatti, another physicist, suggests in *Psychoenergetic Systems* that the way superluminal connectedness can exist is through a higher plane of reality. He suggests that "things" are more connected or events more "correlated" on a plane of reality "above" ours, and that "things" in that plane are connected through an even higher plane. Thus by reaching to a higher plane we may be able to understand how instantaneous connectedness works.

## Conclusion

Physicists state that there are no basic building blocks of matter, rather that the universe is an inseparable whole; a vast web of interacting interweaving probabilities. Bohms work shows that the manifest universe arises out of this whole. I suggest that since we are inseparable parts of that whole, we can enter into a holistic state of being, become the whole, and tap into the creative powers of the universe to instantaneously heal anyone anywhere. Some healers can do this to a certain extent by merging and becoming one with God and the patient.

Becoming a healer means to move toward this universal creative power which we experience as love by reidentifying self with and becoming universal; becoming one with God. One stepping stone to this wholeness is to let go of our limited self definitions based on our Newtonian past of separated parts and to identify ourselves with being energy fields. If we can integrate that reality into our lives in a practical and verifiable way, we can separate fantasy from a possible broader reality. Once we associate ourselves with energy fields, higher consciousness becomes associated with higher frequency and greater coherency.

Using Sarfatti's model, we begin to see a world very much like that described later in this book: the world of the aura and the universal energy field. There we exist in more than one world. Our higher bodies (higher auric frequencies) are of a higher order and are more connected to others' higher bodies than are our physical bodies. As our awareness progresses into higher frequencies and higher bodies, we become more and more connected until we are eventually one with the universe. Using his concept, the meditative experience, then, can be defined as an experience of raising our consciousness to a higher frequency so that it can then experience the reality of our higher bodies, our higher consciousness and the higher worlds we exist in.

So let us look more now at the energy field phenomena to see what experimental science can tell us.

## Chapter 4 Review

1. How have scientific views influenced our self-concepts?
2. Why is the view of a fixed physical world impractical to us now?
3. What was so important about Faraday's and Maxwell's contributions to the ideas about how the world works?
4. What is superluminal connectedness and what is its significance in our daily lives?
5. How can the idea of multidimensional reality help describe the HEF?

### Food For Thought

6. Imagine yourself as a hologram. How does that unlimit you?

# Chapter 5

# HISTORY OF THE SCIENTIFIC INVESTIGATION INTO THE HUMAN ENERGY FIELD

Although mystics have not spoken of energy fields or bioplasmic forms, their traditions over 5,000 years in all the parts of the globe are consistent with the observations scientists have recently begun to make.

## Spiritual Tradition

Adepts of all religions speak of experiencing or seeing light around people's heads. Through such religious practices as meditation and prayer, they reach states of expanded consciousness which open their latent High Sense Perception abilities.

Ancient Indian spiritual tradition, over 5,000 years old, speaks of a universal energy called *Prana*. This universal energy is seen as the basic constituent and source of all life. Prana, the breath of life, moves through all forms and gave them life. Yogis practice manipulating this energy through breathing techniques, meditation and physical exercise to maintain altered states of consciousness and youth far beyond their normal span.

The Chinese, in the 3rd millennium B.C., posited the existence of a vital energy which they called *Ch'i*. All matter, animate and inanimate, is composed of and pervaded with this universal energy. This Ch'i contains two polar forces, the yin and the yang. When the yin and yang are balanced, the living system exhibits physical health; when they are unbalanced, a diseased state results. Overly powerful yang results in excessive organic activity. Predominant yin makes for insufficient functioning. Either imbalance results in physical illness. The ancient art of acupuncture focuses on balancing the yin and the yang.

Kabbalah, the Jewish mystical theosophy which began around 538 B.C., refers to these same energies as the astral light. Christian religious paintings portray Jesus and other spiritual figures surrounded by fields of light. In the Old Testament, there are numerous references to light around people and lights appearing, but over the centuries these phenomena lost their original meaning. For example, Michelangelo's statue of Moses shows *karnaeem* as two horns on his head rather than the two beams of light the word originally referred to. In Hebrew, this word can mean either horn or light.

John White in his book *Future Science* lists 97 different cultures that refer to the auric phenomena with 97 different names.

Many esoteric teachings—the ancient Hindu Vedic texts, the Theosophists, the Rosicrucians, the Native American Medicine People, the Tibetan and Indian Buddhists, the Japanese Zen Buddhists, Madame Blavatsky, and Rudolph

Steiner, to mention a few—describe the Human Energy Field in detail. Recently many with modern scientific training have been able to add observations on a concrete, physical level.

## Scientific Tradition: 500 B.C. Through 19th Century

Throughout history, the idea of a universal energy pervading all nature has been held by many western scientific minds. This vital energy, perceived as a luminous body, was first recorded in the western literature by the Pythagoreans around 500 B.C. They held that its light could produce a variety of effects in the human organism, including the cure of illness.

The scholars Boirac and Liebeault in the early 12th century saw that humans have an energy that can cause an interaction between individuals at a distance. They reported that one person can have a healthful or unhealthful effect on another simply by his presence. The scholar Paracelsus in the middle ages called this energy "Illiaster" and said that "Illiaster" is composed of both a vital force and a vital matter. The mathematician Helmont in the 1800s visualized a universal fluid that pervades all nature and is not a corporeal or a condensable matter, but a pure vital spirit that penetrates all bodies. Leibnitz, the mathematician, wrote that the essential elements of the universe are centers of force containing their own wellspring of motion.

Other properties of the universal energy phenomena were observed in the 1800s by Helmont and Mesmer, who originated Mesmerism, which became hypnotism. They reported that animate and inanimate objects could be charged with this "fluid" and that material bodies could exert influence on each other at a distance. This suggested that a field, in some ways analogous to an electromagnetic field, might exist.

Count Wilhelm Von Reichenbach spent 30 years during the mid–1800s experimenting with the "field," which he called the "odic" force. He found that it exhibited many properties that were similar to the electromagnetic field that James Clerk Maxwell had described early in the 19th century. He also found many properties were unique to the odic force. He determined that the poles of a magnet exhibit not only magnetic polarity, but also a unique polarity associated with this "odic field." Other objects, such as crystals, also exhibit this unique polarity without themselves being magnetic. Poles of the odic force field exhibit the subjective properties of being "hot, red and unpleasant" or "blue, cold and pleasant" to the observations of sensitive individuals. Furthermore, he determined that opposite poles do not attract as in electromagnetism. He found that with the odic force like poles attract—or like attracts like. This is a very important auric phenomenon, as we will see later.

Von Reichenbach studied the relationship between electromagnetic emissions from the sun and associated odic field concentrations. He found that the greatest concentration of this energy lay within the red and blue-violet ranges of the solar spectrum. Von Reichenbach stated that opposite charges produced subjective feelings of warmth and cold in varying degrees of power that he was able to relate to the periodic table through a series of blind tests. All electropositive elements gave the subjects feelings of warmth and produced unpleasant sensations; all electronegative elements fell on the cool, agreeable side, with the degree of intensity of sensation paralleling their position in the periodic table. These sensations varying from warm to cool corresponded with the spectral colors varying from red to indigo.

Von Reichenbach found that the odic field could be conducted through a wire, that the velocity of conduction was very slow (approximately 4 meters/second or 13 feet/second) and that the velocity seemed to depend on the mass density of the material rather than on the electrical conductivity of the material. Further, objects could be charged with this energy in a way similar to charging by the use of an electrical field. Other experiments demonstrated that part of this field could be focused like light through a lens, while another part would flow around the lens similar to the manner in which a candle flame flows around objects placed in its path. This deflected portion of the odic field would also react like a candle flame when subjected to air currents, suggesting the composition is similar to a gaseous fluid. These experiments show the auric field has properties that suggest it to be both particulate in nature like fluid and also energetic like light waves.

Von Reichenbach found that the force in the human body produced a polarity similar to that present in crystals along their major axes. Based on this experimental evidence, he described the left side of the body as a – pole and the right side as a + pole. This is a concept similar to the ancient Chinese yin and yang principles mentioned earlier.

## Observations by 20th Century Medical Doctors

We can see from the preceding paragraphs that studies up to the 20th century were conducted to observe different characteristics of an energy field surrounding humans and other objects. Since 1900 many medical doctors have become interested in the phenomenon as well.

In 1911, Dr. William Kilner, a medical doctor, reported on his studies of the Human Energy Field as seen through colored screens and filters. He described having seen glowing mist around the whole body in three zones: a) a quarter-inch dark layer closest to the skin, surrounded by b) a more vaporous layer an inch wide streaming perpendicularly from the body, and c) somewhat further out, a delicate exterior luminosity with indefinite contours about 6 inches across. Kilner found that the appearance of the "aura" (as he called it) differs considerably from subject to subject depending on age, sex, mental ability and health. Certain diseases showed as patches or irregularities in the aura, which led Kilner to develop a system of diagnosis on the basis of the color, texture, volume and general appearance of the envelope. Some diseases he diagnosed in this way were liver infection, tumors, appendicitis, epilepsy and psychological disturbances like hysteria.

In the mid-1900s, Dr. George De La Warr and Dr. Ruth Drown built new instruments to detect radiations from living tissues. He developed Radionics, a system of detection, diagnosis and healing from a distance, utilizing the human biological energy field. His most impressive works are photographs taken using the patient's hair as an antenna. These photographs showed internal formations of diseases in living tissue, such as tumors and cysts within the liver, tuberculosis of the lungs and malignant brain tumors. Even a live three-month-old fetus was photographed in utero.

Dr. Wilhelm Reich, a psychiatrist and colleague of Freud in the early part of the 20th century, became interested in a universal energy that he named "orgone." He studied the relationship of disturbances of the orgone flow in the human body to physical and psychological illness. Reich developed a psychotherapeutic modality in which Freudian analytic techniques for uncovering the unconscious are integrated with physical techniques for releasing blockages to the natural flow of orgone energy in the body. By releasing these energy blocks, Reich could clear negative mental and emotional states.

In the period of the 1930s through the 1950s, Reich experimented with these energies using the latest electronic and medical instrumentation at that time. He observed this energy pulsating in the sky and around all organic and inanimate objects. He observed pulsations of orgone energy radiating from microorganisms using a specially constructed high-powered microscope.

Reich constructed a variety of physical apparatuses for the study of the orgone field. One was the "accumulator," which was capable of concentrating orgone energy and which he used to charge objects with this energy. He observed that a vacuum discharge tube would conduct a current of electricity at a potential considerably lower than its normal discharge potential after being charged for a long period of time in an accumulator. Further, he claimed to increase the nuclear decay rate of a radioisotope by placing it in an orgone accumulator.

Dr. Lawrence Bendit and Phoebe Bendit made extensive observations of the HEF in the 1930s and related these fields to health, healing and soul development. Their work stresses the importance of a knowledge and understanding of the powerful etheric formative forces which are the foundations of health and healing in the body.

More recently, Dr. Schafica Karagulla has correlated visual observations made by sensitives to physical disorder. For instance, a clairvoyant named Dianne was able to observe the energy patterns of ill people and to describe very accurately what the medical problems were—from brain disorders to obstructions in the colon. These observations of the etheric body reveal a vital energy body or field which forms a matrix which interpenetrates the dense physical body like a sparkling web of light beams. This energetic matrix is the basic pattern upon which the physical matter of the tissues is shaped and anchored. The tissues exist as such only because of this vital field behind them.

Dr. Karagulla also correlated chakra disturbance with illness. For example, the sensitive Dianne described the chakra at the throat of a patient as being overactive, red and dull gray in color. When Dianne looked at the thyroid itself, it was too spongy and soft in texture. The right side of the thyroid was not functioning as well as the left. This patient was diagnosed through normal medical techniques as having Graves' disease, which causes enlarged thyroid, the right being the larger lobe.

Dr. Dora Kunz, President of the American Section of the Theosophical Society, has worked for many years with the medical profession and in healing. She has observed in *The Spiritual Aspects of the Healing Arts* that, "when the vital field is healthy, there is within it a natural autonomous rhythm," and that, "each organ in the body has its corresponding energetic rhythm in the etheric field. Between the spheres of the various organs, the different rhythms interact as if a transfer function were occurring; when the body is whole and healthy, these rhythms transfer easily from organ to organ. However, with pathology, the rhythms as well as the energy levels are changed. For example, the residue of a surgical appendectomy can be perceived in the field. The physical tissues that are now adjacent to each other have an altered energy transfer function from the one that was previously mod-

ulated by the appendix. In physics, this is called impedance matching or mismatching. Each adjacent tissue is 'impedance matched,' which means that the energy can easily flow through all the tissue. Surgery or illness changes the impedance matching so that the energy is to some degree dissipated rather than transferred."

Dr. John Pierrakos has developed a system of diagnosis and treatment of psychological disorders based on visual and pendulum-derived observations of HEF. The information from his observations of the energy bodies is combined with body psychotherapeutic methods developed in Bio-Energetics and with conceptual work developed by Eva Pierrakos. This process, called Core Energetics, is a unified process of inner healing which concentrates working through the defenses of the ego and personality to unblock energies of the body. Core Energetics seeks to balance all the bodies (physical, etheric, emotional, mental and spiritual) to effect a harmonious healing of the whole person.

I conclude from the above, and other, work that light emissions from the human body are closely related to health. I propose that it is very important to find a way to quantify these light emissions with reliable, standardized light measuring instrumentation to make this information available to the medical profession for clinical diagnosis and the energy itself useful for treatment.

My colleagues and I have conducted a number of experiments to measure the HEF. In one, Dr. Richard Dobrin, Dr. John Pierrakos and I measured the light level at a wavelength of around 350 nanometers in a darkroom before, during and after individuals were there. Results show a slight increase of light in the darkroom when people are in it. In one case, the light level actually decreased; someone who was very exhausted and full of despair was in the darkroom. In another experiment, done with the United Nations Parapsychology Club, we were able to show part of the auric field on black and white television, with the use of a device called a colorizer. This device enables one to amplify greatly light intensity variations close to the body. In another experiment, conducted at Drexel University, with Dr. William Eidson and

Karen Gestla (a sensitive who worked with Dr. Rhine at Duke University for many years), in which we succeeded in affecting, either bending or attenuating, a small two-milliwatt laser beam with auric energy. All these experiments helped support the evidence for the existence of the energy fields but were not conclusive. Results were shown nationally on NBC television, but further research was not conducted because of lack of funding.

In Japan, Hiroshi Motoyama has been able to measure low light levels coming from people who have practiced yoga for many years. He did this work in a darkroom, using a low-light-level movie camera.

Dr. Zheng Rongliang, of Lanzhou University in the People's Republic of China, measured energy (called "Qi" or "Ch'i") radiated from the human body by using a biological detector made from a leaf vein connected to a photoquantum device (low-light measuring device). He studied the energy-field emanations of a Qigong Master (Qigong is an ancient Chinese form of health exercise) and the energy field emanations of a clairvoyant. Results of his studies show that the detection system responds to the radiation in the form of a pulse. The pulse emanating from the hand of the Qigong Master is much different than that of the clairvoyant.

At Shanghai Atomic Nuclear Institute of Academia Sinica it was shown that some vital-force emanations from Qigong masters seem to have a very low frequency sound wave that appears as a low-frequency fluctuating carrier wave. In some cases, Qi was also detected as a microparticle flow. The size of these particles was about 60 microns in diameter and they had a velocity of about 20–50 cm/second (or 8–20 inches/second).

Some years ago a group of Soviet scientists from the Bioinformation Institute of A.S. Popow announced the discovery that living organisms emit energy vibrations at a frequency between 300 and 2,000 nanometers. They called this energy the biofield, or bioplasma. They found that persons capable of successful bioenergy transfer have a much wider and stronger biofield. These findings have been confirmed at the Medical Sciences Academy in Moscow, and are sup-ported by research in Great Britain, the Netherlands, Germany and Poland.

The most exciting study I have seen on the human aura was done by Dr. Valorie Hunt and others at UCLA. In a study of the effects of rolfing on the body and psyche ("A Study of Structural Neuromuscular Energy Field and Emotional Approaches"), she recorded the frequency of low millivoltage signals from the body during a series of rolfing sessions. To make these recordings she used elementary electrodes made of silver/silver chloride placed on the skin. Simultaneously, with the recording of the electronic signals, Rev. Rosalyn Bruyere of the Healing Light Center, Glendale, California, observed the auras of both the rolfer and the person being rolfed. Her comments were recorded on the same tape recorder as the electronic data. She gave a running report of the color, size and energy movements of the chakras and auric clouds involved.

The scientists then mathematically analyzed the wave patterns recorded by a Fourier analysis and a sonogram frequency analysis. Both revealed remarkable results. Consistent wave forms and frequencies correlated specifically with the colors Rev. Bruyere reported. In other words, when Rev. Bruyere observed blue in the aura at any specific location, the electronic measurements would always show the characteristic blue wave form and frequency in the same location. Results showed the following color/frequency correlations (Hz=Herz, or cycle/second):

| | |
|---|---|
| Blue | 100–240 Hz plus 800 Hz |
| Green | 240–400 Hz |
| Yellow | 400–600 Hz |
| Orange | 600–740 Hz |
| Red | 640–800 Hz |
| Purple shades | 900 Hz |
| White | 100–1,000 Hz (contains all colors) |

These frequency bands do not correspond to visible light ($4$–$7.5$ x $10^{14}$ Hz), but the colors occur in the same frequency sequence that visible light displays, with blue having the lowest frequency and red the highest. The frequencies measured are a signature of the instrumentation as well as the energy being measured.

Dr. Hunt says, "Throughout the centuries in which sensitives have seen and described the auric emissions, this is the first objective electronic evidence of frequency, amplitude and time, which validates their subjective observation of color discharge."

The fact that the color frequencies discovered here do not duplicate those of light or pigment does not negate the finding. When we realize that what we see as colors are frequencies picked up by the eye, differentiated and allotted a word symbol, then there is nothing to indicate that the eye and the brain processing centers interpret color only in high frequencies. The ultimate criterion for the experience of color is the visual interpretation. However, with finer instruments, improved recording and data reduction techniques, these data, now primarily up to 1,500 Hz, may very readily contain much higher frequencies.

Dr. Hunt also stated that "chakras frequently carried the colors stated in the metaphysical literature, i.e., kundalini-red, hypogastric-orange, spleen-yellow, heart-green, throat-blue, third eye-violet and crown-white. Activity in certain chakras seemed to trigger increased activity in another. The heart chakra was consistently the most active. Subjects had many emotional experiences, images and memory recalls connected with the different body areas rolfed. These findings give credence to the belief that memory of experiences is stored in body tissue."

For example, when someone's legs are being rolfed, he may very well relive early childhood experiences of potty training. He will not only remember the experience, but emotionally relive it. Many times parents try to potty train a child before the child's body has made the brain-muscle connections to actually control the sphincter muscle that regulates elimination. Since the child cannot physiologically control the sphincter, he will compensate by squeezing the thigh muscles. This puts a great deal of stress and strain on the body. Many times this strain is held habitually throughout life, or until deep bodywork like rolfing or bioenergetics is done. Then, when the muscle tension and

strain is released, so is the memory. Another example of holding memory-tension is the tight shoulders that many of us live with. This comes from holding fear or anxiety in the shoulders. You might ask yourself, what is it that you are afraid you will not be able to accomplish, or what do you think will happen if you don't succeed?

## Conclusion

If we define the Human Energy Field as all fields or emanations from the human body, we can see that many well-known components of the HEF have been measured in the laboratory. These are the electrostatic, magnetic, electromagnetic, sonic, thermal and visual components of the HEF. All these measurements are consistent with normal physiological processes of the body and go beyond them to provide a vehicle for psychosomatic functioning.

Dr. Hunt's measurements show definite frequencies for definite colors of the aura. These frequencies may have higher overtones that were not recorded due to the limitations of the laboratory equipment involved.

Measurements listed above also show the HEF to be particulate in nature and to have fluid-like motion, like air or water currents. These particles are very tiny, even subatomic according to some investigators. When charged minute particles move together in clouds they are usually called plasmas by physicists. Plasmas follow certain physical laws that lead physicists to consider them to be a state between energy and matter. Many of the properties of the HEF measured in the laboratory suggest a fifth state of matter which some scientists call "bioplasma."

These studies show that the ordinary model of the body consisting of systems (like the digestive system) is insufficient. An additional model based on the concept of an organizing energy field needs to be developed. The model of a complicated electromagnetic field (EMF) does not completely serve this purpose. Many of the psychic phenomena associated with the HEF, such as precognition or being aware of past life information, cannot be explained with an EMF model.

According to Dr. Valorie Hunt, the body can be "viewed from a quantum concept of energy stemming from the atomic cellular nature of the functioning body, which cuts across all tissues and systems." She suggests that the holographic view of the HEF would be a good one. "The hologram concept emerging in physics and brain research appears to provide a truly unifying cosmic view of reality which demands reinterpretation of all biological findings on another plane."

Marilyn Ferguson declared in *Brain Mind Bulletin* that "the holistic model has been described as the 'emerging paradigm,' an integral theory that would catch all the wonderful wild-life of science and spirit. Here at last is a theory that marries biology to physics in an open system."

## Chapter 5 Review

1. How has the HEF been measured?
2. When did human beings first learn about the auric phenomenon?
3. When was the aura first observed in the 19th century and by whom?
4. How does the phenomenon of the HEF go beyond what today's science knows?
5. From the point of view of theoretical and experimental science today, what is a good model to account for the HEF phenomenon?

*Chapter 6*

# THE UNIVERSAL ENERGY FIELD

When I, as an adult, again began to see the life-energy fields, I became skeptical and confused. I had not yet found the literature (referred to in the previous two chapters), nor had I received any of the guidance referred to in Chapter 3. Of course, as a scientist I knew about energy fields, but they were impersonal and defined by mathematical formulae. Were they really there? Did they have meaning? Was I fabricating my experiences? Was it wishful thinking, or was I experiencing another dimension of reality that had meaning, was orderly and was very helpful in understanding my present life circumstances and, in fact, life as a whole?

I'd read about the miracles of old, but they all happened in the past to someone I didn't know. A lot seemed hearsay and fantasy. The physicist part of me needed observation and control to prove these phenomena "real or unreal." So I began collecting data, i.e., personal experiences, to see if they fit into some logical form or system, as the physical world does. I believed, with Einstein, that "God doesn't play dice with the Universe."

I found the phenomena I observed to be very much like the world with which I was familiar, well ordered in form, shape and color and also clearly based on cause-and-effect relationships. But there was always a little more there, always something left unknown, unexplainable, a mystery. I came to realize how boring life would be without the unknown mystery always dancing before us as we move through . . . what? Time and space? That is how

I used to think. Now I see that we move through personal experiences of "reality"—thinking, feeling, sensing, being, merging, individuating, only to merge again in an infinite dance of transformation as the soul forms, grows and moves toward God.

What I observed correlated with the many esoteric books written on the subject of the aura and energy fields. The colors correlated; the movements, shapes and forms correlated. Most of what I read, I usually read after making my observations, as if that unseen hand made sure I first experienced a phenomenon before reading about it so that I couldn't project any mental image I might form from my reading. I now firmly believe in this experience of guidance, which moves through and permeates my entire life like a song, ever carrying me on to new experiences, new lessons, as I grow and develop as a human being.

## Exercise to "See" the Universal Life-Energy Fields

The easiest way to begin to observe the universal energy field is to simply relax on your back in the grass on a nice sunny day and gaze at the blue sky. After some time you will be able to see the tiny globules of orgone making squiggly patterns against the blue sky. They seem to be tiny white balls, sometimes with a black spot, that appear for a second or two, leave a slight trail mark, and then disappear again. When you continue this observation and expand your vision, you will begin to see that the whole field pulsates in a synchronized rhythm. On sunny days these tiny balls of energy will be bright and move fast. On cloudy days they will be more translucent, move slowly and be fewer in number. In a smoggy city they are fewer, dark, and very slow moving. They are undercharged. The most abundant and most brightly charged globules I observed were in the Swiss Alps, where there are many bright sunny days and the snow covers everything in thick drifts. Apparently sunlight charges the globules.

Now shift your gaze to the edge of treetops against the blue sky. You may see a green haze around the trees. Curiously, you may also notice that there are no globules in this haze. But if you look closer, you will see the globules at the edge of the green haze changing their squiggly pattern and flowing into the aura of the tree, where they disappear. Apparently the tree's aura is absorbing the tiny globules. The green around the tree appears in the leafing stage, during spring and summer. Earlier in the spring, the aura of most trees has a pink-reddish hue, similar to the color of the red buds of the trees.

If you look closely at a house plant, you will see a similar phenomenon. Put the plant under bright lights with a dark background behind it. You may see lines of blue-green flashing up the plant along the leaves in the direction of growth. They will suddenly flash; then the color slowly

Figure 6–1:   The Effect of Lapis on Plant's Aura

fades, only to flash again, perhaps on the opposite side of the plant. These lines will react to your hand, or a piece of crystal, if you bring them near the aura of the plant. As you draw the crystal away from the plant, you will see the aura of the plant and the aura of the crystal stretch to maintain contact. They pull like taffy. (See Figure 6–1.)

I once tried to see the phantom leaf effect, which is so widely talked about in Kirlian photography. Through the methods of Kirlian photography, people have been able to photograph an image of an entire leaf after half of it was cut away. I observed the aura of the leaf. It was a simple aqua-blue. When I cut the leaf, the aura of the entire leaf turned a bloody maroon. I recoiled and apologized to the plant. When the aqua-blue color reestablished itself in a minute or two, it showed definite signs of the missing part, but not as clearly as I have seen on the Kirlian photographs. (See Figure 6–2.)

Inanimate objects also have an aura. Most personal objects become imbued with the energy of the owner and radiate this energy. Gems and crystals show interesting auras with many layered and complicated patterns that can be used in healing. For example, the amethyst has a golden aura, with golden rays streaking out from its naturally faceted points.

## Characteristics of the Universal Energy Field

As stated in Chapter 5, the UEF has been known and observed throughout the ages. It has been studied as far back in history as we are able to reach. Each culture had a different name for the energy field phenomenon and looked at it from its particular viewpoint. When describing what it saw, each culture found similar basic properties in the UEF. As time progressed and the scientific method was developed, western culture began to investigate the UEF more rigorously.

As the state of the art of our scientific equipment becomes more sophisticated, we are able to measure finer qualities of the UEF. From these investigations we can surmise that the

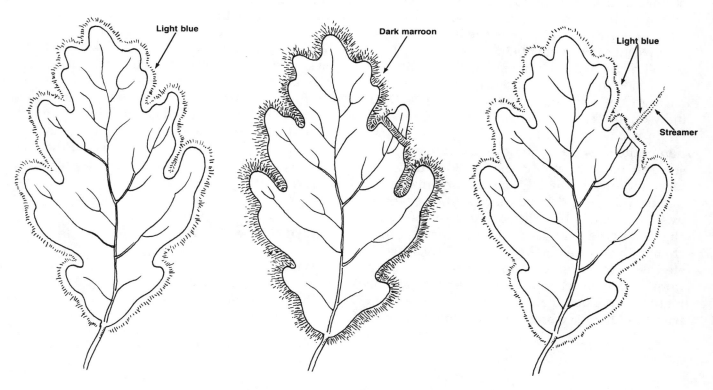

Figure 6–2:  Check of Phantom Leaf Effect

UEF is probably composed of an energy previously undefined by western science, or possibly a matter of a finer substance than we generally considered matter to be. If we define matter as condensed energy, the UEF may exist between the presently considered realm of matter and that of energy. As we have seen, some scientists refer to the phenomenon of the UEF as bioplasma.

Dr. John White and Dr. Stanley Krippner list many properties of the Universal Energy Field: the UEF permeates all space, animate and inanimate objects, and connects all objects to each other; it flows from one object to another; and its density varies inversely with the distance from its source. It also follows the laws of harmonic inductance and sympathetic resonance—the phenomenon that occurs when you strike a tuning fork and one near it will begin to vibrate at the same frequency, giving off the same sound.

Visual observations reveal the field to be highly organized in a series of geometric points, isolated pulsating points of light, spirals, webs of lines, sparks and clouds. It pulsates and can be sensed by touch, taste, smell and with sound and luminosity perceivable to the higher senses.

Investigators of this field state that the UEF is basically synergistic, meaning the simultaneous action of separate agencies that together have greater total effect than the sum of their individual effects. This field is the opposite of entropy, a term used to describe the phenomenon of the slow decay that we so commonly observe in physical reality, the breaking-down of form and order. The HEF has an organizing effect on matter and builds forms. It appears to exist in more than three dimensions. Any changes in the material world are preceded by a change in this field. The UEF is always associated with some form of consciousness, ranging from highly developed to very primitive. The highly developed consciousness is associated with the "higher vibrations" and energy levels.

Thus, we see that, in some way, the UEF is not so different from everything else we know in nature. However, it causes us to reach out with our minds to understand all of the properties that it has. On some levels it is a "normal" thing like salt or a stone; it has properties that we can define with normal scientific methods. On the other hand, if we continue to probe deeper into its nature, it evades the normal scientific explanations. It becomes elusive. We think we have "put it in its place" along with electricity and other not-so-unusual phenomena, but then it slips out of the hand again and causes us to think: "What is it really? But then, what is electricity anyway?"

The UEF exists in more than three dimensions. What does that mean? It is synergistic and builds form. That is against the second law of thermodynamics, which states that entropy is always increasing, which says that disorder in the universe is always increasing and that you cannot get more energy out of something than you put in. You always get a little less energy out of something than you put in. (A perpetual motion machine has never been built.) That is not the case with the UEF. It seems that it is always continuing to create more energy. Like the cornucopia, it always remains filled, no matter how much you take from it. These are exciting concepts and give us a very hopeful view of the future as we risk sinking deeper into the pessimism of the nuclear age. Perhaps someday we will be able to build a machine that can tap into the energy of the UEF and have all the energy we need without threat of harming ourselves.

## Chapter 6 Review

1. What is an aura?
2. Does a penny have an aura?
3. What does not have an aura?
4. Describe the UEF.

# *Chapter 7*

# THE HUMAN ENERGY FIELD, OR HUMAN AURA

The Human Energy Field is the manifestation of universal energy that is intimately involved with human life. It can be described as a luminous body that surrounds and interpenetrates the physical body, emits its own characteristic radiation and is usually called the "aura." The aura is that part of the UEF associated with objects. The human aura, or Human Energy Field (HEF), is that part of the UEF associated with the human body. Based on their observations, researchers have created theoretical models that divide the aura into several layers. These layers are sometimes called *bodies*, and they interpenetrate and surround each other in successive layers. Each succeeding body is composed of finer substances and higher "vibrations" than the body that it surrounds and interpenetrates.

## Exercise to See the Human Aura

The easiest way to start to sense the HEF is through the following exercises. If you are in a group of people, make a circle and holds hands. Allow the energy of your auric field to flow around the circle. Sense this pulsating flow for a while. Which way is it going? See which way your neighbor feels it going. Do they correlate?

Now, without changing anything or moving your hands, stop the flow of energy. Keep it stopped for a while (everyone at once) and then let it flow again. Try it again. Can you feel the

difference? Which do you like better? Now do the same with a partner. Sit opposite each other touching palms together. Let the energy flow naturally. Which way does it go? Send energy out your left palm; then allow it to come into your right. Reverse. Now stop the flow. Next try pushing it out both hands at once. Now suck it in both hands at once. Push, pull and stop are three basic ways to manipulating energy in healing. Practice them.

Now, drop hands; hold your palms about two to five inches apart; slowly move your hands back and forth decreasing and increasing the space between them. Build something up between your hands. Can you feel it? What does it feel like? Now, take your hands further apart, about eight to ten inches. Then slowly bring them back together until you feel a pressure pushing your hands out so that you have to use just a slight amount more force to bring your hands together. You have now touched the edges of one of your energy bodies together. If your hands are one to one-and-a-quarter inches apart, you have touched your etheric body edges together (first layer of the aura). If your hands are three to four inches apart, you have touched the outside edges of your emotional body together (second layer of the aura). Now, very carefully move your hands closer until you can actually feel the outside edge of your emotional body or energy field of your right hand touch your skin of your left hand. Move your right palm about one inch closer to your left palm. Feel the tingling on the back of your left hand as the edge of your energy field touches it. The energy field of your right hand went right through your left hand!

Now, take your hands apart again and hold them at a distance of about seven inches. Point your right index finger at the palm of your left hand, making sure the fingertip is about one half to one inch away from the palm. Now, draw circles on your palms. What do you feel? Does it tickle? What is it?

With the light dim in the room, hold your hand so that the tips of the fingers point toward each other. Hold your hands in front of your face at a distance of about two feet. Make sure there is a plain white wall for a background. Relax your eyes and softly gaze at the space between your fingertips, which should be about one and a half inches apart. Do not look into bright light. Let your eyes relax. What do you see? Move your fingertips closer and then further apart. What is happening in the space between the fingers? What do you see around the hand? Slowly move one hand up and the other down so that different fingers are pointing to each other. What has happened now? About 95% of the people who try this exercise do see something. Everyone feels something. For the answers to the above questions, refer to the end of the chapter.

After you practice these exercises and the ones in Chapter 9 on observing other people's auras, you may begin to see the first few layers of the aura as shown in Figure 7–1A. Later, after you are used to seeing the lower layers, you can practice the higher sense perception exercises as described in Chapters 17, 18 and 19. With more opening in your third eye (sixth chakra), you will begin to see the higher levels of the aura. (Figure 7–1B.)

Now that most of you have felt, seen and experienced the lower levels of the aura, let us go on to describe them.

## The Anatomy of the Aura

There are many systems that people have cre-

ated from their observations to define the auric field. All these systems divide the aura into layers and define the layers by locations, color, brightness, form, density, fluidity and function. Each system is geared to the kind of work the individual is "doing" with the aura. The two systems most similar to mine are the ones used by Jack Schwarz, which has more than seven layers and is described in his book, *Human Energy Systems*, and the system used by Rev. Rosalyn Bruyere of the Healing Light Center in Glendale, California. Her system is a seven-layer system, and is described in her book, *Wheels of Light, A Study of the Chakras.*

## The Seven Layers of the Auric Field

I have observed seven layers during my work as a counselor and a healer. At first I could only see the lower layers, which are the most dense and easiest to see. The longer I worked, the more layers I could perceive. The higher the layer, the more expanded my consciousness needed to be to perceive it. That is, in order to perceive the higher layers, like the fifth, sixth and seventh, I would have to enter into a meditative state, usually with eyes closed. After years of practice, I even began to see beyond the seventh layer, as I will discuss briefly at the end of this chapter.

My observations of the aura revealed to me an interesting dualistic field pattern. Every other layer of the field is highly structured, like standing waves of light patterns, while the layers in-between appear to be composed of colored fluids in constant motion. These fluids flow through the form set by the shimmering standing light waves. The direction of flow is somewhat governed by the standing light form, since the fluid flows along the standing lines of light. The standing forms of light are themselves scintillating, as if they are composed of strings of many tiny, rapidly blinking lights, each blinking at a different rate. These standing light lines appear to have tiny charges moving along them.

Thus, the first, third, fifth and seventh layers all have a definite structure, while the second, fourth and sixth are composed of fluid-like substances that have no particular structure. They take on form by virtue of the fact that they flow through the structure of the odd layers, and thus somewhat take on the form of the structured layers. Each succeeding layer interpenetrates completely all the layers under it, including the physical body. Thus the emotional body extends beyond the etheric body and includes both the etheric and physical bodies. Actually, each body is not a "layer" at all, although that is what we may perceive. It is, rather, a more expansive version of our self that carries within it the other, more limited forms.

From the point of view of the scientist, each layer can be considered to be a level of higher vibrations, occupying the same space as the levels of vibration below it and extending beyond. In order to perceive each consecutive level, the observer must move up in consciousness to each new frequency level. Thus we have seven bodies all occupying the same space at the same time, each one extending out beyond the last, something we are not used to in "normal" daily life. Many people erroneously assume that the aura is like an onion, where you can peel away consecutive layers. It is not.

The structured layers contain all the forms that the physical body has, including internal organs, blood vessels, etc., and additional forms that the physical body does not contain. There is a vertical flow of energy that pulsates up and down the field in the spinal cord. It extends out beyond the physical body above the head and below the coccyx. I call this the main vertical power current. There are swirling cone-shaped vortexes called chakras in the field. Their tips point into the main vertical power current, and their open ends extend to the edge of each layer of the field they are located in.

## The Seven Layers and the Seven Chakras of the Auric Field

Each layer appears different and has its own particular function. Each layer of the aura is associated with a chakra. That is, the first layer is associated with the first chakra, and the second with the second chakra, and so on. These are general concepts and will get much more complicated as we delve more deeply into this subject. For now we will list them to give you a general overall view. The first layer of the field and the first chakra are associated with physical functioning and physical sensation—feeling physical pain or pleasure. The first layer is associated with automatic and autonomic functioning of the body. The second layer and second chakra are in general associated with the emotional aspect of human beings. They are the vehicles through which we have our emotional life and feelings. The third layer is associated with our mental life, with linear thinking. The third chakra is associated with linear thinking. The fourth level, associated with the heart chakra, is the vehicle through which we love, not only our mates, but also humanity in general. The fourth chakra is the chakra that metabolizes the energy of love. The fifth level is the level associated with a higher will more connected with the divine will. The fifth chakra is associated with the power of the word, speaking things into being, listening and taking responsibility for our actions. The sixth level and sixth chakra are associated with celestial love. It is a love that extends beyond the human range of love and encompasses all life. It makes the statement of caring and support for the protection and nurturing of all life. It holds all life forms as precious manifestations of God. The seventh layer and seventh chakra are associated with the higher mind, knowing and integration of our spiritual and physical makeup.

Thus there are specific locations within our energy system for the sensations, emotions, thoughts, memories and other nonphysical experiences that we report to our doctors and therapists. Understanding how our physical symptoms are related to these locations will help us understand the nature of different illnesses and also the nature of both health and disease. Thus the study of the aura can be a bridge between traditional medicine and our psychological concerns.

## Location of the Seven Chakras

The location of the seven major chakras on the physical body shown in Figure 7–2A corresponds to the major nerve plexuses of the physical body in that area of the body.

Dr. David Tansely, a radionics specialist, in his book *Radionics and the Subtle Bodies of Man*, states that the seven major chakras are formed at the points where the standing lines of light cross each other 21 times.

The 21 minor chakras are located at points where the energy strands cross 14 times. (See Figure 7–2B.) They are in the following locations: one in front of each ear, one above each breast, one where the clavicles meet, one in the palm of each hand, one on the sole of each foot,

one just behind each eye (not shown), one related to each gonad, one near the liver, one connected with the stomach, two connected with the spleen, one behind each knee, one near the thymus gland, and one near the solar plexus. These chakras are only about three inches in diameter at one inch distance from the body. The two minor chakras located in the palms are very important in healing. Where the lines of energy cross seven times, even smaller vortices are created. There are many tiny force centers where these lines cross fewer times. Tansely says that these tiny vortices may very well correspond to the acupuncture points of Chinese medicine.

Each major chakra on the front of the body is paired with its counterpart on the back of the

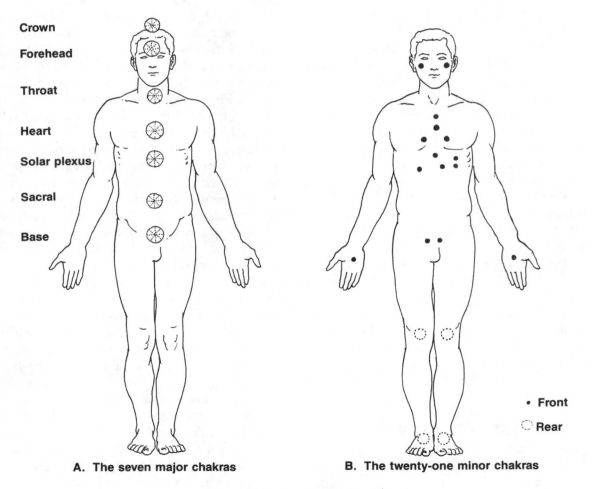

**A. The seven major chakras**

Crown

Forehead

Throat

Heart

Solar plexus

Sacral

Base

**B. The twenty-one minor chakras**

• Front

○ Rear

Figure 7–2:   Location of Chakras
(Diagnostic View)

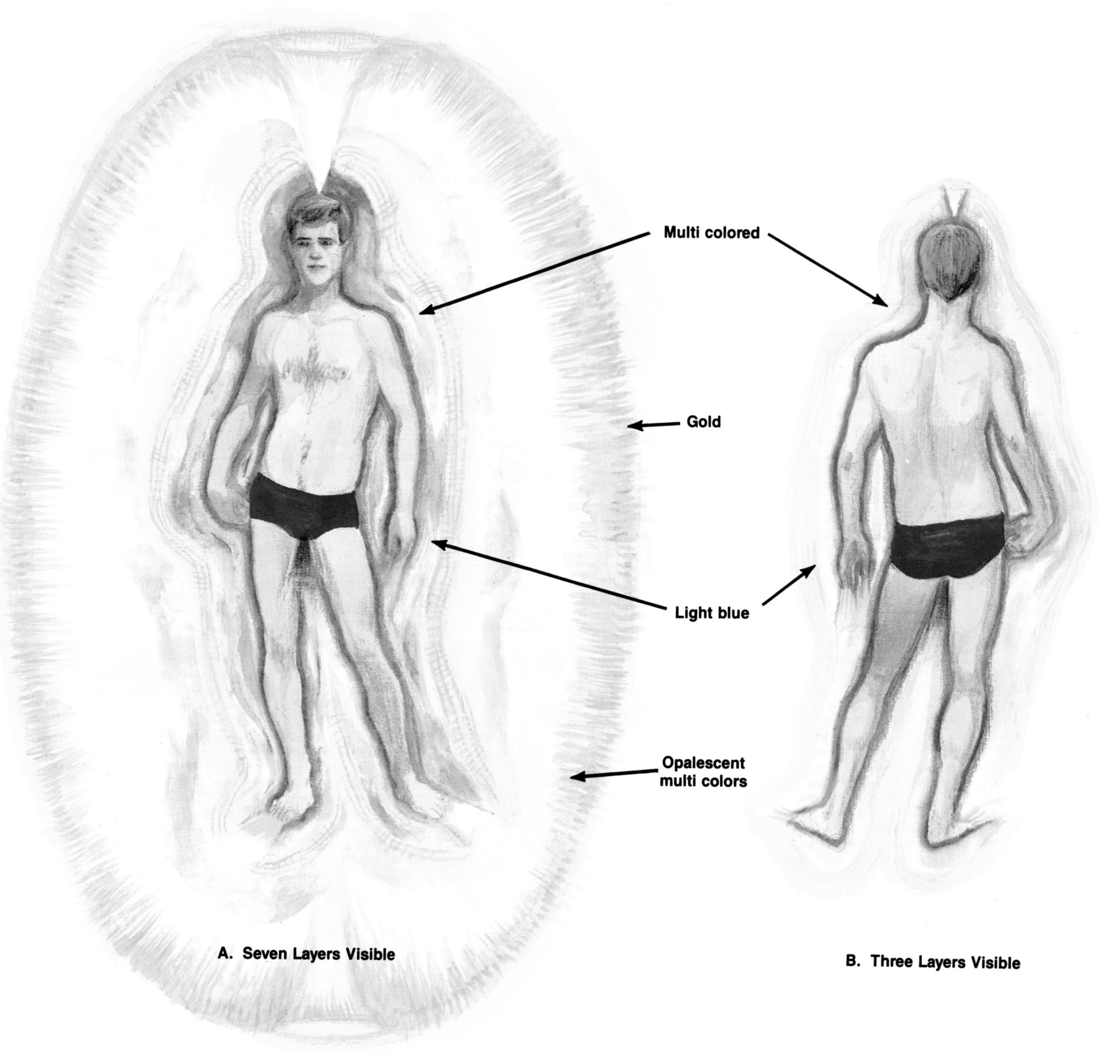

Multi colored

Gold

Light blue

Opalescent
multi colors

B. Three Layers Visible

A. Seven Layers Visible

Figure 7–1: The Normal Aura

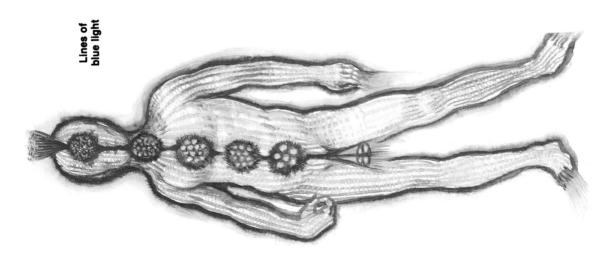

Clouds of
multi-colored light

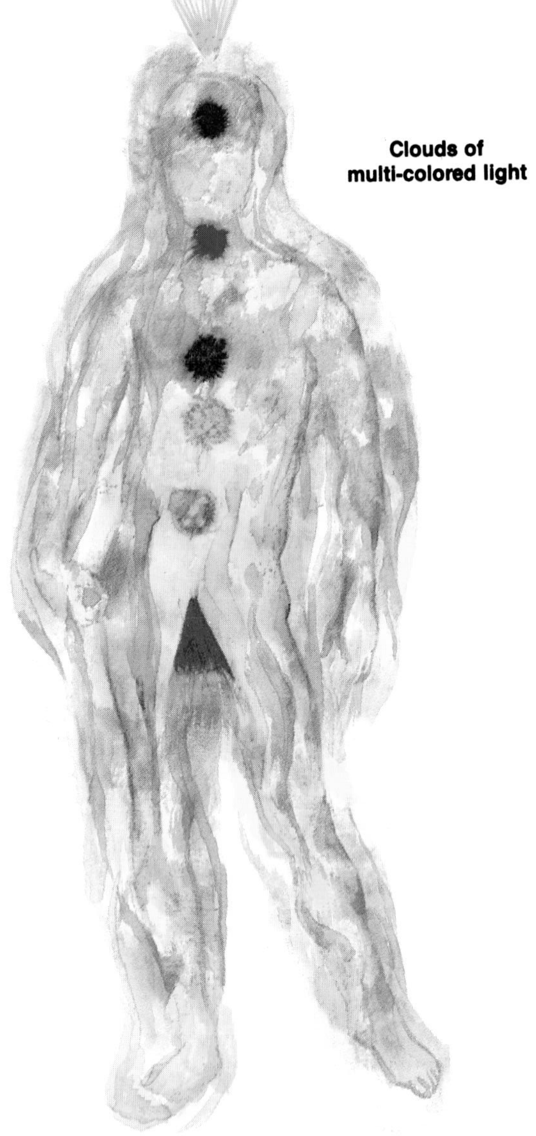

Figure 7-8: The Emotional Body

Lines of
blue light

Figure 7-7: The Etheric Body

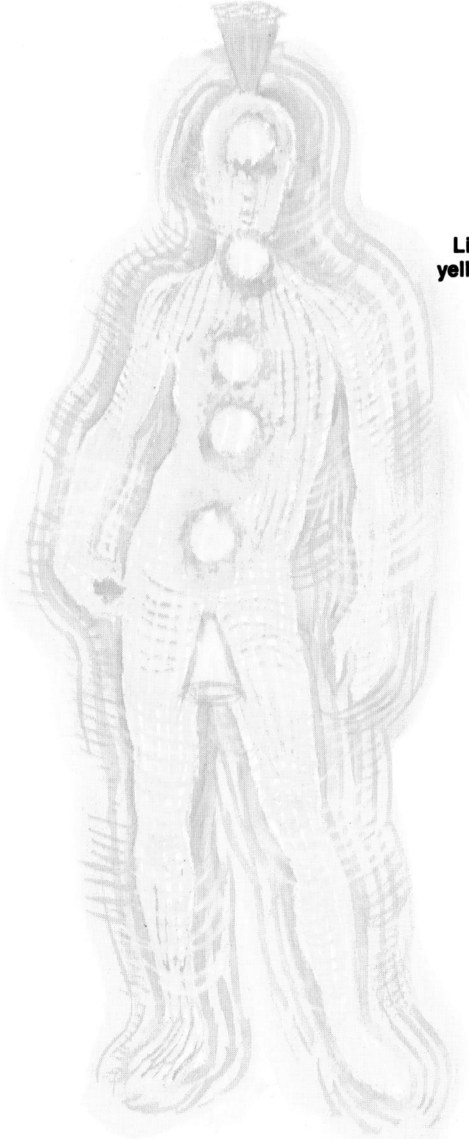

Clouds of
multi-colored light

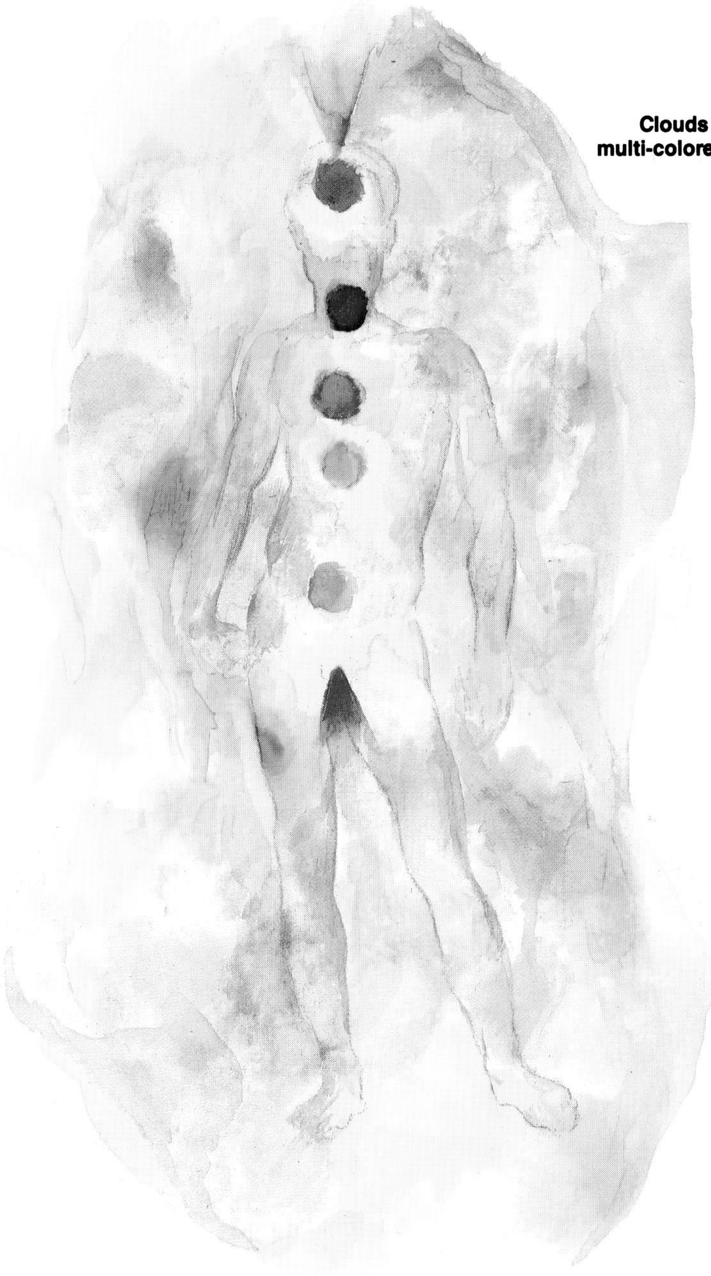

Figure 7-10:  The Astral Body

Lines of
yellow light

Figure 7-9:  The Mental Body

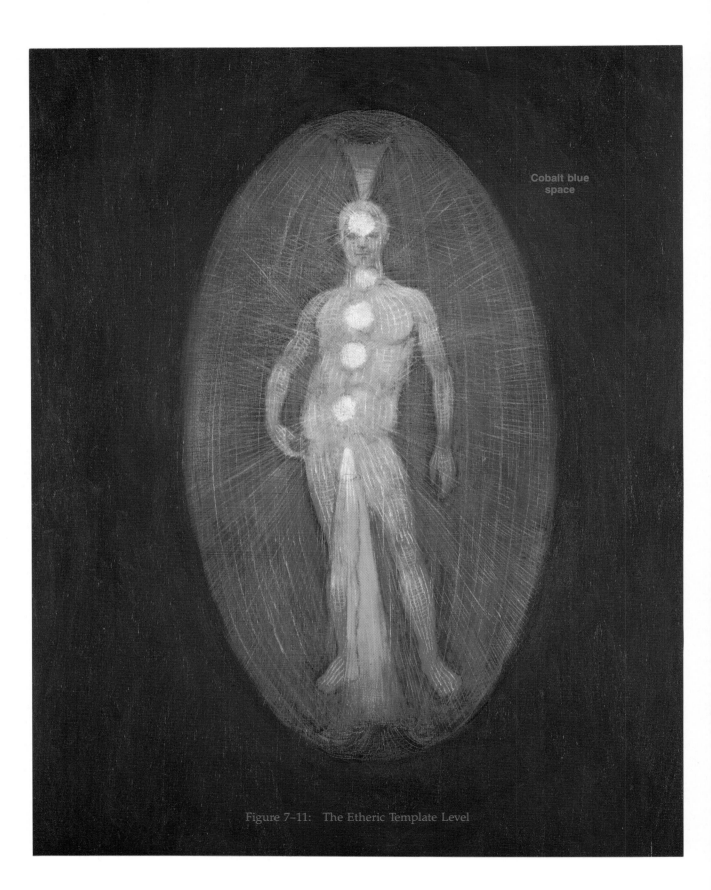

Cobalt blue
space

Figure 7–11: The Etheric Template Level

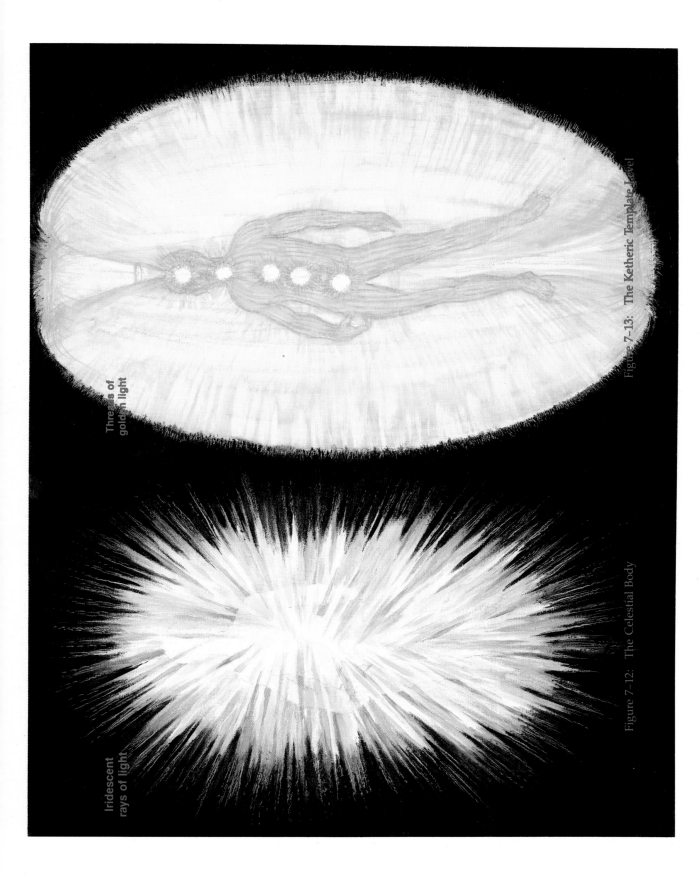

Threads of
golden light

Figure 7-13: The Ketheric Template Level

Iridescent
rays of light

Figure 7-12: The Celestial Body

**A. Normal aura**

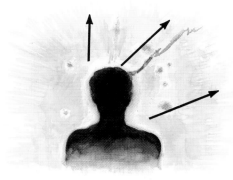

**B. Musician performing**

**C. Man lecturing on his favorite subject**

**D. Man speaking with passion about education**

**E. Woman after core energetics class**

**F. Man who often wears a shirt this color**

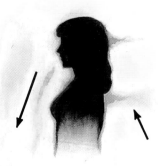

**G. Woman meditating to increase field**

**H. Pregnant woman**
**Soft Pastel Colors are Often Associated With Femininity**

Figure 11–1:  Auras in Motion

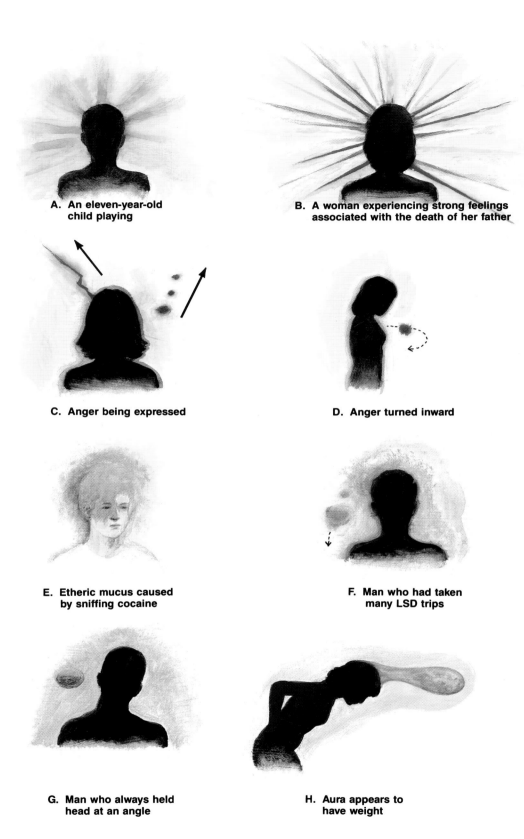

A. An eleven-year-old
   child playing

B. A woman experiencing strong feelings
   associated with the death of her father

C. Anger being expressed

D. Anger turned inward

E. Etheric mucus caused
   by sniffing cocaine

F. Man who had taken
   many LSD trips

G. Man who always held
   head at an angle

H. Aura appears to
   have weight

Figure 11–2:  Auras Seen in Therapy Sessions

Figure 11–5:  Woman Defending by Creating a Pink Cloud of
Energy

Internal scanning

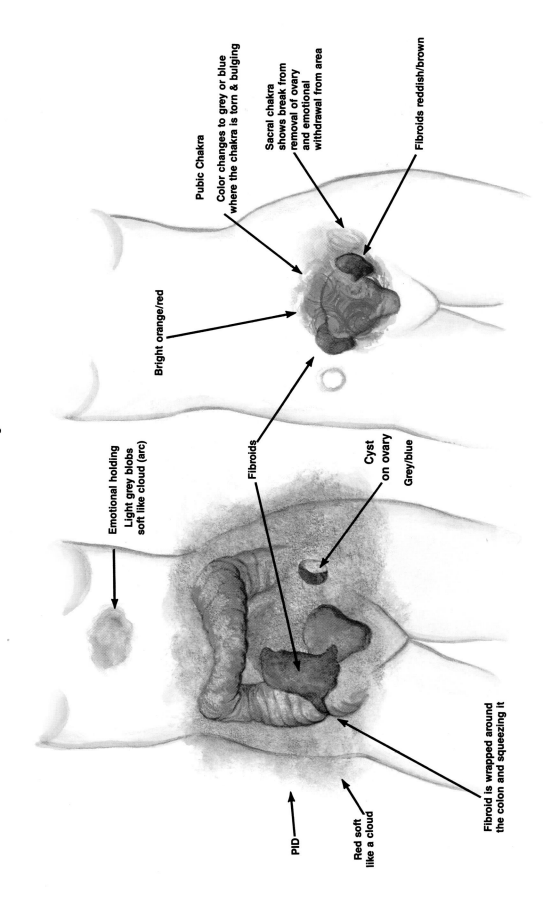

Emotional holding
Light grey blobs
soft like cloud (arc)

Fibroids

Cyst
on ovary

Grey/blue

PID

Red soft
like a cloud

Fibroid is wrapped around
the colon and squeezing it

Pubic Chakra

Color changes to grey or blue
where the chakra is torn & bulging

Sacral chakra
shows break from
removal of ovary
and emotional
withdrawal from area

Fibroids reddish/brown

Bright orange/red

A. Pelvic Inflammatory Disease, ovarian cyst and fibroid

B. Fibroids and disfigured chakra

Figure 18-3: Internal Viewing
(Diagnostic Views)

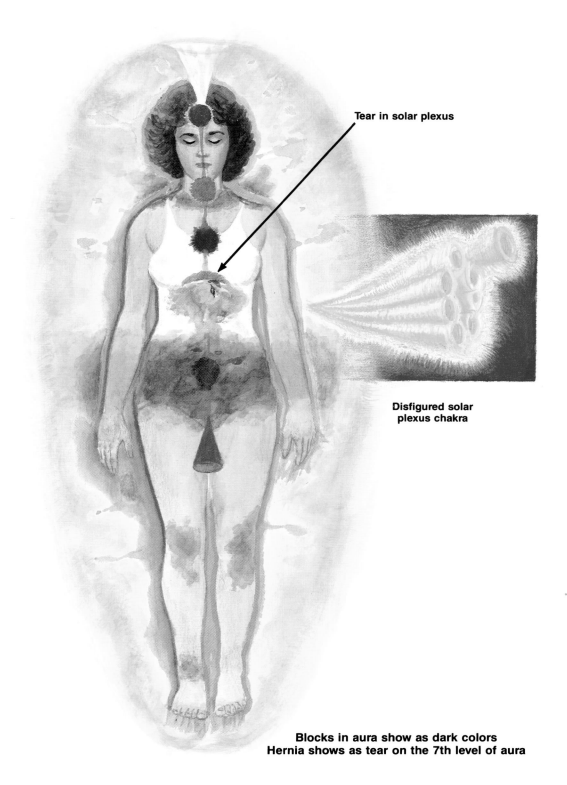

**Tear in solar plexus**

**Disfigured solar plexus chakra**

**Blocks in aura show as dark colors
Hernia shows as tear on the 7th level of aura**

Figure 22–4:   Patient's Aura Before Healing With Insert of
Disfigured Solar Plexus Chakra

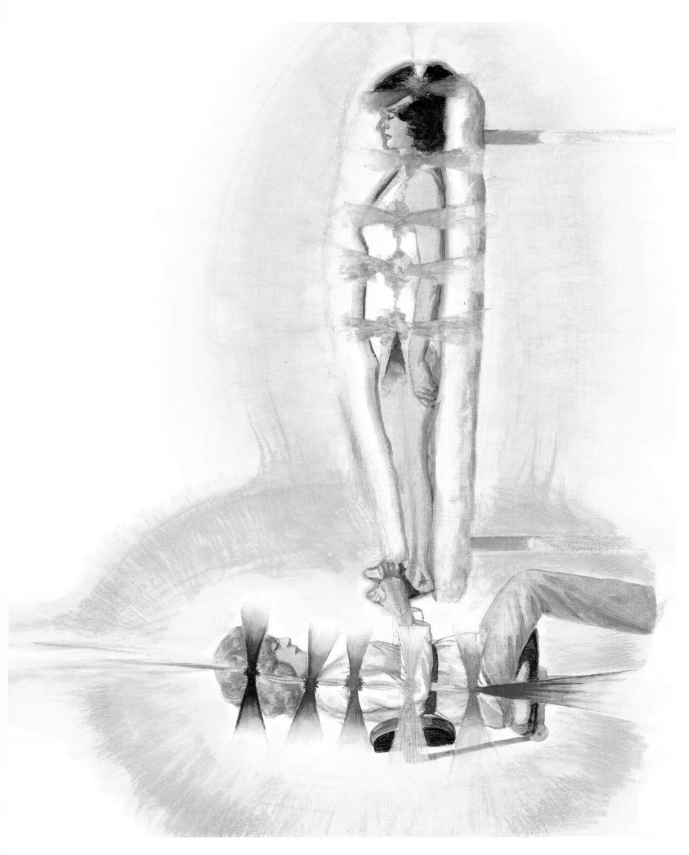

Figure 22-6: Balancing Auric Field of Patient, Healer and Universal Energy Field

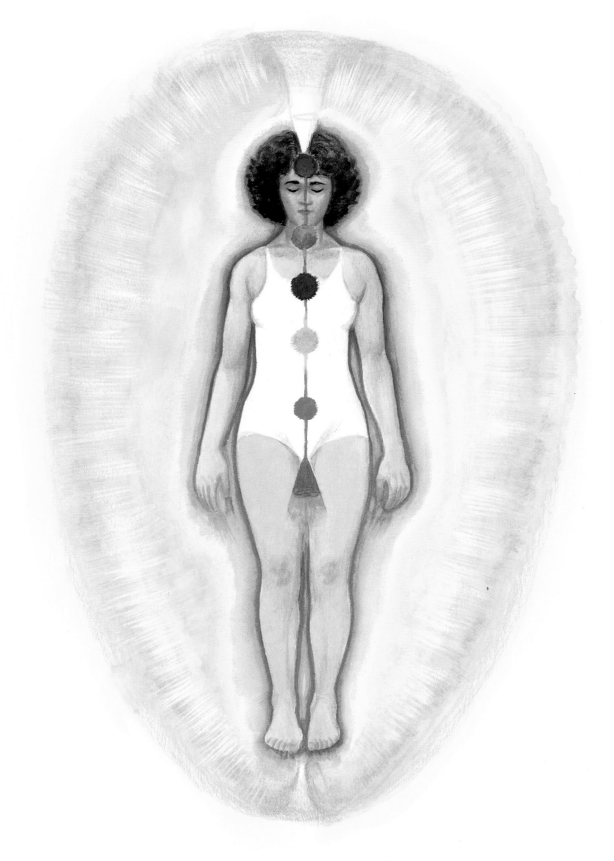

Figure 22–20: Patient's Aura After Healing

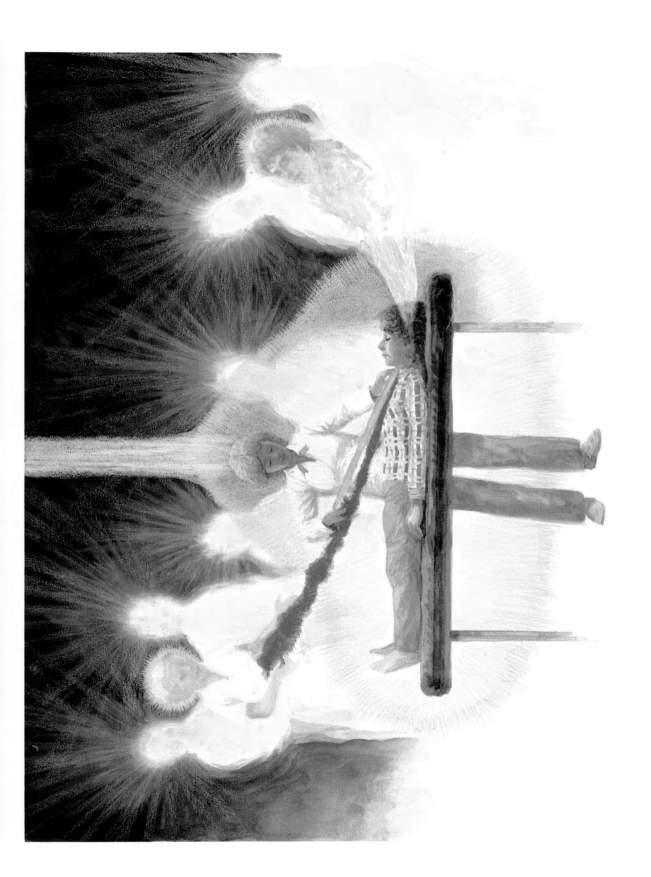

Figure 22–21: Setting an Eighth Level Shield Showing Blue Shield Inserted at Patient's Neck, Patient Out of Body to the Right and Deceased Mother of Patient to the Left.

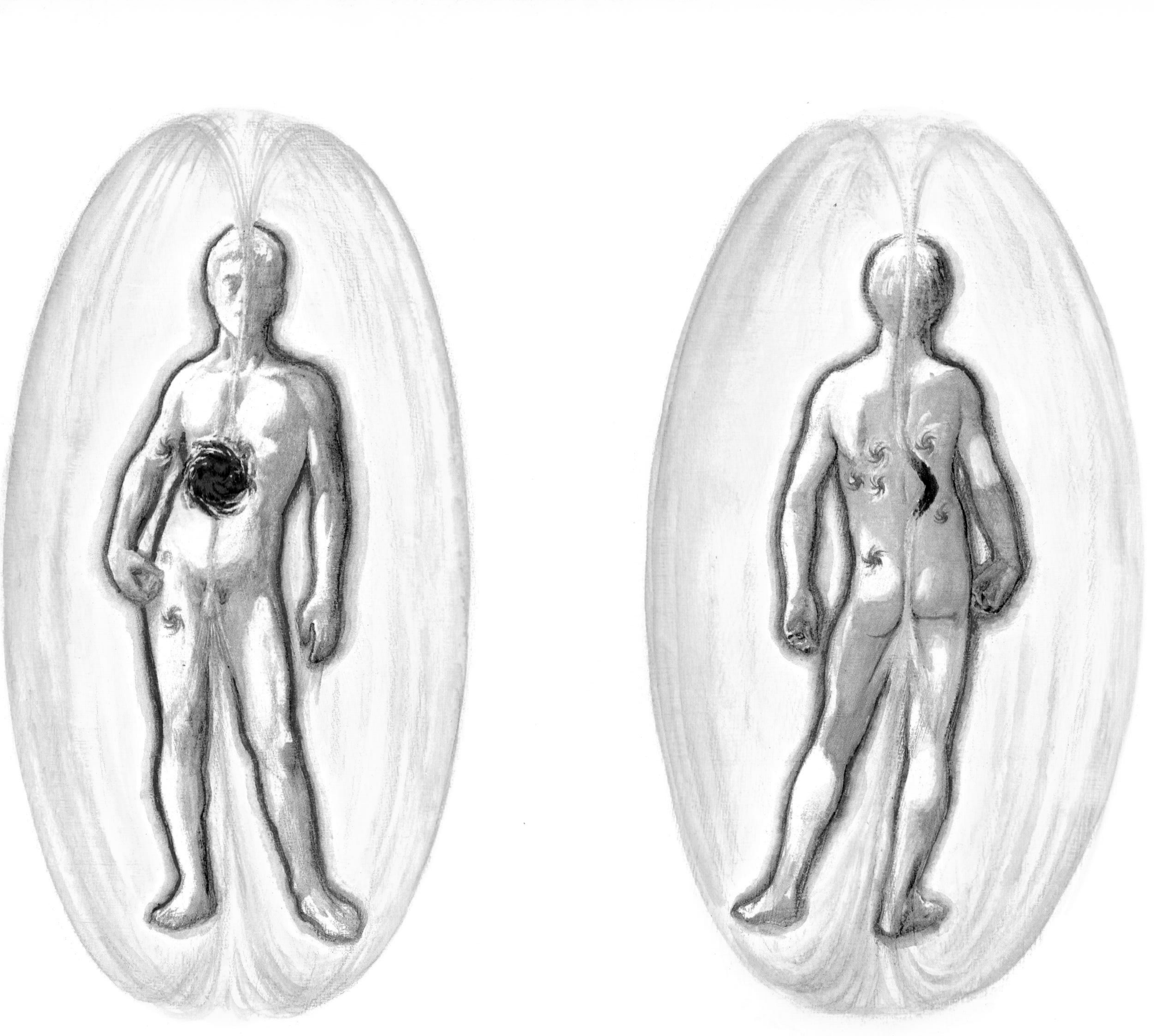

Figure 24-1: Past Life Trauma in the Aura Showing Dark Red Wound on Left

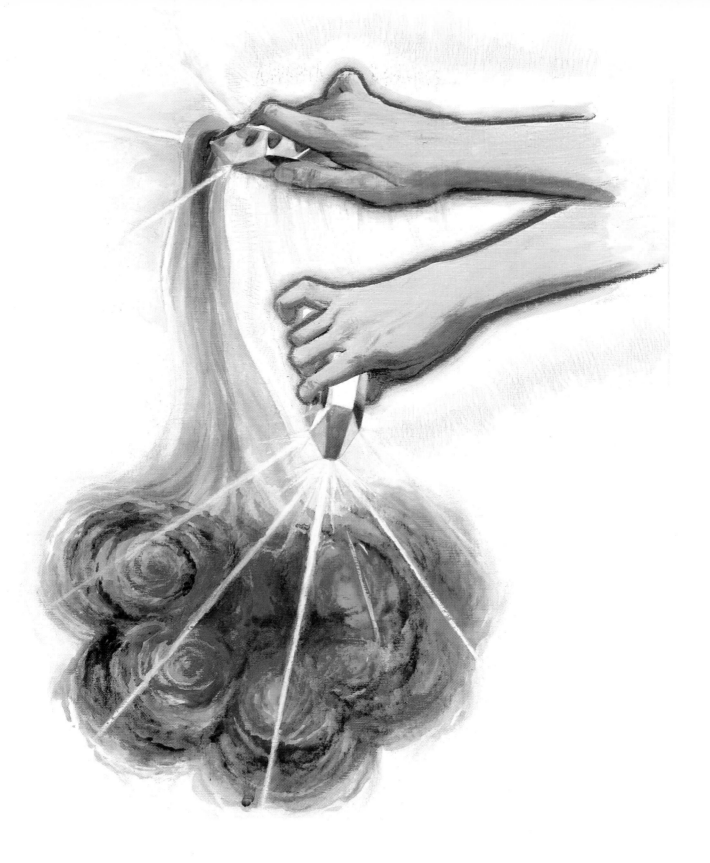

Figure 24-2:  Removing Auric Mucus With a Crystal
Crystal Hooks Mucus and Draws It Out.

Figure 24–6:  Hands of Light

body, and together they are considered to be the front and rear aspect of one chakra. The frontal aspects are related to the person's feelings, the rear ones to her or his will, and the three on the head to a person's mental processes. These are shown in Figure 7–3. Thus chakra #2 has a 2A and 2B component, and #3 has a 3A and 3B component, and so on through the sixth chakra. Chakras 1 and 7 may be considered to be paired if one wishes, because they are the open-ended points of the main vertical power current that runs up and down the spine into which all the chakras point.

The points or tips of the chakras, where they connect to the main power current, are called the roots or the hearts of the chakras. Within these hearts are seals which control exchange of energy between layers of the aura through that chakra. That is, each of the seven chakras has seven layers, each corresponding to a layer of the auric field. Each chakra looks different on each of these layers, as will be described in detail in the descriptions of each layer. In order for certain energy to flow from one layer to another through the chakra, it must pass through the seals in the roots of the chakras. Figure 7–4 shows the auric field with all seven interpenetrating layers, and all seven interpenetrating layers of chakras.

Energy can be seen flowing into all of these chakras from the Universal Energy Field (Figure 7–3). Each swirling vortex of energy appears to suck or entrain energy from the UEF. They appear to function as do fluid vortexes we are familiar with in water or in air such as whirlpools, cyclones, water spouts and hurricanes. The open end of a normal chakra in the first layer of the aura is about six inches in diameter at a distance of one inch from the body.

## The Function of the Seven Chakras

Each of these vortices exchanges energy with the UEF. Thus, when we speak of feeling "open," that is literally true. All the major chakras, minor chakras, lesser chakras and acu-

puncture points are openings for energy to flow into and out of the aura. We are like sponges in the energy sea around us. Since this energy is always associated with a form of consciousness, we experience the energy we exchange in terms of seeing, hearing, feeling, sensing, intuiting or direct knowing.

Therefore, we can see that staying "open" means two things. First, it means metabolizing a lot of energy from the universal field through all the chakras, large and small. Second, it means letting in, and in some way dealing with, all the consciousness that is associated with the energy that is flowing through us. That is not an easy task, and most of us cannot do it. There would simply be too much input. Psychological material related to each chakra is brought to consciousness by increasing one's energy flow through that chakra. Too much psychological material would be released by a sudden flow of energy, and we could not process it all. We therefore work in whatever growth process we are in to open each chakra slowly, so that we have time to process the personal material that is released and integrate the new information into our life.

It is important to open the chakras and increase our energy flow, because the more energy we let flow, the healthier we are. Illness in the system is caused by an imbalance of energy or a blocking of the flow of energy. In other words, a lack of flow in the human energy system eventually leads to disease. It also distorts our perceptions and dampens our feelings and thus interferes with a smooth experience of full life. We are not psychologically prepared, however, to stay open without working and developing our maturity and clarity.

Each of the five senses is associated with a chakra. Touching is associated with the first chakra; hearing, smelling and tasting with the fifth (or throat) chakra; and seeing with the sixth (or third eye) chakra. This is discussed in detail in the chapter on perception.

The chakras of the auric body have three major functions:

1. To vitalize each auric body and, thus, the physical body.

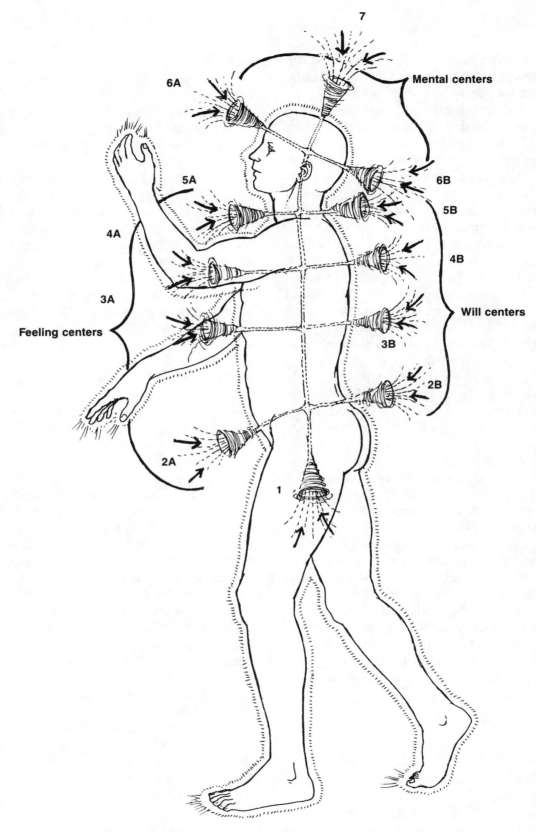

Figure 7–3:  The Seven Major Chakras, Front and Back Views
(Diagnostic View)

46

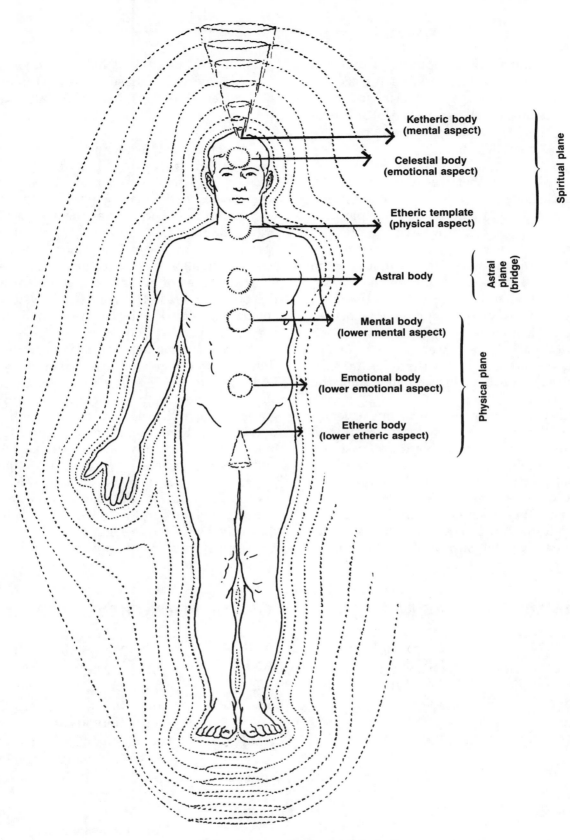

Figure 7–4:  The Seven Layer Auric Body System
(Diagnostic View)

47

2. To bring about the development of different aspects of self-consciousness. Each chakra is related to a specific psychological function. Chapter 11 deals with psychological effects of opening specific chakras in the etheric, emotional and mental bodies.

3. To transmit energy between the auric levels. Each auric layer has its own set of seven major chakras, each located in the same place on the physical body. Since each progressive layer exists in ever increasing octaves of frequency, this is possible. For example, for the fourth chakra, there are really seven chakras, each of a higher frequency band than the lower one. These chakras appear to be nested within each other like nesting glasses. Each chakra on each higher layer extends out farther in the auric field (to the edge of each auric layer) and is slightly broader than the one below it.

Energy is transmitted from one layer to the next through passageways in the tips of the chakras. In most people these passageways are sealed. They open as a result of spiritual purification work and thus the chakras become transmitters of energy from one layer to another. Each chakra in the etheric is directly connected to the same chakra in the next finer body that surrounds and interpenetrates it. The chakras in the emotional body are connected to those in the next finer body, the mental, etc., and so on for all seven layers.

In eastern esoteric literature, each of the chakras is seen as having a certain number of petals. On closer investigation, these petals appear to be small rotating vortices spinning at very high rates. Each vortex metabolizes an energy vibration that resonates at its particular spin frequency. The pelvic chakra, for example, has four small vortices and metabolizes four basic frequencies of energy, and so on for each of the other chakras. The colors observed in each chakra are related to the frequency of energy being metabolized at its particular rate.

Since the chakras serve to vitalize the body, they are directly related to any pathology in the body. Figure 7-5 lists the seven major chakras along the spine with the area of the body each governs. Each chakra is associated with an endocrine gland and major nerve plexus. The chakras absorb the universal or primary energy (ch'i, orgone, prana, etc.), break it up into component parts and then send it along energy rivers called *nadis* to the nervous system, the endocrine glands and then the blood to nourish the body, as shown in Figure 7-6.

The psychodynamic functioning of the cha-

## Figure 7-5
## MAJOR CHAKRAS AND THE AREA OF THE BODY THEY NOURISH

| CHAKRA | NO. OF SMALL VORTICES | ENDOCRINE GLAND | AREA OF BODY GOVERNED |
|---|---|---|---|
| 7-Crown | 972 Violet-White | Pineal | Upper brain, Right eye |
| 6-Head | 96 Indigo | Pituitary | Lower brain, Left eye, Ears, Nose, Nervous system |
| 5-Throat | 16 Blue | Thyroid | Bronchial and vocal apparatus, Lungs, Alimentary canal |
| 4-Heart | 12 Green | Thymus | Heart, Blood, Vagus nerve, Circulatory system |
| 3-Solar Plexus | 10 Yellow | Pancreas | Stomach, Liver, Gall bladder, Nervous system |
| 2-Sacral | 6 Orange | Gonads | Reproductive system |
| 1-Base | 4 Red | Adrenals | Spinal column, Kidneys |

kras, which will be discussed in detail, relates mainly to the first three bodies of the aura, those associated with physical, mental and emotional interactions on the earth plane. For example, when one's heart chakra is functioning properly, one is very good at loving. When the first chakra is functioning healthfully, one usually has a strong will to live and is connected well to the ground. This is the person who is very grounded in his life. When someone's sixth and third chakras are functioning well, he will think clearly. If they are not functioning well, his thoughts will be confused.

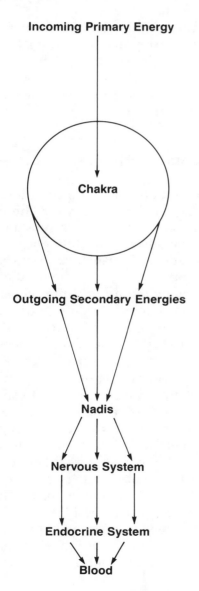

Figure 7–6: Metabolic Path of Incoming Primary Energy

## The Etheric Body (First Layer)

The etheric body (from "ether," the state between energy and matter) is composed of tiny energy lines "like a sparkling web of light beams" similar to the lines on a television screen (Figure 7–7). It has the same structure as the physical body including all the anatomical parts and all the organs.

The etheric body consists of a definite structure of lines of force, or energy matrix, upon which the physical matter of the body tissues is shaped and anchored. The physical tissues exist as such only because of the vital field behind them; that is, the field is prior to, not a result of, the physical body. This relationship has been supported in the observations of plant growth by Dr. John Pierrakos and myself. Through the use of High Sense Perception, we observed that an energy field matrix in the shape of a leaf is projected by the plant prior to the growth of a leaf, and then the leaf grows into that already existing form.

The web-like structure of the etheric body is in constant motion. To clairvoyant vision, sparks of bluish-white light move along its energy lines throughout the entire dense physical body. The etheric body extends from one quarter to two inches beyond the physical body and pulsates about 15–20 cycles per minute.

The color of the etheric body varies from light blue to gray. The light blue color has been connected to a finer form than the gray. That is, a more sensitive person with a sensitive body will tend to have a bluish first layer, whereas a more athletic, robust type of person will tend to have a more grayish etheric body. All the chakras of this layer are the same color as the body. That is, they will also range between blue to gray in color. The chakras look like vortices made of a net of light, just like the rest of the etheric body. One can perceive all the organs of the physical body, but they are formed of this scintillating bluish light. As in the leaf's energy system, this etheric structure sets up the matrix for the cells to grow; i.e., the cells of the body grow along the lines of energy of the etheric matrix, and that matrix is there before the cells grow. If one were to isolate the etheric body and look only at it, it would look like a man or woman made of bluish lines of light in constant scintillation, rather like Spiderman.

By observing the shoulder of someone in dim light against a plain white or plain black or dark blue background, you may be able to see the pulsations of this etheric body. The pulsation rises, say at the shoulder, and then makes its way down the arm, like a wave. If you look more closely, there appears to be a blank space between the shoulder and the blue hazy light; then there is a layer of brighter blue haze that slowly fades as it extends from the body. But be aware that as soon as you see it, it will be gone, because it moves so fast. It will have pulsated down the arm by the time you take a second look to check yourself out. Try again. You will catch the next pulsation.

## The Emotional Body (Second Layer)

The second auric body (Figure 7–8), or next finer after the etheric body, is generally called the emotional body, and is associated with feelings. It roughly follows the outline of the physical body. Its structure is much more fluid than the etheric and does not duplicate the physical body. Rather, it appears to be colored clouds of fine substance in continual fluid motion. It extends one to three inches from the body.

This body interpenetrates the denser bodies that it surrounds. Its colors vary from brilliant clear hues to dark muddy ones, depending on the clarity or confusion of the feeling or energy that produces them. Clear and highly energized feelings such as love, excitement, joy or anger are bright and clear; those feelings that are confused are dark and muddy. As these feelings become energized through personal interaction, body psychotherapy, etc., the colors separate out into their primary hue and brighten. Chapter 9 deals with this process.

This body contains all the colors of the rainbow. Each chakra looks like a vortex of a different color and follows the colors of the rainbow.

The list below shows chakras of the emotional body and their colors.

Chakra 1 = red
       2 = red-orange
       3 = yellow
       4 = bright grass green
       5 = sky blue
       6 = indigo
       7 = white

Chapter 9 gives a number of observations on the emotional body during therapy sessions. In general, the body does appear to be blobs of color moving within the matrix of the etheric field and also extending beyond it a bit. At times a person may throw off color blobs of energy into the air around him. This is especially observable when someone is releasing feelings in a therapy session.

## The Mental Body (Third Layer)

The third aura body is the mental body (Figure 7–9). This body extends beyond the emotional and is composed of still finer substances, all of which are associated with thoughts and mental processes. This body usually appears as a bright yellow light radiating about the head and shoulders and extending around the whole body. It expands and becomes brighter when its owner is concentrating on mental processes. It extends from three to eight inches from the body.

The mental body is also a structured body. It contains the structure of our ideas. This body is mostly yellow. Within this field can be seen thought forms. They appear to be blobs of varying brightness and form. These thought forms have additional colors superimposed on them, actually emanating from the emotional level. The color represents the person's emotion that is connected to the thought form. The clearer and more well-formed the idea, the clearer and more well-formed is the thought form associated with that idea. We enhance these thought forms by focusing on the thoughts they represent. Habitual thoughts become very powerful "well-formed" forces that then affect our lives.

This body has been the hardest for me to observe. This may be partly caused by the fact that human beings are really just beginning to develop the mental body and are just beginning to use their intellects in clear ways. For that reason we are very conscious of mental activity and consider ourselves an analytical society.

## Beyond the Physical World

In the system I use for healing (Figure 7–4), the lower three auric layers are associated with and metabolize energies related to the physical world, and the upper three metabolize energies related to the spiritual world. The fourth layer or astral level, associated with the heart chakra, is the transforming crucible through which all energy must pass when going from one world to the other. That is, the spiritual energy must pass through the fire of the heart to be transformed into the lower physical energies, and the physical energies (of the lower three auric layers) must pass through the transformative fire of the heart to become spiritual energies. In full spectrum healing, discussed in Chapter 22, we use the energies associated with all the layers and all the chakras and pass them through the heart, the center of love.

So far in this discussion, we have focused on the lower three layers. Most of the body psychotherapy I have seen in this country primarily utilizes only the lower three layers and the heart. As soon as one begins to examine the upper four layers of the auric field everything changes, because *as soon as you open your perception to layers above the third you also begin to perceive people or beings who exist in those layers who do not have physical bodies.* From my observations and those of other clairvoyants, there exist layers of reality or other "frequency bands" of reality beyond the physical. The upper four layers of the auric field correspond to four of those layers of reality. Again, I must reiterate that the discussion that follows is only an attempt at a system with which to explain observed phenomena; I'm sure in the future there will be better systems created. This one is useful to me.

ter systems created. This one is useful to me.

In Figure 7–4 I have in general associated the upper three chakras with the physical, emotional and mental functioning of the human being in her spiritual reality. That is because most of us only use that portion of ourselves in those limited types of functions. They are the higher will, the higher feelings of love and the higher knowing, where whole concepts are understood at once. The fourth layer is associated with love. That is the doorway through which we can enter into the other states of reality.

However, the picture is actually more complicated than that. Each of the layers above the third is an entire layer of reality with beings, forms and personal functions that go beyond what we normally call human. Each is an entire world in which we live and have our being. Most of us experience these realities during sleep but do not remember them. Some of us can go into those states of reality by expanding the consciousness through meditative techniques. These meditative techniques open the seals between the roots of the chakra layers and thus provide a doorway for consciousness to travel. For the following discussion, I will focus only on the description of the auric layers and their limited functions. Later on in this book there will be more discussions of the higher layers or "frequencies of reality."

## The Astral Level (Fourth Layer)

The astral body (Figure 7–10) is amorphous and is composed of clouds of color more beautiful than those of the emotional body. The astral body tends to have the same set of colors, but they are usually infused with the rose light of love. It extends out about one half to one foot from the body. The chakras are the same octave of colors as the rainbow of the emotional body, but each is infused with the rose light of love. The heart chakra of a loving person is full of rose light on the astral level.

When people fall in love, beautiful arcs of rose light can be seen between their hearts, and a beautiful rose color is added to the normal golden pulsations I observe in the pituitary gland. When people form relationships with each other, they grow cords out of the chakras that connect them. These cords exist on many levels of the auric field in addition to the astral. The longer and deeper the relationship, the more cords and the stronger they are. When relationships end, those cords are torn, sometimes causing a great deal of pain. The period of "getting over" a relationship is usually a period of disconnecting those cords on the lower levels of the field and rerooting them within the self.

A great deal of interaction takes place between people on the astral level. Great blobs of color of various forms whisk across the room between people. Some of it is pleasant and some not so pleasant. You can feel the difference. You may feel uneasy about someone across the room who is apparently not even aware of your presence; however, on another level a lot is happening. I have seen people standing next to each other in a group pretending not to notice each other, when on the energy level there is a whole communication taking place with lots of energy forms moving between them. You have no doubt experienced this yourself, especially between men and women. It is not just body language; there is an actual energetic phenomenon that can be perceived. For example, when a man or woman fantasize about making love with someone, say in a bar or at a party, there is an actual testing in the energy fields to see if the fields are synchronous and if the people are compatible. More examples of this auric interaction phenomenon will be given in Chapter 9.

## The Etheric Template Body (Fifth Layer)

I call the fifth layer of the aura the etheric template (Figure 7–11) because it contains all the forms that exist on the physical plane in a blueprint or template form. That is, it looks rather like the negative of a photograph. It is the template form for the etheric layer, which as was already stated is the template form for the physical body. The etheric layer of the energy field derives its structure from the etheric template layer. It is the blueprint or the perfect form for the etheric layer to take. It extends from about one and one half to two feet from the body. In disease, when the etheric layer becomes disfigured, etheric template work is needed to provide the support for the etheric layer in its original template form. It is the level at which sound creates matter. It is at this level that sounding in healing is the most effective. This will be discussed in Chapter 23 on healing. To my clairvoyant sight, these forms appear as clear or transparent lines on a cobalt blue background, much like an architect's blueprint, only this blueprint exists in another dimension. It is as if a form is made by completely filling in the background space, and the empty space left creates the form.

An example would be to compare how a sphere is created in Euclidian geometry to the way one is created in etheric space. In Euclidian geometry, to create a sphere one first defines a point. A radius drawn out from that point in all three dimensions will create the surface of a sphere. However, in etheric space, which one might call negative space, to form a sphere the opposite process takes place. An infinite number of planes comes from all directions and fill in all space, except for a spherical area of space left empty. This defines the sphere. It is the area not filled in by all the planes that meet each other that then defines an empty spherical space.

Thus, the etheric template level of the aura creates an empty or negative space in which the first or etheric level of the aura can exist. The etheric template is the template for the etheric body, which then forms the grid structure (structured energy field) upon which the physical body grows. Thus, the etheric template level of the universal energy field contains all the shapes and forms that exist on the physical plane, except on the template level. These forms exist in negative space, creating an empty space in which the etheric grid structure grows and upon which all physical manifestation exists.

By focusing on only the vibratory frequency of the fifth level when observing someone's field, one can isolate only the fifth layer of the aura. When I do this, I see the form of the person's auric field, which extends out to about two and a half feet from the individual. It looks like a narrow oval shape. It contains the entire structure of the field, including chakras, body organs and body form (limbs, etc.), all in negative form. All these structures appear to be formed from transparent lines on a dark blue background, which is solid space. When tuning into this level I also can perceive all other forms in my environment in this perspective. That seems to happen automatically when I switch my perceptual mechanism to this range. That is, my attention is first brought to the general fifth level; then I focus in on the particular person I am observing.

## The Celestial Body (Sixth Layer)

The sixth level is the emotional level of the spiritual plane, called the celestial body (Figure 7-12). It extends about two to two and three-quarter feet from the body. It is the level through which we experience spiritual ecstasy. We can reach it through meditation and many of the other forms of transformation work I have mentioned in this book. When we reach the point of "being" where we know our connection with all the universe, when we see the light and love in everything that exists, when we are immersed in the light and feel we are of it and it is of us and feel that we are one with God, then we have raised our consciousness to the sixth level of the aura.

Unconditional love flows when there is a connection between the open heart chakra and the open celestial chakra. In this connection, we combine the love of humanity, our basic human love for our fellow humans in the flesh, with the spiritual ecstasy found in the spiritual love that goes beyond the physical reality to all the realms of existence. Combining these two creates the experience of unconditional love.

The celestial body appears to me in beautiful shimmering light, composed mostly of pastel colors. This light has a gold-silver shine and opalescent quality, like mother of pearl sequins. Its form is less defined than the etheric template level in that it simply appears to be composed of

light that radiates out from the body like the glow around a candle. Within this glow are also brighter, stronger beams of light.

## The Ketheric Template or Causal Body (Seventh Level)

The seventh level is the mental level of the spiritual plane called the ketheric template (Figure 7-13). It extends from about two and one half to three and one half feet from the body. When we bring our consciousness to the seventh level of the aura, we know that we are one with the Creator. The outer form is the egg shape of the aura body and contains all the auric bodies associated with the present incarnation an individual is undergoing. This body, too, is a highly structured template. It appears to my vision as composed of tiny threads of gold-silver light of very strong durability that hold the whole form of the aura together. It contains a golden grid structure of the physical body and all the chakras.

When "tuning" into the frequency level of the seventh layer, I perceive beautiful golden shimmering light that is pulsating so fast that I use the term "shimmering." It looks like thousands of golden threads. The golden egg form extends out beyond the body some three to three and a half feet depending on the person with the smaller tip beneath the feet and the larger end about three feet above the head. It can expand even more, if the person is very energetic. The outer edge actually looks like an eggshell to me; it appears to have a thickness of about a quarter to a half inch. This outer part of the seventh layer is very strong and resilient, resistant to penetration and protects the field just as an eggshell protects the chick. All the chakras and body forms appear to be made of golden light on this level. This is the strongest, most resilient level of the auric field.

It could be likened to a standing lightwave of intricate shape and form vibrating at an extremely high rate. One can almost hear a sound when looking at it. I'm sure a sound could be heard if one meditated on such a picture. The golden template level also contains the main power current that runs up and down the spine and is the main power current that nourishes the whole body. As this golden power current pulsates up and down the spine, it carries energies through the roots of each chakra and connects the energies that are taken in through each chakra.

The main vertical power current induces other currents at right angles to it to form golden streamers that extend directly outward from the body. These in turn induce other currents that circle around the field, so that the entire auric field and all the levels below it are surrounded and held within this basket-like network. This network shows the power of the golden light, the divine mind that holds the whole field together in its entirety and its integrity.

In addition, in the ketheric template level are also the past life bands within the eggshell. These are colored bands of light which completely encircle the aura and can be found anywhere on the eggshell surface. The band found near the head-neck area is usually the band containing the past life that you are working to clear in your present life circumstance. Jack Schwarz speaks of these bands and how to tell their meaning by their color. Later, in the past life healing section, I will describe how to work with these bands. The ketheric level is the last auric level in the spiritual plane. It contains the life plan and is the last level directly related to this incarnation. Beyond this level is the cosmic plane, the plane that cannot be experienced from the limiting viewpoint of only one incarnation.

## The Cosmic Plane

The two levels above the seventh that I am able to see at this point are the eighth and ninth levels. They are each associated with the eighth and ninth chakras located above the head. Each level appears to be crystalline and composed of very fine high vibrations. The eighth and ninth levels seem to follow the general pattern of alternating between substance (eighth level) and form (ninth level) in that the eighth appears mostly a fluid substance and the ninth appears

to be a crystalline template of everything below it. I have not found references to these levels in the literature, although they may be there. I know very little about these levels, except for certain very powerful healing practices that I have been taught by my guides. I will discuss these methods in Chapter 22.

## Perceiving the Field

It is important to remember that as you open your clairvoyant vision, you will probably perceive only the first layers of the aura. You will also probably not be able to distinguish between layers. You will probably just see colors and forms. As you progress, you will sensitize yourself to higher and higher frequencies so that you can perceive the higher bodies. You will also be able to distinguish layers and be able to focus on the layer of your choice.

Most of the illustrations in the next few chapters show only the lower three or four auric bodies. No distinction is made between the layers. They appear to be mixed within each other and act together in most of the interactions described. Most of the time we have our lower emotions, basic thinking processes and interpersonal feelings mixed together and confused. We are not very good at distinguishing them in ourselves. Some of that mixing even shows in the aura. Many times the mental and emotional bodies appear to act as one confused form. In the following descriptions of the therapeutic processes not much distinction is made in the bodies. However, through the therapeutic process or any other growth process, the layers of one's being become more distinct. The client is much more able to distinguish between base emotions, thought processes and the higher emotions of unconditional love associated with the higher auric levels. This distinction occurs through the process of understanding the cause-and-effect relationships described in Chapter 15. That is, the client begins to understand how his belief system affects the ideas in the mental body, how that, in turn, affects the emotions, then the etheric, and finally the physical body. With this understanding, one can then distin-

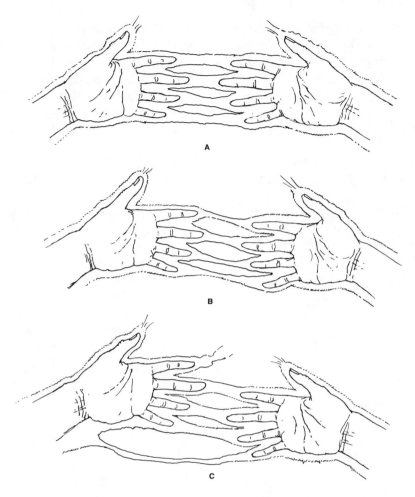

Figure 7–14:   Aura Around Fingertips

guish between layers of the auric field. The layers of the field actually become clearer and more distinct as the client becomes clearer with more self-understanding between physical feelings, emotional feelings and thoughts and acts accordingly.

Later, in the healing sections that follow, it will be very important to distinguish between the layers of the aura.

## Answers to the Questions in Exercises To See the Human Aura

The energy almost always moves from left to right around the circle. It feels very unpleasant to stop, and usually it is impossible to stop the entire flow. The feeling of building something up between your hands is that of a tickling sensation with pressure, somewhat like static electricity. When the energy body edges touch each other, there is a feeling of tingling and of pressure. When the energy body edge touches the skin, there is a feeling of tickling and pressure on the skin surface. When you draw circles on the palm, you can feel the tickling outline of the circle.

Most people see a haze around the fingers and hands when trying to sense the aura. It looks somewhat like the heat wave over a radiator. It is sometimes seen in various colors, such as a blue tint. Usually, most people see it as colorless in the beginning. The energy bodies pull like taffy between the fingers as the haze from each fingertip connects to the haze at the fingertip of the opposite hand. When you move the fingers so that a different fingertip is facing it, the haze will at first follow the old finger and then jump to the closer fingertip. (See Figure 7–14.)

## Chapter 7 Review

1. What is the relationship between the Universal Energy Field and the Human Energy Field?
2. What does the etheric body look like? How does it differ from the emotional body?
3. What are the three main functions of the chakras?
4. Why is a chakra a certain color?
5. Where is the heart of the chakra?
6. What anatomical structures are the chakras related to?
7. Describe the seven lowest layers of the auric field and their functions.
8. Describe the relationship between the chakras and the layers of the aura.
9. Where are the eighth and ninth chakras located?
10. Describe a chakra on the seventh layer of the field.
11. Where is the main vertical power current located?
12. Which layer holds the HEF together?
13. In which layer of the HEF do the emotions appear?

# PART III

# PSYCHODYNAMICS AND THE HUMAN ENERGY FIELD

"The golden light of a candle flame sits upon the throne
of its dark light that clings to the wick."

The Zohar

## Introduction

# THE THERAPEUTIC EXPERIENCE

It was in the psychotherapeutic setting that I first consciously started seeing auras again as an adult. This was a setting where I was not only "allowed" to closely observe people, but I was also encouraged to do so. During my long hours of practice, I observed the dynamics of many people. This was a real privilege, because normal social ethics set very clear boundaries on such behavior. I'm sure you have all had the experience of getting interested in a particular stranger on a bus or in a cafeteria, when after only a short observation that person catches your eye and lets you know in no uncertain terms with a look that you had better stop looking. Now, in the first place, how did he know you were looking? He felt you through the energy field. In the second, why did he tell you to stop? People get very nervous when they are seen. Most of us do not want our personal dynamics to be known by others. Most of us are ashamed of what will be seen if another human being looks closely. We all have problems; we all try to hide at least some of them. In this section, I will discuss how our private experiences, in-cluding our problems, show up in the aura. I will relate that to body psychotherapy and to character structure as defined by bioenergetics. But first let us start at the basis of psychotherapy with childhood development.

There have been a lot of studies done on human growth and development. Erik Erikson is famous for his work on delineating stages of growth and development related to age. These various stages have become a part of our every-day language, such as the oral stage, adolescence, pubescence, etc. None of these studies mention the aura, for it is not known to most people in the field of psychology. When observed, however, the aura is very informative about a person's psychological makeup and her personal growth process. What is developing in the aura at any stage of growth is directly related to the psychological development at that stage. In fact when looked at from the auric point of view, that development can be seen as a natural outcome of what is happening in the auric fields. Let us look at how our energy field usually develops from birth to death.

# Chapter 8

# HUMAN GROWTH AND DEVELOPMENT IN THE AURA

To span the scope of human experience from birth to death and beyond, I will utilize both psychological and metaphysical traditions as resources. If the metaphysics disturbs you, please take it as metaphor.

## Incarnation

The process of incarnation takes a lifetime. It is not something that happens at birth and is then finished. To describe it, we need to use metaphysical terms. Incarnation is organic soul movement in which higher, finer vibrations or soul aspects are continually radiated downward through the finer auric bodies into the more dense ones and then finally into the physical body. These successive energies are utilized by the individual in her growth throughout her life.

Each major stage of life corresponds with new and higher vibrations and the activation of different chakras. At each stage, new energy and consciousness is thus available to the personality for her expansion. Each stage presents new areas of experience and learning. Seen from this point of view, life is full of exciting discovery and challenge to the soul.

The process of incarnating is directed by the higher self. This life pattern, is held in the seventh layer of the aura, the ketheric template level. It is a dynamic template which is constantly changing as the individual makes free-will choices in the process of living and growing. As growth takes place, the individual opens her ability to sustain higher levels of vibrations/energies/consciousness coming into and through her vehicles, her auric bodies and chakras. Thus, she avails herself of ever greater expanded realities as she progresses on her path of life. As each individual progresses, so does the whole of humanity. Each generation is usually able to sustain higher vibrations than the last so that the whole of humanity moves in its evolutionary plan toward higher vibrations and expanded realities. This principle of progression of the human race is mentioned in many religious texts such as the Kabbalah, the Bhagavad Gita, the Upanishads and others.

The incarnation process before conception has been discussed by Madame Blavatsky, and more recently by Alice Bailey, Phoebe Bendit and Eva Pierrakos. According to Pierrakos, the incarnating soul meets with her spirit guides to plan the coming lifetime. In this meeting the soul and the guides consider the tasks she needs to accomplish in soul growth, what karma needs to be met and dealt with, and the negative belief systems she needs to clear through experience. This life work is usually referred to as a person's task.

For example, the person may need to develop leadership. That person, on entering into physical life, will find himself in situations where leadership is a key issue. The circumstances for each person will be entirely different, but the focus would be on leadership. One person may be born into a family with rich leadership heritage, like a long line of respected company presidents or political leaders, whereas another person could be born into a family where leadership is nonexistent and leaders are seen as negative authorities to be put down or rebelled against. The person's task is to learn to accept that issue in a balanced and comfortable way.

According to Eva Pierrakos, the amount of counseling a soul has from her guides in determining her future life circumstances depends on her maturity. Parents are chosen who will provide the needed environmental and physical experience. These choices determine the mixture of energies that will eventually form the physical vehicle in which the soul will incarnate for its task. These energies are very precise and equip the soul with exactly what it needs for its task. The soul takes on both a personal task of personal learning (like leadership) and a "world task," which entails a gift to the world. The design is so unique that by fulfilling the personal task one becomes prepared to fulfill the world task. The personal task frees the soul by releasing energies which are then used for the world task.

For the example mentioned above on leadership, the individual will need to learn that quality or skill before moving into a leadership role in her chosen field of work. She may have felt intimidated from a long line of ancestors who were brilliant leaders, or her reaction to that heritage may be one wholly of inspiration to go forward in her own leadership. Each case is different and very personal according to the uniqueness of the soul which has come to learn.

The life plan contains many probable realities, which allow for wide choices of free will. Interwoven into this life fabric is the action of cause and effect. We create our own reality. This creation emerges from many different parts of our being. Creation is not always easy to understand from a simple cause and effect level, although much of our experience can be understood from that point of view. You literally create what you want. What you want is held in the consciousness, unconsciousness, superconsciousness and collective consciousness. All these creative forces mix to create experience on many levels of our being as we progress through life. What is termed karma is to me long-term cause and effect, also from many different levels of our being. Thus, we create from the personal source and group source, and, of course, there are smaller groups within larger groups all adding to the great fabric of creative life experience. From this point of view it is easy to look at the richness of life with the wonderment of a child.

After the "planning," the soul enters into a process of slowly losing consciousness of the spirit world. At conception an energetic link is formed between the soul and the fertilized egg. At this time an etheric womb also is formed which protects the incoming soul from any outer influences other than those of the mother. As the body grows inside the mother, the soul slowly begins to feel the "drag" of it and slowly becomes consciously connected to the body. At one point, the soul suddenly is aware of this connection; there is a strong flash of conscious energy down into the forming body. The soul then again loses consciousness, only to reawaken bit by bit into the physical. This strong flash of consciousness corresponds with the time of quickening.

## Birth

Birth takes place at a unique time for the incoming soul. At this point, the soul loses its protective etheric womb and is for the first time subjected to the influences of its environment. For the first time, it is alone in the sea of energy which surrounds all of us. It is touched by that field. The greater, stronger fields of the heavenly bodies also, for the first time, influence the soul's new energy field at the time of birth. And, of course, it is at this time that the sea of energy is now influenced by another new field which adds to the greater and enriches it. It is as if another note is sounded and added to the already existing symphony of life.

## Babyhood

The process of slowly awakening to the physical world continues after birth. The baby sleeps frequently during this time; the soul occupies its higher energy bodies. It leaves the physical and etheric bodies disengaged and allows them to be very busy doing the work of body building.

In the early stages of life, the child has the job of becoming used to the limitations of physical sensation and to the three-dimensional world. I have seen many newborns struggling with this process. They still have some awareness in the spiritual world, and I have seen them struggling to let go of spiritual playmates and parent figures and to transfer affections to the new parents. The newborns I have observed have very wide open crown chakras (Figure 8-1). They are struggling to squeeze themselves into the confinements of the tiny body of a baby. When I see them leave the physical body, in their higher bodies, they appear many times to be spirits of about twelve feet tall. They go through an enormous struggle in opening the lower root chakra and connecting to the earth.

One such example of this was a boy born one month later than expected. After a very fast birth, he had a fever. The doctors performed a spinal tap to check for encephalitis. The spinal tap was administered in the region of the sacral

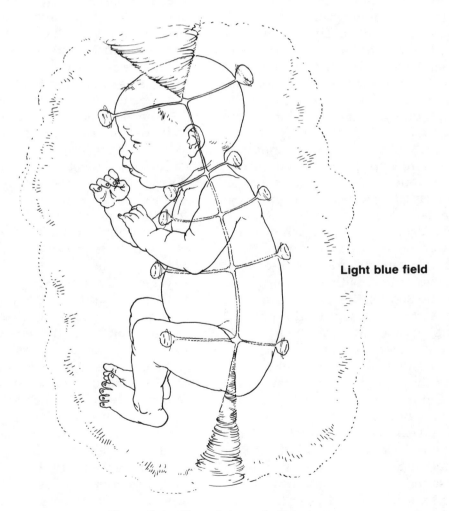

**Light blue field**

Figure 8-1:  Normal Aura of a Baby
(Diagnostic View)

chakra. The child was struggling to let go of two playmates and a spirit woman who did not want to let go either. In his struggle, he would open and connect with the earth whenever his guide was present. Then he would lose contact with his guide, see his playmates and the woman, and struggle fiercely between the two worlds. He felt more affinity with the spirit woman than his own physical mother at those times. In his struggle not to incarnate, he would throw energy out the sacral chakra and to the right to avoid growing roots straight down through the root chakra (first chakra). He was able to do this partly because of the auric hole left from the spinal tap. After a time of struggle, he would again connect with his guide and calm down, open the root and start the incoming process again.

I tried to give him healing. The first time he accepted some, but after that he refused. Whenever I tried to send energy into his aura he made a fuss. He knew what I was up to and wouldn't let me get near him. What I tried to do was to sew the hole in the sacral chakra on the seventh layer of his aura and redirect the energy downward. He wouldn't allow it. I even approached him when he was in deep sleep. When I got to a distance of about one foot, he would wake up and scream fiercely. It was clearly a deep struggle, and he wanted no one to help him with it. One of the secondary physical problems arising from this basic struggle was an intestinal problem from the constant overuse of the solar plexus chakra associated with screaming and crying. He was treated for this problem after he finally made his choice to stay in the physical plane. The astrological chart of this child clearly shows him to be a potential leader.

So, the incoming soul often enters and leaves the body through the crown chakra as it begins working on opening the root chakra to grow roots into the physical plane. The root chakra looks like a very narrow funnel, and the crown chakra looks like a very wide funnel at this stage. The other chakras look like small shallow Chinese tea cups with a narrow line of energy leading back into the body to the spine (Figure 8–1). The general field of a baby is amorphous, formless, and has a bluish or grayish color.

As a baby fixes his attention on an object in the physical plane, the aura tenses and brightens, especially around the head. Then, as his attention fades, the aura fades in color; however, it retains some of the experience in the form of color in the aura. Each experience adds a little color to the aura and enhances its individuality. Thus, the work of aura building is also going on and continues in this way throughout life so that all of one's life experiences can be found there.

After birth there remains a strong energy connection between the mother and child. This connection is sometimes referred to as the germ plasma. It is strongest between mother and child at birth and will remain there throughout life, although it will not be so pronounced as the child grows. This psychic umbilicus is the connection through which children remain in contact with their parents over the years. Many times one is aware of traumatic experiences the other is having, although there may be great distance between them on the physical level.

The field of the child is entirely open and vulnerable to the atmosphere in which he lives. Whether things are "in the open" or not, the child senses what is going on between his parents. The child constantly reacts to his energetic environment in a manner consistent with his temperament. He may have vague fears, fantasies, tantrums or illness. The child's chakras are all open in the sense that there is no protective film over them which screens out the incoming psychic influences. This makes the child very vulnerable and impressionable. Thus, even though the chakras are not developed like those of an adult, and the energy that comes into them is experienced in a vague way, it still goes right into the field of the child, and the child must deal with it in some way. (See Figure 8–2 to compare adult and child's chakra.)

At around the age of seven, a protective screen is formed over the chakra openings that filters out a lot of the incoming influences from the universal energy field. Thus, the child is no longer as vulnerable as before. This stage can be seen as a child grows and individuates. It is near the time of the dawning of reason.

Many times one can see how a younger child sits back and nestles into the lap of the mother

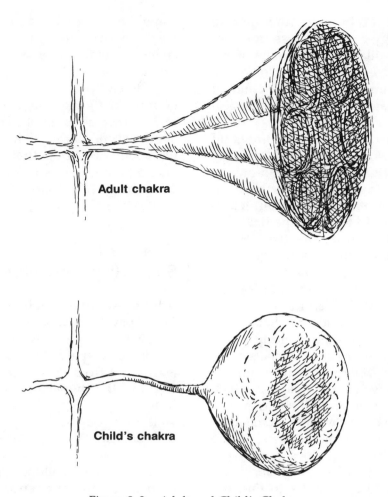

Adult chakra

Child's chakra

Figure 8–2:  Adult and Child's Chakras

or father. The child is being protected from outside influences by the field of the parent. Because of this vulnerability in the child, I am very conservative about allowing children to be in therapy groups with adults. The adult has no idea what it feels like to the child unless he has regressed to that state of vulnerability. I have seen parents unwittingly subject their children to unneeded psychic shock by having them experience group therapy, thinking it to be a progressive thing, or succumbing to group pressures. Adult rage shocks the child's system like physical shock, while grief and depression swamp it like a fog.

In addition to the physical nourishment, breast-feeding gives etheric energy to the child. There is a small chakra in each nipple which supplies the baby with energy. Remember, the baby's chakras are not developed and so do not metabolize all the energies from the universal energy field needed to sustain life.

## Early Childhood

As a child grows and the second chakra begins to develop, the child's emotional life becomes enriched. The child weaves fantasy worlds in which to live, she begins to feel like a separate person from the mother, and these worlds help create that separation. Within these fantasy worlds are the child's possessions. She will send amoeba-like projections from her etheric field out and around these objects. The more important the object in building the fantasy world, the more energy-consciousness from her field with which she will surround it. The object becomes part of the self. When this object is grabbed forcefully from the hand of a child, it tears the field and causes pain, both physical and emotional, to the child.

Beginning around the age of two, the child sees his parents as belonging to him, "me, my daddy, my mommy, etc." The colors red-orange and rosy-pink become more visible in the aura. The child is learning to relate to another, learning a basic kind of love. In terms of the field, the child is able to separate from the field of the mother, with an etheric umbilicus still connecting the two. Thus, the process of separation and independent identity begins. The child creates a fantasy space, lives in it, but still has mommy connected through the etheric umbilicus. She can still look back and see that mommy is not too far away. This space appears to clairvoyant vision as composed of energy mostly from the blue level, or etheric level. It is a space in which the child prefers to play alone, or if a playmate is allowed in, the playmate is carefully watched so as not to allow too much disturbance of the space. At this stage the child does not have a strong enough ego to maintain a real clarity between self and other. She struggles to find her uniqueness, and yet still feels very connected to all things. Personal objects become ways of defining individuation. The private energy space helps this definition. Thus, when another child comes to visit the room of a five to seven year old, the hostess struggles between wanting the communication with another and preserving the image of self. So she struggles to control personal objects that help define who she is and around which she has placed her own energy-consciousness. The struggle here is to recognize and maintain self-individuation and still feel connection to a different "individual."

At around the age of seven, the child begins to weave a lot of gold energy into this space. The space becomes freer, larger, less connected to mommy and more open to visitors. Having a greater sense of self, the child now begins to see her similarities to other humans. She can now allow the "other" a greater self-expression within her private space. A visitor is allowed to create all manner of energy forms within her private space. This makes things more "fun" and "lively" and enhances fantasy life. Children go into the "gang" stage. One of the things that makes this all possible is that, by the age of about seven, all the chakras now have a protective screen over them that filters out many of the energetic influences from the field around her. The child feels "safer" because in her auric bodies she really is.

## Exercise to Sense Psychic Spaces

Adults also infuse their space with their energy. These psychic spaces are safe nests for people in which to live and have their being. Try feeling out psychic spaces that people create. You can learn a lot from these spaces—both about yourself and the owner of the space. Just begin to tune into the spaces that you regularly visit. Walk into your friend's room. How do you feel? Do you like it? Do you want to stay, or do you want to leave?

If you have children, go into each of their rooms. Feel the difference in the energy in each room. How does it match your child? What of him does it express? Is the color right for him, or is it a color that you have imposed upon his space? Think about it.

Try it with different stores that you go into. I find it impossible to stay in some stores because of the energy emanating there.

Now do a little experiment with objects. In a small group of people (preferably people that you don't know a lot about), put their personal objects in the center and choose one that you are attracted to. Hold it in your hand. How does it feel? Heavy, warm, friendly, unfriendly, sad, happy, safe, dangerous, healthy, sick? Do you pick up any images? Give yourself time to tune into them. Check it out with the owner of the object. I bet you are right about some of the things you pick up. Practice and you will do it better next time.

## Latency

As the child grows into latency between seven and puberty, the development of more mental faculties occurs, along with the development of the third chakra. More of the mental color yellow is added to the aura at this time. Although this chakra is opening the mental energies and the child is in school, the mental energies are primarily used to enhance the fantasy life of the child. Here deep teleological urges and connections to the long past development of humanity come into play. The child becomes the Indian chief, the princess, Wonder Woman. These are deep idealistic urges, which reveal the soul's longing and most likely relate to the soul's world task. Within these archetypal forms are found the deep spiritual longings of the individual, the goals and aspirations, as expressed by the qualities played out in the backyard or the school playground. It is now that the first three centers—the physical, emotional and mental centers of the earth plane—are working together to express the first phase of the soul's incarnation.

## Adolescence

The challenge of adolescence, as in all the stages of growth, is to find the self and remain true to the self throughout all the chaos of physical and emotional changes, sweet longings and painful rejections.

As the child approaches puberty, large changes start occurring all through the body and the surrounding energy field. More green is added to the aura and the individual's private space. The space becomes infused with "vibes" from friends. As the heart chakra opens to new levels of feelings, and the dawning of eros and love emerge from deep within the psyche, the beautiful color of rose fill the field. The pituitary (third eye chakra) is activated, and the body begins to mature to that of an adult. All the chakras are affected by these changes. These new higher vibrations are sometimes embraced with excitement by the individual and at other times are loathed because they bring with them new longing and new vulnerability that the individual has not yet experienced. At times, the entire field will be disrupted and the chakras will be completely out of balance, while at other times everything will be flowing in harmony. Thus, the individual goes through great changes of emotional reality, and his actions express this confusion. At one moment he is a child, at another an adult.

The individual now repeats all the stages of growth that he has experienced but with a difference. The first three stages involved the self as the center of the universe. It was me, my daddy, my mommy, my friends, etc. Now it is an "I-thou" relationship. The "I" does not exist alone, and the "I's" welfare now depends on proper adjustments to the "not-I." This is partially caused by the fact that the individual no longer "owns" the love object as he did in the case of his parents or toys. Now his welfare depends on a balancing of his actions to "convince" the loved one to love him, or so he believes. This puts a strain on the psyche between who he thinks he is and who he thinks he ought to be (according to what he thinks she wants him to be, and vice versa). Of course, this was already going on with the parents, but it is brought to the surface more now because at any moment the loved one may choose another, and often does, publicly.

## Adulthood

By the end of adolescence, the chakras and energy pattern used by the individual are now set. All chakras have taken on an adult form. It is at this point that the individual may try to settle down and have no more changes. Some are able to accomplish this and with it cause their lives to stagnate into safe, set, patterns of clearly defined and limited reality. Most people, sufficiently shaken by their life experiences, see that reality is not so easily definable and continue a lifelong search for meaning that leads them through constant challenge to deeper experiences of fulfillment.

In maturity, the "I-thou" expands to include the personal family, which creates its own energy form. More energies flowing through the throat chakra help this personal giving and receiving. As time goes on, the "I-thou" can expand to include the individual and the group. The heart can open to include not only love of the mate and children, but also love of humanity. The color is seen in the aura as a beautiful lilac. This becomes then the integration of the self, the other and the group consciousness. As the third eye opens to higher vibrations, one begins to see the unity of all things and can see at the same time the unique preciousness of each individual soul within that unity.

## Maturity

As the individual approaches old age and death, even more higher-vibration rates can be added to the energy bodies. People's hair turns bright white as the white light coursing through their being increases their affinity with the spirit world. Now, to the "I-thou" relationship is added a very deep personal relationship with God. The lower earthly energy, metabolized through the lower chakras, decreases and is steadily replaced by higher finer energies having much more to do with spirit than life on the physical plane. The person is preparing to return home to the spirit world. When these natural processes are understood and allowed to unfold from within the psyche, serenity and love fill the personal life of the individual. Things fall into place from all the growth that has taken place throughout the years. The solar plexus chakra, especially, becomes more harmonious. The person is able to increase his depth of perception that makes life (despite diminishing physical power) a thing of ever growing interest and richer experience. It is unfortunate that our culture, in general, does not respect and utilize this great resource of wisdom and light as do other cultures like that of the Native American Indians, in which the grandmothers and grandfathers retained the power of decision for the community.

## Death

According to Phoebe Bendit, at death a luminous ray flashes out the top of the head as the person leaves the earth plane through the crown chakra. This experience of going out the crown has often been described as going through the tunnel between life and death. It is seen as a long dark tunnel with a bright light at the end. This "tunnel experience" can also be said to be the soul going up through the main power current of the body along the spine and leaving at the bright light of the crown chakra.

At death, the soul is met by old deceased friends and her spirit guides. At this time, the soul sees her whole life pass by very quickly and clearly so that there can be no mistakes as to just what happened, what choices were made, lessons learned and what lessons still remain for the next incarnation. There follows a time of celebration of a task completed, and some time spent in the spirit world before the next incarnation is taken on.

After people die of a long-term illness, I have often seen them resting, surrounded by white light for some period of time after death. They appear to be taken care of in some kind of hospital on the other side.

I have observed two people who were in the dying process a couple of days before their deaths. In both cases, the people were dying of cancer and had been ill for some time. The lower three bodies were breaking up and coming off the body as opalescent cloudy blobs. This gave the person an opalescent white look. The lower three chakras were also breaking up, with long threads of energy coming out of the solar plexus. The upper four chakras appeared to be very wide open, almost like gaping holes. There was no longer a shield over them. The people who were crossing over spent most of their time out of the body and away. Apparently they were off with their spirit guides somewhere. When the people were in their bodies, there were plenty of spirits around the room. In one case, I saw Azrael guarding the gate. When the person was in deep pain, I asked Azrael why he didn't help her die. He said, "I haven't received my orders yet." (Azrael is the angel of death and looks very strong and beautiful to me, not terrifying as some sources have implied.)

## Heyoan On Death

My guide has been lecturing on the death process, and I would like to quote him here. First he says that death is not what we have understood, but a transition from one state of consciousness to another. Heyoan says that we have already died, in forgetting who we are. Those parts of us that have been forgotten are walled off from reality, and we have come into incarnation to retrieve them. So although we fear death, he says we have already died, and in the incarnation process of reintegrating with our greater being, we actually find more life. He says that the only thing that dies is death.

During our life, we wall off experiences that we wish to forget. We do this so effectively that we do not remember many of them. We begin this walling-off process early in childhood and continue it throughout our life. These walled-off pieces of our consciousness can be seen in the auric field in terms of blocks and will be discussed in the chapter on psychodynamics. Heyoan says that the real death has already occurred in the form of that internal wall.

"As you know, the only thing that separates you from anything is yourself. And the most important thing is that death has already occurred in those portions of yourself that are walled off. That would be perhaps from our vantage point the most clear definition of what the human being considers to be death. It is being walled-off and separate from. It is forgetting. It is forgetting who you are, that is what death is. You have already died. You have in fact incarnated to bring to life those pieces of you that are already in what you call death, if we should ever use that word. Those parts have already died.

"The process of death, that which we would call transition to greater awareness, can be seen as a process in the energetic field. We will describe this now to help you understand the process of death from the auric point of view. There is a washing of the field, there is a clearing, an opening of all the chakras. When you die, you are going to another dimension. There is dissolution in the three lower chakras. There is dissolution of, and note we say dissolution, of the three lower bodies. Those of you who have watched individuals die have seen the opalescent quality of the hands, of the face, of the skin. It is an opalescent mother of pearl as the individual is dying, and the beautiful opalescent clouds are wafting off. Those clouds are the lower energy bodies which serve to hold the physical body together. They are disintegrating. They waft off, and the chakras there are opened and there are cords of energy coming out. The upper chakras are great open holes into other dimensions. So this is the beginning stages of death where the energy field begins to separate. The lower parts of the energy field separate from the upper parts. And then during the three hours or so around the hour of death, there is a washing of the body, a baptism, a spiritual baptism of the body where the energy is flushed through like a fountain right up the main vertical power current. A fountain of golden light flushes through, and all of the blocks are cleansed. And the aura becomes white gold. How will this be experienced by the individual who is dying in terms of memory? You have already heard it. A person sees his or her entire life wash by them. Well that's it. There is a concomitant energy field phenomena of the washing of the aura. All blocks are let go. All forgotten experiences of that lifetime are unblocked. They all flow through the consciousness. Thus, all of the history of that lifetime flows through the consciousness and when the person leaves, the consciousness leaves. It is the dissolution of many of the walls that were created for the process of transformation in this particular lifetime. It is a tremendous integration.

"With the dissolution of the walls of forgetting within you, you remember who you truly are. You become integrated with your greater self and feel the lightness and the vastness of it. Thus death, contrary to popular opinion, is a very wonderful experience. Many of you have read the descriptions of those who have been pronounced clinically dead and have come back to life. They all speak of a tunnel with a brilliant light at the end of it. They speak of meeting a wondrous being at the end of that tunnel. Most have a life review and a discussion of that life with that being. Most reveal that they themselves decided to return to the physical world to complete their learning, even though it was so beautiful where they went. Most of them no longer fear death, but look forward to it as a great release into serenity.

"So it is your wall that separates you from this truth: What you call death is actually transition into light. The death that you imagine you will experience can be found within your wall. Every time you separate yourself in any way, you die a small death. Every time you block your wonderful life force from flowing, you create a small death. Thus as you remember those separated parts of your being and reintegrate them back into yourself, you have already died. You come back to life. As you expand your awareness, the wall between the world, the wall between spiritual reality and physical reality dissolves. Thus death dissolves, it is nothing but the releasing of the wall of illusion when you are ready to move on. And who you are is redefined as the greater reality. You are still your individual self; when you drop your body, you will maintain the essence of self. You can feel that essence of self in the future/past meditations that are given in Chapter 27 (Self Healing). Your physical body dies, but you move into another plane of reality. You maintain that essence of self beyond body, beyond incarnation. And when

you leave your body, you may feel yourself to be a point of gold light, but you will still feel yourself."

## Chapter 8 Review

1. When does a soul take charge of a body?
2. What is the significance of the moment of birth with respect to the HEF?
3. What are the two main differences between the chakras of a small child and those of an adult?
4. What does the aura have to do with childhood development?
5. Why in relation to the aura, does a child scream in pain when someone grabs something out of its hands?
6. Why does a child like to sit inside of an adult's aura?
7. What major developments are happening in the aura during the following stages of development: before birth, birth, babyhood, early childhood, latency, puberty, maturity, middle age, advanced age, death?
8. At what age is the process of incarnation complete?
9. Describe the death experience as witnessed by HSP observers.

### Food For Thought

10. Discuss the relationship of the HEF and a person's personal space.
11. Discuss the relationship of personal boundaries to the HEF.

## Chapter 9

# PSYCHOLOGICAL FUNCTION OF THE SEVEN MAJOR CHAKRAS

As a human being matures and the chakras develop, each represents the psychological patterns evolving in the individual's life. Most of us react to unpleasant experiences by blocking our feeling and stopping a great deal of our natural energy flow. This affects the development and maturation of the chakras, resulting in inhibition of a fully balanced psychological function. For example, if a child is rejected many times when he tries to give love to another, he will probably stop trying to give love. In order to do this, he will probably try to stop the inner feelings of love that he is responding to with action. In order to do this, he will have to stop the energy flow through the heart chakra. When the energy flow through the heart chakra is stopped or slowed down, the development of the heart chakra is affected. Eventually, a physical problem will very likely result.

This same process works for all chakras. Whenever a person blocks whatever experience he is having, he in turn blocks his chakras, which eventually become disfigured. The chakras become "blocked," clogged with stagnated energy, spin irregularly, or backwards (counterclockwise) and even, in the case of disease, become severely distorted or torn.

When the chakras are functioning normally, each will be "open," spinning clockwise to metabolize the particular energies needed from the universal field. A clockwise spin draws energy from the UEF into the chakra, very much like

the right-hand rule in electromagnetism, which states that a changing magnetic field around a wire will induce a current in that wire. Grasping the wire with the right hand, point fingers in the direction of the positive magnetic pole. The thumb will automatically point in the direction of the induced current. The same rules hold true for chakras. If you hold your right hand over a chakra, in such a way that the fingers curl clockwise around the outer edge of the chakra, your thumb points toward the body and in the direction of the "current." Thus we label the chakra "open" to incoming energies. On the contrary, if you curl the fingers of your right hand counterclockwise around a chakra, the thumb will point outward, in the direction of current flow. When the chakra spins counterclockwise, the current is flowing outward from the body, thus interfering with metabolism. In other words, the energies that are needed and that we experience as psychological reality are not flowing into the chakra when it is spinning counterclockwise. We thus label the chakra as "closed" to incoming energies.

Most people I have observed have three or four chakras spinning counterclockwise at any one time. Usually these become more and more open with therapy. Since chakras are not only metabolizers of energy, but also devices that sense energy, they serve to tell us about the world around us. If we "close" chakras, we do not let that information come in. *Thus, when we make our chakras flow counterclockwise, we send our energy out into the world, sense what the energy is that we send out and say that it is the world. This is called projection in psychology.*

The imagined reality that we project onto our world is related to our "image" of what we concluded the world was like through our childhood experiences; and through the mind of the child we were then. Since each chakra is related to a specific psychological function, what we project through each chakra will be within the general area that each chakra functions and will be very personal to each of us because each person's life experience is unique. Thus, by measuring the state of the chakras we can determine one's overall long-term and current life issues.

John Pierrakos and I have related dysfunction in each of the chakras to psychological disorder. Any disturbance in the chakra, as measured by dowsing techniques, shows a dysfunction in that particular area of psychological relating (see Chapter 10 for dowsing technique). Thus, by measuring the state of the chakras, we are able to diagnose the client's psychological needs. I also work directly with the chakras to effect a psychological change. Conversely, we have found that the psychological patterns described by therapists are connected to the human energy field in predictable locations, shapes and colors.

Figure 7-3 shows the location of the seven major energy centers of chakras used for diagnosing psychological states. These are divided into mental centers, will centers and feeling centers. For psychological health, all three types of chakras: reason, will and emotion should be in balance and open. The three chakras in the head and throat area govern the reason; the chakras on the front of the body govern the emotions; their counterparts on the back govern the will. Figure 9-1 gives a table of the major chakras and their psychological function.

Let us look at the general areas of psychological functioning for each chakra. **The first chakra, the coccygeal center (1),** is related to the quantity of physical energy and will to live in the physical reality. It is the location of the first manifestation of the life force in the physical world. When the life force is fully functioning through this center, the person has a powerful will to live in physical reality. When the life force is fully functioning through the three lowest chakras, combined with a powerful flow down the legs, there comes with it a clear and direct statement of physical potency. The coccyx acts as an energy pump on the etheric level, helping direct the flow of energy up the spine.

This statement of physical potency, combined with the will to live, gives the individual a "presence" of power and vitality. He makes a statement, "I am here now," and is well-grounded in physical reality. The "presence" of power and vitality emanates from him in the form of vital energy. He often acts as a generator by energizing those around him, recharging their energy systems. He has a strong will to live.

When the coccygeal center is blocked or closed, most of the physical vitality of the life force is blocked, and the person does not make a strong impression in the physical world. He is not "here." He will avoid physical activity, will be low in energy and may even be "sickly." He will lack physical power.

**The pubic center (chakra 2A)** is related to the quality of love for the opposite sex that the person is able to have. When it is open, it facilitates giving and receiving sexual and physical pleasure. If this center is open, the person will probably enjoy sexual intercourse and probably be orgasmic. However, full body orgasm requires that all centers be open.

**The sacral center (chakra 2B)** is related to the quantity of sexual energy of a person. With this center open, a person feels his sexual power. If he blocks this particular chakra, whatever sexual force and potency he has will be weak and disappointing. He will probably not have much sexual drive, tend to avoid sex and disclaim its importance and pleasure, resulting in undernourishment in that area. Since the orgasm bathes the body in life energy, the body will not be nourished in this way, and it will not receive the psychological nourishment of communion and body contact with another.

**Relationship between chakras 2A and 2B.** The sacral acts as a pair with the pubic chakra. At the two points where the front and rear cen-

## Figure 9–1
# MAJOR CHAKRAS AND ASSOCIATED PSYCHOLOGICAL FUNCTION

| MENTAL CENTERS | ASSOCIATED WITH: |
|---|---|
| 7 Crown Center | Integration of total personality with life, and spiritual aspects of mankind. |
| 6A Forehead Center | Capacity to visualize and understand mental concepts. |
| 6B Mental Executive | Ability to carry out ideas in a practical way. |
| **WILL CENTERS** | |
| 5B Base of Neck | Sense of self, within society and one's profession. |
| 4B Between Shoulder Blades | Ego will, or will towards the outer world. |
| 3B Diaphragmatic Center | Healing, intentionality towards one's health. |
| 2B Sacral Center | Quantity of sexual energy. |
| 1 Coccygeal Center | Quantity of physical energy, will to live. |
| **FEELING CENTERS** | |
| 5A Throat Center | Taking in and assimilating. |
| 4A Heart Center | Heart feelings of love for other human beings, openness to life. |
| 3A Solar Plexus | Great pleasure and expansiveness, spiritual wisdom, and consciousness of universality of life. Who you are within the Universe. |
| 2A Pubic Center | Quality of love for the opposite sex, giving and receiving physical, mental and spiritual pleasure. |

ters come together, in the heart of the chakra, in the spine, the life force exhibits its second most powerful physical urge and purpose—that of the desire for sexual union. This powerful force breaks through the self-imposed barriers between two people and draws them closer to each other.

So, each person's sexuality is connected to his life force. (This is true, of course, of all centers: any of them that is blocked also blocks the life force in that related area.) Since the pelvic area of the body is the source of vitality, any center that is blocked in that area will have the effect of lowering physical and sexual vitality. For the great majority of humanity, the sexual energy moves through, charges and discharges in orgasm through these two sexual chakras.

This movement revitalizes and cleanses the body with an energy bath. It rids the body system of clogged energy, waste products and deep tension. Sexual orgasm is important for the physical well-being of the person.

The mutual letting go into deep communion through giving and receiving in sexual intercourse is one of the main ways humanity has of deeply letting go of the ego "separateness" and experiencing unity. When done with love and respect for the uniqueness of your mate, it is a holy experience culminating from the deep primordial evolutionary urges of mating on the physical level and the deep spiritual yearnings of uniting with Divinity. It is a wedding of both the spiritual and physical aspects of the two human beings.

For those who have already achieved such communion and have passed to other stages along the spiritual path, some spiritual disciplines like Kundalini yoga and Tantric tradition state that this discharge is no longer necessary for the well-being of the person. (Most human beings are not in this category.) Many spiritual practices use meditation to contain, transform and redirect the sexual energy along different energy channels, moving it along the vertical power current up the spine to be transformed into higher vibratory energy which is then used to build the higher spiritual energy bodies. This is a very powerful and potentially dangerous practice and must be done with guidance. Gopi Krishna in his book *Kundalini* speaks of the transformation of his physical seed, the sperm, into spiritual energy, or Kundalini, in this manner. Many spiritual practices advocate holding the sperm or spiritual seed for transformation.

**Blocks in chakras 2A and 2B.** Blocking of the pubic center may result in an inability to achieve orgasm in the woman who is unable to be open to and receive sexual nourishment from her mate. She will probably not be able to connect to her vagina and may not enjoy penetration. She may be more inclined to enjoy clitoral stimulation than penetration. She may also want to always be the aggressive one in the sexual act, i.e., be on top and initiate the majority of the movement. Her distortion here is that she must always be in control. In a healthy state she would want to be active sometimes and receptive at other times, but in this case she unconsciously fears her partner's powers. With gentle, patient caring and acceptance from her mate, she can slowly, over a period of time, open her pubic chakra to receiving and enjoying penetration. She must also go through the deeper feelings of fear and withholding from her mate that accompany her condition to find the images from which such feelings come as described earlier in this chapter. I am not implying that the woman should not be aggressive in sex. I am speaking more about a type of imbalance in giving and receiving.

A severe block in the male in the pubic chakra is usually accompanied by premature orgasm or inability to achieve an erection. The male is afraid on some deep level to give his full sexual power and, thus, withholds it. His energy flow often gets interrupted, clogged or redirected toward the back, out the sacral chakra, so that in orgasm he shoots energy out the posterior second chakra instead of out the penis. This experience is sometimes painful, resulting in an aversion to orgasm and an avoidance of intercourse. This precipitates difficulties on other levels with his mate, as it does with the nonorgasmic woman. Many times, of course, through the law of "like attracts like," these people find each other and share this mutual problem. Too many times the "pseudo" solution has been to blame the other person and try to find another mate. This only perpetuates the situation until the "owner" of the problem has to finally admit ownership. At this point, the work of digging out the originating images or beliefs can begin.

It is a blessing in these cases to have an accepting, understanding and strongly committed mate. If both people, instead of blaming the other, admit their difficulty, they can then focus on giving love, understanding and support to their partner and thus develop a new form of mutuality. This kind of growth takes time and patience. It takes true giving without making demands that one's desires be fulfilled by the other person. Then, as mutual trust and self-respect grow from giving up blame and from giving love, sexuality usually opens up and grows into a nourishing exchange. It is not unusual for one of these centers to be closed when the other is open. Many times this is just how the pairs (front/back) of chakras work in people. There will be an over-functioning in one and an under-functioning in the other, because the person cannot tolerate the power of having both aspects of a chakra functioning at the same time. For example, for some people it is very difficult to feel both tremendous sexual power and be very open to giving and receiving from another in lovemaking. Many times sexual power turns into fantasy rather than allowing the moment to unfold by immersing the self into the partner's depths and personal mysteries. Human beings are infinitely beautiful and complex wonders. Very rarely do we allow ourselves to simply wander uninhibited into that beauty and wonderment. The accompanying psychological problems from imbalance in chakra 2A and 2B result in unsatisfactory life circumstances.

For example, when the rear center is strong in a clockwise direction and the front center is weak or closed, the person will have a strong sex drive and probably a great demand for sexual relations. The problem is that the large amount of sexual energy and drive is not accompanied by an ability to give and receive sexually. Thus, it will be very hard to satisfy a strong drive. If the rear center is strong in a counterclockwise direction, the same is true; however, the drive will probably also be accompanied with negative images, perhaps even violent sexual fantasies. This, of course, makes the drive even harder to satisfy, and the owner of such a configuration may do a lot of sublimating in order to avoid the issue altogether because of shame of such inner feelings. On the other hand, the person may have many sexual partners and then miss the possibility of deep communion between two souls in the sex act. The person may break commitments or not be able to make any commitments regarding sex.

**The solar plexus (chakra 3A)** is associated with the great pleasure that comes from deeply knowing one's unique and connected place within the universe. A person with an open chakra 3A can look up to the starry heavens at night and feel that he belongs. He is firmly grounded in his place within the universe. He is the center of his own unique aspect of expression of the manifest universe and from this he derives spiritual wisdom.

Although the solar plexus chakra is a mental chakra, its healthy functioning is directly related to an individual's emotional life. This is true because the mind or mental processes serve as regulators of the emotional life. The mental understanding of emotions puts them into a framework of order and acceptably defines reality.

If this center is open and functioning harmoniously, he will have a deeply fulfilling emotional life that does not overwhelm him. However, when this center is open but the protective membrane over it torn, he will have great uncontrolled extremes of emotions. He could be influenced by outside sources from the astral which may confuse him. He may get lost in the universe and stars. He will eventually have physical pain in that area from overuse of that chakra and may eventually create a disease, such as adrenal exhaustion.

If this center is closed, he will block his feelings, perhaps not feeling anything. He will not be aware of a deeper meaning to the emotions that lends another dimension to existence. He may not be connected to his own uniqueness within the universe and his greater purpose.

Many times this center serves as a block between the heart and sexuality. If both of those are open and the solar plexus is blocked, the two will function separately; i.e., sex will not be deeply connected to love and vice versa. These two connect very nicely when one is aware of one's firmly rooted existence in the physical universe and of the long historical line of human beings who have served to create the physical vehicle this person now possesses. We must never underestimate how deeply physical a being we each are.

The solar plexus center is a very important center with regard to human connectedness. When a child is born, there remains an etheric umbilicus that is connected between mother and child. These cords represent a human connectedness. Whenever a person creates a relationship with another human being, cords grow between the two 3A chakras. The stronger the connections between the two people, the stronger and greater in number these cords will be. In cases where a relationship is ending, the cords are slowly disconnected.

Cords develop between other chakras of people in relationship also, but the third chakra cords seem to be a reenactment of the dependent child/mother connection and are very important in terms of transactional analysis in the therapeutic process. Transactional analysis is a method to determine the nature of an interaction you have with other persons. Are you interacting with them as a child would to a parent (child/parent)? Or are you interacting as if they are the child and you an adult (adult/child)? Or are you acting as adults? This type of analysis reveals a lot about your personal reactions to other people. The nature of the chakra cords that you build in your first family will be repeated in all the following relationships that you create later. As a child, the child/mother cords represent just that, the child/mother relationship. As an adult, you will most likely grow dependent child/mother cords between you and your mate. As you move through life and mature, you gradually transform the child/mother cords into adult/adult ones.

**The diaphragmatic center (chakra 3B)**, located behind the solar plexus, is associated with one's intention towards one's physical health. If someone has a strong health-love toward his body, and an intent to keep it healthy, this center is open. This center is also known as the Healing Center and is associated with spiritual healing. It is said that in some healers this center is very large and developed. It is also a will center like the one located between the shoulder blades and is usually smaller than the other will centers, except on people who have healing abilities. This center is associated with the solar plexus center, in the front, and is usually open if the solar plexus center is open. If a person has the solar plexus open and therefore is connected to his place in the universe, accepting that he fits as perfectly as each blade of grass, and the "lilies of the field," this person's self-acceptance will manifest on the physical level as physical health. Overall health—mental, emotional and spiritual—requires all centers to be open and balanced.

You will see, as we move through the chakra descriptions, the front and rear aspects of each work together as a pair, and a balance between each is more important than to try to open only one very widely.

**The heart chakra (chakra 4A)** is the center through which we love. Through it flows the energy of connectedness with all life. The more open this center becomes, the greater is our capacity to love an ever widening circle of life. When this center is functioning, we love ourselves, our children, our mates, our families, our pets, our friends, our neighbors, our countrymen, our fellow human beings and all our fellow creatures upon this earth.

Through this center, we connect cords to heart centers of those with whom we have a love relationship. This includes children and parents as well as lovers and mates. You have probably heard the term "heart strings," which refers to these cords. The feelings of love that flow through this chakra often bring tears to our eyes. Once we have experienced this open loving state, we realize how much we have missed it before and we cry. When this chakra is open, the person can see the whole individual within his fellow man. He can see the uniqueness and inner beauty and light in each individual as well as the negative or undeveloped aspects. In the negative state (closed), the person has trouble loving, loving in the sense of giving love without expecting anything in return.

The heart chakra is the most important chakra used in the healing process. All energies metabolized through the chakras travel up the vertical power current through the roots of the chakras and into the heart chakra before moving out of the hands or eyes of the healer. In the healing process, the heart transmutes the earth plane energies to spiritual energies and the spiritual plane energies into earth plane energies to be used by the patient. This will be discussed in greater detail in the chapter on healing.

**Midway between the shoulder blades, chakra 4B** is associated with the ego will, or outer will. This is the center from which we act in the physical world. We go after what we want.

If this center is clockwise, we will have a positive attitude about accomplishing things in life and see other people as supports for those accomplishments. We will then have the experiences to support this view because we live it. We will experience our will and the divine will in agreement. We will see the will of our friends aligned with our will. For example, if you want to write a book, you will envision your friends helping you and it being accepted by the publishers in a way that says, "Yes, this is just what we were looking for."

On the other hand, if this center is counterclockwise, the opposite is true. We will have the misconception that God's will and that of other people is opposed to our will. People will appear to be blocks in our way of getting what we want or in our accomplishing something. We will have to go through them or run them over to get what we want, rather than see them as helping us. We would believe statements like "my will over yours" and "my will over God's." Deep-seated beliefs relating to how the universe functions are involved here.

An image of the universe as a basically hostile place where the strong aggressors will survive, sometimes boils down to "not getting my way means my ultimate survival is at stake." The person functions by control and seeks to make his world safe by controlling others. The solution is for this person to realize how he creates a hostile environment through his aggression, and then to take the chance to let go and see if survival is possible without control. Taking such a chance will eventually lead to experiences of a benign, abundant and safe universe in which the person's existence is supported by the whole.

In another case, this center may be overactive. It could measure very large in a clockwise direction accompanied by a small clockwise or counterclockwise heart chakra. In this case, the person's will isn't particularly negative; it is just used to serve the function the heart center would serve. Instead of being able to let go, trust and love, i.e., run more energy through the heart chakra (4A), the person compensates with his will. He runs more energy through the rear aspect of chakra 4 between the shoulder blades. The person may be saying covertly, "I want my way without having to consider your humanity." This person functions mainly from will rather than love, or power over rather than power from within. It is the distortion from which one would "own" one's mate rather than be an equal.

**The throat chakra (5A),** located at the front of the throat, is associated with taking responsibility for one's personal needs. The newborn is brought to the breast, but must suck before nourishment is gained. This same principle holds throughout life. As the person matures, the fulfillment of his needs rests more and more upon himself. Maturity is reached and this chakra functions properly when one ceases to blame others for one's lacks in life and goes out

to create what one needs and desires.

This center also shows what the state of the person is with respect to receiving whatever is coming toward him. If the center is measured as counterclockwise, the person does not take in what is given to him.

This is usually associated with an image about what it is that is coming to him in the first place. That is, if the person sees the world as a negative, generally hostile place, he will be cautious and have negative expectations about what is coming his way. He may expect hostility, violence or humiliation rather than love and nourishment. Since he sets up a negative force field with his negative expectations, he will attract negative input to him. That is, if he has expectations of violence, he has violence inside of himself and, therefore, attracts it via the law of like attracts like, as explained in Chapter 6 on the nature of the Universal Energy Field.

As the person opens his throat center, he will gradually attract more nourishment until he is able to receive so much that he will be able to keep his throat center open most of the time. In the interim, he may very well attract a negative input shortly after opening the center due to his belief that that is what will come. When he is able to go through this experience, connect to the original cause within himself and find inner trust again, he will reopen his throat center. This process of opening and closing continues until all the misconceptions of receiving or taking in are transformed into trust in a benign nourishing universe.

The aspect of assimilation that occurs at the back of **the fifth chakra (5B), sometimes referred to as the professional center,** is associated with the person's sense of self within the society, his profession and with his peers. If a person is not comfortable in this area of his life, then this discomfort may very well be covered by pride to compensate for lack of self-esteem.

The center at the back of the neck is usually open if one is successful and well suited in one's work and satisfied with that work as one's task in life. If the person has chosen a profession that is both challenging and fulfilling and is giving his best to his work, this center will be in full bloom. He will be professionally successful and will be receiving support for nourishment from his universe. If this is not the case, the person will hold back from giving his best. He will be unsuccessful and conceal his lack of success with his pride. He secretly "knows" he would be "better" if he would either give his best or get a more challenging job. Somehow this person never does either and keeps a defense of pride in order to avoid the real despair underneath. He knows that he is really not succeeding in life. He will probably play the role of the victim, stating how life has not given him the opportunities to let him develop his great talent. This pride needs to be released, and the pain and despair felt and also released.

In this center, we will also uncover the fear of failure that blocks taking the chance to move out and create what one so dearly wants. This also holds true of one's personal friendships and social life in general. By avoiding contact, this person also avoids revealing himself and feeling the fear of not being liked on the one hand, and competition and pride like, "I'm better than you; you are not good enough for me," on the other. Since our feelings of rejection originate inside and we then project them out onto the other, we avoid the other person to avoid rejection. Taking the chance of going for the profession you long for, moving toward the contacts you long for and revealing your feelings about it are ways of releasing these feelings and thus opening this chakra.

**The forehead center (chakra 6A)** is associated with the capacity to visualize and understand mental concepts. This includes the person's concepts of reality and the universe or how he sees the world and how he thinks the world is likely to respond to him. If this center is counterclockwise, one has confused mental concepts, or images about reality that are not true and are usually negative. The person holding them projects them onto the world and creates his world by them. If this center is clogged and weak, the person is usually blocked in his creative ideas simply because the amount of energy flowing through this center is small. If this center is strongly counterclockwise, then this person has the ability to generate strong ideas that are negative. If this is combined with a strongly

functioning executive center, located at the back of the head (chakra 6B), this can create havoc in a person's life.

During the therapy process of purifying or sorting our negative belief images, when an image arises in the energy system and begins to function dominantly, this center will probably spin counterclockwise, even if it is usually clockwise. This therapy process brings the image to the fore and causes it to manifest in the life of the person. With therapeutic help, the person will understand and see the image clearly for what it is. The center will then turn around and will spin clockwise. Usually this type of counterclockwise motion can be detected by the seasoned therapist because of the unstable quality of feeling accompanied by the counterclockwise motion. It will be apparent to the therapist that this is not the normal state of affairs. For example, the chakra may even show a chaotic motion which tells the practitioner that an issue regarding one of his client's concepts of reality is strongly shaking the client's personality.

**At the back of the head, the mental executive center (chakra 6B)** is associated with implementing the creative ideas formulated through the center in the forehead. If the executive will center is open, one's ideas are followed with the appropriate action to cause them to materialize in the physical world. If it is not open, the person has a rough time bringing his ideas into fruition.

It is especially frustrating to have the front center (6A) open and the back one closed. One has many creative ideas, but they never seem to work out. There is usually an accompanying excuse which blames the problem on the outer world. Usually this person simply needs training on how to carry out, step-by-step, what he wants to accomplish. In doing this type of step-by-step work, a lot of feelings will emerge. "I can't stand to wait so long"; "I don't want to take responsibility for this happening"; "I don't want to test this idea in physical reality"; "I don't accept this long process of creation, I just want it to happen without so much work"; "You do the work, I'll be the idea man." This person probably lacked early training in how to take the simple steps in the physical world to accomplish his chosen purpose. He is also probably resistant to being in physical reality and in the position of an apprentice.

On the other hand, if this center is clockwise and the idea center is counterclockwise, we have an even more upsetting situation. Even if the person's basic concepts are not in reality, she will nevertheless proceed to carry the distorted concepts out with a certain amount of success. For example, if you believe this world is a nasty place where "everyone is out for himself so you just take what you want," and you have the ability to do so because you know how to go about it, i.e., your executive will is functioning, then you may act like a criminal. In this case the heart is probably also clogged. Your life will prove your idea to a certain extent. You will be successful to a certain extent until you get caught. Or, with this kind of configuration you may try to make something happen that is simply impossible to do in the physical world. Or, you may be the mover who carries out another person's ideas, whatever they are.

**The crown center (chakra 7)** is related to the person's connection to his spirituality and the integration of his whole being, physical, emotional, mental and spiritual. If this center is closed, the person probably does not have an experiential connection to his spirituality. He probably does not have that "cosmic feeling" and does not understand what people are talking about when they speak of their spiritual experiences. If this center is open, the person probably often experiences his spirituality in a very personal form, unique to that individual. This spirituality is not one defined by dogma or easily related with words. It is rather a state of being, a state of transcendence of the mundane reality into the infinite. It goes beyond the physical world and creates in the individual a sense of wholeness, peace and faith, giving him a sense of purpose to his existence.

## Chapter 9 Review

1. Describe the psychological function of each chakra.
2. Explain what is meant by opened and closed chakras, as described in this chapter.

# Chapter 10

# CHAKRA OR ENERGY CENTER DIAGNOSIS

There are several ways to discern the state of the chakras. In the beginning you will need to explore which practice is easiest and most useful for you.

The best way I have found to start sensing the states of the chakras is to use a pendulum. This device helps increase your sensitivities to the energy flow because it acts as an amplifier. The best pendulums I have found for this purpose are made of beechwood and are pear-shaped. They are one inch in diameter and one and a half inches long. Their energy field is diffused, easily permeated, and also pear-shaped. It is symmetrical around its vertical axis, which is important for this type of measurement. (Beechwood pendulums can be purchased from the Metaphysical Research Group, Archers' Court, Stonestile Lane, Hastings, Sussex, England.)

If you have developed some sensitivity in your hands, or enjoy touching, you can practice sensing the energy flowing in and out of the chakras through feeling them with your hands. This helps to get a sense of whether the energy is freeflowing or clogged, weak or strong. You can do the same thing with an acupuncture point by simply placing your fingertip over it. In this type of sensing, you may even get certain physical feeling responses in your own body that give you the information you wish to know.

Eventually, after you develop your High Sense Perception to a greater degree, you may be able to simply look at the chakras to see how they are spinning (regularly or irregularly) and what their colors are (dark and clogged, washed out and weak, or clear, bright and of a strong tone). You may also be able to see if, and specifically how, they are disfigured. You may eventually be able to perceive them on each layer of the auric field.

But first let us practice using the pendulum.

## Exercise to Diagnose Chakras with a Pendulum

To measure the front chakras, ask your patient to lie on his back. To measure the back chakras, ask the patient to lie on his stomach.

To measure the state of the chakra, hold the pendulum on a string about six inches long over the chakra and empty your mind of all bias as to the state of the chakra. (This is the hardest part and requires practice.) Be sure that the pendulum is as close to the body as possible without touching it. Your energy flows into the field of the pendulum to energize it. This combined field of the pendulum and your energy then interacts with the field of the subject, causing the pendulum to move. (See Figure 10–1.) It will probably move in a circular pattern, circumscribing an imaginary circle above the body of your subject. It may move back and forth in an elliptical movement or a straight line. It may move erratically. The size and direction of the pendulum movement indicates the amount and direction of energy flowing through the chakra.

Dr. John Pierrakos has found that a clockwise movement of the pendulum denotes a psychodynamically open chakra. That means that the feelings and psychological experiences which are governed by and flow through that chakra are well balanced and full in that person's life. If the pendulum moves counterclockwise, that chakra is psychodynamically closed, indicating a problem area in its corresponding psychological aspect. That means that the feelings and psychological experiences which are governed by a flow through that chakra are not balanced, because the energy is blocked, and probably the person has negative experiences associated with them.

The size of the circle made by the pendulum is related to the chakra's strength and the amount of energy flowing through it. It is also related to the amount of energy the healer and the subject have that day. If a larger circle is circumscribed by the pendulum, there is a lot of energy flowing through it. If the circle is small, there is less energy flowing through it.

It is important to keep in mind that the size of the chakra is not the diameter of the circular figure circumscribed by the pendulum, but is indicated by it. The size of the pendulum's circle is a function of the interaction of all three fields, the field of the subject, therapist and pendulum, as mentioned earlier. If the energies of both people are low, all chakras will appear to be smaller. If the energies are high, all chakras will appear to be larger. One must focus on comparison of the relative sizes among the chakras. Health is achieved by balancing the chakras to create an even flow of energy through them all. For health then, all chakras should be about the same size.

There are many variations between the clockwise and counterclockwise basic forms that indicate various psychological states. Figure 10–2 is a table of the various shapes a pendulum circumscribes. Although at first glance this table may seem a bit complicated, it is really quite simple. Each movement circumscribed by the pendulum is a variation between the extremes of

a fully open chakra (clockwise 6″ diameter), C6, or a fully closed chakra, which is counterclockwise, CC6. I rarely find diameters larger than 6 inches unless the person is overusing a particular chakra or is very open after a spiritual experience, when most of the chakras are open. I have measured up to C10 (clockwise with a diameter of 10 inches).

The only exception to falling between C6 and CC6 is the completely still chakra (S) where the pendulum exhibits no movement at all. In this case, either the chakra is reversing its spin, or the individual has so overused or held down and blocked the particular psychological functioning associated with this chakra that it has ceased to spin altogether and no longer metabolizes any energy from the Universal Energy Field. This is a state that, if continued for very long, will most assuredly result in disease, since the body cannot function healthily without being able to make use of outside energy. (See Chapter 15 on the relationship between illness and the chakras.)

Any elliptical swing of the pendulum indicates a right/left side imbalance of energy flow in the body. The designations of left or right refer to the left or right sides of the patient's body, i.e., the pendulum swings upward to the left (CEL) or upwards towards the right (CER) side of the patient's body. This also indicates that one side of the body is stronger than the other. The right side (CER, CCER) represents the active, aggressive, "masculine" or yang nature. The left side (CEL, CCEL) represents the passive, receptive, "feminine" or yin nature of the personality. When the pendulum circumscribes an ellipse slanted up toward the right side of the subject's body, Dr. John Pierrakos has observed that the personality has its masculine aspect more developed than the feminine. This person will probably be "overactive" in the sense that he would be aggressive in moments when receptivity is more appropriate. This will happen with regard to issues directly related to the area of psychological functioning governed by the particular chakra which exhibits elliptical motion.

In any chakra where the elliptical pendulum swing is up toward the left (CEL, CCEL), the person is more likely to be passive in situations

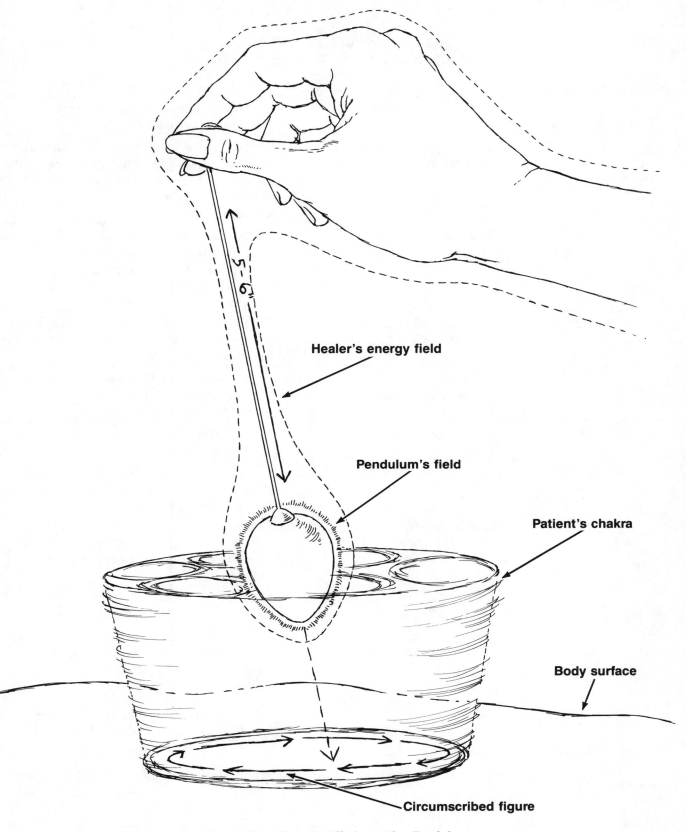

Figure 10–1: Dowsing Chakra with a Pendulum

83

## Figure 10–2
## ENERGY CENTER DIAGNOSIS

| SYMBOL* | NOTATION | MEANING OF SYMBOL | PSYCHOLOGICAL INDICATIONS |
|---|---|---|---|
|  | C6 | clockwise, 6" diameter | Open and harmonious with clear perception of reality. |
|  | CER3 | clockwise, elliptical, right, 3" diameter | Open. Active/receptive split with active side of personality more developed than receptive. Perception of reality biased toward active, masculine or yang side of dualism. |
|  | CEL3 | clockwise, elliptical, left 3" diameter | Open. Active/receptive split with receptive side more developed. Perception of reality biased toward receptive, feminine or yin side of duality. |
|  | CEV3 | clockwise, elliptical, vertical, 3" diameter | Open. With some upward displacement of energy toward the spiritual to avoid interaction with people. |
|  | CEH6 | clockwise, elliptical, horizontal, 6" diameter | Open. With some compacting and holding down of energy to avoid energetic interaction with people. |
|  | CC6 | counterclockwise, 6" diameter | Closed and inharmonious, with active projections of reality. |
|  | CCER3 | counterclockwise, elliptical, right, 3" diameter | Closed. Split, aggressive aspect more developed than passive with projection of a passive, yang biased reality. |
|  | CCEL2 | counterclockwise, elliptical, left 2" diameter | Closed. Split, passive aspect more developed than aggressive with projection of an aggressive biased reality. |
|  | CCEV3 | counterclockwise, elliptical, vertical, 3" diameter | Closed. With upward displacement of energy toward the spiritual to avoid interaction with people. |
|  | CCEH5 | counterclockwise, elliptical, horizontal, 5" diameter | Closed. Some holding down and compacting energy to avoid energetic interaction with people. |
|  | V6 | Vertical, 6" swing | Moving feelings and energy toward the spiritual to avoid personal interaction. |
| | H4 | Horizontal, 4" swing | Holding energy flow and feelings down to avoid personal interactions. Strong block indicated. |

* Remember that the figure symbols are drawn as you are looking at the front of the patient's body.

**Figure 10–2,** Continued

| SYMBOL* | | MEANING OF SYMBOL | PSYCHOLOGICAL INDICATIONS |
|---|---|---|---|
| ↙ | R3 | Right, 3″ swing | Severe aggressive/passive split, aggressive side more developed than passive. |
| ↗ | L4 | Left, 4″ swing | Severe aggressive/passive split, passive side more developed than aggressive. |
| • | S | Still | Chakra not functioning at all, will lead to pathology in physical body. |
| (symbol) | CEAS5 | Clockwise, elliptical, axis shift, 5″ diameter | Tremendous change taking place in person who is actively and deeply working on the issues involved. Probably preoccupied with relevant issues as defined by chakra function. Sensitive chaos. |
| (symbol) | CCEAS6 | Counterclockwise, elliptical, axis shifting, 6″ diameter | Same as CEAS, with negative chaos. |

\* Remember that the figure symbols are drawn as you are looking at the front of the patient's body.

related to issues involved with the particular psychological aspects governed by that chakra. For example, if the will center between the shoulder blades (4B) reads passive (elliptical towards upper left), the person will be unable to reach out for what he wants. This person will remain passive when aggressive action is called for. This person will wait for someone else to do it, or someone else to give it to him. He will also not be able to stand up for his rights or his turn. Many times, a false humility is held up as the reason this person remains passive, but the truth is that he is afraid to be aggressive, usually due to some very deep images about what it means to be aggressive.

The image about aggression comes directly from childhood experience. For example, a child may have had a very aggressive father, who would overpower or humiliate the child every time he reached out for what he wanted. This convinced the child that reaching out for what he wanted was not a good way to get what he wanted. Children are very creative, so the child probably experimented with ways of getting what he wanted, or at least of getting something

as compensation for what he wanted. Whatever way works is what the child will adopt as natural behavior. He will continue this behavior until it no longer works well in his life. Unfortunately, the habit is hard to break, and changing to find new ways takes work, because aggression is seen primarily as negative. Usually under all the passivity is a very hostile aggressive component of the personality that would like to blast out feelings without restraint and take what it wants. If this is done repeatedly in a therapeutic setting, the person will eventually be able to integrate his healthy aggression with the rest of his personality. This aggressive work needs to be done simultaneously with work that turns passivity into healthy receptivity.

The more the circular movement of the pendulum is distorted above any given chakra, the more severe is the psychological distortion. The most severe right/left split is shown by the back and forth movement of the pendulum at a 45 degree angle to the vertical axis of the body (R3, L4 of Figure 10–2). The larger the pendulum movement, the greater the amount of energy contained in the distortion. For example, an R6 measurement for chakra 4B indicates that the person will simply and aggressively take what he wants, no matter what the circumstances are.

The same general rule for measuring severity holds true of the back and forth pendulum swing which is either vertical (parallel to the body's vertical axis [V]) or horizontal (perpendicular to the body's vertical axis [H]). The vertical aspect indicates that the individual is diverting energy upward toward the vertical, which means he's avoiding personal interaction. The horizontal pendulum movement indicates the individual is holding down and compacting the energy flow and feelings to avoid personal interaction. For example, a pendulum reading of V5 at chakra 3A indicates that the person is focusing his personal connection toward the vertical and spirituality, and avoiding a personal relationship with another human being. He defines who he is in the universe from the point of view of a spiritual belief and cuts out the aspect of being connected to another human being. Whereas a pendulum reading of H5 for the same chakra would indicate that the person is not connecting to anyone, not on the spiritual level, not on the human level. This could lead to personal isolation. This particular motion could go into a still chakra (S) from underuse and compaction. Strong physical psychodynamic work is needed in such a case.

When an individual is focusing his psychological work on a particular aspect of his being, either from deciding to do so from an inner place or forced to from some outside circumstance, the particular chakra or chakras involved will probably display chaotic or asymmetrical movement (CEAS, CCEAS) as in Figure 10–2. This movement will cause the pendulum to swing chaotically, usually exhibiting elliptical motion combined with a shifting axis. At first, this movement may confuse the beginner; however, if the pendulum is held over the chakra for a longer period of time, the axis shift will be observable. The circumscribed pattern of the pendulum will look like the last two items in Figure 10–2. Whenever this type of movement is observed, the therapist knows a lot is going on in the client. It is time to work deeply on the issues involved, but at the same time giving the client a lot of personal time and space to do his own self examination/transformation. If he can take a few days off from work at this time and be undisturbed by his daily routine, he will be able to make the best of this period of great personal change. I have regularly observed this phenomenon in people undergoing deep personal transformation work in weeklong intensive retreats.

As the therapist becomes more proficient in use of the pendulum, he will begin to observe more "qualities" in his measurements. The rate of swing (how fast the pendulum moves) indicates the amount of energy being metabolized through the chakra. With practice, the therapist can also "pick up" qualities such as tightness, tension, exuberance, heaviness, sadness, grief, peacefulness and clarity. A fast swing can be fast and tight, indicating overwork, tension and pressure in that area. A fast swing can also be combined with an exuberant feeling, indicating a lot of positive aggression in that area. Thus, by developing more acute senses to the quality of the energy flowing through the chakra, the therapist can be better informed about the client's state. He can tell how stable a chakra is, approximately how long it has been in the state it is in, whether it changes back and forth between two states, and more. A chakra may be open 20% of the time, or 80% of the time. This can be "picked up" by the sensitively trained therapist. This, of course, takes practice with verification.

Chakras go through different phases as they change from closed to open through the intensive work in therapy. The process of changing one's belief system redirects chakra movement. A chakra that is continually closed at a large diameter (CC6) will sometimes, over a period of time, decrease its diameter, turn around and then increase its diameter in the harmonious direction until it becomes C6. Or, more often a CC6 chakra, say in the heart or solar plexus, may, within as little as five minutes of deep crying, turn around to C6. This type of change will not hold long, but, as the person continues his work over a long period of time, the chakra tends to stay "open" longer each time it is opened. This increases its overall percentage time of harmonious functioning, and the person will feel himself being happy for longer periods of time. Over a long time, the chakra will stabilize to the open position and will rarely close. The individual usually then moves on in his process to work on the next disharmoniously functioning chakra that interferes with his daily happiness.

I have found that when a chronically closed chakra opens during a therapy session, it is common that another chakra that is usually open will close briefly in compensation. The personality is not able to tolerate the new "opened" state without some degree of imagined "protection" in the beginning.

## Intensive Retreat Case Study

Now let us examine the chakra configurations actually measured in a case. This is a woman who came to the Phoenicia Pathwork Center in Phoenicia, New York, on two separate occasions to do a weeklong retreat that included very intensive work on herself. The first was in 1979, and the second in 1981. The second time she came, it was with her new husband, and they did very intensive couples work. The chakra measurements were taken before the week's work started, and then again after the week's work was completed. All measurements were taken when the woman was in a very quiet state and had been for some time. They are shown in Figure 10–3. To interpret these readings you will need to use both Figures 7–3 and 9–1 and Figure 10–2 of this chapter on the meaning of each chakra.

As you can see from the readings, the most harmoniously functioning centers are those of the reason, next those of feeling, the worst those of the will. This means that she has a fine mind, which functions well, especially in its concepts of reality (6A) and in the integration of her personality and spirituality (7).

Her mental executive will center (6B) has a right/left split most of the time, meaning that she tends to be aggressive when it is more appropriate to be receptive in any given situation that is related to carrying out her ideas in a step-by-step fashion. She will decide what to do and proceed to do it in a step-by-step way, regardless

## Figure 10–3
## INTENSIVE RETREAT CASE STUDY
### CHAKRA READINGS

| CHAKRA | 1979 | | 1981 | |
| --- | --- | --- | --- | --- |
| | Before retreat | After retreat | Before retreat | After retreat |
| Crown center (7) | C6 | C6 | C5 | C5 |
| Executive will (6B) | CER4 | S | R4 | CER6 |
| Professional will (5B) | CC3 | CER3 | CC3 | C4 |
| Outer ego will (4B) | C5 | C5 | CC5 | C5 |
| Health will (3B) | CER3 | CC3 | CEH4 | C4 |
| Sexual will (2B) | CC4 | CC4 | CC4 | C4 |
| Conceptual (6A) | C4 | C5 | C5 | C5 |
| Receptivity/ responsibility (5A) | L4 | CER4 | C5 | C3 |
| Loving (4A) | C3 | C4 | C4 | C4 |
| Universal knowing (3A) | CC4 | C3 | CC3 | C5 |
| Receptive sexual (2A) | C4 | C4 | CEAS4 | C5 |

of whether or not it is time to start. When she arrived for her first retreat, this center was aggressive. By the time the first retreat was over, this center had calmed down, was no longer aggressive, but rather was still. This configuration of stillness did not hold or change to harmony as it often does over time. Two years later, when she came back, the center was again aggressive; and it did not change during the second retreat. At the time of the last reading, she still had a problem with being over aggressive when carrying out her ideas. This was the only case of no change in her chakras. All the other chakras were balanced by the end of the second retreat.

Her other will centers showed problems, too, with each one of them not functioning at one or another time during the weeks involved. When she arrived in 1979, chakras 5B, 3B and

2B were not functioning properly. This means that she was negatively aggressive in terms of pride (chakra 5B), self-destructiveness (chakra 3B) and dampening her sexual power. She dampened her sexual power by splitting the energy flow in chakra 2B into four parts (the pendulum showed four distinct and separate circles) and using it in negative ways, such as fights with her ex-husband. After the first retreat, the only improvement in her will functioning was in the area of pride, which had let down and become positive functioning in the area of her profession (5B). It still had an overactive component, which took the place of the pride used to compensate for feelings of inadequacy in that area. When she came to the second retreat two years later, she still carried with her the same issues of will. These got resolved during the course of the second intensive retreat, and all the will centers started to function normally.

The feeling centers showed some difficulties, but not as much as the will. The heart center (4A) remained open throughout both years. (She is very good at loving.) The throat center (5A) showed trouble with taking in nourishment and an aggressive denial of her needs. This softened by the end of the first week, and when she came back in two years, it had been resolved, mostly through establishing a very sweet relationship with the man she loves. On the other hand, the solar plexus center (3A), which relates to who you are in the universe, was closed when she first came. It opened during her retreat, but in the second year period, between retreats, it closed again. By the end of the second retreat, it was open again and metabolizing more energy.

You will note that her sexual power center cleared when her relationship with the man she loves became more stable and clearly defined through the work in the couples retreat.

During the first retreat, she opened her feeling centers and began to feel safe in the universal world of feelings. In the second retreat, having done a lot of work on the feeling centers, which were not as blocked as the will centers, she was able to deeply confront her misuse of her will and rebalance it. As you can see from the readings, most of the chakras showed large diameters, which means that the person possessing this energy system has a lot of power.

It is interesting to note that the crown, third eye and heart centers all remained open through the two year period. This means that she is very connected to her spirituality, conceptual reality, and is capable of loving. The overall picture of her personality is that her primary clear function is reason and that she compensates for and defends against vulnerable feelings with the will, which is too aggressive.

As I said earlier, by the end of the second retreat, all centers except the executive will center were functioning well. As long as they stay that way, she will be balanced in her reason, will and emotional functions and will lead a more happy and balanced life.

## Chapter 10 Review

1. What does a pendulum reading at C6 mean for the front aspect of the fourth chakra?
2. What does a pendulum reading of CC5 mean for the rear aspect of the third chakra?
3. What does a pendulum reading of V6 mean for the front aspect of chakra 2?
4. What does a pendulum reading of CC4 mean for the front fifth chakra, physically as well as psychologically?
5. What does a pendulum reading of H5 mean for the rear aspect of chakra 2?

### Food For Thought

6. If you work with someone to open their heart and sex centers and you succeed, why might they close their solar plexus chakra? Is that OK?

## Chapter 11

# OBSERVATIONS OF AURAS
# IN THERAPY SESSIONS

The aura is really the "missing link" between biology and physical medicine and psychotherapy. It's the "place" where all the emotions, thoughts, memories and behavior patterns we discuss so endlessly in therapy are located. They're not just suspended somewhere in our imaginations, but they are located in time and space. Thoughts and emotions move between people in time and space through the human energy field, and learning about it is the way to get a handle on this activity. Let's look at some of the fluid energy flows of auras as people move through their daily lives and then in therapy sessions. We will concentrate on the colorful moving forms of the lower four layers of the aura and return to our discussion of chakras in a later chapter.

## Perceiving Colors in the Field

When one first starts to read auras, the meaning of the colors may not be understood directly. Then, with practice, general meaning of colors will become clear. When the practitioner has more sensitivity through using her gift, she will also read the meaning of the colors she perceives. (Color will be discussed in detail in Chapter 23.)

One of the earliest "explosions" of the human energy field I observed remains one of the most vivid. In 1972 during a bioenergetics-primal scream intensive workshop, I watched Linda light up like a Christmas tree as she screamed about the death of her father from cancer. Bright beams of red, yellow, orange and some blues streamed from her head. I blinked my eyes, but it didn't go away. I squinted; I moved around the room; I looked for the afterimage. The phenomenon was still there. I was seeing something. I could no longer deny the many experiences I had had observing apparent colors around people's heads. I began observing the phenomenon more closely.

As I slowly became more proficient at seeing the aura, I started trying to correlate my findings with the personal state of each subject. I found that people flash bright colors when they are engaged in feelings or actions. When they are quiet, the auric field returns to a stable "normal" state for that person.

In general I have found that the "normal" or "quiescent" aura looks like Figure 7–1. It has a dark bluish-purple or clear pulsating layer out to one quarter inch or as much as one and a half inches from the skin. It is constantly pulsating at the rate of about 15 pulses per minute. The pulsations usually form a wave-like motion down the arms, legs and torso. First it is surrounded by a light blue to gray hazy layer which is much brighter close to the body and fades with distance from the body. The blue color generally turns to a yellow color around the head at about three to four inches in distance. There are usually streamers of the lighter blue coming off the fingertips and toes and out of the top of the head. I have found that most people are able to see the streamers off the tips of the fingers with a few minutes practice and clear instructions. Although most of the time these streamers are blue, their colors vary in the red and purple areas also. They may be any color.

## Exercises to Observe Other People's Auras

Now that you have done the exercises in Chapter 7 observing the aura at your fingertips, let's look at other people's auras.

Again use a darkened room—later evening light, not real dark. You should be able to see each other's faces quite easily. Ask your friend to stand in front of a plain white wall or a screen. Make sure you do not have any lights that you may accidentally look into. You want to relax your eyes.

To see the aura, you want to use your nighttime vision, as when you are walking in the dark and you notice that you can see things better if you do not look directly at them. You are using the rods rather than the cones in your eye. The rods are much more sensitive to low light levels than the cones, which are for daytime and bright color use.

Look at the area of space either near the top of your friend's head or at the neck-shoulder area. Unfocus your eyes so that you are looking at an area of space rather than a fine line. As you softly gaze at a space four to six inches deep around the head, allow the light to come into your eyes. Create a sensation of allowing something to come into your eyes, rather than your eyes reaching out to grasp something as they sometimes do when you try hard to see something. Give yourself plenty of time. Do this with other people, preferably with someone who sees auras so that you can correlate what you see.

You may think you see something, and as soon as you do, it will be gone before you can even say, "That's it!" Make sure that if you look

away at a blank spot on the wall, you do not see the same thing. That is the afterimage effect, in which your eye will hold an image due to a complementary color effect or bright contrast intensity. The auric phenomenon is very fast and doesn't stay. It pulsates. You may see it flow down the arm or flash a color upward and out of the field. You may see a haze around the body that does not look exciting. Don't be disappointed; this is only the beginning.

Pick up a pair of aura goggles at the local holistic book store and follow the instructions you find in them. They help you develop your ability to see and have a cumulative effect on the sensitivity of the eye. Cobalt blue glass is the best color, but hard to get. Most aura goggles are dark purple and work fine.

Don't do any of these exercises too long; you will find yourself getting very tired after a while. I have found that a group of people get very excited when they first see something; then as they continue, doubts come in and each person's energy system tires. Soon you have a room full of very quiet, tired people. So just do a little every day. And check out what you have seen with the illustrations and descriptions that follow.

If a person has a strong feeling, his quiescent aura will suddenly be permeated with another color and form correlating to his emotional state. Then, after the feeling tones down, the aura regains its original general appearance. The length of time this takes varies with the individual and depends on several factors. If the person has not released the feeling, it will remain in his aura (usually faded) until he does. If he releases part of the feeling, that part will be released. The colors and forms may rapidly flash and move out of the auric field, or they may simply fade away over a period of a few minutes or even a few weeks. They may even be colored over or masked by other colors and forms in a layered effect. Some forms, which I will discuss later, stay in the aura for years. Every thought, feeling, and experience a person has affects and changes his aura. Some effect always remains.

Figure 11–1A shows the normal aura of a man. As he sings (Figure 11–1B), his aura expands and brightens. Bright lightning-like flashes and sparks of iridescent blue-violet move off just after the movement of inhaling, before he starts each new line. As the audience becomes more attentive, its general aura expands. Great arcs of light reach out from the singer to the audience, and the two auras connect. Mutual forms begin to build as feelings flow between performer and audience. These energy-consciousness forms relate in structure and color to the mutual thoughts and feelings of the group and the music being created. At the end of the song, these forms are disconnected and broken up by the applause, which acts as an eraser to wipe the field clean for the next creation. Both performer and audience are energized by absorbing the energy created by the music. Some of this energy will be internalized to break blocks held in the body; some of it will be used for the next creation.

As another person lectures on his favorite subject, his aura expands and becomes yellow-gold with silvery-gold or iridescent blue sparks, shown in Figure 11–1C. The same speaker-audience phenomenon occurs, this time with an emphasis on the mental energies, which show up as yellow-gold. After the lecture, his aura remains expanded for some time, as he is high from his work. There has been a mutual exchange of energy consciousness. Some of the audience now vibrates more at his level. Figure 11–1D shows the aura of a man speaking with passion about education. Those who listen will probably pick up some of his pink-maroon color. This occurs by a process of raising one's own vibrations to his level through harmonious induction. Love glows as a soft beautiful rose in the aura. It sometimes also has gold with it. Spiritual feelings have a range of colors: blue for the speaker of truth, purple for spirituality and silvery gold for purity.

People sometimes radiate colors similar to those they like to wear. Figure 11–1E shows a woman after leading a core energetics class (a physical exercise class focused on bringing out feelings to help understand their psychodynamics). This green, which she wears often, is associated with physical health and healing. In another example, Figure 11–1F shows a man who often radiates a lilac color which corres-

ponds to one of his favorite shirts. This color appears to correlate with loving feelings and softness in him. Figure 11–1G shows a woman meditating to increase the energy in her field, which displayed many colors, some of which trickled down her front in fluid motion. Her will center between the shoulder blades was partially visible.

When a woman gets pregnant, her field expands and becomes much brighter. Figure 11–1H shows a woman about six months pregnant with a girl. The mother-to-be has beautiful soft balls of blue, pink, yellow and green rolling over each other down her shoulders.

These are only a few examples of how the human energy field is bound up with and inherently connected to everything we see occurring on a purely physical and psychological level.

## Anger and Other Negative Emotions

Red has always been associated with anger. However, one day my very happy, energetic 11-year-old son, full of joy while playing, looked like Figure 11–1A, with bright red and orange streamers radiating from his head. The quality of the color red is what denotes anger. Bright red orange is not anger; it is related to vibrant life force. The full-blown reaction of the woman in the primal scream workshop is depicted in Figure 11–2B. She is having a large number of feelings all at once, which accounts for so many colors. They are of high intensity, which shows in the aura as brightness and the strong rays emitted off the body in straight lines.

Someone who is angry has a dark red color. When this anger is expressed, it shoots off the person in flashes like bolts of lightning or round sparks that move away from the person, as shown in Figure 11–2C. I have seen this many times in groups and sessions.

In contrast, Figure 11–2D shows an example in which the person did not release her anger and pain. As the red spot emerged from the throat area, it slowly moved outward. A moment later the group leader made a comment to her that was, in my opinion, hurtful. At this point, the red spot quickly moved back toward her body and into her heart area. When it hit her heart, she started crying. The crying was not of the cathartic type. It was rather "poor me, the victim." My interpretation of this event is that she had stabbed herself in her heart with her own anger.

Fear, on the other hand, has a whitish-gray, prickly appearance in the aura, as in white with fear. It is very unpleasant looking and has a repulsive odor. Envy appears to be dark, dirty green and sticky, as in "green with envy." Sadness is dark gray and heavy as in the cartoons of people with dark clouds over their head. Frustration and irritability will probably have dark reddish tones (red with anger), but are mostly apparent from their irregular vibrations that beat against another person's energy field, causing very unpleasant sensations. Usually one's friends react to this interference by trying to elicit a direct expression of negative feelings, which are much more pleasant to deal with. For example, one will say, "Are you angry?" Another will blurt out angrily, "No!" Thus some of this annoying interference is released.

## Effect of Drugs on the Aura

Drugs like LSD, marijuana, cocaine and alcohol are detrimental to the brilliant, healthy colors of the aura and create "etheric mucus," as does disease. Figure 11–2E shows the effect of snorting cocaine on one person's aura. Every time he would snort cocaine on Saturday night, at his Tuesday afternoon session he would have a lot of gray, sticky etheric mucus on the right side of his face and head, while the left side would remain relatively clear. I asked him if he used one nostril more than the other; he thought not. My repeated confrontations—I could tell whenever he did it—and a graphic description of his "etheric snot" helped him stop this habit.

Figure 11–2F shows an aura of a man who had taken many LSD trips and drunk a lot of alcohol. The aura is dirty greenish-brown. The dirty green spot, which slowly moved downward and was not released, correlated to his mixed, undifferentiated, withheld feelings of anger, envy and pain. Had he been able to separate these feelings, understand their basis, express and release them, I'm sure the spot would have separated into brighter clearer shades of the corresponding colors—red, green and gray—and then moved off. However, due to the amount of dark contamination of his field, this man has a lot of energetic cleansing to do to remove his etheric mucus before he can raise his energy level high enough to clarify and move his feelings.

## An "Apparent" Weight in the Aura

Figure 11–2G shows a man who also had indulged for years in drugs like LSD and marijuana, with the resulting dirty green aura. The waste from these experiences appears in the upper right. It appears to exhibit weight because he always held his head at an angle which seemed to balance the form. This form always remained in the same position, week after week. When I pointed it out to him, he was able to see it. (He used a mirror.) In order to remove this form, he would also (in addition to what has already been mentioned) have to get off drugs and cleanse his field. In addition to bodywork, I recommend fasting and a cleansing diet. He would then be able to increase his energy field strength and be able to break into this accumulated waste to dissipate it.

An interesting display of "apparent" weight associated with mucous consistency is shown in Figure 11–2H. This woman had been a "good girl" type for years and finally just reached her rebelliousness. She stopped being so "nice" and got very angry during her session. She knocked down the chairs in the room and even stomped on the tissue box, tearing it to pieces. She left the session feeling liberated. However, the next week she contracted and withdrew very deeply and came into my office with a terrible headache. She moved carefully and held her shoulders up around her ears. At this point, I observed a large "blob" of mucus on top of her head. Apparently the mucus had been released in the earlier session and had accumulated there. (The phenomenon of toxin release from bioenergetic work is well known. Strong energy flow releases toxins held in the tissues. Sometimes people get "sick" after deep work. That sickness is called the "Flukey Flu.") My client was no longer "rebellious," but now exhibited the rather masochistic behavior of self-punishment. I suggested starting the session with physical movement. I asked her to bend forward in a kind of whipping motion with her upper half. As she did so, the mucus ball sprang forward, extending about two and a half feet in front of her. She started to fall forward as if from a large weight (Figure 11–2H). She caught herself, and then the mucus sprang back to her head as if pulled by elastic. She almost fell over backwards. She was too afraid to repeat the movement, so we did a lot of bodywork focusing on feeling her legs, standing firmly on her feet, and feeling connected to the earth supporting her. This process is called *grounding*. By the end of the session the mucus had distributed itself in a thin layer over her body. Her headache was gone. It took several weeks of bodywork to rid her of the entire mucus layer.

## Exercise to Experience Apparent Weight of the Energy Field

An exercise done often in Aikido classes will help you have an experience of the effect of weight in the aura.

Have two people stand on each of your sides. They are going to try to pick you up by grasping your upper arm at the top and at the bottom. When they pick you up for all of these exercises, make sure that they do it in a way that lifts you straight up, rather than pushing you to one side first—that may break your roots.

First do it for practice to see how heavy you feel. Sense how easy/difficult it is for them to pick you up. Now take some time to send your energy field upward. Think "up"; focus on the ceiling. When you have a good focus that you can keep there, ask them to try to pick you up. Was it easier?

Now give yourself time to focus on increasing your connection with the ground. Grow roots from your fingertips and the bottom of your feet into the ground and deep into the earth. Concentrate on the strong and powerful energetic connection you have with the ground. When you have a very good focus, ask them to pick you up again. Are you heavier and harder to pick up? Probably.

## "Dissociated Thought Forms" in the Aura

In the course of my years of bioenergetic practice, I have observed a phenomenon which I refer to as moving spaces of reality. These "spaces" I find similar to those described in the study of topography, where a given "set" or "domain" contains a set of characteristics which then define the mathematical operations that are possible within that domain. In terms of psychodynamics, there exist "spaces of reality" or "belief systems" containing groups of thought forms which are associated with conceptions and misconceptions of reality. Each thought form contains its own definitions of reality, such as, all men are cruel; love is weak; being in control is safe and strong. From my observations, as people move through daily experience they also move through different "spaces" or levels of reality defined by these groups of thought forms. The world is experienced differently in each group or space of reality.

These thought forms are energetic, observable realities which radiate colors at various intensities. Their intensity and definition of form are a result of the energy or importance a person has given them. Thought forms are created, built and maintained by their owners through habitual thoughts. The more definite and clear the thoughts, the more definite the form. The nature and strength of emotions associated with the thoughts give the form its color, intensity and power. These thoughts may or may not be conscious. For example, a thought form can be built from constantly thinking of a fear like "He's going to leave me." The creator of the thought form will act as if it is going to happen. The energy field of the thought form will affect the field of the person it is about in a negative way. It will probably have the effect of pushing the person away. The more this is given power, by putting energy into it either consciously or unconsciously, the more effective it will be in creating the feared result. Usually these thought forms are so naturally a part of the personality that the individual doesn't even notice them. They begin to form in childhood and are based on a child's reasoning, then integrated into the personality. They are like extra baggage a person carries about within himself, not noticing their effect, which is very great. These conglomerate thought forms, or belief systems, attract many "effects" in one's outer reality.

Since these forms are not deeply buried in the unconscious but are on the edge of the consciousness, they can be retrieved through such methods as Core Energetic bodywork, word association games and meditation. When the forms are brought to the focus of the consciousness by expressing the feelings associated with them and releasing those feelings, they are then possible to change. This process allows a clearer view of the assumptions about reality which make up the forms. When the invalid assumptions (remember they are based on logic from childhood) are uncovered, seen and released, they can be replaced by a more mature, clear view of reality, which in turn leads to the creation of positive life experiences.

Within some personalities, these forms are interconnected and the person's consciousness is rarely immersed totally in one space without being aware of most of the others, so the person maintains a high degree of integration in his daily life.

On the other hand, a different type of personality may flow from one space of reality to the other with alacrity, but may not be aware of any connectedness between them. He may not be able to integrate or understand this dynamic flow and thus lives in confusion, especially when a particular chronic cyclical flow is triggered off internally. He may then be caught in an automatic sequential flow from one thought to the next while remaining hopelessly entangled and unable to free himself from this chronic cycle until the whole thing is played out.

He may then move to a different state of reality only because the cyclical action of the thought form has exhausted all of the available energy. He will not know how he moved out of the cyclical pattern and, therefore, will probably be unable to extricate himself from the cycle the next time it is triggered. These states of reality can be euphoric, as in the state in which a person thinks he will accomplish great things and become famous or rich but he is not aware of the tremendous amount of practical work ahead of him before he can attain such a goal. Or it may be an opposite effect, in which the person sees himself in a much worse a state than is the case. In either state, he is not in truth about himself or his life situation. In both states he is probably seeing a part of himself and exaggerating it. He may have the potential to create all the great things he sees for himself in the first state, but much work and time is needed. On the other hand, in the second negative state, he sees the parts of himself that he needs to change, but forgets that change is possible.

William Butler, in his book *How to Read the Aura*, has observed that particular thought forms remain stationary in the energy field until triggered by an internal or external energy input. These forms then move through the aura in a chronic sequence but are not released. They simply play themselves out and become dormant until gaining enough energy to move again. Thought forms gain energy through the individual's habitual semi-conscious thoughts and related feelings. They also gain energy by attracting similar thoughts and feelings from other people. In other words, if you continually judge yourself about something, your actions and feelings will follow your judgments and soon, through both, the people you know will get the picture and agree with you, thus sending you energy in the form of their thoughts and feelings about you which agree with yours. For example, if you keep telling yourself that you are dumb, unworthy, ugly or fat, soon others will agree with you. This energy is added to your personal stockpile until your thought form has enough energy (reaching critical mass) to be triggered. You will then fall into a state in which you are convinced you are dumb, ugly, unworthy, or fat, until the energy in the thought form is dissipated for the time being. Or you may, of course, attract an external event which will trigger it with an explosion of energy. In either case, the process is the same. Such a trigger is not necessarily negative, for if the individual is in a therapeutic process, he may be able to break out of his chronic cycle and break up the cyclical form substantially enough to handle it very well the next time it gets triggered.

If the therapist is able to perceive these realities and describe them or help the client describe them, then the therapist may be able to help the client free himself as he moves from one reality to the next. The therapist's description of each reality state, as the client is experiencing it, will give the client an overview of the whole process. This overview will help the client create for himself an inner objective observer, who can also define each space as he goes in and out of it. From this work, the client and therapist will then be able to define more clearly the client's chronic cycle and find a way out of it together. They can then find a mode to break it next time it starts.

For example, when a particularly schizoid client (see Chapter 13) is stuck in such a form, I simply go to the blackboard and start drawing and labeling these forms the moment he expresses them. As he repeats thoughts out loud, I draw an arrow from the previous thought to the one being expressed. Soon all the cyclical thoughts are depicted on the board. The outer surface of these forms is usually quite limited, meaning that the client experiences a very narrow reality in which definitions and/or distinctions are seen as negative and sometimes flat—such as all other people appearing to be far away or even dangerous. Or the client may completely believe that he is a victim in life. The breaking point comes when the client is able to hold one of the thoughts, which has particularly strong emotional content, long enough to express this emotion. Usually, if the client is able to tolerate the anger or pain associated with the thought, he is able to break out and connect to the deeper levels inside the thought form.

Figure 11–3 shows such an example. In this particular case, as I drew the forms, the client saw the overall picture. This greater understanding helped her center herself and release herself from the chronic cycle. She went into her anger, expressed it, and then saw the deeper issues involved. Much of the outer level of this particular thought form is the mask in which the person does not see or take self-responsibility, but blames others. She does this in order to appear "good." This, of course, leaves her powerless until the deeper reality, which is the heart of the thought form, is reached. When, from childhood trauma, she felt that she was just plain "bad" inside and nothing could be done about it, my client understood that in the future she had the choice of seeing and understanding the whole structure, going first into her anger at feeling trapped, and then into the underlying pain in the thought form. She usually avoided this pain by staying on the surface of the thought form (and, therefore, in unreality). By feeling the pain, she is able to integrate the child inside, who feels "bad," with her inner adult, who knows she is not.

Usually, expressing and releasing the feelings is the key to breaking out of a cyclical thought pattern. Most of the time these forms have become dissociated in the first place in order for the person not to experience the feelings contained in them. The individual spends a lot of effort during his daily life trying to avoid setting the thought form in motion, because it may evoke the unwanted feeling. Even though the person avoids situations that would evoke such feelings, it does not completely work, because he is continually recharging the thought forms. As an individual continues in his therapeutic process, over time the form becomes more and more connected with the rest of the personality; the negative aspects are transformed into positive functions and integrated into the "normal" aura of the person as formless clear bright colors.

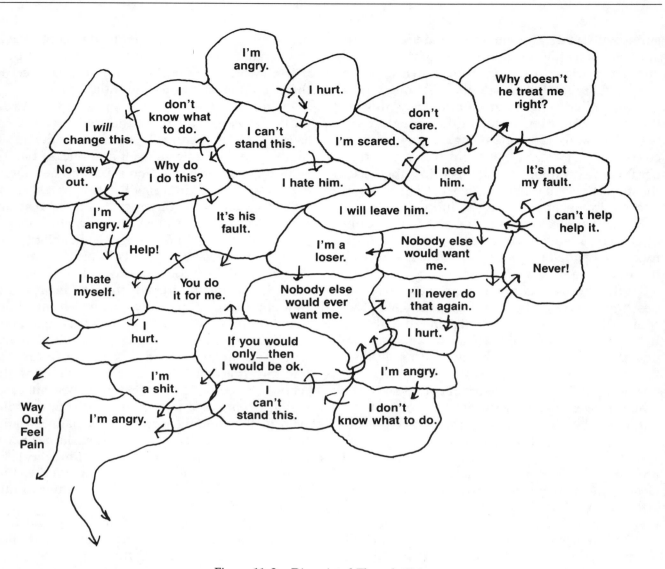

Figure 11–3:  Dissociated Thought Form

## Cleaning the Aura During a Therapy Session

Core energetic therapy is designed to help people release blocks from their auric field through focus and physical exertion. Figure 11–4 illustrates just such a release. By leaning backwards over a padded stool, the muscles of the torso are stretched and begin to relax. This brings about an energetic release, and the block lets go. The client had a strong energy block in the muscles just in front of the spine near the diaphragmatic hinge. While he was working on the bioenerge-

tic stool, this block suddenly released with a burst of energy. The "energy cloud" quickly moved up along the spine. When it reached the head of the client and broke into his consciousness, I observed his going into another space of reality. He began to cry and express early childhood pain. As he expressed his feelings, he released more and more of the energy cloud, and it moved out of his field.

The following is a description of what happens during a typical therapy session. First some background information on the client whom I will call Susan.

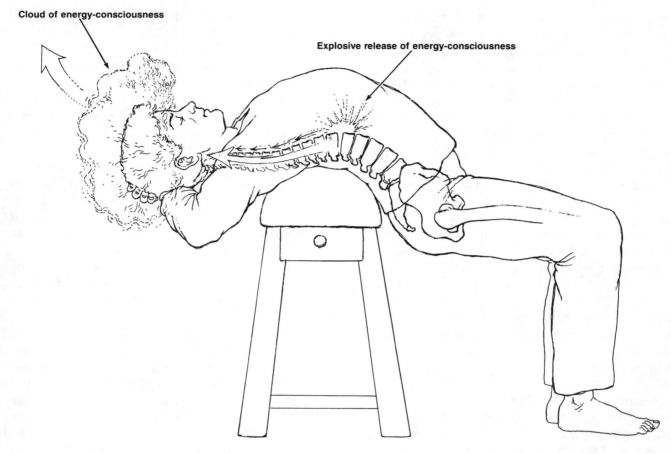

**Cloud of energy-consciousness**

**Explosive release of energy-consciousness**

Figure 11-4:   Man Working on Bioenergetic Stool

Susan was a beautiful blonde woman in her late twenties, a professional therapist, married, with a 2-year-old daughter. She and her husband, also a therapist, had a very nourishing and stable marriage and were leaders among their peers. They met and married very young. Susan's father had died accidentally two weeks before she was born. Her mother was left with a new baby and two young boys to care for. She had little or no income and had to ask other people to take Susan into their home to care for her. Susan grew up in two homes: one a very clean, ordered and strictly Christian home; the other, her mother's disheveled home. Her mother was never able to heal the wound of losing her husband at such an important time. She never married again but had many lovers.

Susan's early marriage satisfied her need for a man to care for her, since she never really had a father. Susan also carried with her the fear that she would never really make a marriage work (like her mother) or that she had to be perfect to do so (as with the religious family).

When Susan came to her session one morning, she was apparently very happy and cheerful. She spoke about her week with her husband. As she spoke and moved her arms, she threw up a pink and white cloud of "happiness" (Figure 11–5). However, this happiness was serving to cover deeper feelings revealed by her energy field. My observations showed there was a block, seen as a dark gray spot in the solar plexus (stomach area), related to fear and other feelings. The secondary block was in the forehead (lighter gray, indicating mental confusion), which directly connected to emotional pain in her heart (red). She displayed a lot of mental activity (high energy) on the sides of the head (yellow). She also had a lot of vibrant life-sexual energy held in her pelvis (red-orange).

As she continued to move her arms and talk cheerfully in a manner that threw up pink and white soft clouds, the bright yellow radiating energy from the sides of the head began to cover over or mask the gray forehead problem area. She was literally convincing herself that she was happy by masking the gray with yellow (mental) energy. When I described what I was seeing, she immediately stopped creating the "false" pink cloud. The gray area in the head regained its original range.

Susan's composure completely changed to fear and emotional pain. Then she began to share what was really going on. Shortly before Susan had come to her weekly session, she had found out that her mother was in the hospital with a kind of paralysis of the eyes. The physician in charge had suggested that it was a symptom of a serious disease, such as multiple sclerosis. Susan was very upset about this situation and needed to have her strength to go through all the various feelings she was having about her mother. By blocking her life-sexual energy in her pelvis and not allowing it to flow down her legs, she was blocking herself off from the ground and her foundation as a human being on the earth. So it was important at this point in the session to move that energy down into the earth and connect her to her energetic foundation, the power in her legs and pelvis.

Through leg and pelvic exercises we started moving the pelvic energy down her legs to build a base for more difficult work. This energy moved rapidly down the legs to connect her with the ground. It then flowed over the whole body and charged the system more evenly. As the pelvic block released, the change in energy gave her a feeling of security within her own sexual and life force feelings. This pelvic block was related to her mother, who did not deal well with her sexual energy. Susan was still afraid of being like Mom. Since Susan had a strong heart-sex connection, there was really no danger of this, which is why the energy moved so rapidly down the legs and into the ground. Once that energy was grounded, Susan knew she could have those pleasurable feelings and still control them so she could choose to do with them what she wanted.

Next, Susan was able to talk about the pain she was feeling in her heart about her mother's illness. She started to cry. This released the red from the heart area. We then proceeded to work on the major block located in her solar plexus, which was related to unfulfilled childhood needs, for which she in turn rejected her mother. Thus her energy field showed her internal conflict. On the one hand, she felt pain and love feelings for her mother, who was at that time very ill, and, on the other, she felt the anger of rejection, as in, "You didn't take care of me; now why should I take care of you?" Bringing this conflict to consciousness and understanding began releasing the gray area in the forehead.

To release the dark spot in the solar plexus took strong bodywork. Susan bent backwards over the bioenergetic stool to stretch and loosen the block. Then she did strenuous movements thrusting the upper half of the body forward and down to regurgitate the block and all it symbolized. It symbolized not only the rejection of her mother, but also Susan's intent to blame her mother for all the deprivation she had ever experienced. Susan maintained a "safe" state of deprivation in her current life; the childhood deprivation had been replaced through habit by self-deprivation. The dark spot (four inches in diameter) in the solar plexus lightened and spread to a larger area (eight inches in diameter), but some of it remained in the energy field, indicating that this issue was not resolved completely. This dark spot would take a long time to release because it contained major life issues.

What I am referring to when I say a "safe" state of deprivation is that she felt comfortable with some deprivation. That seemed normal to her. We human beings feel safest in whatever we consider the norm to be, whether or not it is actually normal; that norm is established in our childhood environment.

For example, with Susan that "norm" was manifesting itself through her living space. As a child there was confusion about her home.

Which was her real home? Neither really was. The problem persisted. She had lived in an unfinished house for almost all of her eight-year marriage. She had never really had a completely finished and furnished home that was hers.

As her therapy progressed, Susan's living space became more harmoniously furnished and beautifully finished. It was truly, in her case, an outer manifestation of an inner state.

From these energy-field observations you are probably beginning to see the connection between illness and psychological problems more clearly. We stop our feelings by blocking our energy flow. This creates stagnated pools of energy in our systems which when held there long enough lead to disease in the physical body. This will be discussed in greater detail in Part IV. The connection between therapy and healing becomes obvious when disease is seen in this way. The broad view of the healer encompasses the totality of the human being. In healing there is no separation between body and mind, emotions and spirit—all need to be in balance to create a healthy human being. The healer focuses on physical, psychological and spiritual misfunction. It is impossible to do healing without affecting the psychological levels of the personality. The more the healer understands the psychodynamics of her clients, the more the healer will be equipped to help the clients heal themselves.

# Chapter 11 Review

1. What is an energy block?
2. How is an energy block created in the HEF?
3. How can you tell when a block in the HEF is released?
4. How can you tell someone is releasing feelings as opposed to holding them?
5. Which happens first—the auric phenomena or the physical?
6. In what color/colors do the following emotions appear in the aura? Fear, anger, love, joy, confusion, envy, hatred.
7. Which color is best in the aura? Vibrant, bright red near the pelvis or nice, rich green near the chest–solar plexus area?
8. What is the effect of marijuana smoking on the aura? Short-term? Long-term?
9. What is a dissociated thought form?

## Food For Thought

10. Do exercises (observing other people's auras) and describe what you see.
11. Trace from beginning to end the cycle of one of the thought forms that you get caught in. What initiated it? What is its origin? How can you break out of it? What deeper feelings does it cover and defend you against feeling?

# Chapter 12

# ENERGY BLOCKS AND DEFENSE SYSTEMS IN THE AURA

After observing many blocks in people's fields, I began to categorize them into types. I found six general types of energy blocks. I also began to notice that people use their fields in defensive ways to protect them from an imagined unpleasant experience. They organized their entire auric fields into what I call an energetic defense system.

First let us look at the six types of energy blocks I have observed.

## Types of Energy Blocks

Figures 12–1 and 12–2 show how these blocks appear to me. The "blah" block (Figure 12–1A) is a result of depressing one's feelings and energy till they stagnate and cause an accumulation of body fluids in that area. The body tends to bloat there. This block usually does not have high energy but is rather of low intensity, which is usually associated with despair. If this block continues, a possible resulting disease would be colitis or angina pectoris. Its color is usually gray-blue. It feels sticky and heavy, like mucus. There is anger there also, usually the blaming kind. The person has given up and feels powerless. For example, a woman who was unhappily married and gave up her career for the marriage had such a block. Now in her fifties, she found it impossible to go back into the business world and start a career. Instead she simply blamed her husband for her unhappiness. She demanded that her daughters do what she had never done. She tried to live her life through them, but of course it didn't work.

The compaction block (Figure 12–1B), which suppresses feelings, on the other hand, contains a lot of accumulated rage, like a volcano. It is dark red in color, usually appearing quite ominous to the observer, who normally does not want to be the recipient of the volcanic eruption. This energy block results in an accumulation of body fat or body muscle in the area. If this compaction continues long enough, it may result in diseases like pelvic inflammatory disease. The person is usually aware of the rage and feels trapped because release of rage is associated with humiliation. One woman I saw concluded in childhood that to have sexual feelings would bring on humiliation. Her father humiliated her with regard to her sexuality when she was young. The result was that she blocked her powerful sexual feelings and held them tightly in her pelvis. The held sexual feelings slowly turned to rage. When the rage was not released, due to fear of humiliation, the accumulation of stagnated energy in her pelvis brought on infection. After years of chronic small infections, she was finally diagnosed as having pelvic inflammatory disease.

The mesh armor (Figure 12–1C) is an effective block in that it helps the person avoid feelings, especially fear, by quickly moving the

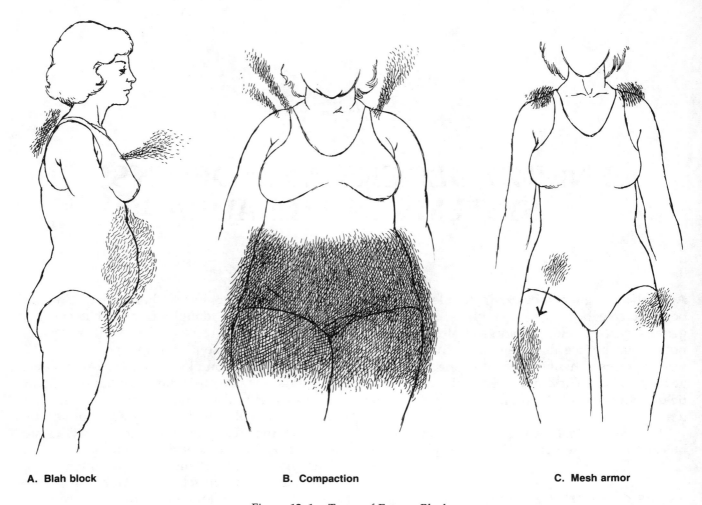

**A. Blah block**          **B. Compaction**          **C. Mesh armor**

Figure 12–1:  Types of Energy Blocks

blocks around when she is challenged either in a life situation or in therapy. For example, if the therapist tries to release a block through exercise or deep massage, the block will simply move to another part of the body. This type of blocking probably will not initiate disease as readily as the other types of blocks. Everything will appear to be wonderful in this patient's life. She will be successful in the world, have a "perfect" marriage and model children, yet she will have the vague sense that something is missing. This person will be able to tolerate deep feelings for only a short period of time before pulling herself out of them. Finally, she will probably create some crisis in her life to break into her deeper feelings. This crisis can take any form, like a

sudden unexpected illness, an accident or an affair.

The plate armor, shown in Figure 12–2A, holds all types of feelings by freezing them. They are held in place around the body by a field of generalized high tension. It effectively helps the person build a well-structured life on the outer level. The body will be well constructed; muscles will tend to be hard. On the personal level, life will not be so fulfilling, because the plate armor effectively nullifies all feelings. This creates high tension all over the body, which can result in several different types of disease: ulcers from overwork or heart problems from physical "pushing" in life without personal nourishment. Because the person cannot

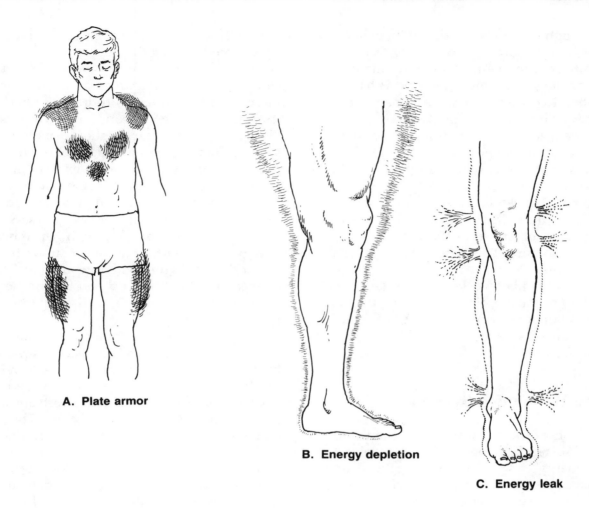

A. Plate armor

B. Energy depletion

C. Energy leak

Figure 12-2: Types of Energy Blocks

feel his body well, e.g., the tension in his long muscles, he will probably overstress his muscles, causing shin splints or tendonitis. This person will also have a "perfect" appearing life that is lacking a deeper personal connection. He will also probably eventually create some kind of life crisis, like those mentioned above, that will help him connect to his deeper reality. A heart attack does this nicely for some men. For example, I know a very successful businessman who owned several magazines with very large circulations. He was so busy working that he became disconnected from his family. After his heart attack, his children came to him and said, "You have to stop or you will die. Teach us to help you run your business." He did, they learned

and the family was brought back together.

The energy depletion block (Figure 12-2B) is simply a decrease of energy flowing down the limb in the direction of the distal end. The person cuts off the limbs by simply not allowing the energy to flow there. This results in weakness of the limb and, in some cases, even physical underdevelopment in that area. This person will avoid use of the limb to avoid the feelings of weakness, and then the deeper associated feelings, like not being able to stand on his own feet in life, or the feeling of failing in life.

The energy leak (Figure 12-2C) occurs when the person squirts his energy out of the joints instead of allowing it to flow down the limb. He does this (unconsciously) to decrease the energy flow through his limbs to the point where he will not have the strength or feeling to respond to certain experiences in his environment. The reason he does not want to respond is based on a childhood conclusion that response is either improper or even dangerous. For example, as a child, if he reached for something he wanted, he may have been slapped on the hand. Again, weakness in the limb (and also poor coordination) results, with avoidance of the use of the limb. Both of these latter types of blocks also result in coldness in the limbs. The person is usually very vulnerable in the areas where the energy leak occurs. This type of block results in joint problems.

Just what kind of blocks a person develops is dependent on many things, including personality and childhood environment. All of us use a combination of several of these blocks. Which are your favorites?

## Energetic Defense Systems

We all create blocks because we see the world as unsafe. We block in patterns that involve our whole energy system. Our energetic defense systems are designed to repel, to defend aggressively or passively against an incoming force. They are designed to show power and thus scare off an aggressor, or they are designed to get us attention indirectly, without admitting that is what we want.

Examples of energetic defense systems which I have observed are shown in Figure 12–3. These defense systems are employed when the individual feels endangered.

With the "porcupine" (usually whitish-gray in color), the person's aura becomes spiny and painful to touch. It is sharp. Many times, when I have put my hand on someone when he did not want it there, I could feel the spines going through my hand. Most people respond to this defense by distancing.

In the "withdrawal" form of defense, the portion of the person's consciousness and aura that is being threatened simply leaves his body in a cloud of light blue energy. The eyes will have a glazed look, although he pretends to be fully there listening to you.

The same is true for the person who is "beside himself." This particular configuration is more long-term than withdrawal, which may last only for a few seconds up to hours. The "beside himself" manifestation usually lasts for a longer period, perhaps days or even years. I have seen people who have been partially out of their bodies for years from some trauma or early surgery. In one case, a young woman had open-heart surgery at the age of two years. She was twenty-one when I worked with her to help her energy fields to seat themselves more firmly in her body. Her higher bodies would partially disconnect and float out, up and behind her. This disconnection resulted in a disconnection from her feelings.

Verbal denial is associated with much energy, usually yellow, in the head, a severe neck block and depleted energy in the lower half, which is pale and still. In order to keep the status quo, the person stays active verbally so as to sustain some feeling of being alive. This verbal exchange keeps the energy flowing in the head.

Oral sucking is closely related to verbal denial in that it is effective in sucking energy from those around in order to fill the person's own field, which he usually is unable to do from the natural surrounding environment. In other words, there is something amiss in the person's ability to metabolize the orgone supply from the surrounding atmosphere, causing him to need predigested energy from others. One can feel this form of sucking in verbal prattle that is boring and exhausting to the recipient, or see it in the "vacuum cleaner" eyes that some people possess. These people love to be around others in some form of socializing. There are other people who need to discharge an excess of energy (masochist types) who make good partners with the oral suckers. Together, they fill each other's needs quite nicely. (See Chapter 13.)

The hooks I have seen on some people's heads usually are on people who have a psychopathic character structure and who are in the process of being confronted by, say, a group of people. They become very threatened in such a

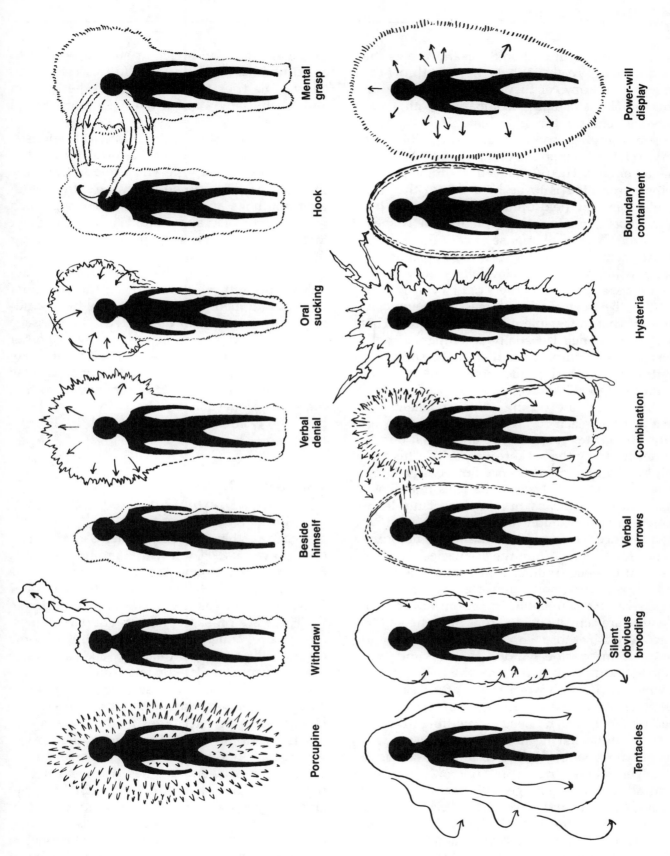

Mental grasp

Power-will display

Hook

Boundary containment

Oral sucking

Hysteria

Verbal denial

Combination

Beside himself

Verbal arrows

Withdrawl

Silent obvious brooding

Porcupine

Tentacles

Figure 12-3: Energetic Defense Systems

105

situation and form a "hook" on the top of the head. If things really get hot, they will throw the "hook" at whomever they see as the aggressor. This "hook" is usually accompanied with a verbal statement. On the other hand, if this type of person wants to confront someone, she may very well try to grasp the other by the head with mental energy. The possible effect on the person being confronted is to be held within the confronter's energy field until the latter is sure her point is being made and accepted as she wishes. This type of defense/offense is very threatening to the recipient because, from all appearances, she is being approached logically with very rational steps leading to the "right" conclusion, but the "between-the-lines" message being conveyed is that the recipient had better agree. This kind of exchange is usually accompanied with the underlying implication that the person being confronted is "bad" and wrong, and the confronter is "good" and right.

"Tentacles" are oozing, slippery, silent and heavy. They reach for your solar plexus in an effort to capture your essence and pull it out, to be devoured by the seeker of security. This person is full of his own essence but doesn't know what to do with it, because he feels that allowing it to move means humiliation. Thus he is caught in despair and even loses touch with his own essence. He may adopt the silent, brooding stance for a while. Then the "tentacles" work at his own essence, pulling him down. The silent brooding is very noisy, however, on the energetic level. He stands out in a room full of people who are actively having fun. Soon he will be surrounded by those who wish to help him, and he will unconsciously, but cleverly and graciously, thank each person for the help offered, saying why it won't work and ask for other suggestions. And so the game goes on. The tentacled person thinks he needs something from the outside, but what he needs is to give out. He may then try verbal arrows to provoke someone to anger. These arrows are not only verbally painful, but also energetically painful, flying through the air and striking the recipient very precisely and effectively. The archer unconsciously hopes this will cause enough pain to elicit anger, which will then give him an excuse

to release his own anger in such a way as to avoid humiliation. In this willful, precise, mental way, he tries to humiliate the other person and, at the same time, avoid having feelings in the lower half of his body.

The person who uses "hysterical defense" will gladly respond to the "arrows" by exploding. The hysterical type will explode in a way that will impinge upon everyone's field with lightning bolts and explosions of color in such fury as to threaten and intimidate with the sheer force of power and chaos. His purpose is to clear the room of everyone.

The person using "boundary containment" will simply remove himself from the situation, while strengthening and thickening his boundary in order to remain unaffected. The message thus conveyed is one of superiority! Another may simply state his supremacy with a strongly ordered, well-controlled, power/will display which blows up and lights up his aura, so that there is no question of who is in charge here, and who is not to be tampered with!

## Exercises to Find Your Major Defense

Try each of these defense systems out; which ones do you use? Try it with a group of people. Everyone walk around the room in each of the defense systems. How familiar is each one? Which ones do you use for different occasions?

There are probably many more defense systems in use. You can undoubtedly think of some others yourself—ones that you use, and ones used by your friends. The important thing to remember is that all of us use them, and that we all agree, whether consciously or unconsciously, to interact with each other in these ways. No one is forced into these interactions; they are all voluntary. On some levels of our personalities, we even enjoy them at times. We need not be frightened when we see them in each other. We always have the choice to respond tolerantly rather than defensively. We must remember that there is always a reason why someone is defending—to protect some vulnerable part of himself that he wishes to keep under control and hidden, either from us or himself, or both. We develop most of these systems early in life. As shown in Chapter 8, the aura of a child is not fully grown any more than his body. It, too, develops and goes through stages of development as the individual grows, and, as it does, basic character patterns, representing both strengths and vulnerabilities, become clear.

## Chapter 12 Review

1. Name and describe six major types of energy blocks.

2. List the major defense systems and how they work. Which do you use? Are the ones you use effective for you? What would be a better way for you to handle your life experience?

### Food For Thought

3. Upon what personal belief system is your major defense based?
4. How would your life be better/worse if you didn't use your defense system?
5. List the types and locations of blocks you have created in your body/energy system. What childhood experiences is each related to?

## Chapter 13

# AURA AND CHAKRA PATTERNS
# OF THE
# MAJOR CHARACTER STRUCTURES

Character structure is a term that many body psychotherapists use to describe certain physical and psychological types of people. After much observation and study, Wilhelm Reich concluded that most of the people he treated could be fitted into five major categories. He found that people with similar childhood experiences and child/parent relations had similar bodies. He also found that people with similar bodies had similar basic psychological dynamics. These dynamics were dependent not only on types of child/parent relations, but also on the age at which the child first experiences life so traumatically that it begins to block its feelings and therefore the flow of energy and to develop the defense system that will become habitual. A trauma experienced in the womb will be energetically blocked or defended against very differently than one experienced in the oral stage of growth, in toilet training or in latency. This is only natural because the individual and his field are so different at different stages of life. (See Chapter 8.)

In this section, I will give some basic descriptions of each character structure, including etiology, body forms and their auric configurations. I will also discuss the nature of the higher self and personal life task of each structure as far as that can be done. Each person's higher self

and life task is unique, but some generalizations can be made.

The higher self of a person is seen as the divine spark within, or the Godself within each individual, the place where we are already one with God. There is a divine spark in every cell of our physical and spiritual being which contains this inner divine consciousness.

The life task is seen in two forms. First, on the personal level, there is a personal task, which has the purpose of learning to express a new part of one's identity. The parts of the soul that are not one with God help form the specific incarnation in order to learn how to be one with the creator and still remain individuated. The world task is a gift that each soul comes into this physical life to give to the world. Many times it is the same as the life's work that comes naturally early on. An artist brings his art, a physician the gift of healing, a musician his music, a mother her nurturing and love, etc. At other times the person has to strive, through many changes of work, to step into what she can finally realize is her life's work. The power and clarity with which the life task is taken on depends a great deal on accomplishing the personal task of learning.

The individual's body is the crystallization in the physical world of the energy fields that surround and are part of each person. These energy fields contain the task of each soul. The character structure can then be seen as the crystallization of the basic problems or personal task a person has elected to incarnate and to solve. The problem (task) is crystallized in the body and held there so that the individual can easily see and work with it. By studying our character structure as it relates to our bodies, we can find the key to heal ourselves and find our personal and world task.

The basic malady I have found in all the people I have ever worked with is self-hatred. Self-hatred is, in my opinion, the basic inner illness in all of us, but just how that self-hatred and nonacceptance of the self manifests is shown in the different character structures. As we work to understand our dynamics on a daily level, we can learn to accept ourselves through this process. We can go through years of living by God's will (the God within), by the truth, and by love—these are all steps to self-realization—but until we can love unconditionally we are not yet home. This means starting with the self. Can we love ourselves unconditionally even though we see our shortcomings? Can we forgive ourselves when we make a mess of things? Can we, after making a mess, get right up and say, "Well, I'll have to learn from that one." "I am a woman/man of God." "I realign myself with the light and keep going through whatever it takes to find my way back to my Godself inside and home." So with that in mind, let us turn to the character structures, knowing that to address the deeper issues that relate to why each of us is a certain type or combination of types of character structure in the first place, will probably take a lifetime.

Working together Drs. Al Lowan and John Pierrakos originally categorized the major aspects of the character structures on the physical and personality levels. To these John Pierrakos added the spiritual and energetic aspects. He changed the meaning of the character structures by adding the spiritual dimension of humankind to the purely biological and disease elements that Reich had developed. As part of this work, Pierrakos related chakra function to the character structures. I carried that work further

and developed the general auric patterns of each character structure, as shown in Figs. 13–5 through 13–8 and the energetic defense systems given in Chapter 12.

Figures 13–1, 13–2 and 13–3 give tables showing the major characteristics of each structure. These tables were compiled by the bioenergetic training class given by Dr. Jim Cox in 1972 and by the core energetic training class given by Dr. John Pierrakos in 1975, in which I was studying. I have added the energy field information from my own work.

## The Schizoid Structure

The first character structure (first in the sense that the major cutoff of life energy flow took place earliest) is called the schizoid structure. In this case, the first traumatic experience took place before or at birth, or within the first few days of life. The trauma is usually centered around some hostility received directly from a parent, such as anger in a parent, a parent not wanting the child or trauma during the birthing process—such as the mother becoming emotionally disconnected from the child and the child feeling abandoned. The range of such events is great; a slight disconnection between mother and child for one child could be very traumatic, whereas it may not have the slightest effect on another. This is related to the nature of the incoming soul and what task it has chosen for itself in this lifetime.

The natural energetic defense used against this trauma at this stage of life is simply to draw back into the spirit world from which the soul is coming. The defense is developed and used for this type of character structure, until it is very easy for the person simply to withdraw into someplace "away," which is into the spirit world. (See Figure 12–3.) This defense becomes habitual, and the person uses it in any situation in which he feels threatened. To compensate for his defense of flying away he tries to hold himself together on the personality level. His basic fault is fear—fear that he has no right to exist. In interacting with others, be they the therapist or friends, he will speak in a depersonalized lan-

# Figure 13–1
## MAJOR ASPECTS OF EACH CHARACTER STRUCTURE
### PERSONALITY MAKEUP

| | SCHIZOID | ORAL | PSYCHOPATHIC | MASOCHISTIC | RIGID |
|---|---|---|---|---|---|
| ARREST OF DEVELOPMENT | Before or at Birth | Babyhood Feeding | Early Childhood | Autonomy Stage | Puberty Genital |
| TRAUMA | Hostile Mother | Abandonment | Seduction Betrayal | Control Forced Feeding & Evacuation | Sexual Denial Betrayal of Heart |
| PATTERN | Hold Together | Hold On | Hold Up | Hold In | Hold Back |
| SEXUALITY | Sex to Feel Life Force, Fantasy | Sex for Closeness & Contact | Hostile/Fragile Homosexual Fantasy | Impotence Strong Interest in Pornography | Sex with Contempt |
| FAULT | Fear | Greed | Untruthfulness | Hatred | Pride |
| DEMANDS THE RIGHT TO | Be/Exist | Be Nurtured & Fulfilled | Be Supported & Encouraged | Be Independent | Have Feelings (Love/Sex) |
| PRESENTING COMPLAINT | Fear/Anxiety | Passivity (Fatigue) | Feelings of Defeat | Tension | No Feelings |
| NEGATIVE INTENT | "I will be split." | "I'll make you give it." "I won't need." | "My will be done." | "I love negativity." | "I won't surrender." |
| DEVICES BEHIND NEGATIVE INTENT | Unity vs. Splitting | Need vs. Abandonment | Will vs. Surrender | Freedom vs. Submission | Sex vs. Love |
| NEEDS TO | Strengthen Boundaries | Own Needs & Stand on Own Two Feet | Trust | Be Assertive Be Free Open Spiritual Connections | Connect Heart to Genitals |

guage, in absolutes, and tend to intellectualize. This only brings on more experience of being separate from life and not truly existing.

When he presents himself for therapy, the presenting complaint will be a great deal of fear and anxiety. In working in therapy, the issue will be that to feel that he exists, he must feel unity, but to survive he believes he must split. Thus he has a negative intent to split. This creates the double bind: "To exist means to die." To resolve this problem in therapy, he needs to strengthen the boundaries that define who he is and to feel his strength in the physical world.

In the therapeutic process, after the client stops trying to be a nice guy to the therapist and begins to work, the first layer of personality encountered will be the blaming part, sometimes called the mask, which says, "I'll reject you before you reject me." After the work of digging deeper into the personality has been done, base emotions sometimes called the lower self or shadow self will say, "You don't exist either." Then, when resolution begins, the more highly-developed part of the personality, sometimes called the higher power or higher self of the personality, emerges to say, "I'm real."

People with schizoid characters can leave their bodies easily and do so quite regularly. On the body level, the result is a body that appears to be a combination of pieces, not firmly held together or integrated. These people are usually tall and thin, but in some cases can have heavy bodies. The tension in the body tends to be in rings around the body. Joints are usually weak, and the body is usually uncoordinated, with cold hands and feet. The person is usually hyperactive and ungrounded. There is a main energy block at the neck, near the base of the skull, which usually looks dark gray blue. There is usually energy squirting out the skull base. Many times there is twisting in the spine, caused by a habitual twisting away from mate-

# Figure 13–2
# MAJOR ASPECTS OF EACH CHARACTER STRUCTURE
## PHYSICAL AND ENERGETIC SYSTEM

|  | SCHIZOID | ORAL | PSYCHOPATHIC | MASOCHISTIC | RIGID |
|---|---|---|---|---|---|
| PHYSICAL BUILD | Elongation Right/Left Imbalances | Thin Collapsed Chest | Inflated Chest Top Heavy | Head Forward Heavy | Rigid Back Pelvis Tipped Back |
| BODY TENSION | "Ring" Tension Uncoordinated Weak Joints | Flaccid Smooth Muscles Hold | Top Half Compacted Lower Half Spastic | Compressed | Spastic Plate Armor Mesh Armor |
| BODY CIRCULATION | Cold Hands/Feet | Cold Chest | Cold Legs/Pelvis | Cold Buttocks | Cold Pelvis |
| ENERGY LEVELS | Hyperactive Ungrounded | Hypoactive Low Energy | Hyperactivity Followed by Collapse | Hypoactive (Internalized Energy) | Hyperactive (High Energy) |
| ENERGY LOCATION | Frozen at the Core | In the Head Generally Depleted | Upper Half of Body | Boiling Inside | On Periphery Withheld from the Core |
| PRIMARY FUNCTIONING CHAKRAS | 7th 6th Front 3rd Front 2nd Rear Asymmetrical | 7th 6th Front 2nd Front Aspect | 7th 6th 4th Rear Aspect | 6th Front 3rd Front | Will Centers 6th Front |
| PSYCHODYNAMICS OF OPEN CHAKRAS | Spiritual Mental Will | Spiritual Mental Love | Mental Will | Mental Feeling Will | Will Mental |
| ENERGETIC DEFENSE SYSTEM | Withdrawal "Porcupine" Beside Himself | Oral Sucking Verbal Denial Hysteria | "Hook" Mental "Grasp" Hysteria | Silent Brooding "Tentacles" | Power/Will Display Boundary Containment |

rial reality as the person partially flies out of the body. The body has weak, thin wrists, ankles and calves and usually is not connected to the ground. One shoulder may be larger than the other (even without playing tennis). Many times the head is held to one side and there is a vague look in the eyes, as if the person is partly somewhere else. He is. He may be sometimes referred to as "flaky." Many of these people started masturbating early in childhood, finding that a way to connect to the life force was through their sexuality. It helped them feel "alive" when they could not connect to others around them.

What the person with a schizoid character has avoided through the use of his defense system is his inner terror, the terror of annihilation.

Of course he could not deal with it as a baby because he was completely dependent upon those whom he found terrifying, or by whom he had felt completely abandoned in his greatest hour of need the birthing process. As a baby the schizoid character felt direct hostility from at least one of his parents, the people he depended on for survival. This experience initiated his existential terror.

The schizoid character can find release from his inner terror of annihilation when he, as an adult, realizes that his terror is now more related to his inner rage than to anything else. This rage comes from continuing to experience the world as a very cold, hostile place where isolation is forced upon anyone who wants to survive. A part of the schizoid being fully believes this to

# Figure 13–3
## MAJOR ASPECTS OF EACH CHARACTER STRUCTURE
### INTERPERSONAL RELATIONS

|  | SCHIZOID | ORAL | PSYCHOPATHIC | MASOCHISTIC | RIGID |
|---|---|---|---|---|---|
| EVOKES | Intellectualization | Mothering | Submission | Teasing | Competition |
| COUNTER TRANSFERENCE REACTION | Withdrawal into Away | Passivity Neediness Dependency | Exertion of Control | Guilt Shame Holding | Withdrawal into a Holding Back |
| COMMUNICATES IN | Absolutes | Questions | Dictates | Whining Disgust | Qualifiers |
| LANGUAGE | Depersonalized | Indirect | Direct Manipulation ("You should.") | Indirect Manipulation (Polite Expressions) | Seductive |
| DOUBLE BIND | "To exist means to die." | "If I ask, it's not love; if I don't ask, I won't get it." | "I have to be right or I die." | "If I get angry, I'll be humiliated; if I don't, I'll be humiliated." | "Either choice is wrong." |
| MASK STATEMENT | "I'll reject you before you reject me." | "I don't need you." "I won't ask." | "I'm right; you're wrong." | "I'll kill (hurt) myself before you do." | "Yes, but. . . ." |
| LOWER SELF STATEMENT | "You don't exist either." | "Take care of me." | "I will control you." | "I will spite and provoke you." | "I won't love you." |
| HIGHER SELF STATEMENT | "I'm real." | "I'm satisfied, fulfilled." | "I give in." | "I'm free." | "I commit." "I love." |

be the essence of material reality. Under this rage is the great pain of knowing that what he needs is loving, warm connection and nourishment from other humans; but in many cases he has not been able to create that in his life.

His terror is that his own rage will cause him to blow apart into pieces that will scatter into the universe. The key for him is to face his own rage little by little without flying away in defense. If he can stand on the ground and allow the terror and rage to come out, he will release the inner pain and the longing for connection with others and make a place for self-love to come in. Self-love takes practice. We all need it no matter what combination of character structures we may be. Self-love comes from living in ways that do not betray oneself. It comes from living according to one's inner truth, whatever that may be. It comes from not betraying oneself. It can be practiced through simple self-love exercises given in the final section.

## The Energy Field of the Schizoid Structure

The schizoid structure is characterized mainly by energy-field discontinuities like imbalances and breaks. The main energy of the person is held deep within the core of the person and is usually frozen there until therapy and healing work is done to free it. Figure 13–4 shows the thin and breaking line of the etheric body of this structure with energy leaks at the joints. Its color is usually very light blue. The next layer and mental bodies are seen to be either tightly held and frozen at times or, at other times, moving around randomly without a balanced energy between front and back, right and left. The field is usually brighter with more energy on one side and on the back of the head. The spiritual bodies of the schizoid are usually strong and bright with many brilliant colors on the sixth layer of the aura, or celestial body. The oval form, or ketheric template layer, is usually very bright in appearance, with a color more of silver than gold. It usually has diffuse boundaries and is not fully inflated with a narrowing of the egg shape at the feet, where there is sometimes weakness.

The aura's imbalance, which is found primarily in the lower three bodies, extends to the chakras in the schizoid person who has not begun process work; many chakras are counterclockwise. This means that they send more energy out than they take in. The disturbed chakras correspond to qualities in the character structure that need transformation. Chakras that are clockwise (open) are usually asymmetrical, meaning that those chakras are also not functioning in a balanced manner even though they are "open." More energy will flow through one part of the chakra than another part. This imbalance is usually lateral; that is, there may be more energy flowing through the right side of the chakra than the left side. The person would therefore tend to be more active or possibly even more aggressive than receptive in the area of life governed by that chakra. This asymmetry has been described in Chapter 10 in terms of active/receptive splitting. A diagonal or elliptical figure measured by the pendulum indicates an asymmetrical chakra that appears to clairvoyant vision as shown in Figure 13–4.

The chakras that are usually open are the rear sexual center (second), the solar plexus (third), the forehead (sixth) and the crown (seventh). The sixth and seventh centers are associated with mental and nonphysical spirituality to which the person is usually very oriented in his life. He also functions through will (second chakra). These chakra configurations are variable and change during a person's transformational work. As the individual opens more to being in the third dimension and living in the physical, more of the chakras open. Many times the rear sex center is not open in the beginning of the work.

The lower part of Figure 13–4 shows the relative degree of bright energy active in the brain area. The brightest, most active place is the occipital or rear area, and the least is the frontal area. The second most active chakra is the third

eye and third ventricle area of the brain, which are connected by a bridge of brightness between the two. Then come the side lobes, which are associated with language. There are large general areas of the brain that appear to have low activity.

The low energy in the frontal area can be seen by the blank, "gone" look often seen in the schizoid. He usually directs his energy up the spine and out the back of the head in the occipital region, creating the energy bulge towards the back of the head. This is a way of avoiding here-and-now contact in the physical plane.

The energetic defense systems primarily used by the schizoid are the porcupine, withdrawal, and being beside oneself, as described in Chapter 12, Figure 12–3. Of course a person with any structure can use the various defenses at various times.

## The Higher Self and Life Task of the Schizoid Character

In the personal growth process, it is always important to be very honest with the self as to the self's shortcomings, to work on them to transform them. But it is not healthy to dwell on the negativities of the self for very long. One must always balance the attention to these parts that need transforming with attention to finding the nature of the higher self, supporting it, enhancing it and allowing it to come forth. After all, that is what transformation is all about, isn't it?

People who are or have some schizoid character in their personality makeup are usually very spiritual people. They have a deep sense of the profound purposes of life. Many times they seek to bring the spiritual reality into the mundane lives of those around them. They are very creative people, with many talents and many creative ideas, who could be compared to a beautiful mansion with many rooms, each room tastefully and richly decorated in a different style, culture or period. Each room is elegant in its own right because the schizoid has had many lifetimes in which he has developed this wide range of talents (decorated rooms). The problem

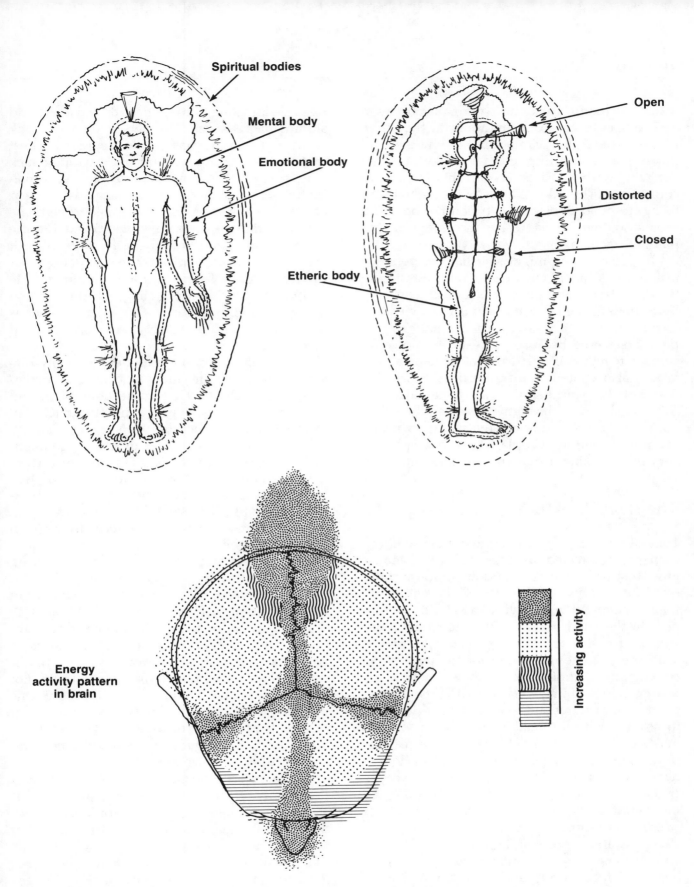

Figure 13–4:  The Aura of the Schizoid Character
(Diagnostic Views)

is that the rooms do not have doorways between each other. To get from one room to the other, the schizoid must climb out a window and down a ladder and up another ladder and into the window of the next room. This is very inconvenient. The schizoid needs to integrate his being, to build doorways between the beautiful rooms so that he has easier access to all the parts of his being.

In general, one might say that the personal task of the schizoid character is related to facing his inner terror and rage, which blocks his ability to materialize his tremendous creativity. His terror and rage actually keep the parts of his person separate because he fears the powerful coming together of all his creative talents. His task is also related to materializing, or making manifest, his spirituality in the material world. This may be done through expressing the spiritual reality through his creativity, e.g., writing, inventions, helping people, etc. These tasks are very individual and must not be generalized.

## The Oral Structure

The oral character is created when normal development is arrested during the oral stage of growth. The cause is abandonment. In childhood he experienced the loss of his mother, either by death, illness or withdrawal. The mother gave to the child, but not enough. Many times she "pretended" to give—or gave in spite of herself. The child compensated for the loss by becoming "independent" too early, many times by talking and walking very early. Thus, he becomes confused about receptivity and is afraid to ask for what he really needs because deep inside he is sure it will not be given. His feelings of needing to be taken care of result in dependency, tendency to cling, grabbiness and decreased aggressiveness. He compensates by independent behavior that collapses under stress. His receptivity then becomes a spiteful passivity, and aggression becomes greed.

The person with an oral structure is basically deprived, feels empty and hollow and doesn't want to take responsibility. The body is undeveloped with long, thin, flaccid muscles and slumps in weakness. The person does not look adult and mature, has a cold depressed chest and shallow breathing, and his eyes may suck your energy. Psychodynamically, the personality holds on and clings to others against the fear of being abandoned. He is not able to be alone and experiences an exaggerated need for the warmth and support of others. He tries to get it from the "outside" in order to compensate for the tremendous feeling of inner emptiness. He suppresses his intense feelings of longing and aggression. His rage over the abandonment is held in. Sexuality is used to get closeness and contact.

The oral person has experienced many disappointments in life, many rejections of his attempts to reach out. He thus becomes bitter and feels that whatever he gets is never enough. He cannot be satisfied because he is trying to satisfy an inner longing which he denies by compensating with something else. On the personality level, he demands to be nurtured and fulfilled. In interacting with others, he will speak in indirect questions that evoke mothering from another. But this does not fill him because he is an adult, not a child.

His presenting complaint when entering therapy is passivity and fatigue. In working in therapy the issue will be to find nourishment in his life. But to get his needs met, he believes he must risk abandonment by or pretense from another. Thus his negative intent will be "I'll make you give it to me" or "I won't need." This in turn creates the double bind, "If I ask, it's not love; if I don't ask, I won't get it." To resolve this problem in therapy, he needs to find and own his needs and to learn to live his life in such a way that his needs get met. He needs to learn to stand on his own two feet.

In the therapeutic process, the first layer of personality encountered will be the mask. It says, "I don't need you" or "I won't ask." After the work of digging deeper into the personality is done, the lower self or shadow self will say, "Take care of me." Then, when resolution begins, the higher self of the personality emerges to say, "I'm satisfied and fulfilled."

## The Energy Field of the Oral Structure

The Oral Character (Figure 13–5) tends to have a depleted field, which is calm and quiet. The main energy is located in the head. The etheric is held tightly near the skin and is also light blue in color. The emotional body is also held in, with not much color, and has a generally depleted quality. The mental body is bright and usually yellowish. The higher levels of the aura are not very bright. The outer egg form (seventh layer) is not entirely inflated, not bright, with a silvery-golden glow more to the silvery side and depleted around the feet area.

The chakras may be mostly closed or de-energized in an oral person who has not done much process work. He will most likely have the crown and the forehead center open, which accounts for his mental and spiritual clarity. If he has done personal growth work, he may have his front sexual center open as well. Thus he is interested in sex and has some sexual feelings.

The configuration of activity in his energy field in the head is shown at the bottom of the page, Figure 13–5. This shows that most of the energy is located in the frontal and side lobes of the brain, and the least energy at the rear in the occipital regions. Thus the oral character is centered on intellectual and verbal activity and not on physical activity.

The defense mechanisms primarily used by the oral are those of verbal denial, oral sucking and possible verbal arrows used to get attention, rather than to provoke rage—that is, unlike the way the verbal arrows are used by the person with a masochistic structure as stated in Chapter 12.

## The Life Task and High Self of the Oral Structure

The oral character needs to learn trust in the abundance of the universe and reverse the process of grabbing. He needs to give. He needs to give up the role of the victim and to acknowl-

edge what he does get. He needs to face his fear of being alone, go deep into the void within and find it teaming with life. When he owns his own needs and stands on his own two feet, then he will be able to say, "I have it," and allow the core energy to open up and flow.

The inner landscape of an oral character is like a fine musical instrument, like a Stradivarius. He needs to finely tune his instrument and compose his own symphony. When he plays his unique melody in the symphony of life, he will be fulfilled.

When the higher self is released, the oral characters can make good use of his intelligence in creative work in the arts or sciences. He will be a natural teacher, because he is very interested in so many things, and can always connect what he knows with love direct from the heart.

## The Displaced or Psychopathic Structure

In his early childhood, the person with a displaced structure experienced a covertly seductive parent of the opposite sex. The parent wanted something from the child. The psychopath was in a triangle with the parents and found it hard to get support from the parent of the same sex. He sided with the parent of the opposite sex, could not get what he needed, felt betrayed and then compensated by manipulating that parent.

His response to that situation was to try to control others anyway he could. To do this he must hold himself up, and even lie if need be. He demands to be supported and encouraged. But in interacting with others he will dictate direct manipulation like, "You should . . ." to evoke submission. This does not lead to support.

In its negative aspect, the person with this structure has a tremendous drive for power and need to dominate others. He has two ways of getting this control: by bullying and overpowering or by undermining through seduction. Many times his sexuality is hostile with a lot of

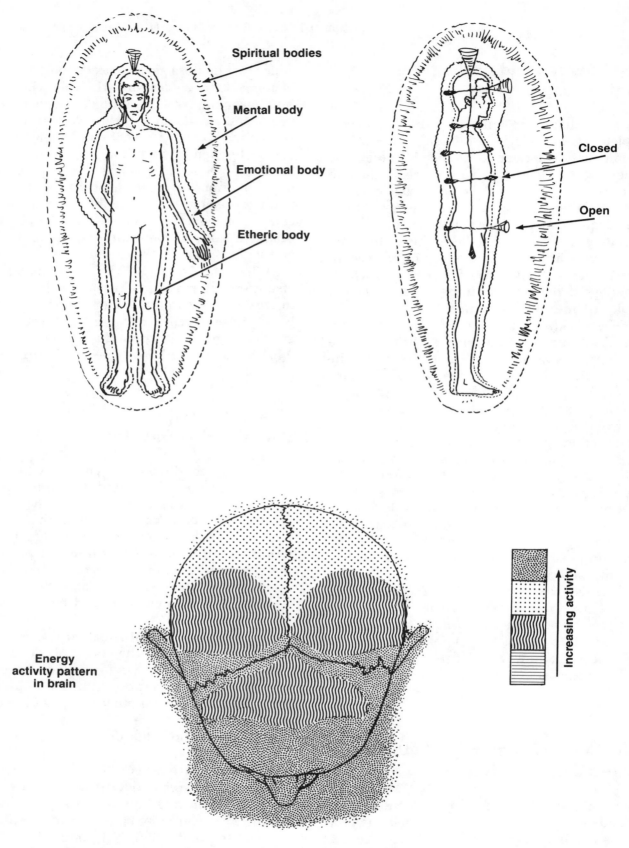

Spiritual bodies

Mental body

Emotional body

Etheric body

Closed

Open

Energy
activity pattern
in brain

Increasing activity

Figure 13–5:  The Aura of the Oral Character
(Diagnostic Views)

fantasy. He has invested in an ideal picture he has of himself and has strong feelings of superiority and contempt, which covers deep inferiority feelings.

His presenting complaint when entering therapy are feelings of defeat. He wants to win. But to be supported means to surrender, and that, he believes, means defeat. Thus his negative intent is, "My will be done." This creates the double bind of, "I have to be right or I die." To resolve this problem in therapy, he needs to learn to trust.

In the therapeutic process, the first layer of personality encountered will be the mask. It says, "I'm right; you're wrong." After digging deeper into the personality, the lower self or shadow self will say, "I will control you." When resolution begins, the higher self of the personality emerges to say, "I give in."

The upper half of the body seems blown up, and there is a lack of flow between the upper and lower half of the body. His pelvis is undercharged, cold and tightly held. There is severe tension in the shoulders, base of skull and eyes; his legs are weak, and he is not grounded.

The psychopathic structure holds up against fear of failure and defeat. He is torn between his dependency on people and his need to control them. He fears being controlled and used and is afraid to be put in the position of victim, which is totally humiliating to him. Sexuality is used in power play; pleasure is secondary to his conquest. He tries not to express his needs by making others need him.

## The Energy Field of the Psychopathic Structure

The main energy is located in the upper half of the body. His energy level is first hyperactive and then collapses. The person with a displaced structure (Figure 13–6) has a general field that is depleted at the bottom in all auric levels and energized at the top; thus the egg shape is distorted in this way also. The etheric decreases in fullness toward the feet and is generally of a darker blue color and stronger tone than that of the schizoid and the oral. The emotional body

also is fuller at the top. The mental body protrudes toward the front of the body more than towards the back, whereas the emotional body may appear to have a bulge at the will center located between the shoulder blades, which is usually greatly enlarged. The higher auric layers are also stronger and brighter on the upper half.

The chakra configuration in a psychopathic structure generally shows open will centers at the shoulder and neck base, with the will centers between the shoulder blades extremely large and overused, open frontal center and crown center, with most of the others closed, especially the feeling centers. The rear sexual center may be partially open. Thus he functions primarily through mental and will energy.

The energy activity in the brain is strong and bright in the frontal lobes. This energy activity decreases towards the back of the head and is very still and usually rather dark in the occipital region. This indicates the person is interested primarily in intellectual pursuits and not in body activity other than in a way that serves the active will. The intellect is also used to serve the will.

It is from these powerful frontal lobes that the psychopath sends out energy arches that reach toward another's head to hold him in the mental grasp type of defense. He also engages in some verbal denial. He may explode into a volcanic rage similar to that used in the hysterical defense system, but in a controlled, balanced energy form that does not contain that same kind of chaos.

## The Life Task and Higher Self of the Psychopathic Character

The psychopath needs to find true surrender by gradually deflating and letting go of his upper half and his tendency to control others and by giving in to his deeper being and sexual feelings. With this, he can satisfy his deep longing to be in reality, make contact with friends and feel like a human being.

The inner landscape of the psychopathic character is full of fantasy and adventures of honor. Here those who win are the ones with

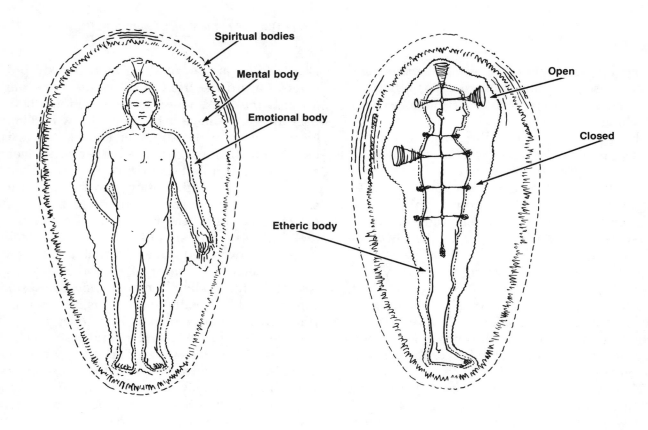

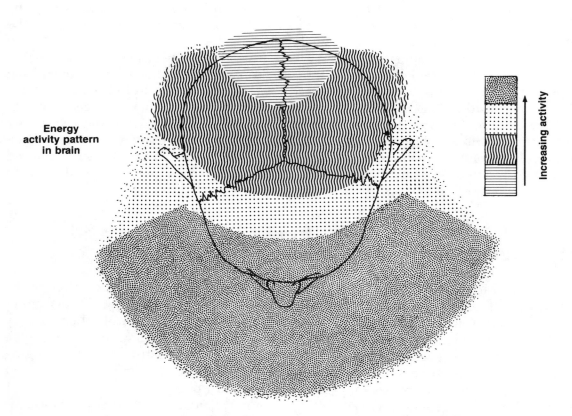

Figure 13–6: The Aura of the Psychopathic Character
(Diagnostic Views)

120

the most truth and honesty. The world revolves around noble values, which are upheld through perseverance and valor. How he longs to bring this into the physical environment of his real world. He will someday.

When his higher self energies are released, he is very honest and has a lot of integrity. His highly developed intellect can be put to use to solve disagreements by helping others find their truth. Through his honesty, he can lead others to their honesty. He is very good in managing complicated projects and has a big heart full of love.

## The Masochistic Structure

In childhood, the love the masochistic personality was given was conditional. His mother was dominating and sacrificing—even to the extent of controlling his eating and excretory functions. The child was made to feel guilty for any self-assertion or attempt to declare his freedom. All his attempts to resist the tremendous pressure put on him were crushed; he now feels trapped, defeated and humiliated. His response to this situation was to hold in his feelings and his creativity. In fact he tried to hold everything in. This lead to anger and hatred. He demands to be independent, but when he interacts with others, he uses polite expressions delivered with whining disgust to indirectly manipulate others. This evokes teasing from others. The teasing then allows him to become angry. He already was angry, but now he has been given the right to express it. Thus he is caught in a cycle that keeps him dependent.

On the negative side, this person is one who suffers, whines and complains, remains submissive on the outside, but will never really submit. Within are blocked strong feelings of spite, negativity, hostility, superiority and fear that he will explode into violent rage. He may be impotent and have a strong interest in pornography. A woman is likely to be nonorgasmic and feel her sexuality is unclean.

His presenting complaint when entering therapy is tension. He wants release from his tension, but unconsciously believes that releasing it and accepting what is inside leads to submission and humiliation. Thus his unconscious negative intent is to remain blocked and to "love negativity." This leads to the double bind of "If I get angry, I'll be humiliated; if I don't, I'll be humiliated." To resolve this problem in therapy, he needs to become assertive, be free and to open his spiritual connectedness.

In the therapeutic process the first layer of personality encountered will be the mask that says, "I'll kill (hurt) myself before you kill (hurt) me." After some therapy work is done exploring this inner landscape, the lower self will become conscious. It says, "I will spite and provoke you." This will eventually release the higher self which resolves the situation with, "I'm free."

Physically he is heavy and compacted with overdeveloped muscles and shortening of the neck and waist. He carries strong tensions in the neck, jaw, throat and pelvis, which is tucked under. His buttocks are cold. His energy is choked in the throat area, and his head thrusts forward.

Psychodynamically, he holds in and gets stuck in a morass in which he whines, complains, holds back feelings and provokes. If his provocation is successful he will have an excuse to explode. He is not conscious of his provocation and thinks he is trying to please.

## The Energy Field of the Masochistic Structure

His main energy is internalized. He is hypoactive and yet boiling inside. The masochistic structure's field (Figure 13–7) is fully inflated. The etheric body is dense, thick, coarse and shaded to the gray colors rather than the blue. The emotional body is full, multicolored and fairly evenly distributed, as is the etheric body. The mental body is large and bright even on the lower part of the body. The intellect and emotions are more integrated. The celestial body is bright all around the body with colors of mauve, maroon and blue. The egg is fully inflated and has a dark golden color. The egg is a bit overweight toward the bottom and forms more of an oval shape than an egg. Its outer edge is

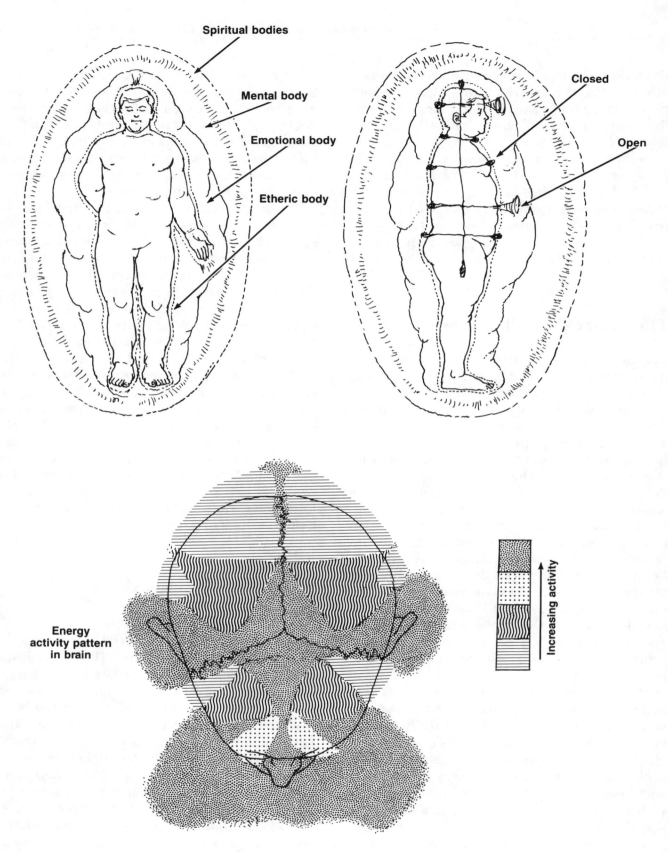

Figure 13–7:   The Aura of the Masochistic Character
(Diagnostic Views)

strongly defined with somewhat too much tension and thickness.

The chakras that are usually open in a masochist before starting core process work are the forehead, the solar plexus and, possibly, a partially opened rear sexual center. He thus functions in the mental, emotional and will aspects of the personality. The energy activity pattern of the brain shows activity in the frontal, parietal and ventricle areas, with some of this activity extending to a small central area in the occiput, which is surrounded by a less active area. Defense systems commonly employed by the masochist are the tentacles, silent obvious brooding and verbal arrows.

## The Life Task and Higher Self of the Masochistic Character

The masochist needs to free himself from humiliation by freeing his aggression. He needs to express himself actively in whatever way suits his fancy whenever he wants to.

The inner landscape of a masochistic character is like filigreed silver and gold. His creative force expresses itself in delicate intricate designs, each of personal distinction and taste. Each nuance is important. When he brings this highly developed creativity out, the world will be awed.

His higher self energies are full of caring for others. He is a natural negotiator. His heart is big. He is very supportive and has a lot to give, both in energy and understanding. He is full of deep compassion and at the same time has a great capacity for fun and joy. He is capable of creative playfulness and lightness. He will bring out all these gifts and excel in whatever he wants to do.

## The Rigid Structure

In childhood, the person with a rigid character structure experienced rejection by the parent of the opposite sex. The child experienced this as a betrayal of love because erotic pleasure, sexual-

ity and love are all the same to the child. To compensate for this rejection, the child decided to control all the feelings involved—pain, rage and good feelings—by holding them back. To surrender is a scary thing for this person, because it means releasing all these feelings again. Thus he will not reach out for his needs directly, but will manipulate to get what he wants. Pride is associated with feelings of love. The rejection of sexual love hurts his pride.

Psychodynamically, the rigid person holds back feelings and actions in order not to look foolish. He tends to be worldly, with a lot of ambition and competitive aggression. He says, "I'm superior, and I know everything." Inside is a deep terror of betrayal; vulnerability is to be avoided at all costs. He is afraid of being hurt.

He holds his head high and backbone straight with pride. He has a high degree of outer control and a strong identification with physical reality. This strong ego position is used as an excuse to avoid letting go. This person fears the involuntary processes within the human being that are not determined by the ego. The inner self of the individual is walled off from the outpouring and inpouring of feelings. He will have sex with contempt, not love.

In holding back his feelings, he only creates more pride. He demands love and sexual feelings from others, but when he interacts with them, he seductively uses qualifiers to remain uncommitted. This leads to competition, not love. His pride is then hurt, and he becomes more competitive. He is in a vicious cycle that does not get him what he wants.

His presenting complaint in therapy (if he comes at all) is that he has no feelings. He wants to surrender to feelings, but he believes they will only hurt, so his negative intent is, "I won't surrender." He chooses sex over love but that doesn't satisfy him. This leads to the double bind of "Either choice is wrong." To surrender will hurt; to remain in pride will not allow feelings. To resolve this problem in therapy, he needs to connect his heart to his genitals.

In the therapeutic process, the mask will say, "Yes, but . . ." After some time, the lower self or shadow self will emerge into the conscious. It will say, "I won't love you." Then as feelings begin to flow as a result of bodywork, the higher self will resolve the situation by stating, "I commit, I love."

The body is harmoniously proportioned, highly energized and integrated. It can have two types of blocks—plate armor, like steel plates on the body, or mesh armor, like a suit of chain mesh over the body. The pelvis is tipped back and cold.

## The Energy Field of the Rigid Structure

The main energy is held on the periphery and away from the core. He is hyperactive. The person with a rigid structure (Figure 13-8) is characterized by his balance and integration, shown in the aura by a strong bright aura that is for the most part evenly distributed over and throughout the body. The etheric field is strong, wide and even, with a bluish-gray color and medium coarseness. The emotional body displays a calm balance and is evenly distributed. It may not be as colorful as some of the other structures if the person has not worked to open his feelings. It may be larger in the back of the person, since all the centers are open there. The mental body is developed and bright. The celestial body may not be very bright if the person has not opened much to unconditional love or his spirituality. The causal or ketheric template egg is strong, resilient, very well shaped and brightly colored—golden-silvery with a predominance of gold.

The chakras of the rigid character that are probably open before beginning process work are the rear will and sexual chakras and the mental chakras. He thus lives primarily by his mind and will. The crown and solar plexus may or may not be open. As the person starts process work and opening to his feelings, the front feeling centers begin to open.

The brain activity pattern shows a lot of activity on the sides and the central rear portion of the brain. In some cases the frontal lobes are just as active, depending on the area of life the person has decided to concentrate on. If it has been intellectual pursuits, then this area will also be as bright and active; if not, it will usually be the second most active area. If the person has pursued development in the arts, like painting or music or other creative forms, I find the side lobes brighter. I find that as people work in their process, grow and become more enlightened, the activity patterns of the brain become more balanced with activity at the side, frontal and occipital area. The bridges begin to build directly through the head to form a cross when observed from the top. When a person begins to develop his spirituality and have spiritual experiences, say in meditation, I find more activity growing in the central brain area.

Energetic defense systems most used by the rigid person are power-will display, boundary containment and sometimes hysteria (shown in Figure 12-3).

## The Life Task and Higher Self of the Rigid Character

The rigid character needs to open the feeling centers and allow his feelings to flow and be seen by others. He needs to share his feelings, whatever they are. This will allow energies to flow into and out of the core of his being and release the uniqueness of the Higher Self.

The inner landscape of the rigid character holds adventure, passion and love. There are mountains to climb, causes to champion and loves to be romanced. Like Icarus, he will fly to the sun. Like Moses, he will lead his people to the promised land. He will inspire others with his love and passion for life. He will then be a natural leader in most any profession he desires. He will be capable of deep contact with others and the universe. He will be able to play in the universe and enjoy life fully.

It is very helpful to keep the general character structure of your patient in mind when giving a healing. This will help you as a healer to approach the healing specifically for each person and to make the healing most efficient. Just approaching the healing in terms of each patient's relationship to boundaries is very helpful.

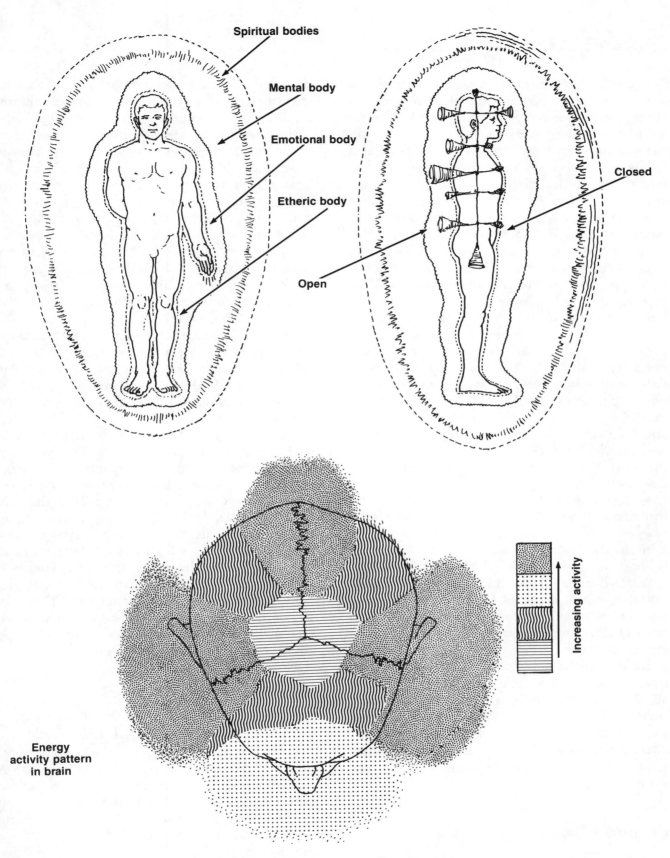

**Spiritual bodies**

**Mental body**

**Emotional body**

**Etheric body**

**Closed**

**Open**

**Increasing activity**

**Energy activity pattern in brain**

Figure 13–8:  The Aura of the Rigid Character
(Diagnostic Views)

125

The person with a schizoid character structure will need to have his boundaries identified and strengthened. He also will need to have his spiritual reality confirmed. High Sense Perception helps a lot with this. The schizoid's aura also needs to be charged up, and he needs to be taught how to hold a charge. The energy leaks need to be stopped. The oral character's aura needs to be charged up and the chakras need to be opened. The boundary needs to be strengthened. The person needs to be taught how it feels to be open, so that he can learn to keep the chakras open through exercise and meditation. The oral person needs a lot of touching. The person with displaced character structure needs to charge the lower half of his field, open the lower chakras and learn to live more through the heart rather than the will. It is very important to be very tender with sexual issues with the displaced character structure. The second chakra must be dealt with with care, understanding and acceptance. The healer must be very sensitive and careful when touching the lower half of the body. The person with a masochistic energy field needs to learn to move and release all the energy he has blocked. His boundaries must be respected above all. Never touch without permission. The more of the healing he can do for himself, the faster and better he will heal. His healing will always be related to creativity, which is hidden inside and needs to be brought out and expressed. The rigid character's aura needs softening. This person needs to open the heart chakra and connect to love and other feelings. The second layer of the aura needs to be activated and its activity brought to consciousness. This must be done slowly by the healer, allowing feelings to be experienced for short periods at a time. The deeper core energies of the personality need to be reached through laying-on of hands. It is important for the healer to lovingly accept the personality when her hands are on the body.

## Beyond Character Structure

As each person works on himself psychodynamically, physically and spiritually, the aura changes. The aura becomes balanced, the chakras open more and more. Images and misconceptions about reality within our negative belief system clear away, creating more lightness, less stagnation and higher vibrations in the energy field. The field becomes more resilient and fluid. Creativity increases as the efficiency of the energy-metabolizing system grows. The field expands and deeper changes begin to occur.

Many people begin to have a beautiful golden-silvery point of light in the center of the head that grows into a brilliant ball of light. As the person develops, this ball grows larger and extends beyond the body. It seems to be the seed kernel that brings light to and develops the celestial body into a brighter more advanced organ, which begins to perceive and thus to interact with reality beyond the physical world. The location of this light seems to be in the root area of the crown and third eye chakras, where the pituitary and pineal glands are located. As the mental body grows brighter, sensitivities to reality beyond the physical develop. One's way of life changes to a natural flow of energy exchange and transformation with the universe. We begin to see ourselves as a unique aspect of the universe, completely integrated with the whole. Our energy system is seen as an energy transformation system, which takes in energy from the environment, breaks it down, transforms it and then resynthesizes it and sends it out into the universe in a higher spiritual state. Thus, we are each living transformation systems. Since the energy we transform has consciousness, we are transforming consciousness. We are truly spiritualizing matter.

## Character Structure and Life Task

Each character structure is a model of a transformation system gone awry. First we block the energy. It becomes clogged and slowed down within our energy systems. We do that by living according to our negative beliefs. We really are out of reality a lot of the time because we live and react to the universe as we think it is, not as it really is. But this does not work for long. We create pain in our lives by doing this. Sooner or later we hear the message that we are doing something wrong. We change ourselves and our energy systems to alleviate the pain. We unclog our systems and transform the energy. In doing this we not only help to clear away our personal negative beliefs, but we also affect those around us in a positive way. We thus transform energy.

When we begin releasing our blocks, we do our personal task. This frees our energy so that we can do what we have always wanted to do in life: that deep longing we have had since childhood, that secret dream, that is one's life task. That which you have wanted to do more than anything in your life is your life task. It is what you came here to do. By clearing away your personal blocks, you pave the way to accomplish your deepest longing. Let your longing lead you. Follow it. It will bring you happiness.

You have designed your body and your energy system as a tool to perform your life task. It is made up of a combination of energy-consciousness that best suits what you have been incarnated to do. No one else has that combination, and no one else wants to do precisely what you want to do. You are unique. When you block the flow of energy in your energy system that you created for your task, you also block your task. The general patterns of blocking that people do is called character structures and defense systems. These are all ways by which you habitually separate yourself from what you came to do on the world task level. They are also direct manifestations of what you don't know about life that you have come here to learn. Therefore you have your lesson crystallized into your body and your energy system. You have built and fashioned your schoolroom according to your own specifications. You live inside it.

As you will learn, energy blocks lead eventually to physical disorder. Conversely, these disorders can be traced to your character structure or the way you block your creative energies. Therefore whatever your illness may be, it is directly related to your life task. Your illness is directly related, through your energy system, to your deepest longing. You are sick because you are not following your deepest longing. So I ask

again, what is it that you most long to do with your life—more than anything else in the world? Find how you stop yourself. Clear away those blocks. Do what you wish to do, and you will get well.

## Exercises to Find Your Character Structure

Observe yourself in a mirror. Which body type does your body look like? Read over each table and each character structure. Then answer questions 7–10.

## Chapter 13 Review

1. Describe the general HEF configuration of each of the five major character structures.
2. Describe the highest qualities of each of the main character structures.
3. According to auric vision, which areas of the brain are most active in each different character structure?

### Food For Thought

4. What is the life task of each character structure?
5. How is character structure related to life task?
6. How is illness related to a person's life task?
7. Proportionately list each character structure that makes up your personality/body self. For example:
   - 50%  Schizoid
   - 20%  Oral
   - 15%  Displaced
   - 5%  Masochistic
   - 10%  Rigid
8. Go through Figure 13–1. Find your personality traits for each item listed.
9. Go through Figure 13–2. Find your physical and energetic traits for each item listed.
10. Go through Figure 13–3. Find how you relate with other people from your character structure for each item listed.

11. From the answers to the preceding three items, what could your personal task be? Your world task?

12. If you have any physical disorders, relate them to question 11 above.

13. Now do items 7–12 for each of your patients.

# PART IV

# THE PERCEPTUAL TOOLS OF THE HEALER

"And though the Lord give you the bread of adversity, and the water of affliction, yet shall not thy teachers be removed into a corner any more, but thine eyes shall see thy teachers.

"And thine ears shall hear a word behind thee, saying, this is the way; walk ye in it, when ye turn to the right hand, and when ye turn to the left."

Isaiah 30:20–21

# THE CAUSE OF ILLNESS

From the perspective of a healer, illness is the result of imbalance. Imbalance is a result of forgetting who you are. Forgetting who you are creates thoughts and actions that lead to an unhealthy lifestyle and eventually to illness. The illness itself is a signal that you are imbalanced because you have forgotten who you are. It is a direct message to you that tells you not only how you are in imbalance but also shows you the steps that will take you back to the real self and health. This information is very specific if you know how to secure access to it.

Illness can thus be understood as a lesson you have given yourself to help you remember who you are. Immediately you will think of all kinds of exceptions to this statement. But most of them will limit you to a perception of reality that only includes this particular lifetime and only life in the physical body. My scope is, however, a more transcendental one. The above statements can only be understood in a whole and healthy way if you already accept yourself as existing beyond the physical dimensions of time and space. The statements can only be felt as loving, if they also include you as a part of the whole, and therefore the whole. They are based upon the idea that individuation and wholeness are the same. That is, a priori the whole is made up of the individual parts, and the individual parts are therefore not only part of the whole, but like a hologram are in fact the whole.

During my own personal growth process that took place over the years while I was making energy-field observations as a counselor, two major changes occurred that drastically changed my way of working with people. The first was that I began to receive guidance during sessions from spiritual teachers as to what to do in the sessions, and I began to look and ask for specific kinds of information pertaining to different levels of the aura. The second was that I began to develop what I call "internal vision"; that is, I could see into the body somewhat like an x-ray machine. My practice slowly turned from that of a counselor to that of a spiritual healer.

Healing became first an extension of the therapy and then the central core of all therapy because it reaches all the dimensions of the soul and body far beyond that which the therapy was able to do. My work became clear. I was healing the soul or becoming a channel to help the soul remember who it is and where it is headed in those times it forgets and gets off track in disease or illness. This work has, for me, become very fulfilling, full of ecstasy in the experience of high energies and angelic beings who come to heal. At the same time, it is challenging to face the pain of terrible physical illness, which the healer must experience to some extent in order to heal. I had to let myself see the tremendous energy and soul imbalances that many people live with. Humanity carries with it terrible pain, loneliness and deep longing to be free. The work of the healer is a work of love. The healer reaches into these painful areas of the soul and gently reawakens hope. S/he gently reawakens the ancient memory of who the soul is. S/he touches the spark of God in each cell of the body and gently reminds it that it is already God and, already being God, it inexorably flows with the Universal Will towards health and wholeness.

In the next few chapters, I will discuss the process of illness and the process of healing as seen from the point of view of the Spiritual Teachers. I will share with you some of my experiences of spiritual guidance in the professional setting and discuss in detail High Sense Perception, how it works and how you can learn it. I will also present Heyoan's view of reality. All of this is important to understand in order to learn the healing techniques presented in Part V.

# Chapter 14

# THE SEPARATION OF REALITY

As can be seen in Chapter 4, the idea presented by Newtonian mechanics that the universe is composed of separated building blocks of matter became outmoded in the early 20th century. Much evidence has been presented by our scientists that shows that we are all always interconnected. We are not separate beings; we are individuated beings. It is only our old Newtonian habits of thinking that lead us to these concepts of separation from the whole. They simply are not true. Let me show you an example of what interpreting self-responsibility from the point of view of separateness can do.

Suppose a small child contracts AIDS from a blood transfusion, for example. If that event is interpreted from the separation point of view, one may say, "Oh, poor victim." From the popularized version of self-responsibility one might say, "Oh, he created it, so it is his fault." But from holism one would say, "Oh, what a hard lesson that brave soul and family have chosen to learn from their greater reality. What can I do to best help them? How can I best love them? How can I help them remember who they are?" Anyone who approaches life in this manner finds no contradictions between responsibility and love and a great deal of difference between responsibility and blame.

The view from individuation and holism promises respect and acceptance of whatever other fellow human beings experience. On the contrary, statements like "Oh, you created your cancer; I wouldn't do a thing like that" are made from the perspective of separation, not individuation. Separation promotes fear and victimhood; fear and victimhood only support the illusion of powerlessness. Responsibility and acceptance promote power, power from within to create your reality. For if you unconsciously had something to do with making things the way they are, then you can have a great deal to do with creating things the way you want them to be. Let us look at the processes of forgetting more clearly.

As children, only a small portion of our internal experience is verified by those around us. This creates an internal struggle between self-preservation and confirmation from others. As children, we needed a lot of confirmation; we were in a learning stage and that learning was based on confirmation from the outside world. As a result we either created secret fantasy worlds, or we rejected much of our unconfirmed inner reality and found a way to store it for later verification. Another way to explain the process is that we blocked off our experiences, be they images, thoughts or feelings. Blocking effectively walls us off from that portion of experience, at least temporarily. We wall ourselves off from ourselves. This is another way of saying we forget who we are. In Chapters 9 and 10 we dealt extensively with blocks in the auric field. The effect of these blocks when seen from the auric point of view is to disrupt the healthy flow of energy throughout the auric field and eventually to cause disease. They become what is sometimes called stagnated soul-substance. They are "blobs" of energy-consciousness that are cut off from the rest of us. Let us look at this process using the Gestalt idea of the wall.

Whenever you experience discomfort, you are in some way experiencing the wall you built up between the greater integrated you and a part of yourself. That wall serves to hold back a portion of yourself that you do not want to enter into your experience of the moment. With time, the wall grows stronger, and you forget that it is a portion of yourself that is walled off, i.e., you have created more forgetting. It begins to appear that what is walled off is something from the outside, that the wall appears to hold back some dreaded force from the outside. These internal walls are created over eons of soul experiences. The longer they stand, the more they appear to be keeping something other than self away from the self. The longer they stand, the more they appear to create safety, but the more they solidify the experience of separation.

## Exercises to Explore Your Inner Wall

To explore your walls, you can use the following exercise. Bring to memory a particularly unpleasant situation, either one you are struggling with currently or an unresolved one from the past. Begin to experience what that situation felt like, picture it in your mind, hear the words or sounds associated with that experience. Find within that experience the fear it contains. Fear is the feeling of being separated. As you are able to bring yourself back into that state of fear, begin to perceive also a wall of fear. Feel it, taste it, see it, smell it. What is its texture, its color. Is it light or dark, sharp or hard? What is it made of? Become the wall. What does it think, say, see, feel? What does this portion of your consciousness believe about reality?

Heyoan has given the following explanation of the wall:

"We will go back to the idea of the wall that you yourself have fashioned in order to maintain what you considered at the time of fashioning an inner equilibrium, but that actually maintains an outer disequilibrium, as in a dike, or in locks, where one level of water is higher than the other. So you may see yourself behind this wall and a great flood, a great pressure of power of some form on the outside, with you inside. *Your wall then makes up for that which you feel you are lacking on the inner level.* In other words there is this great power coming towards you and you think you have less power than it has. Then you make a wall to protect you as, when in the medieval ages, the walls of the castles were being stormed. You who are inside the wall must first explore the essence of this wall, for it is fashioned of you. It is fashioned of your essence and it is full of statements, statements of what you must do in order to remain safe. Now, the wonderful point about all of this is that this wall is fashioned of your essence and contains power within it. That power can be transformed and redistributed as a foundation for the power of the inner self. Or it can be seen as a stairway into the inner self where that power already exists. That is another way of saying it, depending upon which metaphor suits you best. And so you sit behind your wall of safety, and at the same time you sit in your wall of safety, because you are that wall. It is, then, the bridge of consciousness between what you as the wall say and what you as the inner person who is being protected say.

## Exercise to Dissolve Your Wall

Hold a conversation between you the wall and you the person inside. When that is thoroughly done, then we suggest you hold the same conversation between you and what is beyond the wall and even the wall and that which is beyond and continue these conversations until there becomes a flow through that wall.

"Now you can see this wall symbolically on the psychodynamic stage. You can also see it as representative of that wall between who you are and who you think you are, for you are that power on the other side of the wall, too, in whatever form it is. You have power within it, not power over it. The wall represents the belief in power over, the power of separation, which is one of the greatest maladies of the earth plane at this time, the disease of power over. And so, if you can find this metaphor within you and without you on not only the psychodynamic level but the spiritual level and the world level, you can use it as a tool for self exploration and healing. You can use it as a tool for remembering who you are."

Let us look at the wall from the auric field point of view. As was said earlier, the wall can be seen as an energy block in the aura. In the process of going into the wall, experiencing it and enlivening it, you are also enlightening the block. The block seen in the auric field begins to move and stops disrupting the natural energy flow.

These blocks exist on all the levels of the aura. They affect each other from layer to layer. Let us now look at how a block in one layer of the aura—which, of course, would be expressed in the reality of that layer, i.e., thought, belief or feeling—can eventually cause an illness in the physical body.

## Chapter 14 Review

1. What is the cause of illness?

### Food For Thought

2. What is the nature of your inner wall?
3. Hold a conversation with your wall. What does your wall say? What does the part of you that sits behind the wall say? What does the part of you that sits without the wall say? What is the wall protecting you against? What is the nature of your power that you have locked away in your wall? How can you release it?

## Chapter 15

# FROM ENERGY BLOCK
# TO PHYSICAL DISEASE

## Dimension of Energy
## and Consciousness

Looking at ourselves with a broader perspective than we did before, we see that we are much more than our physical bodies. We are composed of layer upon layer of energy and consciousness. We may sense that internally. A clear graphic description of our self-experience of feelings and thoughts is presented in this chapter.

Our inner spark of divinity exists in a much higher plane of reality and advanced consciousness than that of our everyday consciousness. We are this higher consciousness just as much as we are our everyday consciousness. This higher consciousness can be tapped into with practice. Once it is found, it is no surprise. One has the sensation of "Oh, yes! I knew that all along." Our divine spark has supreme wisdom; we can use it to guide our daily life, growth and development.

Since the aura is the medium through which creative impulses from our higher realities are precipitated down into the physical reality, we can use the auric field to bring our consciousness back up (in vibration) through its layers into the reality of the Godself. To do this, we need to know more specifically how these creative impulses are transmitted, layer by layer, into our physical world to help create our daily experience of life.

First, let us consider again just what the aura is. It is much more than a medium or a field. It is life itself. Each layer is a body, just as real, alive and functioning as is our physical body. Each body exists in a conscious reality that is in some ways like, and in some ways unlike, the physical reality. Each layer is, in a sense, in a world of its own, yet these worlds are interconnecting and exist immersed within the same space in which we experience our physical reality.

Figure 15-1 lists the planes of reality in which we exist and which correlate with each of the auric layers or bodies shown in Chapter 7. The physical plane is composed of four levels: the physical, etheric, emotional and mental levels. The astral plane is the bridge between the spiritual and physical, and the spiritual plane is above it and has gradations of enlightenment within it. As already stated in Chapter 7, we have at least three layers in our spiritual bodies—the etheric template level, the celestial level and the ketheric template level.

Creation or manifestation takes place when a concept or a belief is transmitted from its source in the high levels down into the more dense levels of reality until it becomes crystalized into physical reality. We create according to our beliefs. Of course what is taking place on the lower layers also affects the higher ones. In order to understand the process of creating health or disease, let us look again more closely at how con-

## Figure 15-1
## PLANES OF REALITY IN WHICH WE EXIST
(as related to the layers of the aura)

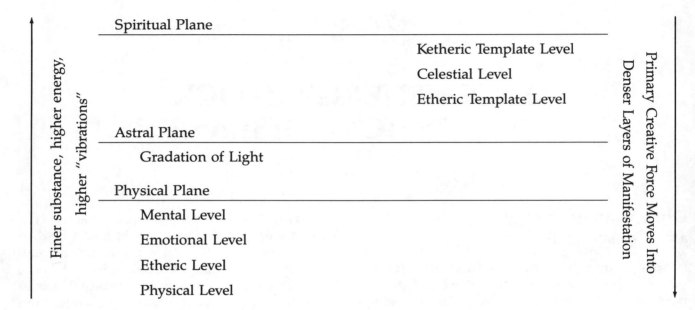

sciousness manifests on each layer of the auric field.

Figure 15-2 lists how consciousness expresses itself on each auric layer and the statement that consciousness makes. On the physical level, consciousness takes the form of instinct, automatic reflexes and the automatic functioning of internal organs. Here consciousness makes the statement, "I exist." At the etheric level, consciousness is expressed in terms of sensations like physical pleasure or pain. Unpleasurable sensations such as cold and hunger are signals that something is needed to rebalance our energy in order to flow once again in harmony. At the emotional level, consciousness is expressed in basic primal emotions and reactions like fear, anger and love. Most of these emotions relate to the self. On the mental level, consciousness is expressed in terms of rational thinking. This is the plane of the linear analytic mind.

On the astral level, consciousness is experienced as strong emotions that extend beyond the self and the other to encompass humanity. The astral plane, an entirely different world, is the plane where astral travel takes place, and, as described by people who have experienced it, that plane differs from the physical plane in the following ways: objects have fluid form; light is radiated from objects rather than being primarily reflected off them; and to travel, one need only concentrate on where one wants to go and stay focused on that place. The direction shifts with the focus, so that if you shift your focus, you shift your direction. Concentration power is very important on this plane!

The differences and similarities between the physical and astral planes would not be surprising to the physicist, since the laws that govern the astral plane would be based on natural law governing a medium of finer substance, higher energy and faster vibrations. These laws would, of course, correlate with those we know in our physical world. I propose that our physical laws are, in fact, simply special cases of general laws, the cosmic or universal laws which govern the entire universe.

On the spiritual plane there is yet another world with its own reality, one that seems, from my limited view of it, to be far more beautiful,

## Figure 15–2
## HEALTHY AND UNHEALTHY FUNCTION IN THE AURIC LEVELS

| Level | Expression of Consciousness | Statement Consciousness Makes |
|---|---|---|
| 7 Ketheric Level | Higher Concepts | I know. I am. |
| 6 Celestial Level | Higher Feelings | I love universally. |
| 5 Etheric Template Level | Higher Will | I will. |
| 4 Astral Level | I-Thou Emotions | I love humanly. |
| 3 Mental Level | Thinking | I think. |
| 2 Emotional Level | Personal Emotions | I feel emotionally. |
| 1 Etheric Level | Physical Sensation | I feel physically. |
| Physical Level | Physical Functioning | I exist. I am becoming. |

The basic primary creative force is initiated in the highest spiritual body and is then moved into the astral body. Or, from another point of view, one might say that the finer substances and energies in the spiritual bodies induce harmonic resonance in the astral which then induces harmonic resonance in the lower three bodies. This process continues all the way down into the frequency level of the physical body. (The phenomenon of harmonic induction is that which occurs when you strike one tuning fork and another in the room will sound.) Each body expresses this impulse in terms of its conscious reality at its own level. For example, a creative impulse from the spiritual moving into the astral will be expressed in terms of broad feelings. As it moves into the lower frequency layers, it will be first expressed in terms of thoughts, then specific feelings, then physical sensation, and the physical body will respond automatically through the autonomic nervous system. It will either relax if it reads a positive impulse or will contract if it receives a negative one.

## The Creative Process of Health

Health is maintained when the creative force coming from human spiritual reality is directed according to universal or cosmic law (Figure 15–3). When the ketheric body is aligned with greater spiritual reality, it manifests the divine knowing of that reality. The statement made is, "I know I am one with God." It is the experience of being one with the creator, yet being individuated at the same time. This reality then induces the feeling of universal love in the celestial body. This feeling of being one with God in turn creates an alignment of the individual will in the etheric template with the Divine will. This in turn is expressed in the astral level as love for humanity. The experience of love for humanity will influence the mental layer and inform the perceptions of reality in the mental body. This vibration in the mental body is then transmitted by the laws of harmonic induction and sympathetic resonance down into the matter and energy of the emotional body, which then expresses itself as feelings. If perception of

full of light and loving than ours. On the fifth layer, the etheric template, consciousness expresses itself as higher will, with which we will things into being through the power of naming and defining them. On the celestial level, consciousness expresses itself as higher feelings like universal love, that is, love that goes beyond human beings and friends into a universal love for all life. On the seventh level, consciousness is expressed in higher concepts of knowing or belief systems. This is where the initial creative impulse begins from our knowing, not just linear knowing, but integrated knowing.

## Figure 15–3
## THE CREATIVE PROCESS OF HEALTH

KETHERIC TEMPLATE BODY . . . . Divine Knowing:   I know I am one with God.

CELESTIAL BODY. . . . . . . . . . . . . . . Divine Loving:   I love life universally.

ETHERIC TEMPLATE BODY . . . . . . . . . Divine Will:   Thy will and mine are one.

ASTRAL BODY . . . . . . . . . . . . . . . . . . . Loving:   I love humanity.

MENTAL BODY . . . . . . . . . . . . . . . . Clear Thinking:   Clear thinking used to implement love and will

EMOTIONAL BODY . . . . . . . . . . . . . . . Real Feeling:   Natural unblocked flow of feelings corresponding with Divine Reality, creates: love

ETHERIC BODY . . . . . . . . . . . . . . . . . . . . . . I exist:   Natural metabolism of energy, which maintains the structure and function of the etheric body; yin/yang balanced, creates: We're OK.

PHYSICAL BODY . . . . . . . . . . . . . . . . . . . . Beingness:   Natural metabolism of chemical energies, balanced physical systems, creates: physical health.

reality is consistent with cosmic law, the feelings will be harmonious and accepted by the person and allowed to flow. They will not be blocked.

This flow then is transmitted down into the etheric body, which responds in a natural harmony. The result is pleasurable body sensations that promote natural metabolism of energy from the Universal Energy Field. This energy is needed to nourish the etheric body and to maintain its structure and function. A natural balance of the yin/yang energies in the etheric body is also maintained. With this balance, the natural sensitivity in the body, coming from the natural flow of feelings, leads to increased awareness of body sensations, which in turn leads to following proper diet and exercise. The healthy etheric

## Figure 15–4
## THE DYNAMIC PROCESS OF DISEASE

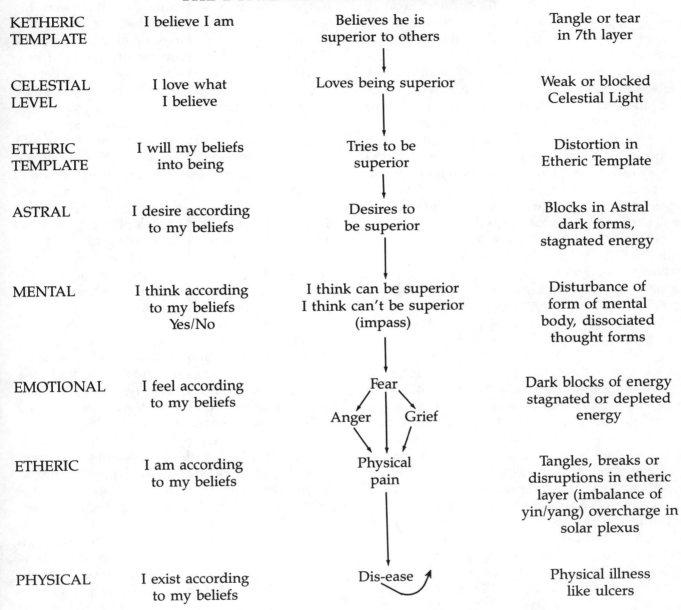

| | | | |
|---|---|---|---|
| KETHERIC TEMPLATE | I believe I am | Believes he is superior to others | Tangle or tear in 7th layer |
| CELESTIAL LEVEL | I love what I believe | Loves being superior | Weak or blocked Celestial Light |
| ETHERIC TEMPLATE | I will my beliefs into being | Tries to be superior | Distortion in Etheric Template |
| ASTRAL | I desire according to my beliefs | Desires to be superior | Blocks in Astral dark forms, stagnated energy |
| MENTAL | I think according to my beliefs Yes/No | I think can be superior I think can't be superior (impass) | Disturbance of form of mental body, dissociated thought forms |
| EMOTIONAL | I feel according to my beliefs | Fear / Anger Grief | Dark blocks of energy stagnated or depleted energy |
| ETHERIC | I am according to my beliefs | Physical pain | Tangles, breaks or disruptions in etheric layer (imbalance of yin/yang) overcharge in solar plexus |
| PHYSICAL | I exist according to my beliefs | Dis-ease | Physical illness like ulcers |

body then supports and maintains a healthy physical body, in which the chemical and physical systems remain balanced and functioning normally, perpetuating physical health. In the healthy system, the energies in each body remain balanced and support the balance in the other bodies. Health is thus maintained; i.e., health attracts more health.

## The Dynamic Processes of Disease

In the diseased system (Figure 15–4) the same step-down process is at work. However, after the primary creative force moves out from human spiritual reality, it becomes distorted and then acts against universal law. This distortion occurs when the primary creative impulse impinges upon an energy block or distortion within the aura. As soon as the primary creative impulse becomes distorted on its way into the denser layers of the auric bodies, it continues to be distorted as it is transmitted to succeeding levels. I have seen the primary distortions as high as the seventh layer of the aura, where they appeared as tears or tangled lines of light. These "spiritual distortions" are always related to belief systems acquired in this lifetime, or in other lifetimes, and are therefore karmic. I see karma simply as life experience created from belief systems that have been carried over from one lifetime to the next until they are cleared and realigned with the greater reality.

A distorted seventh layer is related to a distorted belief system. An example could be, "I believe I am superior." This distortion affects the celestial layer by blocking celestial love and distorting it. Then the person may love being superior. Light on the celestial level might appear very weak. This will affect the fifth layer of the field, which will be distorted. The person will try to be superior. The astral level will respond with the desire to be superior, which will cause blocks or dark blobs of stagnating energy in the astral body. The mental body will give the person the thought that he is superior. Luckily nobody can fool himself all the time, so sooner or later the opposite is brought to mind. If I'm not superior, then I must be inferior. A mental impasse is created in the person, which is also a distortion in the structure of the mental body. There is a splitting of the life force into two directly opposing currents, and the person falls into a dualistic split. Another example of this conflict is, "I can't do it" yet "I can do it." Thus, we have a mental impasse set up in the mental body. This impasse is expressed in energy and vibrations. If the impasse is not solved by the individual, it may become a dissociated thought form and fall into unconsciousness. This will affect the emotional body (through inducted vibration as described earlier) and cause fear, because the person cannot solve the problem. This fear is based on unreality and is unacceptable to the person. It is therefore blocked and after some time may also become unconscious.

Since there is no longer a free flow of feelings in the emotional body, where more dark blobs of stagnated or very weak energy will appear, this disruption will be precipitated down into the etheric body in the form of tangled or torn lines of light force. Since these are the lines of force, or the grid structure, upon which the cells of the physical body grow, the problem of the etheric body will be transmitted into the physical body and become disease in the physical body.

In our example (Figure 15–4), this fear could disrupt the etheric at the solar plexus, causing an overcharge of yin in that area if the person is not able to solve this particular dilemma. This disruption, if allowed to continue, will cause a disruption of the metabolism of chemical energies in the physical body, causing physical systems to become imbalanced and eventually diseased. In our example, the overcharge of yin in the solar plexus could cause increased acidity in the stomach and eventually ulcers.

Thus, in the diseased system the imbalanced energies in the higher bodies are progressively transmitted down into the lower bodies, eventually causing disease in the physical body. In the diseased system, the sensitivity to the body sensations is decreased and can lead to insensitivity to the body's needs, manifesting through improper diet, for example, which can create a negative feedback loop of more imbalanced energies. Each body that is disrupted or imbalanced also has a disruptive effect on the neighbor above it. This disease tends to create more disease.

The observations I have made through High Sense Perception show that *on the even-numbered layers of the field, disease takes the form of the blocks described earlier in this book—undercharged, overcharged or clogged dark energy. On the structured layers of the field, disease takes the form of disfiguration, disruption or entanglement. There may be holes in the grid structure on any of the odd-numbered layers of the aura.* Drugs affect the aura a great deal. I have seen dark energy forms in the liver left from drugs taken for various previous diseases. Hepatitis leaves an orange-yellow color in the liver years after the disease is supposedly cured. I have seen the radiopaque dye used to observe the spine that was injected into the spinal column to diagnose injury ten years after injection although it is supposed to be cleared by the body in a month or two. Chemotherapy clogs the whole auric field, but especially the liver, with greenish-brown mucus-like energy. Radiation therapy frays the structured layers of the auric field like a burned nylon stocking. Surgery causes scars in the first layer of the field and sometimes all the way to the seventh layer. These scars, disfigurations and clogs can be healed by helping the physical body heal itself; if they are left distorted, the physical body will have a much more difficult time healing itself. When an organ is removed, the etheric organ can still be reconstructed and serve to keep harmony in the auric bodies above the physical body. I would imagine that someday, with more knowledge of the auric field and biochemistry, we may be able to cause organs that have been removed to grow again.

Since the chakras are the points of maximum energy intake, they are very important focal points of balance within the energy system. If a chakra is imbalanced, disease will result. The more imbalanced a chakra is, the more serious the disease. As shown in Chapter 8, Figure 8-2, the chakras appear to be vortices of energy made up of a number of smaller spiral cones of energy. Adult chakras have a protective screen over them. In a healthy system these spiral cones spin rhythmically in synchronicity with the others, drawing energy from the UEF into their center for the body's use. Each cone is "tuned" to a specific frequency that the body needs to function healthfully. However, in a diseased system these vortices do not work synchronistically. The spiral cones of energy that make up these vortices may be fast or slow, jerky or lopsided. Sometimes breaks in the energy pattern can be observed. A spiral cone may be fully or partially collapsed or inverted. These disturbances are related to some dysfunction or pathology of the physical body in that area. For example, in a case of brain disorder, Schafica Karagula observed in *Breakthrough to Creativity* that one of the smaller vortices of the crown chakra was drooping down instead of standing upward in a manner she had found to be normal. The matrix within the brain of the individual

also showed "gaps" where the energy had to jump across. This "spark gap" corresponded to the part of the brain that had been surgically removed. John Pierrakos in "The Case of the Broken Heart" reports observing disorder in the heart chakras of patients with angina pectoris and coronary heart disease. The chakras, instead of being bright, whirling vortices, appeared to be clogged with a dark, sluggish substance.

Some specific examples of my observations of disfigured chakras are given in Figure 15-5. The first (Figure 15-5A) shows the configuration of every hiatal hernia I have observed. The solar plexus chakra has eight smaller vortices. The small vortex located on the left side of the body, in the upper left quadrant, looks like a spring that has been sprung. This disfiguration appears all the way out to the seventh layer of the field. Figure 15-5B shows the tip of one of the smaller vortices has been pulled out. I have witnessed this in many chakras. It appears in the first chakra when there has been some damage to the coccyx. It appears in the solar plexus chakra when there has been a severe psychological trauma. Many times it appears as postsurgical trauma in a chakra in the area where the surgery has been performed. Figure 15-5C is a clogged chakra. Everyone who has angina has clogged, darkened energy in the heart chakra. The three people who have AIDS that I have observed have the first and the second chakras clogged, and sometimes the entire field, including all seven layers, depending on how far the disease has progressed. A torn chakra, like that shown in Figure 15-5D, has appeared in every cancer patient I have seen. Again the configurations listed here go out to the seventh layer. A chakra can be torn, and the cancer may not appear in the body until two or more years later. The protective shield is completely ripped away from this chakra. In people who have very serious forms of cancer, I have seen the seventh layer torn from the feet all the way through chakras one, two and three and into the heart chakra. The effect of a torn seventh layer is loss of a lot of energy from the field. In addition to energy loss, the patient is subject to all kinds of outside influences that affect him not only psychologi-

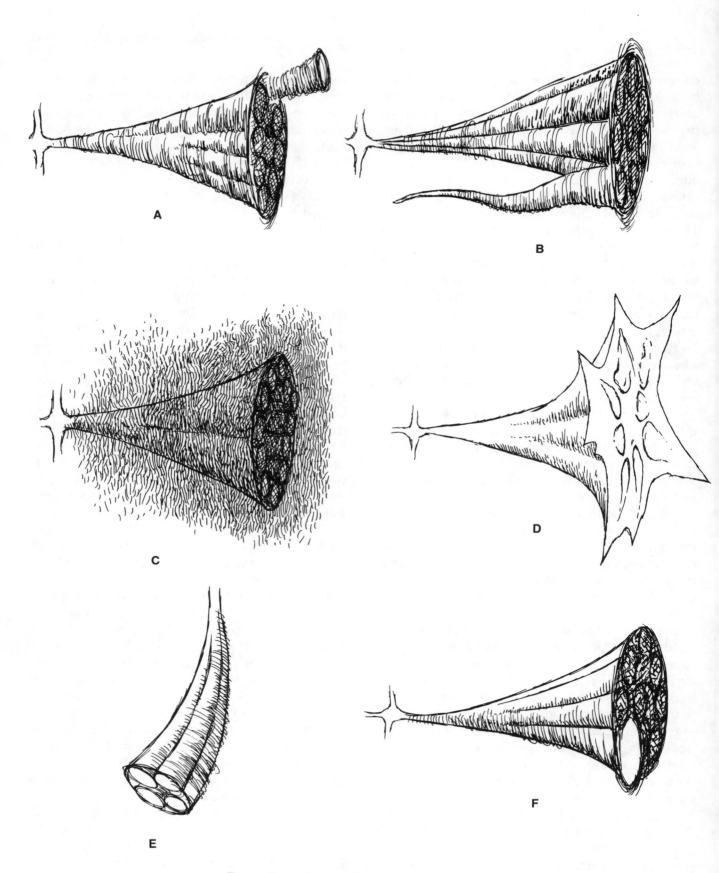

Figure 15–5: Chakras That Have Been Disfigured

144

cally, but physically. The field is unable to repel incoming energies that are not healthy for the system to assimilate. Figure 15–5E shows an example where the entire chakra is pulled to one side. I have seen this often in the first chakra, where people have connected their energy to the ground mainly through one leg, while the other leg is weak. This is also usually associated with a coccyx that has been jammed over to one side.

I am beginning to think that each vortex of a chakra supplies a specific organ with energy. I have noticed that every time there is a disturbance in the pancreas, there is also a disturbance in a certain vortex on the left side of the solar plexus chakra just below the one associated with hiatal hernia, whereas when the disturbance is in the liver, a different vortex in the same chakra is affected, one near the liver.

Figure 15–5F shows a disfiguration that occurred from a heavy therapy marathon. After spending a week in group therapy with her son who is a drug addict, this woman came home with one vortex of the solar plexus chakra wedged open. It was pale with almost no spin and no protective screen. Since I saw the problem the week after the experience, I was able to repair the aura before additional damage occurred. If I had not, eventually this woman would have had problems in the liver, the organ related to the weakened vortex, or she would have healed it somehow herself.

There are many more configurations that can occur. Many, as you can see, are simple structural misalignments. I have seen chakras that are actually pulled inside out, greatly expanded or greatly reduced in size. All eventually result in disease, and all are related to an energy-consciousness or expression of the individual's belief system and experience, as discussed earlier. In other words, disease at any layer of the field will express itself in that level of consciousness. Each expression is some form of pain, be it physical, emotional, mental or spiritual. Pain is the built-in mechanism that alerts us to correct a situation. It brings our attention to the fact that something is wrong and makes us do something about it. If we have not listened to ourselves before, if we have continued to ignore what we know we want or need to do, eventually pain will help us do it. Pain teaches us to ask for help and healing and is, therefore, a key to the education of the soul.

## Exercise to Find the Personal Meaning of Your Illness

A key question in this healing-education process is: "What does this illness mean to me? What is the message to me from my body? How have I forgotten who I am?" The disease is a specific answer to the question, "How does this pain serve me?"

We all create disease to some extent in our physical bodies. If you look back at the original cause, it is always based on forgetting who we are. As long as we believe that we must be separated in order to individuate, we will continue to create disease. Again, we are right back to where we started from—the holistic or holographic view of the universe.

## Chapter 15 Review

1. What is the relationship between psychosomatic illness and the aura?
2. What is the basic cause of all disease as seen from the HEF point of view?
3. Describe how disease is created through the Human Energy Field.

### Food For Thought

4. Take a few minutes to meditate on how the disease process may be occurring in your body. Describe it.
5. How have our beliefs shaped our experiences and what role does our HEF play in this creation?

# Chapter 16

# THE PROCESS OF HEALING, AN OVERVIEW

What the healer has to offer the patient and the medical profession are three things: a different and broadened view of the causes and cures of disease; access to information about any given life or medical situation that may not be available through other means; and working directly with the patient to enhance the patient's healing abilities. No matter how miraculous the result, the healer really induces the patient to heal himself through natural processes, even though they are beyond what is considered to be natural for those who are not familiar with healing. Your body and your energy system move naturally toward health. The healer has ways and means to evoke health. The physician, of course, also works with these principles. But with the burden of so many impersonal cases, and constantly being faced with illness, many medical doctors become oriented towards the cure of a specific set of symptoms, which sometimes may not be the same as orientation towards health. To the healer, health not only means health in the physical body, but also balance and harmony in all parts of life.

The process of healing is really a process of remembering—remembering who you are. Within the aura the process of healing is a process that rebalances the energies in each body. When all the energies in each body are balanced, health occurs. The soul has learned its particular lesson and, therefore, has more cosmic truth.

There are two major approaches to healing today. One is "inner" healing, which establishes balance and health in all levels of the person by focusing on and dealing directly with the physical, emotional, mental and spiritual aspects of the human being, how he creates his belief systems and reality. The other is "outer" healing, which helps reestablish balance in the different layers of the aura, including the physical body systems, by applying energy distilled from the Universal Energy Field.

I suggest the "inner" healing is most important but that the "outer" healing methods are needed to supplement this process.

## The Process of Inner Healing

The process of inner healing rebalances the energies in each body by focusing on the expression of that imbalance, correcting it and repairing the appropriate layer of the aura through laying-on of hands. (See Figure 16–1.) This realignment in each body helps reestablish balance in the others.

The process of inner healing, called full spectrum healing, is discussed at length in Chapter 22. Here we will briefly describe it.

In the healing of the ketheric template level, the faulty belief system is brought to consciousness and challenged. Healing is done on the seventh layer of the field. This healing consists

## Figure 16-1
## THE PROCESS OF INNER HEALING

| | | |
|---|---|---|
| KETHERIC TEMPLATE BODY | 7th layer healing | Challenges faulty belief system. |
| CELESTIAL BODY | 6th layer healing | Sits in Universal Love. |
| ETHERIC TEMPLATE BODY | 5th layer surgery | Realigns individual will to Divine Will. |
| ASTRAL BODY | 4th layer chelation, love | Gives love and acceptance. |
| MENTAL BODY | Chelation and repatterning of thinking | Challenges dualistic thinking patterns. |
| EMOTIONAL BODY | Chelation and redirection of emotional flow | Reexperiences blocked feelings and pain to release energetic flow of feelings. |
| ETHERIC BODY | Chelation and structure repair | Releases energy flow and vibrations in etheric body. Restructures it. Rebalances metabolism of orgone in etheric. |
| PHYSICAL BODY | Massage | Revitalizes and nourishes physical body with energy, rebalances chemical processes, which rebalance physical systems. Health. |

mainly of repairing and restructuring this body wherever needed. Repair of the seventh layer automatically opens the sixth layer for more celestial love.

On the celestial level, the healer sits in celestial or universal love and simply channels it to the patient.

On the etheric template level, the auric body is realigned through spiritual surgery. This has the effect of realigning the will to the Divine Will.

On the astral level, healing takes place through chelation and love. The healer sits in the reality of love of humanity and channels energy to the patient. This allows the mental level to begin relaxing and letting go of some defenses.

On the mental layer, the healer challenges the faulty thinking processes that create imbalance on that level. These thinking processes are based on the logic of the child who experienced the trauma. When the adult becomes aware of them, they are easily seen for what they are and can be replaced by more mature thinking processes. The healer works to restructure that layer of the auric field by helping the client to imagine new solutions to old problems.

On the emotional layer, using a chelation technique, the healer helps the client to clear blocked feelings. Sometimes the patient relives old traumas and experiences all the blocked feelings during the healing. Sometimes the traumas are removed without the patient's becoming aware of them.

On the etheric layer, there is straightening and repair to be done to restructure that layer, to reestablish a sense of well-being and strength.

To work directly on the physical body, exercises, body positions and voice are used to release physical blocks, for example, muscle tension, fat or weakness.

In the process of full spectrum healing, all the bodies are worked on together. This process is done in private sessions or sometimes in groups with a healer. In this process, health in the physical body usually appears last, after the other bodies have been balanced. This may take one session or a year of sessions.

You may wonder how healers can do all this. It is because they have access to an enormous amount of information through an expanded state of consciousness.

## The Process of Outer Healing

To enhance and accelerate this basic healing, outer healing methods are used (and in many cases very much needed), for the physical symptoms generated by the faulty belief systems cannot be left alone until the belief system is corrected. It is sometimes necessary to provide outer healing to save the person's life. However, if the "inner" healing is not also done and the faulty belief system not challenged, illness will again precipitate into the physical body, even after present symptoms have been removed.

With the advancement of the practice of holistic medicine, many healing methods are being developed and are proving to be reliable. Many physicians are emphasizing diet, food supplements like vitamins and minerals, exercise and health maintenance programs to keep people healthy. Health care professionals like homeopaths, chiropractors, acupuncturists, kinesiologists, masseuses and other body workers are practicing all over the country to help people maintain their health. People are becoming more conscious of regular fitness programs of exercise and regular health checkups to catch any possible difficulty before it becomes serious.

Laying-on of hands healing is now being practiced around the country in many forms. People are interested in shamanism and other ancient forms of healing. Psychic surgeons regularly visit this country and work with hundreds of people. We are in a health care revolution. Why?

With the advent of modern technology and the loss of the family doctor, medicine became depersonalized. The family doctor took responsibility for a family's health by being familiar with the family's history, sometimes for generations. Today a physician can't even remember the names of his patients because he has so many. With this change to what is many times a wonderful technology that saves many lives, the physician cannot possibly take responsibility for each patient's health. That responsibility has fallen back on the patient himself, where it ought to be. This is the basis for the health care revolution. Many people want to take more responsibility now for their health. To make this change a smooth one, the best way is to integrate the methods that are available, so that healing can become very personal again, as it was at one time in our history.

## How Healers and Physicians Can Work Together

With healers and physicians working together, it is possible to take advantage of the best technology and the best personal attention available for each patient. Let us see how it would work.

Healers can assist physicians in the three ways mentioned in the introduction to this section. They are: giving a broader view of the causative factors involved in any illness; providing information that cannot be obtained through the present standard methods or that cannot be obtained by those methods in the time required; and providing laying-on of hands to balance the energy system of the patient and to enhance and accelerate the healing. Many times this last effort helps the patient gain the strength necessary to save his life.

In clinical practice, the healer can work directly with physician and patient in making the first diagnosis to pinpoint the problem, give an overall view of how the energy system is out of balance (and thus how serious the problem is), provide a broader view of the causative factors involved and work with the patient on the meaning the illness has in his life.

The healer's methods of diagnosis will be discussed in the next chapter. The healer can receive recommendations through use of High Sense Perception about the kinds and amounts of specific drugs to be taken, supplementary healing techniques, diet, food supplements and exercise. The healer can follow the case with the doctor and again through the use of High Sense Perception, make recommendations as to how that dosage and other supplements need to be changed week to week, day to day, or even hour to hour. In this fashion, the healer and physician together can achieve a level of "fine-tuning" in the care of the patient never before imagined. The healer can observe the patient's energy field to tell how the drug or other healing methods used are affecting the patient overall.

I have done a little of this work and it has been very effective. I have met a healer, Mietek Wirkus, who worked in this way for three years with physicians in a clinic affiliated with the "IZICS" Medical Society in Warsaw, Poland, that was set up specifically to do this work. It was very successful and is still in operation. Records kept by this clinic show that laying-on of hands, called bioenergotherapy (BET), is most effective in nervous system diseases and the diseases which were consequences of migraine, in healing bronchial asthma, noctural enuresis, hemicrania, nervous illness, psychosomatic diseases, gastric ulcer, some kinds of allergies, liquidation of ovarian cysts, benign tumor, sterility, arthritic pains, and other kinds of pain. BET helps to relieve the pain caused by cancer and decrease the amount of pain medication or tranquilizers taken by the patient. Good effect has also been observed in treatment of deaf children. In almost every case the doctors discovered that after BET treatment, patients became more quiet and relaxed, pain was gone or relieved, and the rehabilitation process (especially after surgery or infection) was accelerated. In this country, many healers are beginning to

work with physicians. Dr. Dolores Krieger introduced laying-on of hands to the nurses at New York Medical Center years ago, and they practice it in the hospital. Rosalyn Bruyere, director of the Healing Light Center in Glendale, California, has entry to many hospitals to practice healing and is involved with several research projects to determine the effectiveness of laying-on of hands for various types of illness.

Another type of research would be through the use of High Sense Perception to help researchers find the causes and cures of illnesses that now seem incurable, such as cancer. With internal vision, which is discussed in the next chapter, the healer can observe the disease process at work inside the body. What a wonderful tool to assist research!

With the use of High Sense Perception, the healer can tell which of the many holistic healing methods will work best for each patient by observing its effect on the aura. By recommending that the patient focus on the most effective methods for him, healing will be accelerated. For example, in my observations I have noted that different methods or remedies work on different levels of the auric field. Aubrey Westlake in his book *The Pattern of Health* has designated which of the Bach Flower remedies heal which auric levels. I have observed that the higher the potency of the homeopathic remedy, the higher the auric body it affects. The higher potencies above 1M work on the higher four layers of the auric field and the lower potencies work on the lower auric levels. Because of the tremendous power of the higher potencies, young practitioners are always taught to start with the lower potencies (lower energy bodies) first, and then work up into the higher bodies when the correct remedy is found. In the process of laying-on of hands, many healers are able to choose which body to work on. The same holds true for self-healing meditation, where one can work on all of the bodies. Radionics is a method to distill the healing energies from the UEF with the use of machines which generate "rates" or "frequencies." Along with radiathesia, radionics broadcasts energies through the UEF to patients located at considerable distances from the practitioners. A blood sample or a piece of hair from the patient is generally used as an "antenna." The radionics practitioner can choose which auric layer to work with.

Chiropractic certainly reaches up through the first three levels of the aura, as do herbs, vitamins, drugs and surgery. Of course laying-on of hands, healing meditations and healing with light, color, sound and crystals all reach the upper levels of the auric field. Through research, we could learn more about how to use them for the best results.

Many books have been written on these types of healing. For further reading, I suggest the following books: *The Science of Homeopathy* by George Vithoulkas, M.D., *Dimensions of Radionics* by David Tansely, M.D., *Chiropractic, A Modern Way to Health* by Julius Dontenfass, M.D., *Traditional Acupuncture: The Law of the Five Elements* by Dianne M. Connelly, Ph.D.

The medical profession in this country has focused primarily on the physical body and has become expert in this field, especially in specific organ and organ-system diseases. Drugs and surgery are the major methods applied. One of the major problems in the use of drugs and surgery in healing is the tremendous side effects which they very often create. Drugs are prescribed from knowledge of the physical body's functioning, but they also contain energies in the higher realms which then, of course, affect the higher bodies. The effects of these drugs on the higher bodies have not been studied directly when the drugs are tested for use. Rather, the effects of these higher energies are only seen when they are finally precipitated down into the physical body. I have seen the aftereffect of drugs remaining in the aura for as many as ten years after the drug was taken. For example, a drug that was once used to cure hepatitis was seen to be causing immune deficiencies five years later. A red dye placed in the spinal column for exploratory purposes was inhibiting the healing of spinal nerves ten years later.

## Toward a Holistic System of Healing

I believe the holistic healing systems of the fu-ture will combine the tremendous body of the "analyzed" knowledge of the traditional medical profession with the "synthesized" knowledge of the higher body energy systems. The future holistic healing systems will diagnose and prescribe healing for all the energy bodies and the physical body simultaneously as needed by the patient and incorporate both the inner and the outer healing processes. Medical doctors, chiropractors, homeopaths, healers, therapists, acupuncturists, etc. will all work together to aid the healing process. The patient will be seen as a soul on its journey back home to the true self, the Godself, and disease will be seen as one of the ways to point the traveler in the right direction.

To do this, we need to use the analytic methods developed by the medical profession to delve into the mysteries of the higher body in order to gain a practical knowledge of their functioning and structure. We need joint research projects in which the higher body healing methods are tested along with current allopathic scientific medicine to see the combined effects. How do allopathic drugs and homeopathic remedies work together? Which are in harmony with each other, supporting and enhancing a cure? Which are inimical and should not be used together?

We must concentrate on finding a detection method to observe the energy bodies. Since the etheric is of the coarsest matter, is most like the physical body and is probably the easiest to detect, we should concentrate first on it. What a tremendous tool we would have if we could produce a picture of the grid structure of the etheric to show energy balances and imbalances. With this information and further study, we could then find more practical and efficient methods to rebalance the energies in the etheric. In the future we would move on to discover methods to apply to the higher bodies.

*Thus we could heal the disorder before it is precipitated into the physical body as physical disease.*

Most of all, I would seek to teach health care professionals, especially physicians, to perceive the fields, so that they also can see the disease process in action inside the living body of the patient. Some physicians are already reaching out for help. They send their hardest cases to healers. Usually they do it covertly. It is time to come out of the closet and work openly as teams.

With highly trained and qualified people able to see the inner processes of the body by simply looking, imagine how far those people could carry medical research. Rather than placing the emphasis on observing animals in a laboratory, research could be focused on the actual patient and his personal needs. When one is able to access directly ("read") the kind of treatment a patient needs, programs will be designed on a personal level for each individual's healing.

Heyoan has stated that "the precise substance given in the precise dosage at the precise time for each individual acts as a transmutive substance to create health in the most efficient way, with the least side effects, and in the shortest time possible." Health here is not just physical health; it is complete balance at all levels.

Given such a potential, let us now look at the many different ways of securing information on all levels of the aura.

## Chapter 16 Review

1. Describe the process of inner healing.
2. Describe the process of outer healing.
3. Upon what levels of the HEF do medicines work?
4. Upon what levels of the HEF are the effects of medicine tested in normal medical practices?
5. How is the potency of a homeopathic remedy related to the aura? Upon what auric levels do what homeopathic remedies act?

### Food For Thought

6. What are the major effects of understanding the disease process through the HEF on medical practices? Include applications, psychodynamic functioning, patient responsibility and self-perception.
7. How can healing through the auric fields be integrated into normal medical procedures?

## Chapter 17

# DIRECT ACCESS OF INFORMATION

Accessing information beyond the normal means can help a healing enormously. It is possible to get almost any kind of information one needs through this method. Direct access means just what it implies. You directly connect with and receive the information that you wish to have. This process has been labeled High Sense Perception, clairaudience, clairvoyance, clairsentience or psychic reading. Let us take a clearer look at just what that process is.

The information coming to you comes through your five senses. These have been labeled traditionally as sight, touch, taste, hearing and smell. Most people have developed some of these means to access information more than others. Your internal processes of thinking, feeling and being have a great deal to do with your modes of accessing information as the neurolinguistic programmers Richard Bandler and John Grinder have stated in their book, *Frogs to Princes*. Your internal experience runs through certain habitual channels. You may work primarily with a combination of visual and kinesthetic processes, or auditory and kinesthetic, or visual and auditory. Any combination is possible. You use different combinations for different internal process. You may know whether or not you think primarily in pictures, sounds or feelings. I recommend that you find out, because the way you access through the normal senses is the way that I would recommend that you begin learning to develop your High Sense Perception.

For example, if I am given a name, first I hear the name, then I search kinesthetically in all directions until I feel a connection being made to that person. From that point I see pictures and hear information about the person who was named. Several years ago I could not do that.

The first High Sense I developed was the kinesthetic one. I spent many hours doing body psychotherapy, touching people and their energy fields. Then my discernment moved into "seeing." I began seeing things that correlated to what I was feeling. After a lot of practice I began to hear information. Each of these ways of access can be learned through exercises and meditations. By entering into a calm quiet state and concentrating on one of your senses, you enhance it. It only takes practice. The hard part is to learn to enter into a calm state and stay focused on your purpose.

## Exercises to Enhance Your Perceptions

**To enhance your kinesthetic sense,** sit in a comfortable meditative position and focus on feeling the inside of your body. Focus on body parts and organs. If it helps, touch the part of your body you are focusing on. If you tend to be visual, you may want to look at the body part. If you tend to be auditory, you may want to listen to your breathing or heartbeat to help you focus.

Now do the same for the space around you. With eyes closed, sit and feel the room you are in. Focus on, reach for or beam towards different locations in the room and different objects. If you need help, open your eyes or touch the objects in the room, then go back to simply sitting and feeling. Now have a friend lead you blindfolded into an unfamiliar room. Sit and feel the space kinesthetically the same way you tuned into your body. What have you learned about the room? Take the blindfold off and check it out. Do the same for people, animals and plants.

**To enhance your visual sense,** sit again for meditation and, with eyes closed, look at the inside of your body. If you have trouble doing this, find the sense that will help you. Touch the part or listen to your internal processes until you can get a picture of it. Now do the same for the room. First, with eyes open, examine details in the room; then, with eyes closed, create a picture of the room in your mind. Now go to an unfamiliar room and start with eyes closed. What can you "see"?

Remember, we are speaking of visual perception. This is different from the process of visualization, which is a creative act in which you visualize what you want to create.

**To enhance your auditory sense,** sit in meditation. Listen to the inside of your body. Again, if you need help with this sense, put your hand on the part you are listening to and feel it, or look at it. Then go outside and listen to all the sounds around you. If you do this in the woods, you will begin to hear the synchronicity of the sounds. Together they make a symphony. Listen even more closely. What else can you hear? Sounds that don't exist? Listen more carefully— someday they may have meaning for you. Itzhak Bentov in his book *Stalking the Wild Pendulum* writes of a high-pitched sound that many meditators hear. It is above the normal range of hearing. He was able to measure the frequency of this sound.

As I developed my "seeing" abilities, I discovered that the pictures came in two forms. One is symbolic, the other literal. In the case of the symbolic picture, one simply sees an image that has meaning to the person for whom one is "reading." For example, one might see a nebula swirling in the sky or a large chocolate cake. In the case of the literal picture, one sees pictures of events or things. One can witness an experience that the patient had in the past. In both the symbolic vision and the "reading" of an event, the healer takes the position of witness. That is, the healer enters into that time frame and witnesses events as they occurred. The same is true for the symbolic vision. The healer watches the vision unfold and describes it as it is unfolding. I call this receptive channelling. It is very important that the vision not be interpreted or disturbed by the healer as it unfolds. The meaning the vision has may be different for the healer and the patient. For example, if you see a symbolic picture, say of a scene of a blue car driving down the road, you don't immediately say, "Oh, what does that mean?" You just watch the car drive down the road and let the scene unfold before you. In this process, you will gather information piece by piece and will slowly build an understandable picture. You may not know if the picture has symbolic meaning or if it is literal (i.e., something that actually happened or may happen) until later. This type of information receiving takes a lot of faith. You may take as long as a half to one hour to build that picture into something that is understandable.

On the other hand, some readers use their own symbols and give readings by interpreting them. This works only with a lot of practice, because the reader must first build a clear set of symbols through which she can receive information.

In another type of literal seeing the healer sees a picture of an internal organ of the patient. The picture either appears on a screen in the healer's mind, which I call the mind-screen, or appears to be located inside the patient's body, as if the healer can see through the layers of the body and into the organ like an x-ray machine. This type of seeing I have labeled internal vision. It is a very powerful tool to help describe an illness. With internal vision you use active direct access. This means you go after some specific information you wish to access. For example, by using internal viewing I can look wherever in the body I wish to. I can decide where to look, at what depth, at what level of the aura and in what resolution or size, macro- to microscopic.

## Long-distance Perception

I have found that direct access works whether the person is in the same room with you or at a distance. The longest-distance aura reading I gave was during a phone conversation between New York City and Italy. At this point in my experience, my long-distance readings appear to be pretty accurate, but the healings are not as powerful as when I am in the room with the person.

## Direct Access and Precognition

There have been many times when people have asked my guide questions regarding the future. He always responds by saying that it is possible to talk about probable future reality, but not absolute future realities, because all of us have free will to create what we want in the future. He also says he will not predict the future, but then he goes ahead many times and answers the question that has been asked. So far most of these possible futures have occurred. For example, Heyoan has told someone that perhaps she would be interested in getting involved with the United Nations. She has since received two invitations that got her involved with the UN. Another person was told that he could get involved with the diplomatic service of Mexico and that he would make a contact when on vacation in Portugal. It happened. Others were told that they needed to finish certain things in their lives because they would probably be moving. They are moving now, although they had not thought of it before. At the beginning of one particular healing, I was told that the person had cancer and was going to die. She did. It was not even suspected when she came to the healing, and it was not found until after four CAT scans, and about four months later. The CAT scan results showed the same shape, size and location of cancer tumor I had seen with internal vision. Of course I was very upset when I accessed this information. I did not tell the patient. I told her to go to her physician immediately. Unfortunately, I had no access to the physician. Experiences like these bring up issues of where the

responsibility of the healer lies, which will be discussed later in this book.

The best measuring of the process of direct access of information is the work done on remote viewing by Russell Targ and Harold Puthoff of Stanford Research Institute. They found that a viewer in the basement of the lab at Stanford could fairly accurately draw a map of the location of a target team of people, who were sent to various predetermined points. Targ and Puthoff began their experiments with known psychics and then found that anyone they chose, even the most skeptical, could do it. I believe that what I am doing is very similar, only applied to healing.

In short, I believe most people can use some kind of direct accessing of information in their daily lives. What information would help you run your profession better? You can probably perceive it through the use of your own Higher Sense Perception. All of this is another way of saying that the human being has many ways to receive information and guidance—if we will only ask for it or be open to receiving it.

Direct access of information has many implications for the future. If we, as a species are learning to access information as evidence suggests, it will affect our entire educational system, and of course the society in which we live. We will go to school not only to learn deductive and inductive reasoning, to gather information and enhance memory, but *we will also go to school to learn how to access anything we want to know at a moment's notice.* Rather than spending hours memorizing things, we will learn how to access the information already stored in the "memory" of the universal energy field. In esoteric terms this information storage is called the akashic records. These records are the energetic imprint fixed within the universal hologram of everything that has ever happened or has ever been known. In this type of brain function, information is not stored in our minds; it is simply accessed. In this type of brain function, to remember means to tune in again to the universal hologram and to read the information again, not to search one's own mind to retrieve the information.

Since this information exists outside the limitation of linear time, as shown in Chapter 4, we will probably to some degree be able to read the future, as Nostradamus did when he predicted the rise of a dictator named Histler in Europe some two hundred years before Hitler.

## Chapter 17 Review

1. What are the main ways of directly accessing information?
2. Describe ways to enhance your visual, auditory and kinesthetic senses.
3. If a person is kinesthetic, which type of meditation and direct access would be best for him to focus on?
4. What is the difference between actively looking at the aura and perceiving it symbolically?
5. Does direct accessing of information work at a distance? How far? Using physics, what explanations is there for this phenomenon?
6. What is the difference between active and receptive channelling or accessing of information?

## Food For Thought

7. Are you primarily visual, auditory or kinesthetic?

# Chapter 18

# INTERNAL VISION

My first internal vision experience happened early one morning as I was lying in bed observing the interesting muscle and bone structure on the back of my husband's neck as he lay asleep on his side beside me. I thought it was very interesting the way the muscles connected into the cervical vertebrae. Suddenly I became aware of what I was doing and quickly cut off such seeing. I would not "return" to that level of reality for some time, saying that I had made it all up. Of course, eventually, it came back. I began "seeing" inside my clients. At first it was disconcerting, but my internal vision persisted and so did I. The internal viewing correlated with other information I could obtain about the patients, either from them or their physicians.

Internal vision is the human version of the x-ray or nuclear magnetic resonance (NMR) process and is just as sophisticated. Internal vision includes the ability to look into the body at whatever depth and resolution (within a certain range) one wants to see. It is a new way of perceiving things. If I want to see an organ, I focus on it. If I want to see inside the organ or a specific part of it, I focus on that. If I want to see a microorganism that is invading the body, I focus on that. I receive pictures of these things that look like normal pictures. For example, a good healthy liver looks dark red, just as it does with normal vision. If the liver has been or is jaundiced, it will look a sickly yellow-brown. If the person has had or is having chemotherapy, the liver usually looks green-brown. Microorga-

nisms look somewhat the way they look under the microscope.

My experiences of internal viewing, which happened spontaneously at first, later became more controllable. I began to understand that to see this way I had to be in a particularly open state, in which my third eye (sixth chakra) was activated and the rest of my mind was in a comparatively calm, focused state. I later found techniques that would bring on this state, so I could look inside the body when I chose to, provided I was able to get into that mental and emotional state. If I was tired, I might not be able to do so, partly because it is harder to focus and quiet the mind when one is tired. It is also harder to raise one's vibrational rate when one is tired. I also discovered that whether or not my eyes were open mattered little, except for the interference of additional information that would come through the open eyes. Sometimes this additional information helps the focus; sometimes it hinders it. For example, I sometimes use my eyes to help me focus my mind on where I am looking. At other times, I will close my eyes in an effort to shut out other information that may be distracting my attention.

## Examples of Internal Viewing

An example of such viewing is shown in Figure 18–1. The upper left shows the front exterior au-

**Front view**

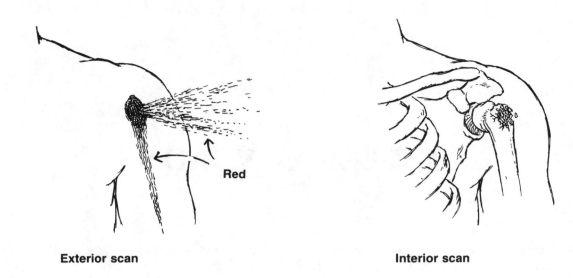

Red

Exterior scan                    Interior scan

**Back view**

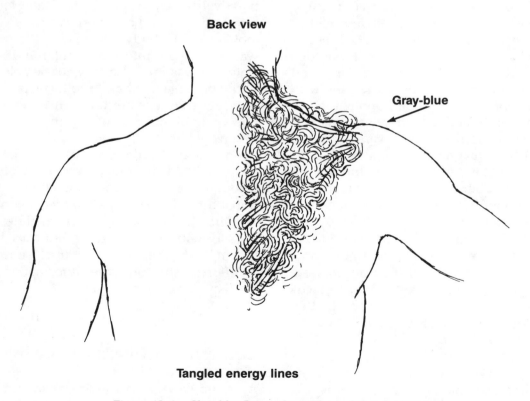

Gray-blue

**Tangled energy lines**

Figure 18–1:  Shoulder Injury Seen Through Internal Vision
(Diagnostic Views)

ric view, the upper right shows the interior view and the lower illustration shows the rear external view. In this case, a friend of mine fell on the ice and hurt her shoulder. As I worked on her, I could see the "auric hemorrhage" out the front of the shoulder where she was losing energy. The rear area lines of energy along the trapezius muscle were tangled up and needed to be straightened. I cupped my right hand over the hemorrhage to stop it and combed out the tangles on the back. As I was doing this, I could see the crushed end of the humerus, which was later confirmed by x-rays. This "short" (half hour) session healed the hemorrhage and the tangles to help a faster healing of the crushed bone.

Another example, shown in Figure 18–2, is an ovarian cyst which I observed to be about the size of a tennis ball, 7 cm in diameter. On January 3 (Figure 18–2A), it looked dark bluish gray. This cyst had already been diagnosed by a physician, but the PID (Pelvic Inflammatory Disease) which showed up as dark red in the aura had not. By January 15 (Figure 18–2B), the cyst had shrunk to four centimeters, and the PID had been diagnosed by the physician. By January 21 (Figure 18–2C), it was two centimeters, but getting blacker, and showed a strange spiral configuration connected to it. The patient was on a cleansing diet that was clearing away the problem. (I was not administering healing at this time; I was only observing the progress.) On January 29 (Figure 18–2D), the cyst grew to three centimeters, the size of a quarter, at the onset of menses (a common occurrence with cysts). By February 6 (Figure 18–2E), the cyst was down to one centimeter; by March 3 (Figure 18–2F), it was completely gone, with a lot of good, healthy premenstrual energy to take its place. All these observations correlated in size with that of a physician's observations by pelvic examination.

Because of the darkness of the cyst's appearance in the aura on January 21, both the physician and I advised that this woman take antibiotics. This type of illness, pelvic inflammatory disease (PID), over a long period of time (three years in this case) has been known to pre-

cede the development of cancer, which we wanted to prevent by getting rid of the infection. The patient remained on a cleansing diet throughout the treatment. She may very well have been completely free of infection without the antibiotic, but we did not want to take a chance. To my internal vision the cyst was almost black. In its early stage, cancer looks dark gray-blue. As it progresses, it turns to black in the aura. Later, white spots appear in the black. When the white spots sparkle and move out like a volcano, the cancer has metastasized. In this case, the cyst was getting too dark to wait for the cleansing diet alone to do the work needed.

Figure 18–3A shows another case of PID, ovarian cyst and a fibroid tumor. As you can see, with HSP cysts are easily distinguishable from fibroid tumors, which show up in the field as reddish brown.

Figure 18–3B shows an example of the use of remote internal viewing. At the end of one of my classes, a student asked if I would give her friend, who had two fibroids, a healing. As she asked, I immediately saw an internal view of her friend's pelvic region. I drew it on the blackboard. Two months later that drawing was confirmed when I gave the patient a healing. What I had seen was confirmed by the physician's diagnosis. She had two relatively small fibroid tumors which appeared reddish brown in the aura. The one on the right was higher up and on the outside of the uterus, whereas the one on the left was lower and partially embedded in the uterus. What I had not seen remotely, but observed during the healing, was that the front second chakra had a break in it, probably partially due to the removal of the left ovary. This chakra was most likely disturbed before the ovary was removed, causing the dysfunction in the first place. I am sure that the surgery caused more trauma to the chakra. Adding to the surgical trauma, women usually withdraw their energy from the area where an ovary has been removed because they do not want to feel the emotional pain of losing an ovary. This type of blocking inhibits the natural healing process in that area of the body, only to make the trauma worse eventually.

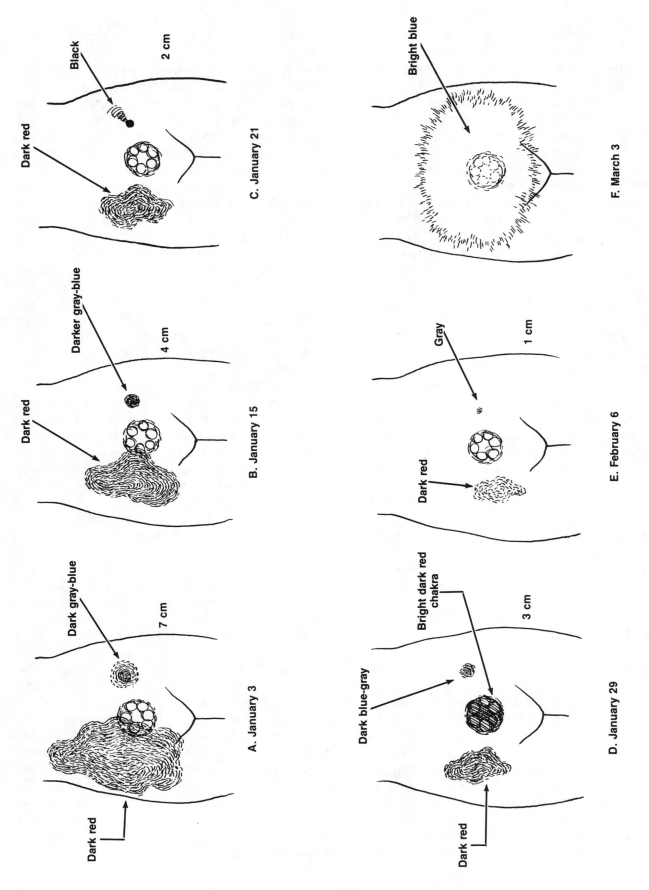

Figure 18–2: Healing of Pelvic Inflammatory Disease and Ovarian Cyst (Internal View) (Diagnostic Views)

A. January 3

Dark gray-blue

7 cm

Dark red

B. January 15

Darker gray-blue

Dark red

4 cm

C. January 21

Black

Dark red

2 cm

D. January 29

Bright dark red chakra

Dark blue-gray

3 cm

Dark red

E. February 6

Gray

Dark red

1 cm

F. March 3

Bright blue

160

## Precognition with Internal Viewing

An example of precognition, or warning from the spirit teachers, happened one day when I was going to visit a friend. I was three blocks from her office when I was told that she wouldn't be there, that she might have had a heart attack and that I was needed to give her a healing. I found the office locked, so I went to her apartment where I found her in a state of physical pain, holding her left arm to her body. She had spent the morning in the emergency room having cardiograms. Figure 18–4 shows what my vision revealed to me. There was emotional pain and fear held in the throat and solar plexus, and there was stagnated energy in the heart area, which permeated her body and then went straight back through to the rear aspect of the heart chakra. Thoracic vertebra #5 (T5) was displaced to the left. This vertebra is not associated with the nerves that innervate the heart, but is located at the root of the heart chakra. I could also observe a weakness in the aorta just above the heart. As we worked together to clear the stagnated energy around the heart, my friend let go the emotional holding in the throat and solar plexus areas by sharing her pain with me and crying. The dark energy cleared; T5 went back into place. She felt a lot better. The weakness in the aorta was still there when I left, but has cleared considerably with time.

## Microscopic Internal Vision

Two examples of microscopic internal viewing are shown in Figure 18–5A and B. Figure 18–5A shows the tiny rod-shaped organisms that permeated the shoulder/arm area of a person who had been diagnosed as having a leprosy-like infection. I could see these organisms penetrating this area—both muscle and bone. As we worked to heal, a very strong lavender and then silver light flowed into the body and filled the infected area. The light caused the organisms to vibrate at a high rate. It appeared to knock them loose. Then the energy flow turned around and sucked them out of the body.

In the case of an AML (acute myeloblastic leukemia) patient named Rose, who had been on chemotherapy, I could see strange-looking, flat, white, seedlike objects that appeared to be squishing the red blood cells (Figure 18–5B). About a year before she came to me, she had been told by several physicians that she would probably die within two weeks. At that time she was immediately put into intensive care and went on chemotherapy. She said that when they told her of the remaining two weeks, she saw a white-gold light in the room and knew that she was not going to die. On the label of every bottle of fluid, including the chemotherapy, that went into her during her hospital stay she wrote "pure love." She had no side effects from the chemotherapy. She went into remission.

When she became an outpatient and continued her chemotherapy, she also started having channelling sessions with a friend of mine, Pat Rodegast, who channels a guide named Emmanuel. Emmanuel told Rose to stop chemotherapy because it was making her sick. The physicians said if she stopped chemotherapy, she would die very quickly because her blood tests showed she was still in remission—not cured. It was not an easy thing to do, but she decided to stop. At this point she came to me, and I saw the seedlike objects in her blood. During the first healing, the seedlike objects were knocked loose with a blast of lavender and then silver light, then were all sucked out. Her next blood test showed her blood to be completely clear and normal for the first time since her diagnosis.

I clearly was not the main instrument in her healing; my role was one of support and clearing the blood. Thanks to the internal viewing, I could reassure her that there was nothing abnormal in her blood. This continued to be corroborated by her blood tests until we decided it was no longer important for her to see me and have this support. It was not easy for her to stand up for her truth. She needed this support because at the time the medical doctors, in all their sincerity, were quite afraid that she would die very quickly if she went off chemotherapy and told her this regularly. This is not meant to criticize the medical doctors; they were doing all

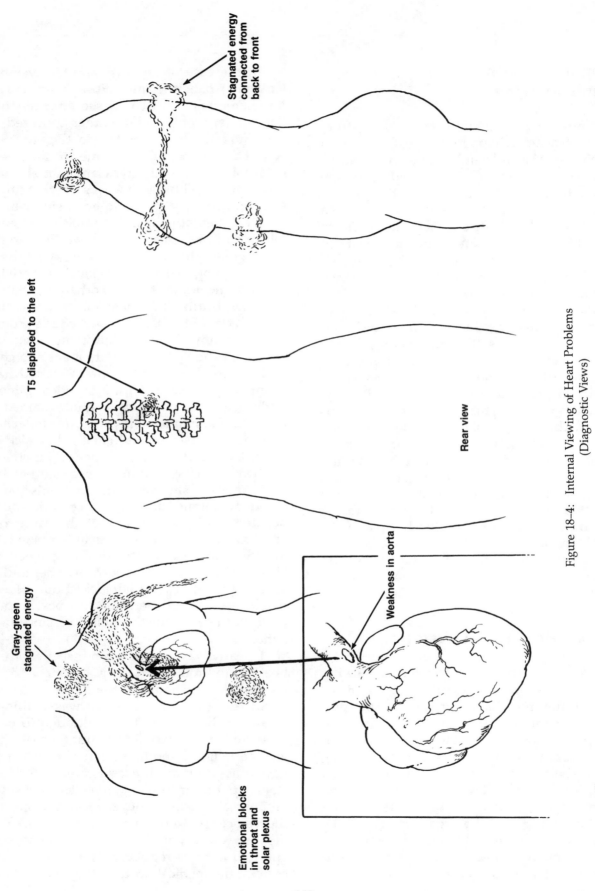

Stagnated energy connected from back to front

T5 displaced to the left

Rear view

Gray-green stagnated energy

Weakness in aorta

Emotional blocks in throat and solar plexus

162

Figure 18-4: Internal Viewing of Heart Problems
(Diagnostic Views)

they could do to save her life. But in this case there were other factors at work of which they were not aware. I, as a healer, had access to that information. They did not. This is an example where open collaboration between spiritual healers and medical doctors would serve the patients well. We have a lot to give to each other to aid the healing process.

## The Process of Internal Viewing

I have the following explanation of how this kind of seeing works. I have observed the path of light coming into the body with my internal or x-ray vision. And what I have seen is this. Light enters both through the third eye and

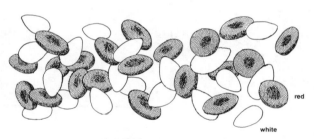

**B. The blood of a leukemia patient**

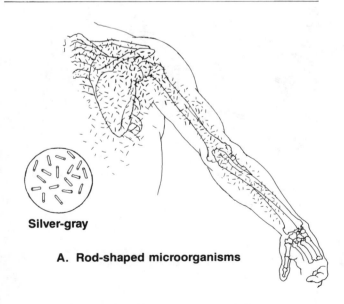

Silver-gray

**A. Rod-shaped microorganisms**

Figure 18–5: Microscopic Internal Vision

through the physical eyes and flows along the optic nerves as shown in Figure 18–6. This light is of higher vibration than visible light and can pass through skin. The light passes through the optic chiasm and goes round the pituitary, which sits right behind the optic chiasm. The light then takes two paths. One path goes to the occipital lobes for normal vision, and the other into the thalamus for oculomotor control. It has been my observation that by certain meditative and breathing techniques, one can cause the pituitary to start vibrating and radiating gold auric light (or rose light if the person is in love). This vibration and gold light increase the amount of light branching into the thalamus area. According to my seeing, this auric light arcs over the bottom of the corpus callosum and is directed into the pineal gland, which acts as a detector for internal vision. By breathing in a certain controlled manner that rasps air against the upper back throat and soft palate, located just the other side of the pituitary, I can stimulate the pituitary into this vibration. This meditative breathing also helps to focus my mind and to quiet it. It also brings gold light up the back of my spine from the base and rose light up the front. These two streams arc over each other in the thalamus area. This brings more energy to the central forehead and central areas of the brain with which I see. The subjective feeling of this type of seeing is allowing something (energy, information) to come into the third eye region of the head. This type of vision brings with it the ability to scan to whatever depth one chooses, with a wide range of resolution, down to the cellular and even viral level.

My subjective feeling is that I have a scanner inside my head. It is located at the central brain area behind my third eye and about two inches back, where a line straight back from the third eye would intersect a line drawn between my temples. This seems to be the heart of the scanner. From this point, I can look in any direction I choose without moving my head; however, it usually helps to look directly at whatever I am scanning.

When a patient comes to me, I do a very general scan over the entire body to pick up areas of interest. I am attracted to the areas of the

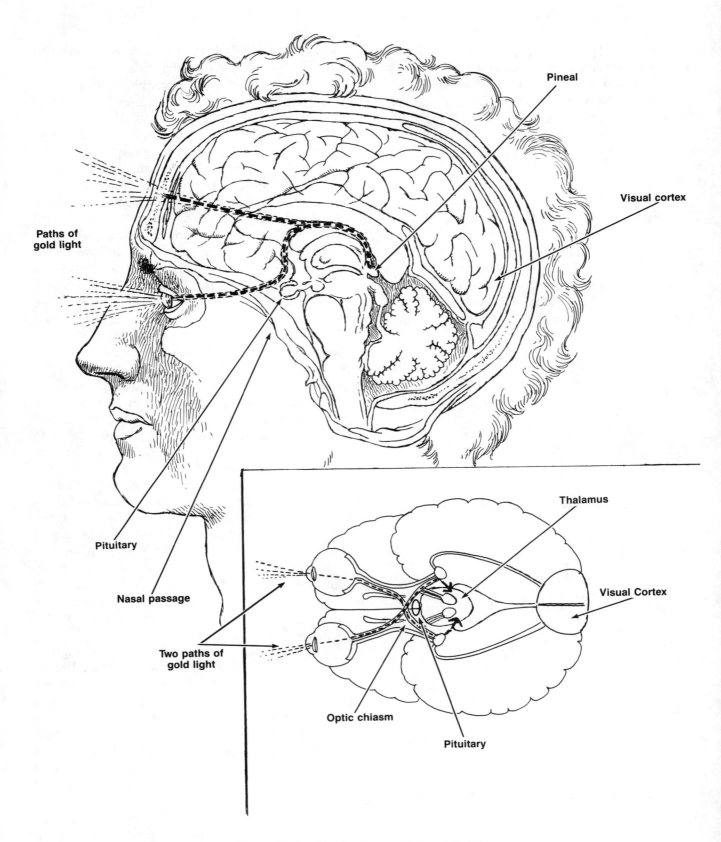

Figure 18–6:  The Anatomy of Internal Viewing

164

body that need attention. Then I tune in more finely to that area and scan it at a finer resolution. To do fine scanning, I sometimes put my hands on the area in question. I find it easier to see this way.

Sometimes I use another method. I just ask to see a picture of what the problem is, and I will receive a mental picture of the situation.

## Exercises to Establish Internal Vision

### 1. Traveling through the body.

The best way to practice learning internal vision is through deep relaxation exercises that include what is called traveling through the body.

First, lie down and loosen all tight clothing. Deep breathe and relax. Try it again. Now take a deep breath and tense your whole body as tightly as you can. Hold your breath; then breathe out and let all the tension go. Do it again. Now repeat the tension-breath exercise, but tense your body only half as tight, equally all over the body. Breathe out and let go.

Now, take a deep breath, and relax as you let it go. Repeat three times without tensing your body. Visualize the tension oozing off your body like thick honey onto the surface beneath you. Feel your heart slow down to a nice, slow, healthy beat.

Now, imagine yourself very tiny, like a point of light, and enter your body wherever you choose. Your tiny self flows to your left shoulder, relaxing all the tension as it goes. Your tiny self flows down your left arm and into your hand relaxing all the tension with a slight tingling sensation, warmth and energy. Your left arm is heavy and warm.

Now your tiny self flows back up your left arm and down into your left leg relaxing all the tension there, then up your left leg into your right leg and back up into your right arm. Your whole body is heavy and warm. Now you begin to explore your body systems with your tiny self. Enter your heart and follow the blood as it is pumped through your body. Does that system look well? Does it feel healthy? Now, travel

through your lungs and look at the lung tissues. Go into your digestive organs. Follow the course that food takes as it enters your body. Go from your mouth down your esophagus into your stomach. How does it look? Is it getting enough energy? Is it balanced in the amount of digestive enzymes it needs? Now, follow the food out of your stomach into the lower stomach, then into the small intestine, and then into the large intestine. Is everything well? Now, go back up into your liver, your pancreas, your spleen. Are they all functioning well? Travel through your genitals. Are they getting the loving care they deserve?

If there is any place in your body that you are concerned with, send the tiny self into that area with love and energy. Take a good look at that area. If it is lacking in anything, let your tiny self do something about it. If it needs to be cleaned out, clean it out. If it needs energy, let the tiny self send it energy.

When you have satisfied yourself with the exploration and care of your body, allow the tiny self to grow to your normal size and merge with your real self.

You can return to this type of self-exploration any time you wish.

Bring yourself back to a normal state of awareness, but allow yourself to remain deeply relaxed, self-confident and aware. You have been scanning your own body.

### 2. Scanning a friend.

Sit opposite a friend in a chair. One person can be the observer, and the other open to being observed. Do a meditation to silence the mind. Gently allow yourself to focus on your friend. Keep your eyes closed. Remember what it felt like to travel through your own body. Now you can visually travel through your friend's body. This will feel a bit different, because you are scanning from outside the body this time.

First, scan the body to find an area you are attracted to. You may use your hands at first, but do not touch your friend. Later you will not need to use your hands. When you are drawn intuitively to an area on your friend, simply put more of your focus there. Allow yourself to focus on the organs of that area. Believe what you see. You may get a color, a texture, a sensation or just a vague sense of something. Allow the pictures to come into your head.

When you feel satisfied with what you've found, allow yourself to be drawn to another area of the body and repeat. If you are not drawn to another part of the body, just start scanning the body.

You can scan the body by body area or, if you are familiar with anatomy (which you ought to learn if you want to be a healer), scan the body systems. Note what you see in your mind.

When you are satisfied with your exploration, slowly come back into yourself and open your eyes.

Discuss what you were able to pick up with your friend. How does what you picked up correlate with what she knows about herself? What doesn't correlate? Can you explain why? Perhaps the answer is in your assumptions. Perhaps the problem is in your own body. Perhaps you are right and your friend doesn't know about the situation you "saw." Now switch roles and let your friend observe you. Let yourself be passive to make it easier for her.

### 3. Meditation to open your third eye scanner.

An exercise suggested by one of my teachers, the Rev. C.B., is to lie on your back or sit with your back straight. Make sure you are comfortable. Take a deep breath through your nose. First, fill your lower abdomen with air, then your middle chest, and then your upper chest. Now open your mouth as wide as you can. Hold the back of your tongue toward the back of your throat and hold your throat in such a way as to allow the air to escape only if it rasps against the upper back part of your throat near the soft palate. Try to get it to rasp as far back as you can. The rasping sound should be fine, not gurgly. Do not throw your head back. Keep it directly on top of your spine. Slowly allow the air to escape from your body, first the air in the lower abdomen, then in the middle chest, and then in the upper chest. Let all the air out. Take a breath and relax. Repeat the rasping breath. When you

get the hang of it, add the following visualization.

As the breath leaves your body, visualize a golden stream of light start in the rear pelvic area and run up your spine into the central brain area. Repeat three times with three rasping breaths. Now focus on the front of your body. The stream of light looks pink on the front of the body. Repeat three times with three rasping breaths. Notice that the two streams of light arc over and into the center of the brain.

Once you have learned this exercise, do not do this more than three to four breaths for each side of your body or you may get very dizzy. Please treat this last exercise with a great deal of respect since it is very powerful. Take everything at a slow pace. You cannot speed up your evolution in a nonorganic way. It never works (although most of us wish it would).

Many times during a healing I do quick breathing exercises that help me raise my vibrations and energy so that I can see into the aura better, see higher levels of the aura and also transmit higher frequencies through my field. To do this, I rasp the air against the upper back part of my throat, but I do it by taking very short, fast breaths through my nose. Because I have practiced the above exercises so many times, this is now easy for me to do. I also sometimes take long, steady, even, in/out breaths without pause, and rasp air on the back of my throat to center my focus, clear my mind and balance my energy field. I call this breathing technique the *nasal rasp breath*.

When High Sense Vision is coupled with High Sense Hearing, information received becomes even more useful.

## Finding the Cause of the Illness: Rolling Backwards in Time

I have discovered a way to "read" the cause of a particular physical problem. It combines two techniques. The first is the normal way we evoke memory. Simply remember back to when you were younger. Now pick a certain age, or a certain place you have lived in, and remember it. Now remember an even earlier time. What is your internal process to evoke memory? What does it feel like? When I remember something of my past, I use my mind in a particular way. I know what it feels like. I hold memories in either feelings, pictures or sounds. *It is easy to "roll backwards" in time; we all do it. Most of us believe we can only do it for ourselves, and not for others. That is just a limited belief.* I have discovered that it is this internal process, of rolling backwards in time, that is used to "read" the past history of an illness.

The second technique is to use kinesthetic connection and internal vision. First, I connect with the particular body part in question using my kinesthetic sense. Then I get a picture of the problem area to describe its present condition. I hold the connection and then roll backwards in time, reading the past and witnessing the history of the body part. As I keep witnessing back into the past, I finally "read" the cause of the problem. For example, I will see a trauma occur to a body part at an earlier time in the patient's life. Then I will see another, at an even earlier

time, and so on. Most serious illnesses result from a long series of such traumas. I simply keep going backwards until a time before any trauma occurred to that part of the body. The first trauma that occurred is the initiating cause of the present problem.

## Chapter 18 Review

1. What can be seen with use of internal viewing? Where in the body can you see? What depth?
2. With internal viewing, what size ranges of objects can a viewer perceive?
3. Can internal vision be used at a distance?
4. List three exercises to learn internal viewing.
5. What endocrine gland is the sensor for internal viewing?

### Food For Thought

6. What is the difference between visualizing and perceiving?

## Chapter 19

# HIGH AUDITORY PERCEPTION AND COMMUNICATION WITH SPIRITUAL TEACHERS

The information I received auditorially was at first general, and then with practice it became specific. For example, I would hear words of love and assurance for the individual who had come for a healing. Later this information would get as specific as naming people, diseases a patient had, or in some cases a diet, vitamins, remedies or drugs that would benefit the patient. Many people who chose to follow these verbal instructions became well.

The best way I know to enhance High Auditory Perception is to sit for guidance. Take pencil and paper, sit in a comfortable meditative position, center yourself and lift your consciousness. Formulate a question in your mind as clearly as you can. Focus now on wanting to know the truth about that question, no matter what the answer is. Then write the question on the paper. Set the pen and paper down within reaching distance. Focus and silence the mind. Wait for an answer to come to you. After some time in silence you will begin to receive an answer. That answer will come in the form of pictures, feelings, general concepts, words or even smells. Write down the answer, no matter what it is. You may think it is irrelevant, but keep writing. The form through which the information comes will vary. Stay with it and write. The writing will eventually begin to orient the incoming informa-

tion to sounds. Focus on hearing directly the words that are coming to you. Practice, practice, practice. Write everything that comes to you. Do not leave anything out. After you are finished writing, put the paper aside for at least four hours. Later, go back and read what you have written. You will find it of interest. Keep a notebook for this purpose.

After I did this every morning at sunrise for three months, the verbal information came so quickly that I couldn't write fast enough. The voice suggested that I buy a typewriter. Soon I couldn't type fast enough. The voice suggested that I buy a tape recorder. I did. At first, it was hard to go from writing to speaking the words out loud. The sound of my voice interfered with the quiet I, by that time, was able to hold in my mind. With practice I became clear again. The next step was to do it for another person, and then in front of a group. This was especially embarrassing, because the way verbal channelling works is that the channeller can only hear the first few words of what is going to be said. It takes a lot of faith to jump into the beginning of a sentence, and allow the unknown rest of it to flow out.

The experience of accessing information verbally inevitably leads to the question, "Who is talking?" I certainly hear a voice. Is it one I make up, or does it have another source? Best place to find out? Ask the voice! I did. It said, "My name is Heyoan, your spiritual guide."

What does Heyoan mean?

"The Wind Whispering Truth Through the Centuries."

Where does it come from?

"Kenya."

It is true that I had seen visions of spirits and angels before, but I had categorized them as visions. Now they were talking to me. Soon I could feel their touch, and sometimes when I saw them in the room, I could smell a wonderful fragrance. Just a metaphor, or reality? All of my personal reality comes to me through my senses, and now that they are expanded, a greater, broader reality exists for me. Others with expanded sense perceptions experience it too. To me it is real. You can only decide from your experience.

Receiving information from a guide is different in that you enter into the metaphor that you are asking for information from a person who is wiser and more advanced than you are. The information that comes through is beyond your understanding, but if you allow it to continue to come through, you will eventually understand it. Channelling a guide can give information beyond the linear mind and can touch people very deeply; it reaches the soul beyond the human limitations. Usually, in the beginning of a reading my guide Heyoan will speak. That means I am doing a passive direct access. Then at a certain point, Heyoan will suggest that the patient ask questions to make things clearer. I feel that this is the best sequence because guides usually know more about where the problems really lie than we do. They go right under an individual's defense and into the heart of the matter. Therefore, when Heyoan starts a reading, we don't waste time getting to the deeper information that is waiting to assist us.

I also ask Heyoan questions during readings. I usually do this silently. I can ask for a picture of the situation or any specific part of the body, or I can ask to have a certain problem described. I even ask questions like, "Is this cancer?" Usually I get pretty specific answers, but it is not always easy, especially if I am uneasy about what the answer might be. It is then that I will block the information coming through. Then I must recenter to go on. Now it is time for you to try it.

## Exercises to Receive Spiritual Guidance

Sit in a meditative position with your back straight, but with a slight hollow in the small of your back. You may sit in a chair, using the back of the chair to rest on, or you may prefer the yoga position of sitting on a pillow on the floor with your legs crossed. Be sure it is a comfortable position for you.

1. If you are a kinesthetic type, close your eyes and simply follow your breath as it flows into and out of your body. Now and then you may want to repeat a reminder to yourself, "Following breath to center." With your mind's eye, follow your breath into your body and all the way to your center. Your senses may become heightened, and you may want to start following the energy flow throughout your body.

2. If you are a visual type, imagine a golden tube up and down your spine where the main power current of the aura is. Visualize a white-golden ball above your head. As you calmly breathe, the ball slowly sinks down through the tube and into the central part of your body to the solar plexus. Then watch the golden ball grow like a sun inside your solar plexus.

You may want to continue the growth of the golden ball on the solar plexus. Allow it to first fill your body with golden light. Then let it fill your auric field with golden light. Continue the expansion to fill the room you are in. If you are meditating in a circle of people, see their golden balls expand to create a golden ring, filling the room. Let it expand, growing larger than the room, to the size building you are in, the area outside the building, the town or city, the state, the country, the continent, the earth, and beyond. Do this slowly. Move your consciousness to expand the golden ball of light out to the moon and the stars. Fill the universe with bright golden light. See yourself as part of that universe and as one with it and therefore one with God.

Now, keep the light just as bright and bring it back in, step by step, just as you sent it out. Fill your being with all that light and knowledge of the universe. Be sure to do this slowly, going step by step back in. Feel the tremendous charge your auric field has now. You have also brought back into your field the knowledge that you are one with the Creator.

3. If you are an auditory type, you may simply want to use a mantra for the entire meditation. You may want to use a sacred name as the mantra, such as Om, Sat-Nam, Jesus or "Be still and know that I am God." Or you may want to sound a note. I find that on some days it takes more effort to center myself, so I may use a combination of the above meditations to get my mind free of its chatter. On another day, all I need is a simple mantra.

For more meditations and practices for getting into that quiet self-accepting state and to increase your sensitivity, I highly recommend the exercises in the book *Voluntary Controls* by Jack Schwarz. This book contains a whole series of such exercises geared to the western mind and is very effective.

Now that you are centered and your mind is quiet, you are ready to sit for spiritual guidance.

## Channelling Personal Spiritual Teachers for Guidance

Each person has several guides who stay with him and guide him throughout many lifetimes. In addition, one has teacher-guides who stay during times of specific learning and are chosen because of that specific learning. For example, if you are learning to be an artist, you are bound to have a few artist-type guides around for inspiration. In whatever kind of creative work you are involved in, I am sure you are inspired by guides who are connected to that type of work in the spirit world, where the forms are more perfect and beautiful than we are able to manifest on the earth plane.

To contact your guide, simply sit in the quiet, peaceful understanding that you are one with God, that a spark of God exists in every part of your being and that you are perfectly safe. This attitude allows you to reach a state of inner quiet that allows you to hear.

In general, when entering a lifted state for guidance, I go through the following internal experience.

I feel an excitement because I sense the presence of a guide full of light and love. Then I become aware of a beam of white light above me, and I start lifting myself up into it. (One might say, I go up into it with my mind's eye.) My excitement diminishes as I become aware of a pink cloud of love coming down over me. I become filled with a feeling of love and security. I then feel myself being lifted into a higher state of consciousness. At this point, my body may make a few adjustments, like the pelvis curling under more (to the forward position), and my backbone straightening more. I may involuntarily yawn to help my throat chakra open. (This is the chakra through which one hears one's guides.)

After more lifting, I enter into a state of holy serenity. Then I will usually both hear and see the guides. Throughout the beginning of the reading I will continue lifting. I usually have about three teachers that guide me. The person who has come to me for help will usually be accompanied by his guide or guides.

*It is the experience of light, love and serenity that confirms your connection to the guides. If you do not have it when trying to channel, then you are most likely not connected to your guides.*

The guide will communicate in whatever form is easiest for you to receive. It will either be in a general concept, direct words, symbolic pictures or direct pictures of happenings like past experiences or past lives. When one form of communication does not reach you, or you become afraid of what is being conveyed, the guides will simply shift to another form or approach the subject from another angle. For example, if I fear that the words that are coming through have a certain meaning, or if someone has asked a particularly controversial question, I will "run away" from that place of inner peace and harmony and no longer be able to hear what the guide is saying. I then have to take a minute or two to find that place inside again. If I cannot pick up the words again, the guides will probably send me a general concept that I then try to explain in my own words. This slowly merges with their words again, and I am "back on line." If that doesn't work, they will come in with a picture that I will begin describing and allow the client to help find the meaning of the symbolic picture for himself.

My internal experiences of verbal channelling is as follows. I sit in a cross-legged position, palms down on my thighs. First I center myself. To me this means kinesthetically anchoring in my body. It feels as if I build a strong energetic foundation around my lower half. Once this foundation is set, I begin to lift my consciousness by kinesthetically feeling it raise and visually focus upward into the light. I also turn my palms upward when I do this. At a certain point when I am lifted, contact with the guide is made. Again I feel it kinesthetically. I see the guide behind my right shoulder, and I hear the first few words from that direction. When I and the guide are ready to begin, I lift my hands and hold fingertips together in front of my solar plexus or my heart. This balances my energy field and helps maintain a lifted state. The rasp nasal breath also helps. At this point, I usually begin to channel verbally. At first the words come from the right shoulder area. The more connected to the channelling process I become, the closer-in the words are. The guide also appears to come closer. Soon, there is no lag time between hearing and speaking the words, and the apparent direction they are coming from moves to above and inside my head. The guide also visually appears to fit over me like a glove. The guide begins to move my arms and hands in coordination with the conversation. "He" also uses my hands to balance my energy field and to run energy into my chakras while "he" is talking. This keeps the energy high and focused. My personality self seems to be floating off and above, listening and watching it all. At the same time, I feel merged with the guide, as if I am the guide. As the guide I feel much bigger than the personality me, Barbara.

At the end of the conversation, my experience is one of the guide lightly disconnecting and lifting off, while my consciousness sinks downwards into my body and my personality self. At this point I am usually quite shy.

## The Chakra Senses

So far I have mentioned only accessing through four of the normal five senses of sight, sound, feel and smell. It is rare, but I suppose one could channel through taste also. In studying the accessing process, I have seen that each mode or sense is related to a chakra; i.e., we access information through the sensing mechanism of each chakra. Figure 19–1 lists the seven chakras and the sense that is active through each one. When I observe someone channelling, I am able to perceive which chakra they are using to get their information. That chakra is usually very active and has more energy running through it when they are channelling. Note that we do not normally distinguish between the kinesthetic sense, feeling and intuition, but in my opinion, they are very different as described in Figure 19–1. We also don't call loving a sense, but I believe it is. Just begin to pay more attention to what is going on when you are loving or "sensing love." Loving is not in the same category as other feelings. Of course loving is more than just a sense. It is also a way of being in synchronicity with other human beings.

The kind of information you receive through each of your chakras is different. The first chakra yields kinesthetic information—feelings in your body like a feeling of balance or imbalance, shivers running up and down the spine, physical pain in a body part, a feeling of illness or health, safety or danger. This information can be utilized by the healer to know what state the patient is in. If the healer feels illness, and she knows it is not hers, she will know that it is the patient's. She may feel the patient's leg pain in her own leg or in her hand when she places it on the patient's leg. All this kind of information comes through the first chakra and can be used very successfully if the healer clears herself so that her own body is a sounding board. She can

**Figure 19–1**
## SENSES OF THE SEVEN CHAKRAS

| Chakra | Chakra Perception | Nature of Information | Meditation Practice |
|---|---|---|---|
| 7 | Knowing whole concept | Receiving a whole concept that goes beyond each of the senses listed below | Be still and know I am God |
| 6 | Seeing Visualizing | Seeing clear pictures, either symbolic or literal | Messianic or Christ Consciousness |
| 5 | Hearing Speaking | Hearing sounds, words or music and also taste and smell | Sounding Listening |
| 4 | Loving | A sense of loving another | Rose light of love Love a flower |
| 3 | Intuition | A vague sense of knowing that is not specific—a vague sense of size, shape and intent of being that is sensual | One-pointedness of mind |
| 2 | Emotional | Emotional feeling—joy, fear, anger | Meditate on peaceful sense of well-being |
| 1 | Touch Movement and presence Kinesthetic | Kinesthetic feeling in your body—like feeling of balance, shivers, hair standing on end, energy running, physical pleasure or pain | Walking Meditation Touching Deep relaxation |

distinguish between her body and the body of her patient. If the healer feels pain in her leg, she had better be aware of whether it was there before the patient arrived or if she is picking it up from the patient. Of course there are disadvantages to this method of accessing information. One tires very fast of feeling everyone else's physical pain.

The second chakra yields information about emotional states, either of the healer or others. Again the healer must use her own energy field to distinguish between her own emotional feelings and those of the patient. This can be learned with practice and a lot of good feedback. For example, the healer will sense what the client feels emotionally about the pain in her leg. The client may be angry about being sick, or she may be very fearful about it. She may be afraid that the leg pain really indicates a very serious condition. It is important to use this information because all illness is accompanied by emotional feelings that need to be cleared in some way.

The third chakra gives vague information such as when someone says, "I thought you were going to call, and you did" or "My intuition tells me that I shouldn't fly on that plane today; something might happen." If one is sensing beings from another level, and the third chakra is being used to sense them, the person will get a vague sense of another presence in the room, its location, its general shape and size and its intent, i.e., friendly or unfriendly. The first chakra would reveal kinesthetic information about the presence, and the second would reveal the feelings of the being. In the example of the leg pain, the third chakra will give a vague idea of what deeper meaning the pain has in the client's life and also some intuition of its causes.

The fourth chakra yields feelings of love. Love that reaches out beyond the self, mate or family to humanity and life itself. When you are sensing with the fourth chakra, you can sense another's love and the quality and quantity of that love, whether they be in a physical body or not. One can feel the collective love of humanity. In the example of leg pain, one would feel love for the client and the client's quality of love for herself. The chakra also gives the sense of connectedness to all creatures who have ever had leg pain.

The fifth chakra gives the sense of sounds, music, words, smells and taste. This information can be very specific, depending upon which level of the auric field it is coming from. (See next section.) For example, for the client with the pain in her leg, the healer may very well receive a description of the problem in physiological terms like "It is phlebitis" or "It is a strained muscle due to a new pair of shoes that cause the leg to twist when the client is walking." The fifth chakra may also reveal a sound that would be very effective to use on the leg for healing it.

The sixth chakra reveals pictures. These pictures can be either symbolic, with a very personal meaning for the patient, or literal. Literal pictures are pictures of events that have happened, are happening or will happen. They are also images of things that exist. When I say images, I don't necessarily mean you see them as you do with your eyes, but you do receive a picture in your mind that gives a strong enough impression and allows you to observe it in a way that might allow you to draw or reproduce it if you wished. For example, in the case of the leg pain, the sixth chakra might reveal an image of the blood clot associated with phlebitis, or the healer might simply see the strained muscle, depending on what the cause of the pain is. The image could appear on a screen in the healer's mind, as on TV, or it could appear to be coming directly from inside the leg, as it would to nor-

mal sight. The sixth chakra could also reveal a symbolic picture that would have some meaning for the client but most likely not much meaning for the healer. The symbolic picture would appear on the healer's mind-screen. The sixth chakra could also reveal, in picture form, the patient's past experience that is connected to the leg pain, such as an image of a child falling off a tricycle and bumping her leg right where the pain is now, say twenty years later. This kind of direct access is rather like watching a movie.

Note that I have been referring to receiving pictures. Perceiving means receiving. Perception is receiving what is already there, either in symbolic form or in literal form. Visualizing is an entirely different function. The process of visualization is actively creating. In visualization you create a picture in your mind and give it energy. If you continue to hold it clearly in your mind and give it energy, you can eventually create it in your life. You have thus given it form and substance. The clearer the image and the more emotional energy you project into it, the more you will be able to create it in your life.

The seventh chakra reveals information in the form of a whole concept. This information goes beyond the limited human senses and communication system. The channeller, after absorbing and deeply understanding the concept, must then use her own words to describe what she understands. Many times, as I start to explain something in my own words, Heyoan will come in (from the fifth) and explain it in much clearer words than I can. The whole concept gives a complete sense of knowing. It is the experience of being one with the concept. In our leg pain example, the seventh chakra will reveal the whole life situation that the leg pain is associated with.

## Chakra Sense of Different Levels of Reality

Now that you have an idea of the information coming through each of the chakras, let us look at the different levels of reality that were discussed in Chapters 7 and 15. There I discussed the physical level of reality, the astral, the etheric template level, the celestial level, the ketheric template level and the beings who exist on each of these levels. I also stated that there are levels beyond the seventh. In order to perceive on any one of these levels, the chakra through which you wish to perceive must be opened on that level. If you want to see any particular auric layer, then you must open your sixth chakra to that layer. If you want to see the first level of the auric field, you must open your sixth chakra on the first level of your aura. If you want to see the second level of the aura, you must open your sixth chakra on the second layer of your aura. When beginners start to see the aura, they usually see the first layer, because they open their sixth chakra on the first level of their aura. As they progress, they open the sixth chakra on the next consecutive layer and can then see that layer.

Opening the chakras on levels above the fourth also means that you will start to perceive beings on other planes of existence. This is rather disruptive to your personal life when it first occurs and takes some getting used to. For example, many times you must choose between carrying on the conversation you are having and stopping and listening to the guide who is trying to talk to you at the same time. I have spent a lot of time in this double world existence. Someone who perceives the presence of beings, and responds to them, appears very flaky to those who don't.

In order to hear a being who lives on the astral level you must open your fifth chakra on the astral level. If you want to hear a guide on the fifth level, then you must open your fifth chakra on the fifth level of your auric field. If you want to see an astral guide, then you must open your sixth chakra on the fourth level. To see a fifth level guide, you must open your sixth chakra on the fifth level, and so on.

As was stated in Chapter 7, there are doors or seals between the chakra levels deep within the hearts of the chakras. These seals or doors must be opened in order to move from one level to the next. This is done by raising the vibra-tional level of your energy system. To increase and maintain your field at a higher vibrational level means purification work. You must keep your field clear and highly cleared to perceive the higher levels of the auric field. Doing this also means increased sensitivity in your daily life. This means a lot of self-care in terms of diet, exercise and spiritual practices—to be discussed further in Part VI.

Each level represents another octave higher in vibration than the one below it. To bring your conscious awareness to a higher level means to increase the vibrational rate at which your awareness functions. This is not necessarily an easy task, for as you have seen in the material presented in the chapters on psychodynamics, every increase in energy in the system knocks loose blocks that take you through experiences that you have buried within your subconscious because the events were too threatening to be felt at the time they occurred.

## Meditations to Enhance Experience of Each of Your Auric Levels

I have found different meditation practices that will enhance your experience of each of your auric levels. These are also given in Figure 19-1. To enhance your experience on the first layer of your aura, do walking or touching meditations or deep relaxation. To enhance your experience of the second layer of your aura, meditate on a peaceful sense of well-being. To enhance your experience of the third level of your auric field, do one-pointedness-of-mind exercises. To enhance your experience of your fourth level, meditate on the rose light of love or focus on loving a flower. To enhance your experience of being at the fifth level of your auric field, use sounding or listening meditations. To enhance your experience of your celestial body, meditate on becoming one with the Messianic or Christ Consciousness. To experience your seventh layer of being, sit in meditation and use the mantra, "Be still and know that I am God."

# Chapter 19 Review

1. What is a good way to learn High Auditory Perception?
2. How can you sit for spiritual guidance? Practice it at least three times this week.
3. In what forms will your guides try to communicate with you? Describe the process.
4. Describe the sense associated with each of the seven chakras.
5. If you want to "see" a guide on the ketheric template level, which chakra do you need to open on what level of the auric field?
6. If you want to "hear" a guide on the astral level, which chakra do you need to open on what level of the auric field?
7. If I were to say that I had a vague sense that a being was in a certain corner of the room and that being was not very friendly, through what chakra would I be sensing it? Upon what level of the auric field would that being exist?
8. How do you open a particular chakra on a particular level of your field?
9. What is the main difference between internal viewing and channelling-guided information?

## Food For Thought

10. How would your life be different if you sought and followed guidance more?
11. What are your main resistances to actively seeking guidance in your life?
12. Ask for guidance to learn how to utilize guidance better in your life. What is the answer?
13. What is your negative belief or image of what bad things will happen to you if you follow guidance? How does that relate to your childhood experiences with authorities? How does that relate to your relationship to or image of God?
14. How can precognition work if we have free will?
15. How can using this kind of perception change your life?
16. What is the difference between visualizing and perceiving?

# Chapter 20

# HEYOAN'S METAPHOR OF REALITY

## The Cone of Perception

In the last chapter I discussed opening your perception to higher levels of reality by increasing the vibratory rate of your auric field. This idea was based on the concept of a multidimensional universe composed of levels of vibrational rates existing within the same space. The more advanced or refined that level of reality, the higher the vibrational rate. I would now like to discuss this multi-dimensional universe in terms of levels of perception.

Heyoan says that each of us has a cone of perception through which we perceive reality. One can use the metaphor of frequency to explain this concept, meaning that each of us is able to perceive within a certain frequency range.

As humans, we tend to define reality by what we can perceive. This perception not only includes all the normal human perceptions, but also the extensions of those perceptions through the instruments we have built like the microscope and the telescope. Everything inside our perceptual cone we accept as real, and everything outside that cone isn't real. If we can't perceive it, then it doesn't exist.

Each time we build a new instrument, we increase our cone of perception, and more things are perceived and therefore become real. The same thing is happening here with High Sense Perception, but the instrument in this case is our own body and energy system. As we perceive more things through High Sense Perception, more things become real to us.

I have attempted to draw a graph using the familiar bell-shaped curve to help describe this phenomenon (Figure 20–1A). The vertical axis shows clarity of perception, and the horizontal depicts frequency range of perception. The bell-shaped curve shown in the middle of the graph can be used to depict the normal perceptual range of a human being, a group of human beings or, for that matter, the whole of humanity. Most of us have clear perceptions as defined by the dotted lines. Outside the dotted lines, our clarity is so low that we tend to discount what we perceive. However, if we accept everything we perceive, then the space under the bell-shaped curve also defines what we call the real universe. The dashed line shows the increase in perception that our instruments give us. We, at least most of us, accept that as reality also.

Let us look at this from the point of view of what is called the Brahman and the Maya of the Buddhist tradition. Maya is the manifest world, which according to Buddhism is illusion. Brahman is the basic reality that lies beneath Maya and supports what is manifest. It is not to be confused with Brahmin, the educated priest class in the Hindu caste system. Meditation is practiced in Buddhism in order to get beyond the illusion of Maya which encompasses all pain and to become Brahman or enlightened. Here we have a concept very similar to the cone of perception. Figure 20–1B shows the cone of per-

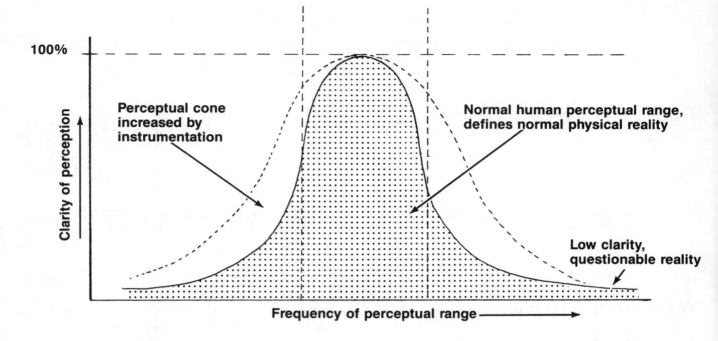

**A. Graphic depiction of our perceptual cone**

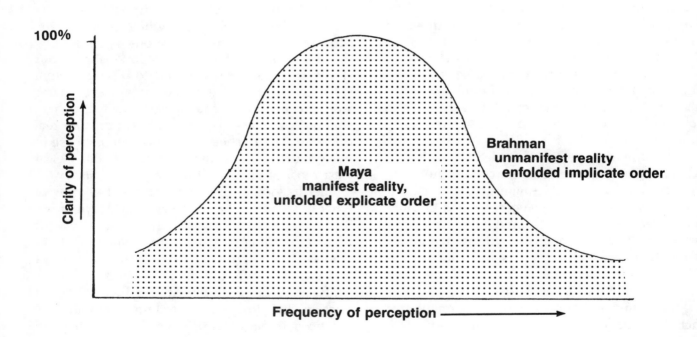

**B. Spiritual interpretation of our cone of perception**

Figure 20–1: Our Perceptual Cone

178

ception again, now interpreted from the point of view of Brahman and Maya. The manifest world of Maya lies within our cone of perception, while the unmanifest world of Brahman lies outside the cone of perception. Physicist David Bohm's Explicate Unfolded Order (see Chapter 4) lies within our cone of perception, and his Implicate Enfolded Order lies outside our cone of perception.

Figure 20–2A shows the effect that High Sense Perception has. I have now labeled what we used to call unreal and nonexistent as the spiritual reality. As we increase our perceptual range to a higher levels of vibration, more of the spiritual (nonphysical) world becomes real to us. The more we use our HSP, the more we are able to perceive (which makes more of the spiritual world accessible to us), the more we come out of illusion and into Brahman or enlightenment. From this point of view, the line of the bell-shaped curve becomes the veil between the spiritual and the material worlds. Heyoan says healing is ultimately dissolving the veil between the spiritual and material worlds.

Another very important point is that, since our self-definitions are based on what we define as real, as our reality broadens, so do we. Figure 20–2B again shows the bell-shaped curve, but now I have labeled it in terms of self-definition. Inside the curve we have a limited self-definition—who we think we are based on our limited view of reality. Outside, we have a self-definition without limits, which is ultimately God. The line of the curve becomes the veil between who we think we are and who we really are. Heyoan repeatedly has said that these two veils (between the spiritual and material worlds and between who we think we are and who we really are) are the same. It is also the veil between what we call life and death. When we know we are spirit, we do not cease to live at death; rather we simply leave our physical body, the vehicle which we as spirit made in order to incarnate in the first place. At a person's death I have witnessed (with HSP) his spirit leaving the body to join other spirits in the room. At death the veil dissolves, and we go home to who we really are.

## The Manifest World

During a reading some time ago Heyoan led me through an experience that explained manifestation. Here is the transcript of that tape.

Heyoan: "And what then is manifestation? It is related to the ability to sense what has been manifest. That ability relates to the One and relates to each person's individuation and where her sensing window is. What is perceived within that window of sensing is what you have defined as the manifest world. When that narrow view through which you sense manifestation expands, then the manifest world expands. For example, when you begin to hear our voice, then you can experience more of the manifest world. That world appears to be less solid or thinner, but it is still of the manifest. The appearance of thinness has more to do with your ability to sense higher frequencies than the reality of higher frequencies having a quality of thinness. This limitation on your sensing, which makes the higher realities appear thinner, also gives you the impression that the higher frequencies appear to be fading back into the unmanifest. However, that is not the case."

Barbara: "So what I am seeing is this whole range of sensing into what we call manifest. It is simply a set of sensing, when you call it manifest. As that range becomes higher and wider, or (one could use the analogy) the more the angle of view increases, or the more our experience broadens, then we are able to sense more of what we call the unmanifest world . . . Oh, it works both ways, so that when one expands to lower vibrations, the same is also true."

Heyoan: "For some reason or other, humanity has chosen to see or describe the lower vibrations as negativity, as darkness, as unpleasant forms. That is one way to do it, although it is simply based on the dualistic nature of the human being and his perception mechanism. It is part of the sensing system that then sees the lower vibrations as negative."

Barbara: "What about the whole long human evolutionary scale?"

Heyoan: "In terms of evolution, we would be speaking simply of the ability to expand the

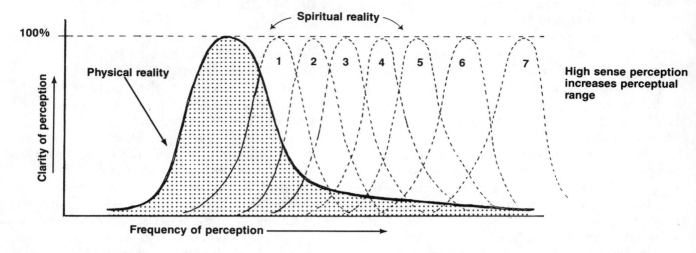

**A. Cone of perception increased by high sense perception**

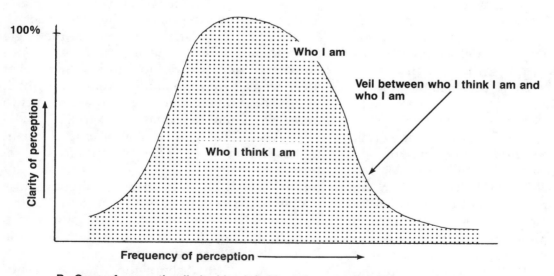

**B. Cone of perception limited by definition of personal reality**

Figure 20–2: Defining the Boundaries of Our Perceptual Cone

180

sensing window. One might say that concrete reality falls within the largest part of the bell-shaped curve of your perception. People tend to disbelieve their perceptions when they reach out beyond one standard deviation, or beyond the maximum part of the bell curve. As humanity progresses along its evolutionary path, the bell curve of perception becomes wider and wider. [See Figure 20–1.] The bell curve of perception could be considered to be a curve that shows the limitations of the human mind in this time of its evolution. We would seek to have the entire range of perception of the human mind functioning at the peak of the bell curve over all frequencies of perception so that expanded reality becomes as concrete as, say, this tape recorder you are holding. The bell curve of perception would then expand to its peak until it becomes flat. When the whole is reached, the manifest and unmanifest become one.

"Another way to say it is: As you expand your cone of perception, our world becomes more and more manifest to you and you will then relate to it as part of the manifest world. Thus, as you continue to expand your perception through your personal evolution, more and more of the Universe becomes manifest to you and you approach the Universal Oneness. In a sense, you are coming back home.

"Through the expansion of perceived reality, the human being could and does then choose what frequency to perceive in and even exist in the manifest universe. It is a tool for understanding the implicate order. This process is the game of life, one might say. When the implicate and the explicate order become one, due to the expansion of perception in the human being, then the state of enlightenment is reached.

"For example, let us use this analogy: white chalk drawing on a white board could be like the unmanifest. A blackboard with white chalk could be like the unmanifest first breaking into dualism. A cream board with colored chalk could be like the multi-dimensional universe. These could be seen as steps in the evolutionary process of perception of the human being, or of who you are, or of the God/Goddess within perceiving him/her self. Thus, as we reach into broader dimensions of reality, the colors become more distinct and more dimensional, as in multi-dimensional colors within each other.

"That is what this discussion is all about: teaching a new perception (High Sense Perception) in humankind. Your internal vision gives you the choice of where to look, and what size, and in what frequency band. Would you look at the physical manifestation, or what you call the physical reality? Or do you want to look at the lower etheric, or the emotional, or up into the higher etheric, or even the ninth or eighth levels of the aura? Where do you choose to place your perception? You also decide on the resolution. Do you choose to look at a microorganism or do you choose to look at a macroorganism? The manifest God chooses to manifest only through perception, that is, chooses upon which part of the face of the dark to manifest through perceptions. There are beings among you who cannot see you and whom you cannot see. They have chosen to live in a different window of perception. Do you understand, my dear?"

Barbara: "No, I'm getting tired. This talk is too linear."

Heyoan: "That is because we are again squeezing this information into your narrow perception. Allow your perception to expand as we lead you into another realm of light. As you enter this room, see the lightness, feel the joy. . . ."

From here I was led into what appeared to be higher and higher realms. Each realm was more magnificent than the one before. Each was harder and harder to perceive. Each was becoming apparently thinner and of less form. My guide Heyoan led me.

We reached as high as I could perceive, at which point Heyoan said, "And here we stand before the door of the Holy of Holies, where every human longs to enter."

I could see my past lifetimes floating by beneath me as the wafted scent of jasmine in the night air. As each did, I could feel a pull to look back into the reality. Each time that pull felt like falling. I tried to stay with a sense of being, beyond Barbara, beyond time, beyond lifetimes . . .

I tried to reach into the door of the Holy of Holies.

Heyoan: "It is not a matter of trying to reach; it is a matter of allowing oneself to be where one already is. There is tremendous room here. It is a state of being beyond time and space. No need to rush. This is what the soul is asking for."

Then I found myself entering a door between two paws of the Great Sphinx. Before me sat Heyoan on a throne.

Heyoan: "So, my dear, when you speak of healing, know that healing is opening the doors of perception so that one can enter into the Holy of Holies and be one with the Creator. It is nothing more, nothing less than that. It is a process, step-by-step, in that direction. Enlightenment is the goal; healing is a by-product. So, whenever a soul comes to you for healing, know deep inside that this is what the soul is asking for.

"Remember that whenever someone comes to you for help or healing, their words come through their doorway of perception. It may be a narrow one, or a broad one. A sore toe, a life-threatening illness, or a seeking of the Truth, that which is asked comes through the doorway of perception, but that which needs to be given is simply this: It is the answer to the longing of the soul. The soul is saying, 'Help me find my way back home. Help me find my way into the Holy of Holies, into the peace of the ages, into the Wind Whispering Truth Through the Centuries.' "

At this point during the meditation, I shuddered and wept with joy. Heyoan had often told me that the meaning of Heyoan is the "Wind Whispering Truth Through the Centuries." Now

I understood. Through the meditation Heyoan had led me into an understanding that I and Heyoan are one. I could experience this with every cell of my body, that I am Truth Whispering Through the Centuries.

Heyoan continued: "And so here I sit, Heyoan, crown of jewels, each being a truth, a known truth. So here I exist, have always existed and will always exist; beyond space and time, beyond confusion; manifest, yet unmanifest; known, but not known. And so sit you here also every one of you. You simply long to know this, from where you stand within your limited perception."

## Chapter 20 Review

1. Explain the concept of the window of perception.

### Food For Thought

2. Given Heyoan's description of reality here, discuss the relationship between your inner wall of fear as described in Chapter 14, the wall between who you think you are, and who you really are; the veil between the spiritual and material worlds; and the veil between life and death.
3. What is death?
4. From Heyoan's last statement, what is the relationship between your guide and you? How is that different from your higher self? Your Divine spark?

# PART V

# SPIRITUAL HEALING

"Even greater miracles than these,
ye shall do also."

Jesus

*Introduction*

# YOUR ENERGY FIELD IS
# YOUR INSTRUMENT

Now that we have a good idea of what healing is all about from the personal, human, scientific and spiritual levels, let us explore the various healing techniques I have learned throughout my years of practice.

As always, healing starts at home. The first prerequisite for any healer is self-care. If you do healing and don't take care of yourself, you will probably get sick faster than in any other situation. This is because healing requires a lot of work from your energy field, in addition to its importance for your own life. What I mean by this is that in addition to keeping you healthy and balanced, your field will be used as a conduit for the healing energies that are needed by others. Your field may not necessarily need the frequencies that you will be transmitting, but your field will have to transmit them anyway. In order to transmit a certain frequency required in healing, your field must vibrate in that frequency or its harmonic. Thus in order to give healing, you will run your field like a roller coaster. You will be constantly varying its frequency of vibration. You will be constantly transmitting different intensities of light. This will affect you. It will be good in the sense that it will speed up your own evolutionary process, because changes in frequency and intensity will break your normal holding patterns and will release the blocks in your field. It may deplete you if you do not keep yourself in top condition. In

healing, you do not generate the energy you transmit, but you must first raise your frequency to that needed by the patient in order to entrain the energy from the Universal Energy Field. This is called harmonic induction and takes a lot of energy and focus to do. As long as your voltage of energy is higher than the patient's, you will transmit to him. If, however, you try to heal when you are very tired, the voltage you are able to produce may be weaker than the patient's. Current flows from a high voltage to a lower one. In this way you could pick up negative energies of disease from your patients. If you are very healthy, your system will just clear them by energizing them or by repelling them. If you are worn out, you may take longer to clear the low energies you pick up. If you already have a tendency toward a particular illness, you could exacerbate your own situation. On the other hand, if you take care of yourself, healing someone with the same particular disease that you have tendencies toward may very well help you learn to generate the frequencies needed to cure yourself.

Studies done by Hiroshi Motoyama measured the strength of a healer's and a patient's acupuncture lines before and after healing. In many cases, the healer's lines for a particular organ were low after the healing. However, they recovered their original strength a few hours later. Motoyama also showed that usually the

185

healer's heart meridian was stronger after a healing, indicating that the heart chakra was always used in healing, as will be discussed in the following chapters.

In the following section I will discuss healing techniques for different layers of the aura, present some examples of healings and give techniques for self-care of the healer.

*Chapter 21*

# PREPARATION FOR HEALING

## Preparing the Healer

In preparing to give a healing, the healer must first open and align herself with the cosmic forces. This means not only just before the healing, but in her life in general. She must be dedicated to the truth and be meticulously honest with herself in all areas of her being. She needs the support of friends and some form of spiritual discipline or purification process. She needs teachers, both spiritual and physical. She needs to keep her own body healthy through exercise and healthy nourishment, balanced diet (including high intake of vitamins and minerals, which the body uses more of when running high energy), resting and playing. Through this nourishment, she maintains her own physical vehicle in a condition that allows her to raise her vibrations to reach up and out to the universal energy field and those spiritual healing energies that will then flow through her. She must first raise her own vibrations to connect with the healing energies before channelling can take place.

Before starting a day of healing, it is good to do some form of physical exercise in the morning, as well as a meditation to center oneself and open the chakras. This does not have to take a long time. Thirty to forty-five minutes is sufficient. The following exercises are the ones that I find very effective. I change them periodically to suit the constantly changing needs of my energy system.

## Daily Exercises for the Healer to Open Acupuncture Lines

1. Lie flat on your back with your arms at your sides, palms facing upwards. Move your feet slightly apart to a comfortable position. Close your eyes. Relax your whole body by focusing on each part of it, one after another. Breathe naturally. Focus on your breath and count—one in, one out, two in, two out, and so on—for five minutes. If your mind starts to wander, bring it back to the counting; if the number is forgotten, start at one again.

As your attention is kept for a few minutes on counting breaths, your mind and body are gradually relaxed.

2. The best exercise to start the day can be done before you get out of bed (if it doesn't bother your sleeping partner, but it probably will). Lie flat on your back, spread your arms out perpendicular to your body and bring your knees up with your feet flat on the bed. Keeping your shoulders down, allow your knees to fall to the right while you roll your head to look left. Now bring your knees up and let them fall to the left while you roll your head to the right. Repeat this movement until your back feels well stretched out.

Joint exercises are especially good to create a smooth flow of energy in the acupuncture channels through adjustment of the joints. Since all the meridians flow through the joints, moving the joints activates the meridians. These joint exercises were developed by Hiroshi Motoyama to open the acupuncture channels. They are given in his pamphlet, "The Functional Relationship Between Yoga Asanas and Acupuncture Meridians."

3. Sit erect on the floor with your legs stretched straight out in front. Place your hands on the floor beside your hips and lean backwards using your straight arms for support. Place your attention in the toes. Move only the toes of both feet. Slowly flex and extend them without moving your legs or ankles. Repeat ten times. See Figure 21-1A.

4. Remain in the sitting position described above. Flex and extend your ankle joints as far as possible. Repeat ten times. See Figure 21-1B.

5. You are still in the sitting position given in #3. Separate your legs slightly. Keeping your heels in contact with the floor, rotate your ankles ten times in each direction.

6. Still sitting in the starting position, bend and raise the right leg as much as possible at the knee bringing the heel near the right buttock. Straighten the right leg without allowing the heel or toe to touch the ground. Repeat ten times and then do the same process with the left leg. See Figure 21-1C.

7. In the same sitting position, hold the thigh near the trunk with both hands and rotate the lower leg in a circular motion about the knee ten times clockwise and then ten times counterclockwise. Repeat the same procedure with the left leg.

8. Bend the left leg and place the left foot on the right thigh. Hold the left knee with the left hand and place the right hand on the left angle. Gently move the bent leg up and down with the left hand, relaxing the muscles of the left leg as much as possible. Repeat the same process with the right knee. See Figure 21-1D.

9. Sitting in the same position as in #8, rotate the right knee around the right hip joint ten times clockwise and then ten times counterclockwise. Repeat the same process with the left knee. See Figure 21-1E.

10. Sitting in the starting position with legs stretched out, raise the arms forward to shoulder height. Stretch and tense the fingers of both hands. Close the fingers over the thumbs to make a tight fist. Repeat ten times. See Figure 21-1F.

11. Maintain the position in #10 above. Flex and extend the wrists. Repeat ten times. See Figure 21-1G.

12. From the same position as in #10, rotate the wrists ten times clockwise and ten times counterclockwise.

13. Taking the same position as #10 above, stretch out the hands with the palms upwards. Bend both arms at the elbows and touch the shoulders with the fingertips and straighten the arms again. Repeat ten times and then perform the same exercise ten times but with the arms extended sideways. See Figure 21-1H.

14. Remaining in the same position with the fingertips in constant contact with the shoulders, lift elbows as high as possible. Then lower them. Repeat ten times. Now point elbows forward. Repeat. See Figure 21-1I.

15. In same position as #14 above, make a circular movement of the elbows by rotating the shoulder joints. Do this ten times clockwise and then ten times counterclockwise. Make the circular movement of each elbow as large as possible, bringing the two elbows together in front of the chest. See Figure 21-1J.

Once you learn these exercises, you can probably do the fingers/toes, ankles/wrist at the same time.

16. Now do several sit-ups, breathing out each time you sit up. Do at least ten to start with. Work your way up to twenty.

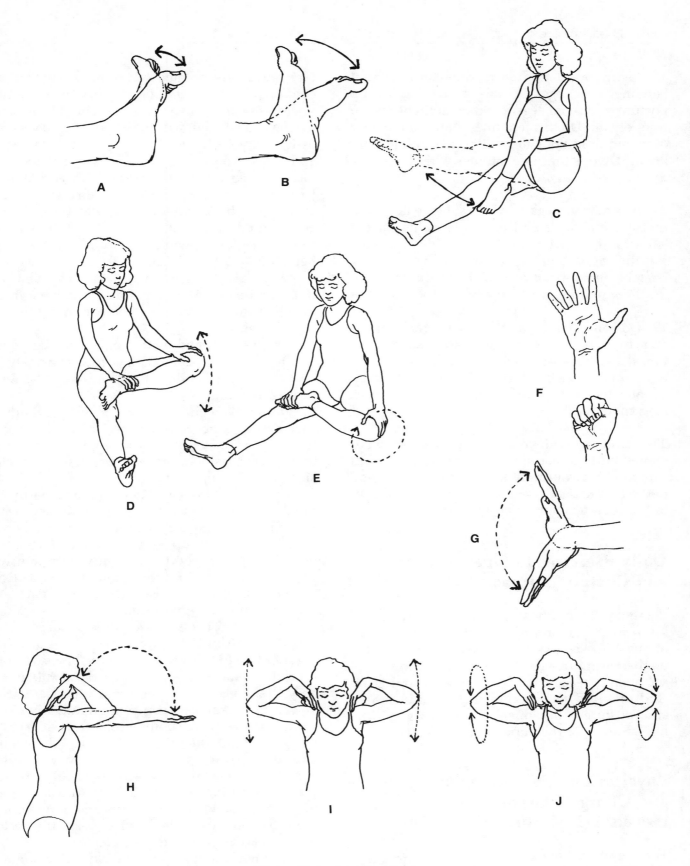

Figure 21–1: Joint Exercises

189

17. Reach over and touch your toes without bending your legs. Do this from a sitting up posture with your legs together, straight and in front of you. Do this ten times. Now simply stay over and hold your toes without bending your knees. Do this for three minutes without getting up.

18. Spread your legs as wide as they will go and repeat the above exercise, first reaching for the left toes, then switch to the right side and reach for the right toes. Now repeat by reaching straight out in front of you. Hold this position for three minutes without getting up.

19. Do some head and neck rolls. First look up and then down with your face. Repeat ten times. Now look to each side ten times. Then roll your head around first clockwise and then counterclockwise several times till your neck feels more flexible.

20. Stand up. With your body straight and your feet about two feet apart, bend over to the left side reaching your right arm over your head and to the left. Repeat several times. Now bend over to the right reaching over with your left arm.

## Daily Exercises to Open and Charge Chakras

There are three different sets of exercises that I know to charge and open chakras. The first set of physical exercises opens the chakras very well on the lower three levels of the aura. The second set opens the chakras well on the astral level. And the third set is a combination of breathing and postures that open the chakras on the higher levels of the auric field.

## Physical Exercises to Open and Charge Chakras (Levels 1–3 of Auric Field)

These exercises are shown in Figure 21–2.
Chakra 1. Stand with feet wide apart and toes and knees pointed out to an angle that is comfortable for your knees. Now bend your knees as deeply as you can. You should eventually be able to go down so that your buttocks are as low as your knees. Move up and down several times. Now add a swing motion to your pelvis. Push your pelvis as far forward and as far back as you can. Emphasize the forward movement. Rock back and forth this way three times as you go down. Stay down and rock back and forth three times while you have your knees bent; then rock back and forth three times on the way up. The most important movement of this exercise is the rocking when your knees are deeply bent. Repeat the whole thing at least three times.

Chakra 2. Stand with your feet shoulder width apart and parallel. Now rock your pelvis back and forth bending the knees slightly. Repeat several times.

Now make believe you are inside a cylinder that needs to be polished. Polish it with your hips. Put your hands on your hips. Move then in a circular fashion, making sure you polish all sides of the cylinder evenly.

Chakra 3. Jumping. This requires a partner. Hold each other's hands firmly. While one person supports, the other jumps up and down. Bring your knees up as high as possible into your chest when you jump. Jump continuously without stopping for several minutes. Rest. Do not bend over to rest. Switch, let your partner jump while you support him.

Chakra 4. This is an isometric posture exercise. Get on your hands and knees as shown in Figure 21–2. In this position, your elbows do not touch the floor. Your arms are used as a fulcrum. Vary the angle of your legs and buttocks until you feel pressure between your shoulder blades (some men with big shoulder muscles will feel it more in the shoulders, so be careful). When you succeed in getting pressure between your shoulder blades, then put isometric pressure in that place by pushing your whole body forward for a while, then pull backward. You can do this from the hips and legs. This exercise works the back of the heart chakra or the will center.

For the front of the heart chakra, find something large and round like a barrel, a soft couch back, or a bioenergetic stool to lean backwards over. Lean backwards over it, with your feet firmly planted. Relax and let the muscles of your chest stretch out.

Chakra 5. Head and neck rolls. Move your head several times in the following directions. Facing forward, up and down, side to side. Up to the left, then down to the right. Reverse. All the way up to the right, all the way down to the left. Now roll your neck and head all the way around several times in both directions.

The throat chakra also responds very well to sound. Sing! Make any kind of noise you like to, if you don't sing.

Chakra 6. Repeat the movements for chakra 5 with the eyes.

Chakra 7. Rub the crown of your head in a clockwise direction with your right hand.

## Visualization to Open Chakras (Level 4 of Auric Field)

To do this exercise, sit in a comfortable chair or in the lotus position on a pillow on the floor. Keep your back straight. First, after calming the mind with one of your meditation exercises, bring your awareness to your first chakra. Visualize it as a vortex of red light spinning clockwise. (Clockwise as defined by looking at the chakra from the outside of your body.) It is positioned directly under you with the larger end of the spinning cone open to the earth and the tip of the cone pointing into the bottom of your spine. As you watch it spinning, breathe in red. Breathe out red. Visualize the breath as red on the inbreath. On the outbreath, do not visualize, just watch what color it is. Repeat until you can clearly see red both on the inbreath and on the outbreath. If the color red is either lighter or muddy on the outbreath, that means you need to balance your red energies. If it is lighter, you need more red in your field. If it is muddy, you need to clean your lower chakra. Do this by repeating the exercise until the ingoing and outgoing colors are the same. This is true for all the chakras.

Maintaining your picture of the first chakra, move to the second located about two inches above your pubic bone. Visualize two vortices. One on the front of your body and one on the back of your body. See them spinning clockwise with with a bright red-orange color. Breathe in red-orange. Breathe it out. Repeat. Check to make sure the ingoing and outgoing colors are the same before moving on.

Maintaining the visualization of the first two chakras, move up to the third at the solar plexus. Here visualize two yellow spinning vortices. Breathe in yellow. Breathe it out. Repeat until the yellow is bright on the inbreath and outbreath.

Move to the heart. See the clockwise spinning vortices in green. Breathe green in and out until the colors are balanced. Look down to make sure you can see all the other chakras (that you have already charged) spinning before moving to the throat chakra.

At the throat, breathe in and out blue through the clockwise spinning vortices.

At the third eye chakra, see the clockwise spinning vortices on the front and back of the head as violet. Repeat the breathing exercises.

Then move to the crown. It is opalescent white and sits on top of your head. It spins clockwise. Breathe in white. Breathe it out. Repeat. See all seven chakras spinning clockwise. See the vertical power current flowing up and down your spine. It pulsates with your in breath. As you breathe in, it pulsates up. As you breathe out, it pulsates down. See all the chakras connected to it at their tips, with the crown chakra forming the top entrance and exit, and the root chakra forming the base entrance and exit for energy to flow through your field. See the pulsating energy flowing in through all your chakras with your inbreath. Your whole field is now filled with a lot of light energy. This is a good exercise to do before healing to open and charge all your chakras.

## Breathing and Posture Exercises to Charge and Open Chakras (Levels 5–7 of Auric Field)

The most powerful exercises I have seen to charge up the auric field, brighten it, clear it and

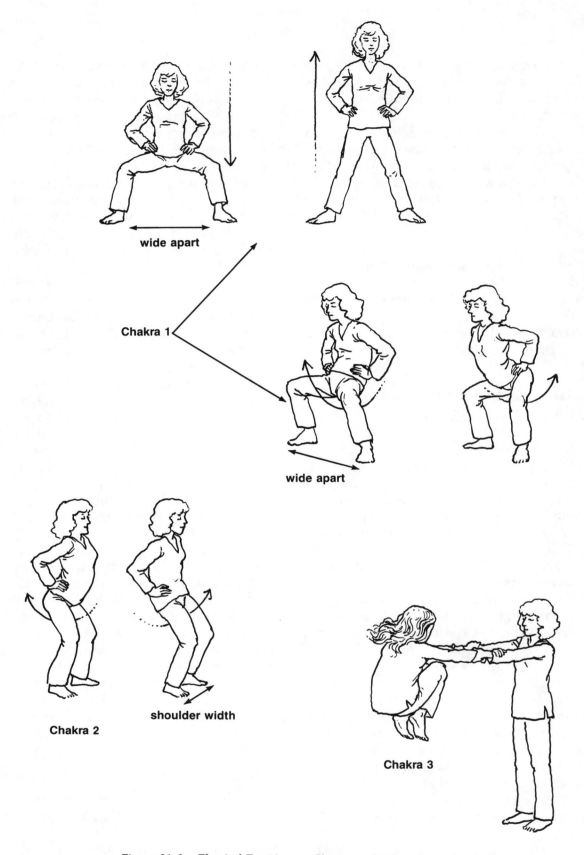

**wide apart**

**Chakra 1**

**wide apart**

**Chakra 2**

**shoulder width**

**Chakra 3**

Figure 21–2:  Physical Exercises to Charge and Open Chakras

192

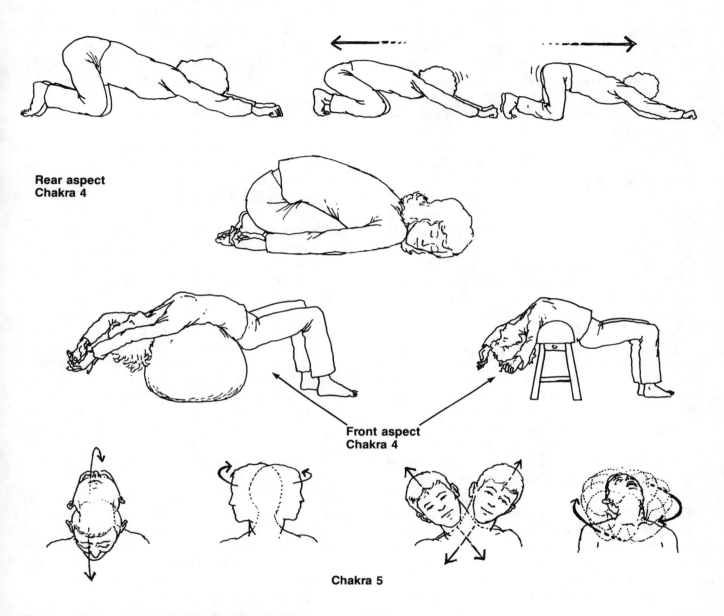

**Rear aspect
Chakra 4**

**Front aspect
Chakra 4**

**Chakra 5**

**Chakra 6. Repeat above movements for chakra 5 using eyes rather than head.**

**Chakra 7. Stand on your head.**

Figure 21–2: Physical Exercises to Charge and Open Chakras (continued)

193

strengthen it are those taught by the Kundalini Yoga people, who focus on position, breathing and spine flexibility. I would recommend that you learn them directly from a Kundalini Ashram if you have the opportunity. If not, I have simplified some of what they teach to add to this book. These are shown in Figure 21–3.

Chakra 1. Sit on the floor on your heels. Place the hands flat on the thighs. Flex spine forward in pelvic area with the inhale, and backward with the exhale. If you like, use a mantra with each breath. Repeat several times.

Chakra 2. Sit on the floor with your legs crossed. Grab the ankles with both hands and deeply inhale. Flex the spine forward and lift the chest; rotate the top of the pelvis back. On exhale, flex the spine backwards and the pelvis forwards near your "sit bones." Repeat several times, using a mantra if you like.

Chakra 2—Another Pose. Lying on back, prop yourself up on your elbows. Raise both legs about one foot above the floor. Open legs and breathe in; as you breathe out, cross legs at knees keeping legs straight. Repeat several times. Slightly raise legs and repeat again. Do this until your legs are about two and a half feet above the floor, then lower them following the same procedure. Rest. Repeat several times.

Chakra 3. Sit with crossed legs; grasp the shoulders with fingers in front, and thumbs in back. Inhale and twist to the left; exhale and twist to the right. Breathing is long and deep. Make sure spine is straight. Repeat several times and reverse direction. Repeat again. Rest one minute.

Repeat entire exercise sitting on the knees.

Chakra 3—Another Pose. Lie on back with legs together and raise the heels six inches. Raise the head and shoulders six inches; look at your toes; point to your toes with your fingertips, arms straight. In this position pant breath through your nose to a count of 30. Relax; rest for a count of 30. Repeat several times.

Chakra 4. Sitting up with legs crossed, lock fingers in a bear grip at the heart center, elbow pointing out to the sides. Elbows move in a see-saw motion. Breath long and deeply with the motion. Continue several times, and inhale, exhale and pull on the grip. Relax one minute.

Repeat sitting on your heels. This raises the energy higher.

Be sure to tuck in your pelvis.

Chakra 5. Sit with crossed legs, grasp knees firmly. Keep the elbows straight. Begin to flex the upper spine. Inhale forward; exhale back. Repeat several times. Rest.

Now flex spine by shrugging shoulders up with inhale and down with exhale. Repeat several times. Inhale and hold 15 seconds with shoulders pressed up. Relax.

Repeat the above exercises while sitting on the heels.

Chakra 6. Sitting with crossed legs, lock fingers in bear grip at throat level. Inhale; hold your breath; then squeeze your abdomen and sphincters and push energy up, as if you were pushing toothpaste up out of the tube. Exhale the energy out the top of your head, as you raise your arms above your head, holding same bear grip. Repeat.

Repeat sitting on your heels.

Chakra 7. Sit with crossed legs with arms stretched over the head. Interlock the fingers except for the two index fingers, which point straight up. Take an inbreath by pulling the navel point in, saying "sat." Let the breath out, saying "nam" while relaxing the navel point. Repeat in rapid breaths for several minutes. Then inhale and squeeze the energy from the base of the spine to the top of the head by squeezing and holding the sphincter muscles first, and then the stomach muscles. Hold your breath. Then let it out maintaining all muscle contractions. Relax. Rest. If "sat nam" does not feel right for you, use a different mantra.

Repeat, sitting on your heels. Rest.

Repeat without using mantra. Instead take short fast pant breaths through the nose.

Chakra 7—Another Pose. Sit with legs crossed. Hold arms up at a 60-degree angle with wrists and elbows straight, palms facing up. Pant breathe through the nose, with a rasping breath against upper back part of throat for about one minute. Inhale, hold the breath and pump the abdomen in and out 16 times. Exhale; relax. Repeat two or three times. Rest.

## Color Breathing Meditation to Charge Aura

With your feet parallel and shoulder width apart, slowly bend and unbend your knees. Each time you bend your knees and go down, breathe out. As you come up, breathe in. Allow yourself to go down as far as you can without having your heels come up. Relax your arms. Keep your back straight and do not bend forward. Allow the lower half of your pelvis to jut forward a bit.

Now stretch your arms out in front of you, palms down. Add a circular motion with your hands to the up-and-down motion you are already making. Your arms are stretched out as far as possible on the upward motion. As you reach the top of your movement, bring your arms into the body (palms down) and allow them to remain close to your body on the downward motion. At the bottom of your movement, again stretch your arms out. (See Figure 21–4.)

Add a visualization to this movement. You will breathe in colors from the earth up through your hands and feet and in from the air all around you. As you breathe out, you will breathe out the colors. Breathe each color several times.

Start with red. When you reach the bottom of the next movement, breathe in red. See the whole balloon of your aura fill up with red. After you reach the top of your movement and begin moving down, breathe the color out. Now try it again. Can you see the red clearly with your mind's eye? If not, repeat the exercise till you do. Colors that are hard to visualize are most likely the ones you need in your energy field. Again, as in exercise 22, just watch the color as you breathe out; don't control it. When it is bright and clear, move on to the next color.

Now breathe in orange as you move upward. Let it come into you from the earth up into your feet, into your hands and into you from the air all around you. If you have trouble visualizing these colors in your mind, get some color samples to look at; or it might be easier for you to do this with your eyes closed. Repeat the exercise with orange again.

Continue the exercise through the following sequence of colors: yellow, green, blue, violet and white. Make sure you see the whole egg form of your aura filled with each color before moving to the next color. These are good colors for each of the chakras. If you would like to add even higher vibrations to your aura, continue with the following colors: silver, gold, platinum and crystalline; then come back down to white. All colors of this second group should have an opalescent quality.

## Vibrating Exercise for Grounding

Vibrating your body means to hold your body in a position of tension that sets up involuntary physical vibrations in the body. This will increase energy flow and release blocks. These exercises are well known in core and bioenergetic therapy.

Stand with your feet parallel and shoulder width apart. After you complete the aura charging exercises given above, stand and again simply breathe out when you go down and in when you go up. Bend your knees as much as you can; let your legs begin to feel tired. If you keep doing this long enough, your legs will begin to physically vibrate in an involuntary way. If they do not, start a vibration by quickly bouncing up and down on your heels. Allow the vibrations to work up into the upper part of your legs and your pelvis. With practice, these vibrations will spread over your whole body. This is a very good way to create a strong energy flow throughout your body. Once you get the feel of it, you can devise exercises to cause any part of your body to vibrate in order to increase the en-

Figure 21-3: Breathing/Posture Exercises to Charge and Open Chakras

196

Figure 21-3: Breathing/Posture Exercises to Charge and Open Chakras (continued)

197

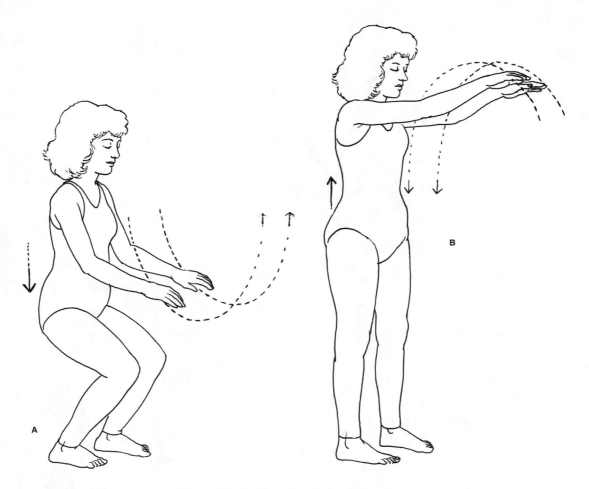

Figure 21–4:  Standing Color Meditation

ergy flow through that part. In this case, one usually needs the pelvis to vibrate in order to enhance the earthly energies flowing through the first and second chakras. Later, when you are in a healing situation, you can slowly roll your pelvis back and forth (while in a sitting position), then add a little short, fast vibration to the rolling motion. This should help the pelvis vibrate. You will feel the increased energy flow throughout your whole body.

## Sitting Meditations for Centering

Now sit for meditation for 10 to 15 minutes. Be sure your back is straight and comfortable.

A good mantra to repeat to yourself to si-lence the mind for this meditation is: "Be still and know that I am God." Simply keep your consciousness focused on that mantra. If your mind wanders, simply bring it back.

Another good meditation to still the mind is simply counting to ten. Count one on the in-breath, two on the outbreath, three on the in-breath, four on the outbreath, until you reach ten. The hard part is that every time you allow your mind to wander and think another thought other than the counting, you go back to one and start all over again! This type of meditation really lets us know just how sloppy our minds are! Very few people can get to ten on the first try!

Now you are ready (after a large glass of wa-ter) to begin a day of healing.

## Caring for the Healing Space

It is important to work in a clean room that has been cleared of low energies, bad vibes or dead orgone energy (DOR) as Wilhelm Reich called it. If possible choose a room that is full of direct sunlight and has access to open air. You may also keep the room clean by smoking it in the Native American Indian tradition with sweetgrass and cedar or with sage and cedar.

To smoke a room with cedar and sage, put some dried green cedar and dried sage plant into a container and set it afire. It is a Native American Indian tradition to use an abalone shell for the smoking so that all four elements—fire, earth, air and water—are represented. However, if you do not have an abalone shell, you can use a frying pan. When a large amount of the cedar and sage are burning, put out the fire. A lid works best. There will be a great deal of smoke, sending it into all the corners of the room. It is also a Native American Indian custom to start at the easternmost part of the house or room and cover the room in a sunrise direction (clockwise). Be sure that a door is open before you start the smoking. The smoke attracts the DOR energy and carries it out the door.

To complete the smoking, you can give a small offering of corn meal into the fire as a thank you. To learn more about these Native American Indian traditions, I refer you to Oh-Shinnah of the Four Corners Foundation, 632 Oak Street, San Francisco, California 94117. Oh-Shinnah, by the way, smokes each of her patients before working with them. This clears away a lot of the DOR before she starts. You can smoke yourself if you feel clogged. Some people burn epsom salts by pouring a little alcohol over them in a saucepan and then lighting it. Using the saucepan, walk around the room, patient or yourself.

Crystals sitting around the room help collect dead orgone energy. They are then cleaned by simply putting them in a bowl of one-quarter teaspoon sea salt and one pint spring water to soak overnight. Negative ion generators also help clear the room. Never work in a room without ventilation or with fluorescent lights. These lights generate a frequency that interferes with the normal pulsation of the aura causing a beat frequency to be set up in the field. The spectral range is also unhealthy.

If you work in an unventilated or fluorescent lighted room, you will probably get sick. You will start accumulating DOR in your body; your vibrations will slow down and slowly get weaker. Eventually you will have to stop your work, probably for several month's time until your energy system can clear itself out again. You may not even notice your energy frequencies decreasing because your sensitivity will decrease with them.

## Caring for the Healer

If you find yourself accumulating DOR in your body, **to clean your aura** take a 20-minute bath in a warm tub of one pound sea salt and one pound baking soda. This may make you very weak as it draws large quantities of energy out of the body, so be prepared to rest afterward to replenish yourself. Lying in the sunshine helps recharge your system. Just how long to take a sunbath entirely depends on your system. Be intuitive; trust when your body says it has had enough. You may have to take these baths several times per week to clear yourself.

One should always drink a full glass of spring water after each healing; so should the patient. Running water through your system helps carry away the DOR and prevents bloating. Bloating, paradoxically, is caused by not drinking enough water in the first place. Your body will retain the water in an effort to hold the DOR in the water rather than let it go deeper into the tissues of your body.

Crystals also help protect the healer's energy system. A clear quartz or amethyst crystal can be worn over the solar plexus to strengthen your field and make it less permeable. Rosy quartz helps protect the heart when worn over the heart chakra. There is much to be said about healing with crystals. I generally use four crystals on the client in healing, in addition to the ones I wear, which are an amethyst and a rosy quartz. I put a large rosy quartz in the left hand (heart meridian) of the patient and a large clear quartz in the right hand. These soak up DOR that is released in the healing. I use a large amethyst with iron deposits in it on the second or first chakras to keep the patient's field pulsating strongly. The iron helps keep the patient grounded. The crystals tend to hold the patient in the body. A smoky quartz at the solar plexus is very good for this.

If you wear a crystal, you should be sure that you wear the right one for your body. If the crystal is too strong, it will increase your field vibrations and eventually deplete your field, because your basic metabolism rate will not be strong enough to keep up with the rate that the crystal induced on your field; i.e., you will not be able to supply enough energy to your field to keep up the higher vibrations. You will eventually lose energy. If, however, you choose a crystal that is slightly stronger than your field, you will then enhance your field.

If you wear a crystal that vibrates slower than your field, it will put a drag force on your field and slow your vibrations down. You simply need to be aware of how each crystal affects you. As you become stronger you will be able to wear stronger crystals. You will also need different crystals at different times of your life, depending on the circumstances.

Crystals in the form of old jewels or keepsakes have imbued the energy of their former owners in them and should be thoroughly cleaned for a week in one-quarter teaspoon sea salt to one quart of spring water or in ocean water. Many crystal workshops are being presented now. I suggest if you want to use crystals, attend one and learn about them before using them.

I use a massage table and a secretary's chair when healing. This way I do not have to stand all day, and my back gets plenty of support. The wheels on the chair allow free movement, and I can stand or sit whenever appropriate during a healing. I also use oil to anoint the feet. This helps the energy enter the body.

One of the most important things a healer needs to stay healthy is private personal time and space. This is not easy, for most healers are in great demand by their patients. It is imperative that the healer be able to say, "No, I need time for myself now," no matter how great the demand is. This means that when you need time you give it to yourself **no matter what.** If you do not, you will get depleted and have to stop practicing for a while anyway. Don't wait till there is nothing more to give. Rest now. Give time to your hobbies and other personal pleasures. It is very important that a healer lead a full personal life that provides for her needs. If she does not, she will eventually try to get those needs met by her patients. She will develop dependencies on her patients, which will then interfere with the healing process. The golden rule for the healer is: *first, the self and what nourishes the self; then, deep pause for consideration; then, the nourishment of others.* Healers who do not do this will eventually suffer from burnout and may risk disease from energy depletion.

## Chapter 21 Review

1. Describe exercises to open acupuncture channels. Why do they work?
2. Describe exercises to clear the healer's auric field.
3. What two things should a healer do before beginning a healing?
4. Why must a healer drink a lot of water?
5. How can you clear a room of dead orgone energy (DOR)? Give three ways.
6. Why does a healer need to care for the healing space? Her own energy system? What will happen if she doesn't?
7. How can you prevent yourself from picking up DOR in a healing? In normal life circumstances?
8. What three things does a healing space need to keep it clean?
9. Why is it usually easier to heal in a healing space than in the home of a patient?
10. How can you clear your field if you have picked up DOR in a healing?
11. Describe at least three ways to heal with crystals.
12. How can you get sick from wearing a crystal? What effect does it have?

*Chapter 22*

# FULL SPECTRUM HEALING

An important thing to know about healing is that one heals or works on different layers of the aura in a healing and that for each layer the work is very different from that for other layers. This will be understood more as I go into a detailed description of what takes place in a healing. The other main point is that the energies for healing do go through the fire crucible of the heart chakra for transformation from spirit to matter and from matter to spirit, as stated earlier in Chapter 16.

## Exercises to Gather Energy for a Day of Healing

Before you begin a session with any patient, it is important to align yourself with the highest energies available and to do several of the exercises given in the last chapter to clear and charge all your chakras to allow the energy to come into your field. Do these meditation exercises for several months until you are comfortable with them. Before you begin a day of healings, it is very important for you to gather energy and focus on your purposes. Meditate the evening before or the morning of the healing day. Allow one minute per patient. Hold your mind completely blank while drawing in energy for one minute for each patient. Another technique is to focus your mind, without other thoughts, on each patient while drawing in energy. Again concentration time is one minute per patient. Visualize or feel energy flowing into you. You

also need to have lots of experience in discernment, which is discussed in Chapter 19. Be sure you are supported by a few friends who are experienced in these matters. These two things (discernment and support) are not electives but prerequisites for anyone who wants to be a channel during healing. This is very profound work and should never be taken lightly or as a party game. Misuse of these techniques can, and often does, lead to very unpleasant experiences, which have the possibility of causing harm to the person trying to channel without the appropriate spiritual discipline. Channelling is actually a by-product of spiritual discipline. Once these requirements are fulfilled, one can proceed with the exercise to let the guides come into your field given later in this chapter. For now, do exercises in Chapter 21 before meeting with your patient.

After greeting your patient, be sure to describe briefly what you will be doing if the person has not worked with you before. It is important that the healer communicate as much as possible in the patient's language. Be as simple as possible. If you discover the patient already understands a lot regarding the aura and healing, then talk at that level of understanding. Quickly determine the general level of understanding about healing and the aura to establish common ground for communication. This will set the patient at ease so you can begin work.

In a healing session, I usually work with the lower auric bodies first and then move on to the higher bodies. A brief outline of the healing sequence, given in Figure 22–1, may be useful as you follow the detailed description below.

## Figure 22–1
# HEALING SEQUENCE

1. General analysis of the patient's energy system
2. Alignment of the three energy systems to be used in the healing: that of the healer, patient and guides and the Universal Energy Field
3. Healing the lower four bodies (1st, 2nd, 3rd and 4th layers of the aura)
   A. Chelation: Charging and clearing the patient's aura
   B. Spine cleaning
   C. Cleansing specific areas of the patient's aura
4. Healing the etheric template (spiritual surgery) (5th layer of aura)
5. Healing the ketheric (7th layer of aura) template (restructuring)
   A. Ketheric template organ restructuring
   B. Ketheric template chakra restructuring
6. Healing of the celestial level (6th layer of aura)
7. Healing from the cosmic level (8th and 9th layers of aura)

## DETAILED HEALING SEQUENCE

### 1. General Analysis of Patient's Energy System

To begin a healing for the first time, I usually do a quick energetic body analysis to determine how the patient utilizes his energy system in general, noting the physical characteristics of the body to determine character structure. Once I can see that structure, I know I will probably be working a lot with the chakras that are habitually blocked. I simply have the person stand with his feet parallel and shoulder width apart. I then ask him to bend and unbend the knees while breathing in harmony with this movement. This reveals a lot about how the person directs and misdirects his energy, which ultimately causes the physical problem. For example, the energy will usually not be flowing

evenly up the legs; it is usually stronger on one side of the body than another; there are areas of the body that get more energy than others. All these imbalances are related to emotional and mental issues the person needs to meet and work through. For example, someone who is afraid to love will probably send more energy to the rear part of the body near the heart area (the will center), misdirecting energy that is needed to nourish the loving heart center.

After getting a good idea of how the person utilizes his system, I used to do a chakra analysis by dowsing with the pendulum. Now I simply psychially "read" the problem.

For the beginner, I suggest that you look at the structure of the physical body. Compare it to what you have learned about character structure. Which character structures are most predominant? What, then, will be the psychodynamics involved? Which chakras are most likely to be misfunctioning? Review the tables in Chapter 13. This information reveals a lot about the balance of reason, will and emotion and about the active and receptive principles in the personality. It also tells a lot about the way the person is functioning in each of the areas that each chakra represents psychodynamically. Look at the structure of the physical body. All this information can be used to guide the person to a deeper understanding of the self and how he functions from day to day.

I now ask the patient to remove his shoes and any jewelry (which may interfere with his normal lines of energy) and lie on my massage table on his back. (At this point you may wish to do a chakra reading with your pendulum as given in Chapter 10.) I usually get out my crystals if it feels appropriate for the patient. As mentioned in the last chapter, when I use crystals, I put a large rose quartz crystal in the left hand of the patient and a large clear quartz in the right hand. I use a large amethyst with iron deposits in it on the second or first chakras to keep the patient's field pulsating strongly and to keep the person grounded in the body. A fourth crystal is my scoop. It is a clear quartz crystal about one and a half inches wide by three and a half inches long. A larger one gets very heavy in the hand, and a smaller one cannot take as much energy out. This crystal has a very strong beam of white light coming out its tip that acts like a laser beam in cutting loose accumulated junk in the aura. I use it in the "cleansing" part of the healing.

## 2. Alignment of Energy System of Healer, Patient and Guides

It is very important before first making contact physically with the patient to align oneself with the ever present higher energies. To do this, I again bring my energy quickly up the chakras as described in exercise 22. I make an affirmation to align myself with the Christ and the universal forces of light. I pray, either silently or out loud. "I pray to be a channel for love, truth and healing in the name of the Christ and the universal forces of light." If you do not have a connection with the Christ, please use the connection that you do have to the Universal Wholeness, God, the Light, the Holy of Holies, etc. I then silence my mind by closing my eyes and taking long, low, deep breaths through the nose while rasping the air against the soft palate. I sit at the patient's feet and hold my thumbs on the solar plexus reflex point on the bottom of the feet. This point, as defined by the system of foot reflexology, is located on the bottom of the foot just below the ball of the foot. (See Figure 22–2.) I then focus on my patient to adjust the three energy systems involved: his, mine and the greater forces of light. This can be done by scanning up through the crown of the healer's body and then up through the body of the patient to his crown. After this is done, one may make a quick survey of the organs of the body through touching the reflex points on the feet and sensing the state of the energy of each. The most important ones usually turn out to be the major organs of the body and the spine.

The imbalanced points on the bottom of the foot will feel either too soft or too hard. The flesh of the foot may stay indented after you have pushed it with your finger tip, needing more resiliency. It may be too resilient and not indent at all. It may feel like a muscle spasm. Another way to describe the feeling you may pick up from imbalanced points in terms of energy flow is that they will feel as if a little fountain of energy is squirting out of them or a little vortex of energy is going into the skin at that point. The same is true for imbalanced acupuncture points. The acupuncture points look like little vortexes of energy or tiny chakras. An imbalanced acupuncture point will have energy squirting out of it, or it will feel like a tiny whirlpool that sucks energy in. You may want to run energy specifically into the points that need it.

### A. Channelling for Healing

As you progress through the healing sequence, you may add another dimension to the channelling used to receive information. In channelling for the healing itself, you allow the guides to utilize more of your energy field in two major ways. The first is simply to allow different levels or vibrations of light to be channelled through your field. Usually these colors and intensities are chosen by the guide. The person channelling simply keeps aligned with the white light or Christ light. A second way is to allow the guides to partially come into your field and do work on the patient's field through direct manipulation. In both case, allow your hands to be guided by the spiritual teacher. In the first case, the guidance and hand movements are general and may begin as soon as you put your hands on the patient's feet. In the second, they are both very intricate and very precise and are usually done on the higher levels of the field (5–7). Many times the guide will reach his hand through the healer's hand and beyond, going right into the body of the patient. This requires the utmost attention of the healer to what the guides are doing, so as not to interfere. For example on fifth auric level healing, if your just get tired of holding your hand or moving it in a certain way and you want to stop, you must make it very clear to the guide and give him time to adjust the healing to allow for such an energetic break. Drawing a hand away prematurely usually causes an energetic shock to the patient, who will usually jump. Then you have to go back and fix up the disruption you have caused. With experience you will become familiar with sequences of energetic phasing that allow pauses if necessary.

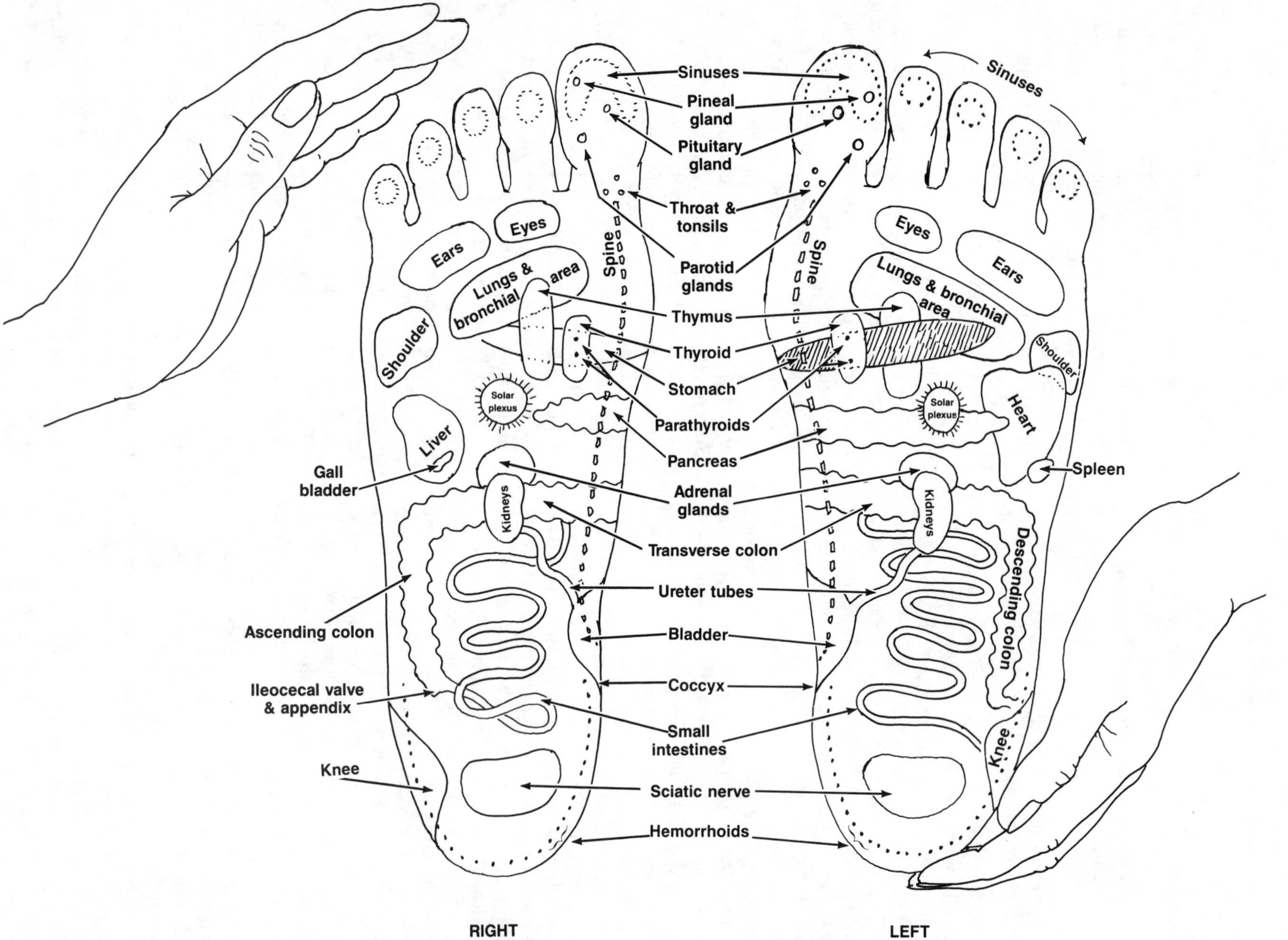

Figure 22-2: Main Points of Foot Reflexology

LEFT

RIGHT

Sinuses
Ears
Eyes
Shoulder
Heart
Spleen
Knee
Lungs & bronchial area
Solar plexus
Descending colon
Kidneys
Spine

Sinuses
Pineal gland
Pituitary gland
Throat & tonsils
Parotid glands
Thymus
Thyroid
Stomach
Parathyroids
Pancreas
Adrenal glands
Transverse colon
Ureter tubes
Bladder
Coccyx
Small intestines
Sciatic nerve
Hemorrhoids

Eyes
Ears
Shoulder
Liver
Lungs & bronchial area
Solar plexus
Kidneys
Spine

Gall bladder
Ascending colon
Ileocecal valve & appendix
Knee

### 3. Healing the Lower Four Auric Layers

#### A. *Chelation: Charging and Clearing the Patient's Aura*

To "chelate," derived from the Greek word *chele*, or "claw," means to claw out. Rev. Rosalyn Bruyere, who founded and developed this technique, adapted this word to mean simply to clear the field of the patient by removing auric debris. Chelation also fills the aura up with energy, as in blowing up a balloon, and generally balances it. This is done by running energy into the body in steps starting at the feet. It is best to run energy in the most natural way; that creates balance and health in the whole system. Energy is therefore run into the body from the feet up because energy is normally drawn up from the earth through the first chakra and the two chakras on the bottom of the feet. These earth energies are always needed in healing the physical body because they are of the lower physical vibrations. Thus you are pouring energy into a depleted system in the most natural way it goes. This way, the energy body takes in the energy and carries it to where it is needed. On the other hand, if you start at the area of complaint, the energy body may very well carry the energy to another location before it actually begins nourishing the area of entry. Since that is not a natural flow, it is not as efficient. Please see the chelation chart in Figure 22–3. Succeeding figures in this chapter will show how one person's aura changed through a complete healing.

When Mary first came to me, her auric field was clogged, dull and imbalanced (Figure 22–4). There were blocks shown as dark red and brownish colors at her knees, pelvic area, solar plexus and shoulders. She had disfiguration in the solar plexus chakra that looked as if the small vortex in the upper left section was protruding like a spring that had been sprung. This disfiguration extended through the fifth and seventh layers of the field. This configuration is associated with a hiatal hernia. Mary complained of pain in that area of her body and also had problems in her personal life in connecting deeply with people. The process of healing, which took place over a few weeks, not only rebalanced, charged and restructured her energy field, but also helped Mary to learn to connect to people better. This was done through channelling information about her childhood experiences in which she had learned to block her energy field habitually and thus eventually created her psychological and physical problem.

Let us now go over each step of the healing as if you are the healer.

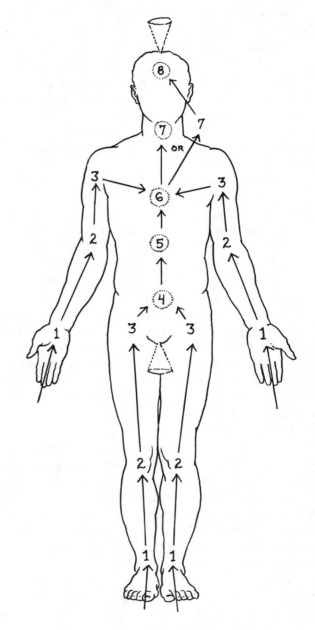

Figure 22–3: Chelation Chart

Sit with your hands on the feet of the patient (Mary) until the general field is cleared and balanced (Figure 22-5). Energy flowing from this position activates the whole field. Do not try to control the color you are channelling; allow it to flow automatically. If you focus on a color, you will probably interfere rather than help, because the fields are smarter than your linear mind.

As long as you clear your field so that your chakras are clear and can thus metabolize all colors from the Universal Energy Field, the field of the patient will simply absorb what it needs. If one of your chakras is blocked, then you will have difficulty channelling the color or frequency of light that is transmitted through that chakra. If this is the case, repeat the chakra opening exercise till all your chakras are open. Figure 22-6 shows the flow of energy into the healer's chakras through the healer's vertical power current into the heart chakra and then out through the healer's arms and hands into the patient's auric field.

As the energy is flowing, clearing, charging and generally rebalancing the energy field of the patient, you will probably feel it flowing through your hands. It is as if a fountain flows forth from them. It may feel warm or tingling to you. You may feel the pulsations which are slow and rhythmic. If you are sensitive in this way, you will sense the changes in this flow. Sometimes there will be more energy flowing up one side of the body. Then the frequency of pulsation will change, and so will either the direction of flow or the general location the energy is filling in the patient's energy field. At this point, the flow is into general auric body areas.

After several minutes work, the intensity of flow will diminish, and there will simply be an equal flow of energy up both sides of the body. This means that the overall field is generally balanced, and you are ready to move to the next position. Note that Mary's aura as shown in Figure 22-5 is already a lot clearer than her presenting aura shown in Figure 22-4.

Now, move around to the right side of the patient. With one hand always on the patient's body, to maintain the connection, put your right hand on the bottom of the patient's left foot and your left hand on the patient's left ankle. You will have to reach across the patient's body to do this (Figure 22-7). Allow energy to flow from your right hand to your left hand through the foot of your patient. First the flow of energy may be weak; then as the rivers of energy flow fill up, the flow of energy becomes strong. As the foot fills with energy, the flow between your hands will again decrease. Now move your hands to the right foot and ankle and repeat the same procedure. Fill it with energy the way you did the left foot. Now move your right hand to the left ankle of the patient and your left hand to her left knee. Run energy from your right hand through the patient's lower left leg and into your left hand. At first the flow may be weak and probably stronger on one side of the leg than the other. When the filling is complete, move to the right ankle/knee position (Figure 22-8). As you chelate between the ankle and knee, the dark clouds on the right thigh and hip clear, and the field there brightens. Then some of the darkness on the left side of the solar plexus begins to clear. Continue working up the legs, joint to joint, knee to hip, left side, right side (Figure 22-9). As you continue to work up the body, the patient's aura will continue to clear and she will enter into an altered state of consciousness. Move from the hip to the second chakra (Figure 22-10). Now the patient's field in the pelvic area clears, especially in the area between your hands. In this position your right hand is on the patient's hip and your left is in the center of the second chakra right above the pubic bone. Repeat on each side of the body. You will be aware of the changes clearing in the aura by the rising and falling of energy flow as you move from one place to the next. As you place your hands on a new place, the energy will first flow slowly until the connection between your field and the patient's is made. The flow will increase and peak, then slowly decrease, and either stop or continue at a very low rate. This means it is time to move. The energy flow will feel like tingling or heat waves. Always make sure you get an even flow of energy up both sides of any part of the body before moving on. This includes both sides of each leg as well as both sides of the body.

After the second chakra is thoroughly

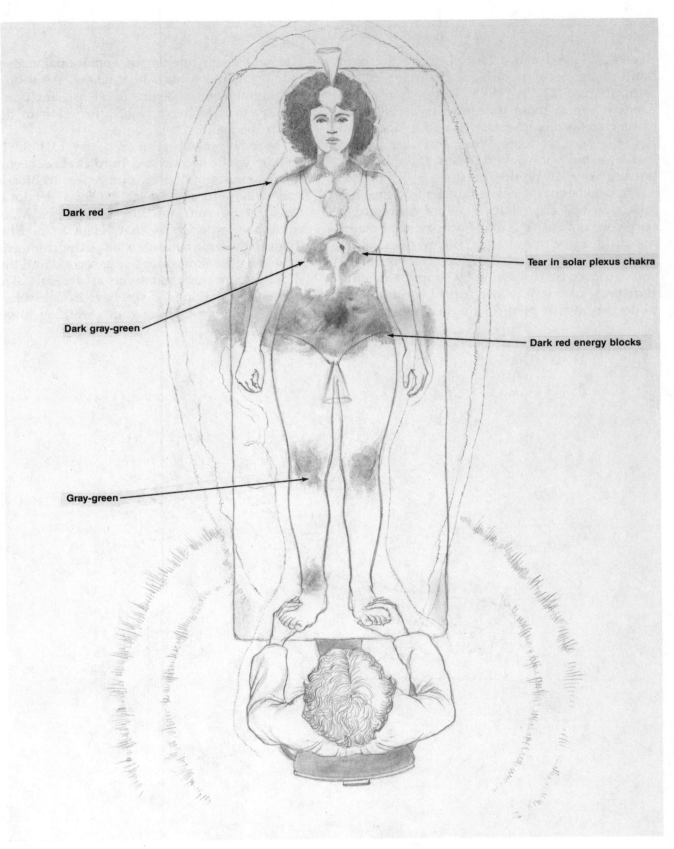

**Dark red**

**Tear in solar plexus chakra**

**Dark gray-green**

**Dark red energy blocks**

**Gray-green**

Figure 22–5: Balancing Right and Left Sides of the Body and Beginning To Run Energy into feet

207

cleared, charged and balanced, move the right hand to the second chakra and the left to the third (Figure 22–11). With Mary, you would need to spend more time on the second and third chakras because they are the ones that have the most blockage. When you have cleared this area, put your right hand on the third chakra and your left on the fourth.

As you begin to chelate directly into the chakras, you will enter into a deeper communion with your patient. You may find yourself breathing at the same rate she is. This means you are "mirrored." Once you have become mirrored, you can pace her breathing by simply changing your own; hers will follow. It may be important to do this at this point in the healing, because you will begin opening up emotional material when you move into the chakras. As soon as emotional material begins to release, the person will try to hold her breath in an effort to hold down the feelings.

Mary is now beginning to try to hold her feelings as the second and third chakras become more connected. You encourage her to breathe. She does; and she cries. She feels her loneliness. So do you. You may feel or see Mary's childhood experiences that relate to it. Share them with her. She understands the connection now and cries some more. Her second and third chakra open and clear more as a result of expressing her feelings. If you have trouble tolerating the feelings, change your breathing to stop

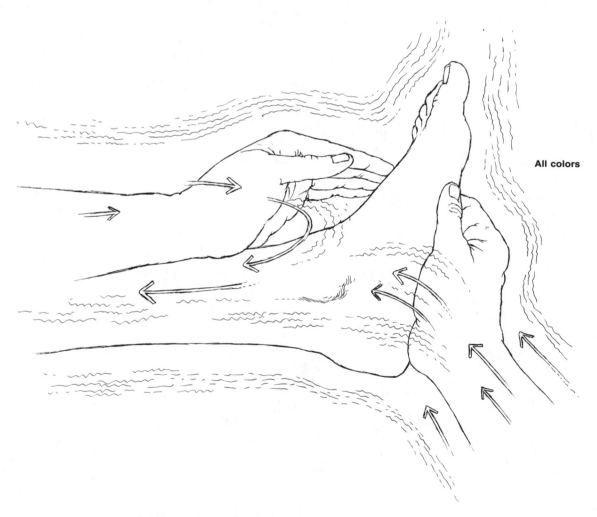

Figure 22–7: Energy Flow During Chelation of Auric Field

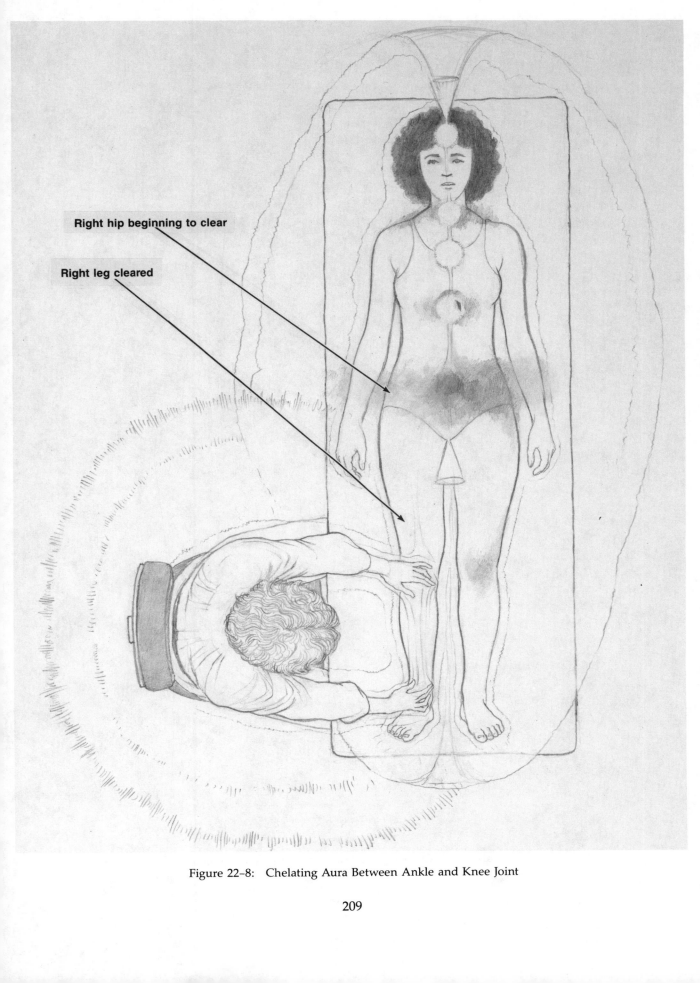

**Right hip beginning to clear**

**Right leg cleared**

Figure 22–8:   Chelating Aura Between Ankle and Knee Joint

209

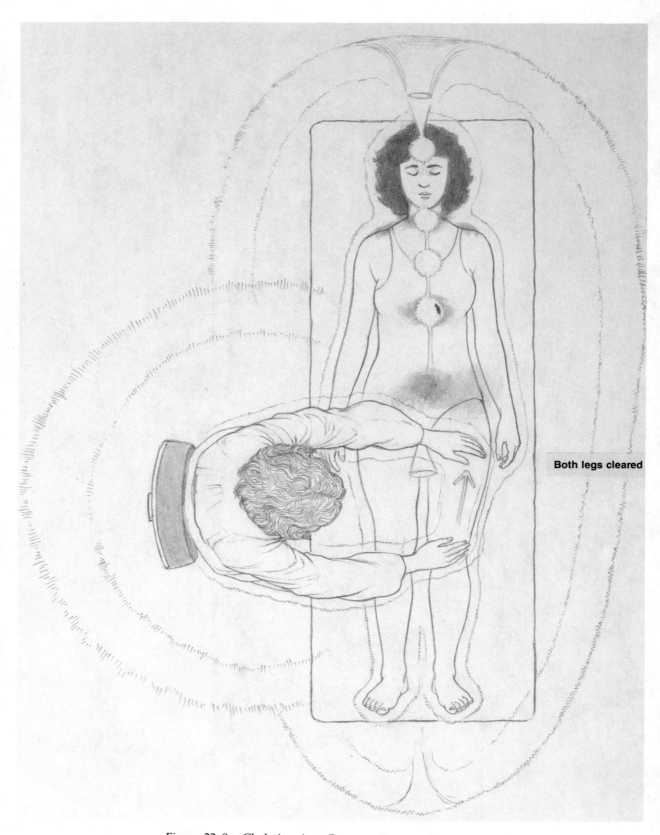

Both legs cleared

Figure 22–9: Chelating Aura Between Knee and Hip Joint

210

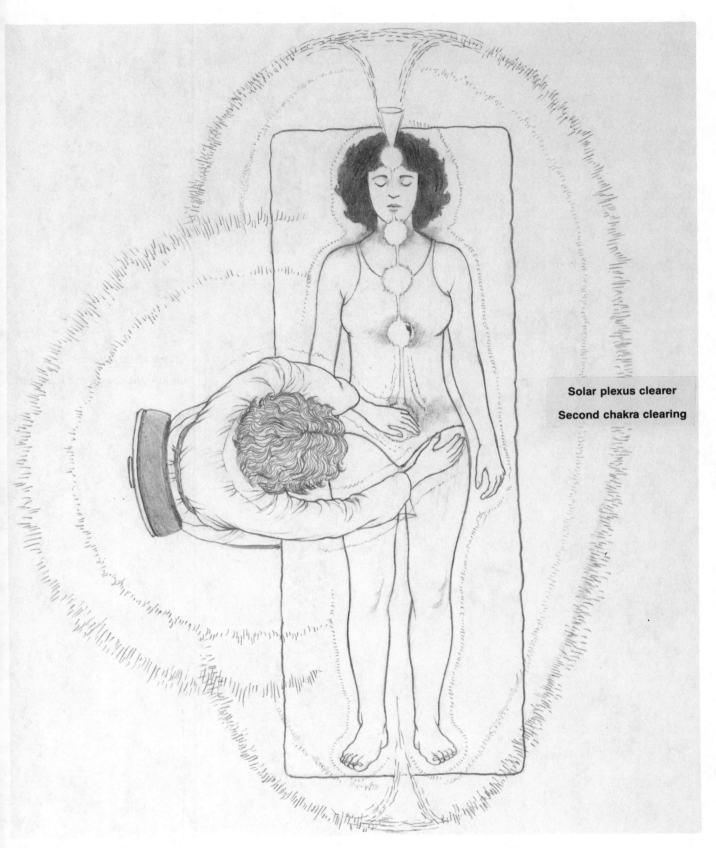

Solar plexus clearer

Second chakra clearing

Figure 22–10:   Chelating Aura Between Hip Joint and Second Chakra

211

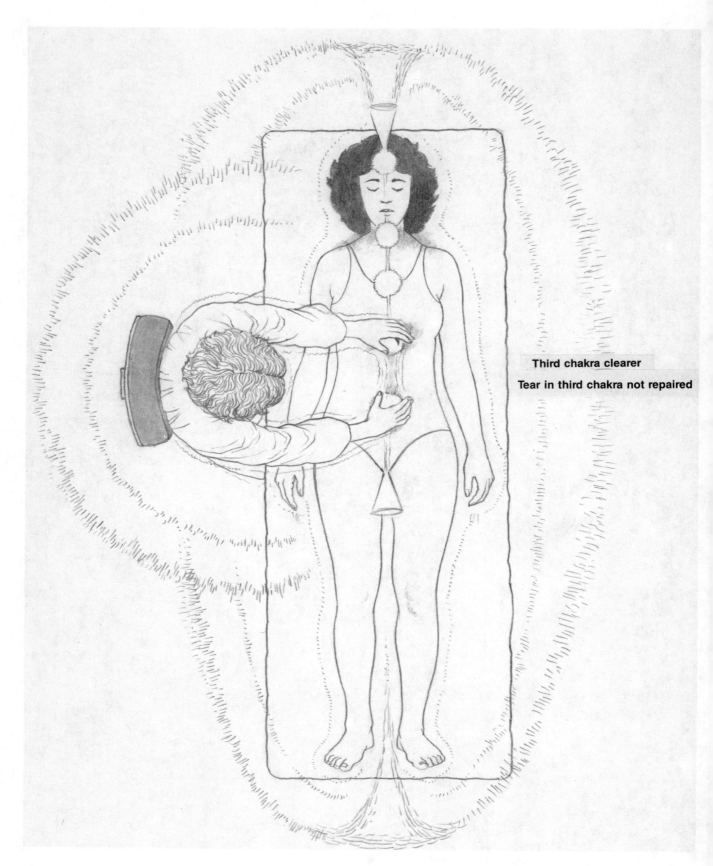

Third chakra clearer

Tear in third chakra not repaired

Figure 22–11:   Chelating Aura Between Second and Third Chakra

212

pacing and lift your consciousness to a higher lever. Continue to send energy. As Mary's chakras clear, she becomes calm and quiet. Figure 22–12 shows that the chelation has cleared the lower four levels of Mary's field, but it has not repaired the tear. The third chakra will need special attention on the fifth and seventh layers where the tear is. To chelate chakras four, five and six simply continue up the body, putting your left hand on the upper chakra and your right on the lower one. When you get to the fifth chakra, most patients are more comfortable if you put your left hand under the neck instead of on top of it. Then after that is finished, move each hand to each shoulder, as you slip your body into a sitting position above the head of your patient. Balance the right and left sides of Mary's energy field. Then slowly move your hands up the sides of the neck to the temples, running energy all the while. At this point, if you are a student, you will move to sixth level healing described under point six. Do sixth level healing and a closure on the seventh level as described under the heading Sealing Ketheric Template Level. In the beginning do not expect to do any more than this until you become more proficient in healing. At first, this will probably take you a good hour to complete. After many hours of practice, you will begin to perceive the upper layers of the auric field and will then begin to work on them as described under points four and five. Even later, you may perceive above the seventh layer and begin to work on the eight and ninth levels as described under points seven in the text that follows.

I ask all new students to do a complete chelation to ensure that they will not miss anything that needs to be cleared this way. Later, when they become more proficient in both running energy and perceiving the field, they will no longer need to chelate all the chakras. They will know how far up it is necessary to chelate. For heart patients it is important to reverse-chelate. That is, you draw energy away from the heart chakra, because usually it is clogged with dark energy.

At this point I will give a few more pointers about chelation. Remember, you are channelling, not radiating. This means that you raise your vibrations to the level of energy that is needed and then you simply connect yourself to the Universal Energy Field and let it flow (like putting an electrical plug into a wall socket). If you don't heal in this manner, you will get tired very fast. You cannot radiate or direct enough energy from inside your own field to heal; you must channel it. (Your job in channelling is only to raise your level of vibrations so that you can complete the circuit with the UEF.) To raise your vibrations to a higher energy level, the chakra opening exercises that you have done are very useful. By preparing for a healing ahead of time, you will start at a high energy and frequency level. Throughout the healing you will slowly rise to higher and higher levels simply because you are in a lifted state of consciousness. Most likely, the longer you stay in it, the higher you will be able to get, especially if you stay centered and focused with good breathing. The best type of breathing I use is taking long, continuous in- and outbreaths, with very little pause in the middle. Breathing is done through the nose, rasping the air against the soft palate, as in the exercises given in Chapter 18. You can also focus on expanding your auric field. The most important thing to do is to remain in a sensitive synchronic flow with the energy fields around you. A pause in energy flow may indicate that a higher frequency is about to come through. Wait a bit. If it doesn't come, then move on as stated earlier. As you become more attuned, you will begin to feel changes in frequency of the energy flowing through you. Eventually you will be able to hold certain frequency levels by adjusting your breath and focus.

Hold your hands, slightly tensed, firmly on the body; direct the energy that you are receiving with all your chakras through your hands and into the body. You may want to vibrate your body to get your chakras pumping more energy, using exercise 25 described in Chapter 21.

In this part of the healing, you are probably using the energy through your lower chakras more than through your upper chakras. A lot of energy also comes up from the earth through the bottom of the feet. Be sure to have your feet well planted on the floor. Visualize growing roots to the center of the earth and drawing en-

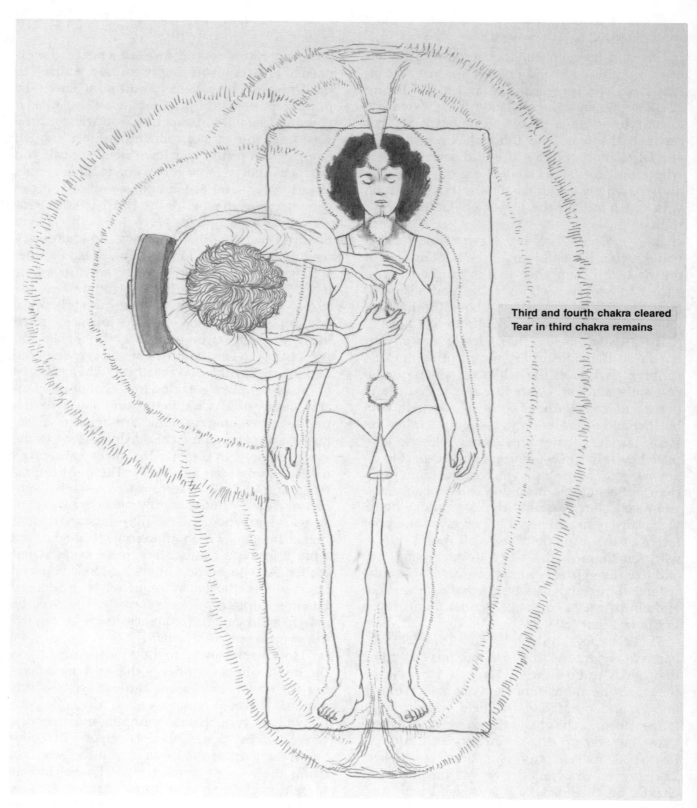

Third and fourth chakra cleared
Tear in third chakra remains

Figure 22-12:  Chelating Aura Between Third and Fourth Chakra

214

ergy up through those roots. This process nourishes and charges the lower energy bodies. Always make sure your body is in a comfortable position to ensure free flow of energy.

The patient's energy system will take the energy and automatically move it to the area in the body where it is needed. For example, although your hands may be at the feet, the energy could be going up the spine and into the back of the head. While the chelation is being done and to prepare the patient for more specific work, the healer can use this vital time to read the patient psychically and communicate with the patient. This is the time the patient starts opening up and sharing personal history more deeply. A greater mutual trust occurs as soon as the healer puts her hands on the patient. The healer will also continue to scan the body for problem areas.

In Mary's case, her aura has cleared and is much lighter, as can be seen in Figure 22–12. During the chelation of the second, third and fourth chakra area, her emotional release has brought her into a deeply relaxed state. The first four levels of her field are clear enough to support fifth and seventh layer work. Another patient might not be, even after a full chelation through the sixth chakra, and might still need to have his field cleared more in specific locations of heavy disturbance. There are two major ways of such clearing. One is a spine cleaning. The other is either to push or scoop auric waste out of specific areas.

### B. Spine Cleaning

At this point the patient may need a spine cleaning. (See Figure 22–13.) It is, in general, a good thing to do since it cleans the main vertical power current in the auric field. However, given a one hour session, most times I do not do it unless there is a spinal problem because other things are usually more important and a normal spine will clear during chelation. Part of this technique was taught to me by my teacher C.B.

To do a spine cleaning, ask the patient to roll over onto the front of his body. Be sure you have a table with a face plate or nose hole so that the patient can look straight down. He should not have his head turned to the side for this work.

Massage the area of the sacrum. Using the thumbs, massage the foramens (small holes in the bone through which nerves pass) in the sacrum. (That is the area above the gluteus maximus where the dimples are.) Look up the sacrum in an anatomy book if you don't know what this part of the body looks like. It is a triangle-shaped set of fused bones with the tip pointed downward that has five foramens along each side of the triangle. The last lumbar vertebra sits upon it, and the tailbone extends downward from its lower tip. Make small circles with your thumbs in the area of the foramens of the sacrum. You will be sending red-orange energy through your thumbs. Work in this way all the way up the spine, from the right side of the patient's body, using your thumbs on each side of each vertebra. Circling clockwise with the right thumb and counterclockwise with the left usually works best.

Now cup your hands together over the second chakra. Channel red-orange energy from your hands into the chakra while making a slow clockwise movement with your hands. To do this you must be able to hold your energy flow at the red-orange frequency. This technique is taught in Chapter 23 on healing with color. Charge the chakra. When it is charged, begin to move your hands up the spine. Let the light turn to a blue laser-like beam as your hands leave the second chakra. Be sure you do not "drop" the energetic connection as you move up the spine. You will have to position your body in a way so that you can move comfortably along with your hands as they move up the spine.

With your blue laser light, you are cleaning the spine and pushing all the clogged energy out the top of the head through the crown chakra. Repeat the whole sequence at least three times and until the main power current is cleaned. You may want to lightly tap the fourth and fifth chakras to help them open.

### C. Cleansing Specific Areas of the Patient's Aura

During the chelation you will begin to sense through High Sense Perception where you will work next on the physical body. As you become

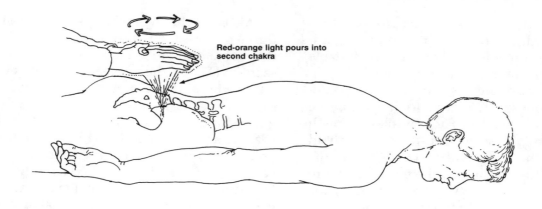

Red-orange light pours into second chakra

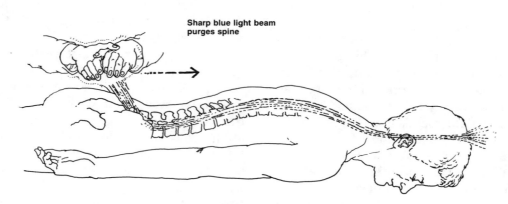

Sharp blue light beam purges spine

Figure 22–13:   Spine Cleaning    (Diagnostic View)

more advanced, you probably won't need to chelate through all the chakras before you start working more directly on an area of clogged energy. After a lot of practice you should at least chelate up through the heart before concentrating on one area. (Allow yourself to be led intuitively.) More direct work is done by running energy into a clogged aura to energize it and knock the stagnated energy loose and/or by directly pulling the clogged auric mucus out with the hands.

To run energy directly into a specific area, you can use your hands either apart or together. With your hands on either side of the block (front to back on bottom to top of the body), you

can direct the energy to move out of one area and into another by pushing with your right hand and pulling with the left (or vice versa). (See Chapter 7 for push/pull/stop techniques.) At times, this is right to do; at other times, you will feel it more appropriate to use both hands together. Either technique directs the energy directly into a block and cuts deep into the aura. Each also floods new energy deep into the aura and is a good method to fill the chakras. Figure 22–14 illustrates both hand positions. For the closed hand method, cup hands together with crossed thumbs and palms facing downward over the area into which you are directing the energy. Make sure your hands come together

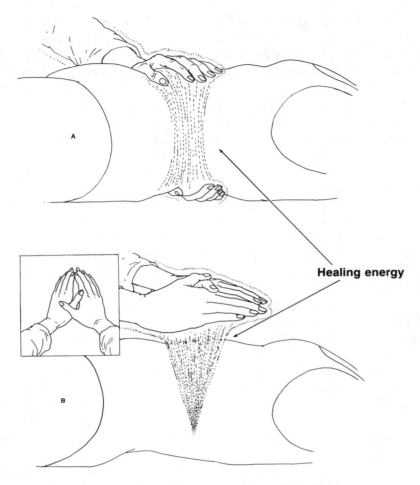

**Healing energy**

Figure 22–14:   Running Energy Deep into Auric Field

solidly, leaving no space between them or between your fingers. Fingers should be slightly cupped. Vibrate your hands to increase energy flow.

You will find that by doing this you can direct energy like a beam of light deep into the body. It can fill, or it can knock things loose. The guides will direct you as to what is needed and run the appropriate energy through. If they are using this technique to knock blocks loose, then they will shortly change the frequency that they are sending through and probably reverse the energy flow and suck the block out. Simply allow your hands to move as needed to accommodate the outward pull. You may want to lift your hand with the dead orgone energy and allow the guides to lift it off your hand.

Another technique is to use your etheric hands to pull the blocked energy out of the patient's field. To pull this energy out, imagine that your etheric fingers appear to get very long, or the etheric parts of the fingers grow long and penetrate the body of the patient and simply scoop up the energy like a shovel or rake it together to be scooped up. You simply pull it up and out of the aura and hold it in your hand while the guides enlighten it, i.e., energize it until it turns into white light, and let it go (that way you don't get your room full of dead energy). Then you, as healer go in for the next handful.

When appropriate, you can also pull clogged energy out with the use of a crystal scoop, which catches the energy and pulls it out (see

Chapter 24). A crystal is a very powerful tool in this kind of work, as it acts like a laser beam: it goes in, cuts and collects the energy, which you then pull out and let the guides turn to white light.

It is not always good to use crystals. Some people are just too sensitive for this kind of cutting action. Never use crystals after the ketheric template work (a higher level work to be explained later) is done. Using them then could just tear out the template work. The patient should not need crystal work after the template work; it should have all been done beforehand (that is, on any given area of the body). In Mary's case described earlier, no crystals were used.

While this work is being done, the healer can scan the auric layers to see if the chakras or organs need restructuring on the template levels. The guides will choose whether to work on the etheric template level (fifth) or the ketheric template level (seventh). The template work can only be done after a good deal of cleaning on the first four layers of the aura has been completed. In fact, if the aura is very dirty, sometimes it is hard to see the etheric template level through the dark energy.

If the guides decide to do ketheric template work (seventh layer), the healer must take the crystals away from the patient because the crystals help hold the patient in his body. For the ketheric template work, it is necessary for the patient to partially leave the body; otherwise the patient may experience a great deal of pain and the work could not be done. I tried to sew up a small tear in the seventh layer once without removing the crystals from the patient's body. The patient began to scream in pain after about two seconds work (my hands were not touching the body). I quickly removed the crystals, finished the sewing and healed the large red inflammation I caused on levels 1, 2, 3 and 4 by the clearing techniques described above.

If the guides decide to do etheric template work (fifth layer) at this point in the healing, it is not necessary to remove the crystals. I believe that this is because the etheric template works in negative space and is not connected to the body in a "feeling" way.

### D. Exercise to Let the Guides Come into Your Field to Work

If you are having trouble letting the guides come into your field, I suggest the following exercise. (This exercise can also be done before the healing starts if you wish.) It is only to be done after you have charged your field with exercise 22 (visualization) in Chapter 21.

Now that your field is charged and balanced, repeat the above exercise and change it slightly to help facilitate the entrance of the guides into your field for healing.

If you have your hands on someone, gently remove them before doing this. Go back to your own first chakra. See it spinning red. Breathe the color twice. On the second inbreath, raise your consciousness to the second chakra and allow the red to turn to red-orange. Breathe out red-orange.

Focus on the second chakra. Breathe in red-orange. Breathe it out. Breathe in red-orange again and let it turn to yellow while raising your mind's eye to the third chakra. Breathe in yellow. Breathe it out. Breathe in yellow and let it turn to green as you move up to the heart chakra. Breathe in green; breathe it out. Breathe in green; lift yourself to the throat chakra; let the green become blue. Breathe in blue; breathe it out. Breathe in blue and lift yourself to the third eye as the blue turns to indigo. Breathe in violet; breathe it out. Breathe in indigo and let it go to white as you lift yourself to your crown and out the top of your head. As you lift through the crown, allow the guides to come into your field through the rear aspect of the throat chakra. You will feel them come around over your shoulders and down into your arms, like an overlay.

You may feel your field become much fuller. At this point, you may be able to see a guide's arms interpenetrating yours and the light streaming from them. Relax. Get used to the feeling. If you feel the urge to put your hands on an area of your body, do so. (Later, help a friend. Allow your hands to be guided to a place on a friend's body that needs healing. It may not be where you think.) Let the beautiful healing energy stream forth from your hands in love. Never be afraid to put your hands on another with love.

## 4. Healing the Etheric Template Level of the Aura (Fifth Layer of Auric Field)

If the guides decide to do etheric template work, the healer will be signaled simply to lay hands on the body in two places, usually over two chakras, and to allow the hands to rest there. From this point on, the guides control everything that goes on, and the healer is largely passive.

As I progressed in the etheric template healing work, I began to witness whole operations taking place. At first, I found this hard to believe because they appeared to be so similar to an operation on the physical level performed by surgeons in the operating room of a hospital. I also, of course, thought I was projecting the whole thing. I asked two friends of mine who are very clairvoyant to come and sit in on some healings to see if our experiences correlated. They did.

This is what we regularly saw: As I allowed my hands to passively rest upon the patient's body, my etheric hands would detach themselves from my physical hands and sink deep into the patient's body. Then the hands of the guides who do etheric template work (whom I call the surgeons) would reach through my etheric hands and literally perform an operation. When they did that, the size of my etheric hands would expand greatly.

To do an operation, the guides would stick tubes through my arms, down through my hands and into the body of the patient. Apparently, they use all the same equipment that a normal surgeon does—scalpels, clamps, scissors, needles, syringes, etc. They cut, scrape things away, cut things out, do transplants and sew things back up again. At one point, I saw a large syringe float down my arm and into the body of a patient whose spinal nerves were being rejuvenated and sewn back together. I looked up at my friend and asked, "Did you see that?" She said, "Yes," and went on to describe the same scene I was witnessing. Since then, we have done many healings together, always correlating what we see.

All this work is done on the fifth level of the auric field. This layer appears to exist in negative space, as was described in Chapter 7. To me through my High Sense Perception negative space is similar to a negative of a photograph where all the dark areas are light, and all the light areas look dark. In negative space, all the areas that we expect to be empty are filled, and all those that we expect to be filled appear to be empty. On this level, all of what would be empty space looks dark cobalt blue, and all the auric lines appear to be empty spaces within that cobalt blue field. Once one has entered into that level of reality, it seems perfectly normal.

The fifth level is the template for all form that exists on the physical plane. If a form is disrupted in the auric field, it will have to be reestablished on the fifth level of the field for it to regain its healthy form on the physical plane. Thus all auric surgery must be done on the fifth layer of the field. Etheric surgery, then, is essentially the task of creating a new negative space for the etheric body of the patient to grow into and become well.

During this type of operation, which I have called spiritual surgery, the healer cannot under any circumstances move her hands. In fact, most of the time the hands are so paralyzed it would be fairly hard to do anyway. Whenever I have tried, it was a great effort. It takes a lot of patience to simply sit there, sometimes for 45 minutes, while the guides do their work.

After the guides are finished, they will sterilize their work and begin slowly closing up the incision. The etheric hands of the healer slowly begin to surface and merge with the healer's physical hands. Again, this takes patience. (Sometimes I get bored.) Finally, the hand on the lower part of the patient's body (usually my right hand) comes loose, and the guides usually direct me to bring it up the body to the left hand. I then slowly remove the left hand and then, step by step, with delicate hand and finger movements I reconnect the newly restructured area of the etheric template with the template of the part of the body around it. This is done by slowly moving the hand up through the chakras. The healer's hands do not move away from the body until the incision is closed and the new and old fields are reconnected.

Let us return to the patient, Mary. For the last parts of the chelation, Mary has been lying on the healing table in a serene relaxed state.

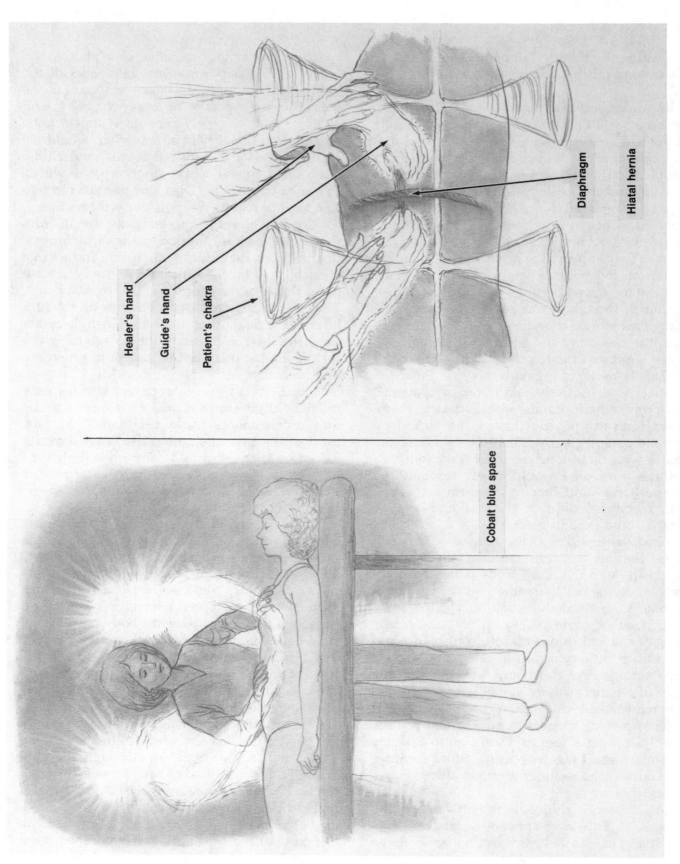

Healer's hand

Guide's hand

Patient's chakra

Diaphragm

Hiatal hernia

Cobalt blue space

Figure 22-15: Etheric Template Healing: Spiritual Surgery

220

She has drifted a bit out of her body and is resting. The auric field is continuing to utilize the energy it has received to heal itself. Mary is ready for etheric template work on her hiatal hernia. As you place your hands upon the third and fourth chakra (Figure 22–15), your etheric hands begin to float downward and you begin to become more aware of the inside of the body through whatever your best way of accessing is. You feel, hear or see it. You are sitting in negative space, but it feels completely normal. Your energy field around your body expands as your vibrational rate increases. You sense a presence behind you, maybe even more than one. Gently, ever so gently, the guides slip through your auric field. It feels very familiar, very comfortable, and most of all, it feels wonderful. You have been lifted to a state of angelic serenity. You are at peace with the universe. As you sit in surrender to your own higher creative power, you observe the guide's hands slipping into the body of your patient through your etheric hands. You watch them sewing up the hernia in the diaphragm. At first you are incredulous, but then it all seems so natural that you simply allow it to happen. What is important here is that the patient gets well. You trust in knowledge that goes beyond your normal, narrow self-definitions and allows the healing to take place. The guides repair the tear and reconnect the new restructured template with the rest of the fifth layer template. Then you feel them beginning to withdraw their energy. You will be surprised how deep your etheric hands were into the field of the patient. You didn't notice it so much going in, but now as the energy field begins to pull out, you will feel it moving outward. The patient may notice it too at this point. Next, you will feel yourself gaining more control over your right hand. Its connection to your patient's aura loosens, and you begin to slowly withdraw it. When it is fully withdrawn, flex your fingers a bit to exercise the hand. Now with your right hand sink into the fourth chakra and loosen the left hand. Slowly, gently remove the left hand. You are ready to move to seventh layer work. But first, a few more tips on etheric template healing.

During etheric template surgery, the guides control the color frequencies, direction of flow and location of the work. The more you trust and follow, the more they will be able to do. In addition to "normal" surgical procedures, they sometimes direct you, the healer, to hold both hands and arms across the body very still and ask you to raise yourself to higher vibrations and allow the strong force of lavender and even sometimes silver to come through. You must not move under this circumstance as the flow is very strong and will disrupt not only your patient's field, but yours as well. After sufficient energy has been poured through to knock the configuration loose, the guides then reverse the energy flow and suck the loosened energy back up and out. This is a higher level of healing and probably uses sixth level energies. It removes specific etheric template forms from the field, like the psychic forms of viruses, bacteria or, in one case, white seedlike objects from the blood of a leukemia patient so that they cannot regenerate themselves in the person's physical body.

From time to time, a small group of us who have developed High Sense Perception meet to give mutual support to each other in regard to our personal lives and dealing with all the issues that arise in our lives from being clairvoyant, clairaudient or clairsentient. We also do exchange healings with each other (we each become the patient). This work is very productive because not only do the healers see what is going on, but so does the patient. This work has verified many of my perceptions and also helps create a clear framework with which to describe these experiences. We are learning how to look into each layer of the aura, what that experience is like and what new healing procedures can come from the information we receive.

### 5. Healing the Ketheric Template or Restructuring the Golden Auric Grid (Seventh Layer of Auric Field)

Many times when the auric field is disfigured on the fifth level, it is disfigured on the seventh level as well. So ketheric template restructuring needs to be done. It is usually done before the healer concentrates on the sixth level healing, although, by this time in the healing some sixth level frequencies have automatically come through. Seventh level work is very different from fifth level work in that the healer is very active. In the fifth level the healer's main task is surrender and following. Here the challenge to the healer is to be very active in breathing and in finger and hand movement, yet still remain highly sensitized and focused at a high frequency level. It takes a great deal of mind focus and breath control to reach the seventh level. The golden light at this level is very strong and resilient. Many times it appears to be tiny golden threads that are extremely strong.

The guides of the patient always come to healings and assist. If you are alert, you will see them walk into the healing room with the patient. At this point in the healing they usually pull the patient out of his body and care for him so that a deep relaxation can take place and allow for the template work to be done. Usually the patient's experience is that of floating in a peaceful state. He usually is not aware of how deeply he has moved into an altered state of consciousness until he gets up or tries to stand up at the end of the healing.

Ketheric template work, which restructures the seventh layer with golden light, consists of two major parts: cleaning and restructuring the grid structure of the organs, muscles, nerves or other parts of the body and cleaning and restructuring the chakras. The guide's hands work directly through the healer's hands in an overlay manner. The guides come down over the shoulders and into the hands and arms of the healer. Tiny golden threads come out of the fingers of the healer, which move very rapidly as guided. The golden threads move much more rapidly than the healer's intricate rapid finger movements. To restructure the ketheric grid of an organ, the guides usually remove the grid structure of the organ from the body. This can happen only if the consciousness of the patient allows it. I am referring to the deeper consciousness, not the conscious awareness. At these moments, the patient is in an altered state, communicating with his guides, which he may

or may not remember when returning to the body.

### A. Ketheric Template Organ Restructuring

The hands of the healer will move with tremendous light-force and a strong burst of energy to remove the ketheric field of the organ. The organ then floats above the body where it is cleaned and restructured by more rapid finger movements, which are weaving the blue etheric grid onto the golden template with white-gold threads. The space inside the body is cleansed and sterilized with light before the organ is replaced. When the restructuring and sterilizing is completed, the organ simply slips back into the body. It feels almost as if it were sucked back in. It is then sewn back into place and filled with blue light to energize it. The area is then usually filled with a cottony, soothing white light that acts as an internal anesthetic. Then the whole area is usually covered with a golden energy bandage for protection.

Examples of such a healing are shown in the Figures 22–16 and 22–17. I received a phone call from a client who had a lump in her breast. Her doctors could not tell if it was an infection or a tumor. They had tried to aspirate it, but could not, and therefore had scheduled surgery. As I was speaking on the phone with her, I immediately got a picture in my mind of a dark red lump in her left breast with dark gray spots extending up under her armpit where her lymph nodes would be. To check my "seeing," I asked her if the lump was located in the left breast slightly below and to the left of the nipple. With that affirmed, I went on to tell her that I was quite sure it was not cancer and was some sort of infection like mastitis. I could tell this because of the color of dark red, which indicates infection. I also heard the guides telling me that it was a form of mastitis. However, I also saw that the axillary lymph nodes were very dark gray. This disturbed me. I told her that the primary problem was not the lump in the breast, but the clogged lymph nodes, and that she needed to do some cleansing of her whole body and this particular system. In surgery a few days later, the doctors removed the infected mammary

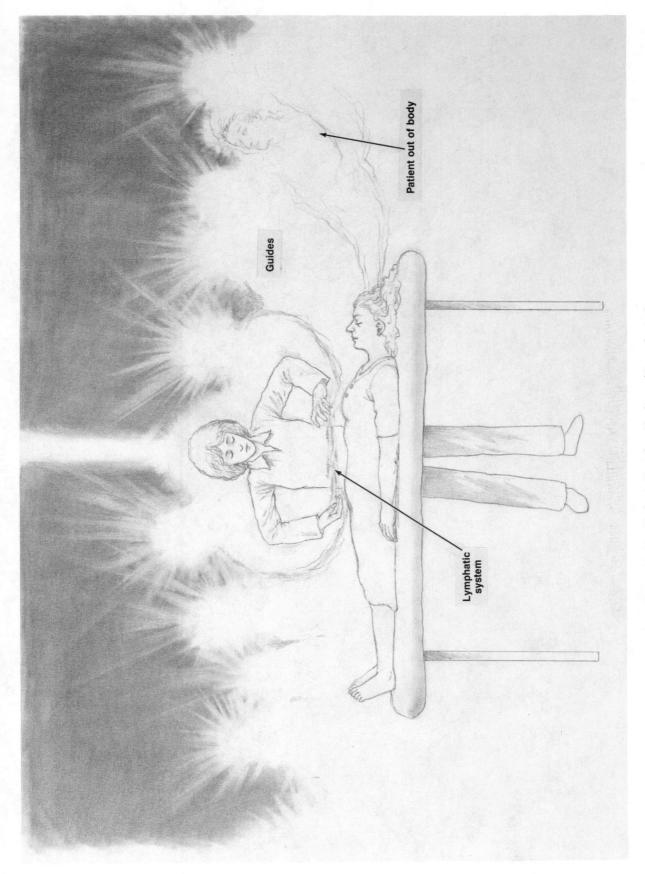

223

Figure 22–16: Ketheric Template Healing of Lymphatic System

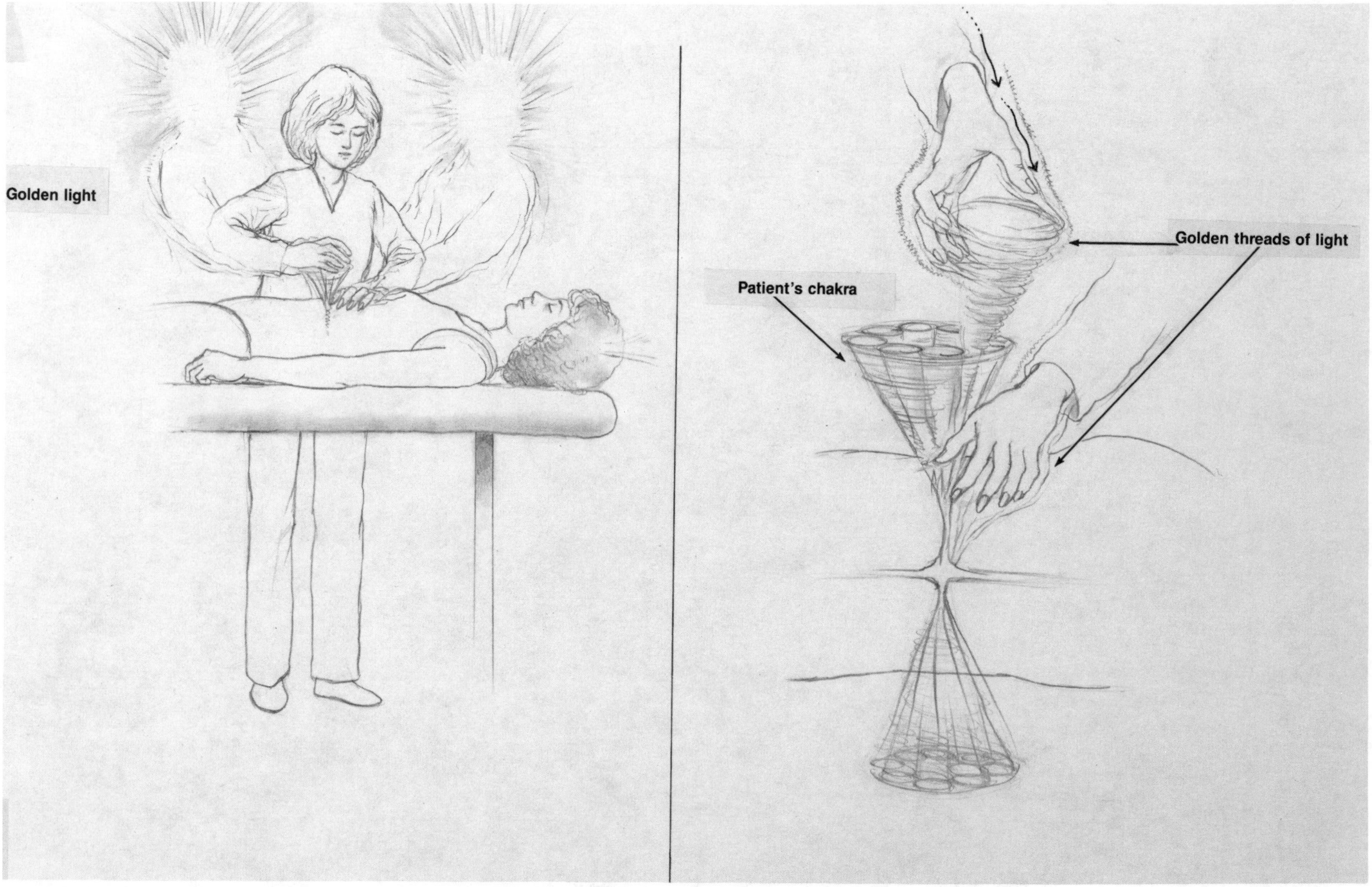

Golden threads of light

Patient's chakra

Golden light

Figure 22-17: Ketheric Template Healing: Spiritual Surgery

224

glands and diagnosed her as having mastitis infection due to clogged-up lymph nodes.

When she came in for a healing about three days after the operation, her system looked very clogged. She had massive clogging of the lymphatic system all over her body, which showed up in dark green areas on either side of her sternum and on the left side of her abdomen. Her whole field was slightly gray. The red area on the left breast had mostly cleared, leaving only the scar showing as a bright red streak in the aura, with fainter red around it left from the operation. After the normal chelation and cleaning work had been done on the lower bodies, the guides removed her entire lymphatic system and cleaned it off before replacing it in the manner described earlier (Figure 22–16). Her whole torso was recharged and shielded with first blue light and then gold light, leaving the lymphatic system (on the seventh layer) looking very clear and golden. The red streak had disappeared. Note that Figure 22–16 shows the guides working through the healer cleaning the lymphatic system, with the patient's guides at her head holding her out of her body while the template work is done.

*B. Ketheric Template Chakra Restructuring*

A similar sequence happens in the chakra structuring, but the chakras are never removed. There are several major ways that chakras become damaged. They can be torn open, the screen over them may be damaged, a vortex can be clogged and slowed in its spinning motion, the point of the chakra may not be seated correctly into the heart or root area of the chakra or a vortex may be sticking out or flopping over and look like a spring that has sprung. The whole chakra can be almost gone, or a small part of it can be affected. For example, in the case of Mary with her hiatal hernia, one of the small vortexes of the solar plexus looked typically like a sprung spring. To heal this, you need to push it back in and sew it down, restructure the protective screen and give it a protective cover in order to allow it to heal over a period of

time. All this is done with the guides directing your hands and healing light. Your hands will move automatically.

Let us return to the patient Mary, who is now lifted out of her body, in an altered state, and in the care of her spiritual teachers. Since you have finished the fifth level healing and can perceive the tear on the seventh layer, you know it is time to move your consciousness up to the seventh level to work. You begin by increasing your nasal rasping breath rate. As your breathing rate increases, you focus your mind as much as you can on lifting your consciousness. Don't worry about hyperventilation; you will be using all the energy you pull in for healing. As you lift up into the seventh layer, you begin to experience Divine Mind, where all that is is understood to be perfection. Soon gold light begins to pour out of your hands, as the guides reconnect through your seventh layer (Figure 22–17). Your hands move almost involuntarily over Mary's third chakra. You begin to see the gold light threads sewing the small vortex in Mary's chakra. Your fingers are moving as rapidly as possible; the golden threads move thousands of times faster. The golden light forces the disfigured vortex to return to its normal position. You don't believe how much energy is flowing through you. You wonder if your body can tolerate it. You continue breathing as the protective shield is restructured. You may wonder if Mary is noticing all this and wants to know what is going on, but you can't talk. There is too much to do to keep all of your being focused. Finally the work is completed, and the chakra is normal. Your breathing is slowing down. You are glad it is over. Your hand may hurt, but you feel wonderful.

Very swiftly, you chelate lightly through the upper chakras and take a position at the head of the massage table. Put your hands on each side of Mary's head, gently run energy into her temples to balance any remaining right/left imbalance. Now that the fifth and seventh layers are restructured and can hold the auric form, it is time to recharge it on the sixth level, with celestial love.

### 6. Healing on the Celestial Level (Sixth Layer of Auric Field)

To heal on the sixth layer of the auric field, you will be working primarily through your heart, third eye and crown chakras. Cup your hands over the patient's third eye with fingers together and thumbs crossed over each other; raise your vibrations to reach up for the light and then let it flow down through and in front of you into the central brain area of your patient (Figure 22–18). Psychically reach for the highest spiritual reality you know by first connecting through the heart with universal love and then reaching up with that consciousness for the light. It is very important to go through the heart and wait till you enter into a state of universal love before going up through the crown, otherwise the healing can become very mental. It must be accompanied by deeply loving every particle of being of the patient, Mary. Being connected to the Messianic consciousness or universal love entails holding someone in your heart and entering into a state of total acceptance and positive will for her well-being and continued existence. It is a celebration in love of the existence of the person. This means that you must enter into this state of being, not just imagine it. Maintaining this state, reach for the light and the highest, broadest spiritual reality you can experience.

To raise your vibrations, you use both the active and the receptive principles. First, strive simply to increase the frequency of your vibrations. This is done through breathing, rasping air across the back of the throat, through meditative focus and by reaching up with the mind's eye into the light. Subjectively, it feels as if you look up into the light and reach for it. You feel lighter and less attached to your body as you go up. It feels like a part of your consciousness literally goes up the spine and stretches up from your body and into the white light. Your feelings become more and more pleasurable as you enter into the light. You feel more and more universal safety and love surrounding you and interpenetrating you. Your mind expands and you can understand broad concepts that you cannot understand in a normal state. You can accept a greater reality, and it is easier for the guides to get concepts through to you because you are not so prejudiced about the nature of the world; i.e., you have removed some of the blocks from your brain. Each step higher into the light releases you more. As you practice through the years, you are able to channel higher and higher energies and concepts.

Now that you have accomplished a certain degree of liftedness, stop reaching and allow the white light to permeate your auric field, which has been raised to a vibration in harmony with the white light. It will flow down through your field into that of the patient.

After the white light flows down into the central brain area of the patient and that area's vibrations are raised to that frequency, go up to the next level of vibration. When the patient has reached that level, move up to the next, and in this step-by-step fashion, the central brain area of the patient lights up. The patient's aura fills with white-gold light that is infused with opalescent colors. The patient sometimes sees spiritual images during this phase of the healing or "falls asleep." (To me, this simply means she does not yet have the capacity to retain the memory of that experience when coming back to a normal state of reality. Some day she will, and this process helps develop it.)

Because this way of channelling is so strong, you must lightly flick your hands to break the connection to the sixth chakra before moving on to the next step in the healing process. After lighting up the thalamus area of the brain and filling the aura with white light, if there is time, I generally do some work directly on the outer levels of the aura. With palms up, tracing paths with my fingers, I usually comb out the light rays of the celestial body. This motion is similar to running your fingers through hair as you pull it away from the head. You begin with your hands near the skin and move outward perpendicular to the body, as if you are lifting the aura up. This gives the patient a light feeling and enhances the celestial body by adding light to it and broadening it. If you have time, try it. Mary will enjoy it.

Figure 22-18: Celestial Level Healing (Sixth Layer)

## 7. Sealing Ketheric Template Level

After the celestial level is brightened and broadened, I then move to the ketheric, the eggshell form that seems to protect the aura. I smooth, straighten and strengthen this form by moving my hands over its outer edge. It may be too narrow around the feet, too broad in places, have lumps or restrictive bands in it. (Some of these bands are related to past lives and will be discussed in Chapter 24). It may be thin in places and even have breaks or holes in it. These need to be repaired, and the whole form needs to regain the shape of an egg with a nice, firm shell. I do these things through simple manipulation. If something is a lump, I smooth it out. If it needs light, I run energy into it until it lights up. If it needs to be strengthened, I run strengthening energy into it. The outer levels of the aura move and are manipulated very easily, so this part of the healing takes a very short time.

To complete the healing on the seventh level of the aura, I reach out over the patient's head and bring my hands together. My hands are about two and a half feet above the head in the eggshell shield of the aura. I then make a large sweeping motion around the entire body of the patient. My left hand moves around to the left, and my right hand moves around to the right. Energy flows in an arc from my hands that reach from above the head to below the feet of the patient, enhancing the entire seventh level of the aura. As I slowly move my hands to circumscribe a circle of golden light around the chest of the patient, the entire eggshell level of the aura is strengthened.

To strengthen Mary's seventh layer and put her in a protective shield to allow the healing to continue to work in her aura, lift your hands above her body. You are still sitting in a position above her head as shown in Figure 22–19. The height of the seventh layer varies between two and one half to three feet above the body. If you can't see it, sensitively feel with your hands in the space above Mary. You will feel a very subtle pressure as you move into the seventh layer. Hold your hands, thumbs together, palms down at the outer edge of Mary's auric field. You will need your rasping breath to hold your energy

level and your consciousness at the seventh layer. Now run golden light out of your hands creating an arc from the head to the feet in Mary's seventh layer. Hold the arc steady and slowly widen it by moving your hands apart to encircle the body. Your right hand moves to the right and your left arcs to the left. Complete the circle all around so that you have traced a whole egg shell around Mary.

When this is completed, I break the connection between my field and that of the patient's with a soft brisk shake of the hands and move to the right side of the patient. I now reconnect with the seventh layer from the outside. (When I was doing the healing before this, I was connected into the energy system. Now I have broken away and am no longer part of that flow.) Gently placing my hands on the outside of the eggshell seventh layer, I silently honor my patient and turn her healing back over to her. I honor who she is, her power to create health and balance in her life, and my small part in reminding her of who she are. I then break contact with the field again, sit down and come back to a normal waking state of consciousness. (By the time I enter into seventh layer healing, I am also in a very high altered state of consciousness.) I pour myself back into my body, much like putting a hand into a glove. I concentrate on being inside every part of my body. I honor my incarnation, who I am and what I have come here for. I allow any healing energy that I may need to come through my body at this time.

This last procedure helps the healer let go of her patient, so that she will not "carry" her with her all week. It is also good to honor the self in this way, so that the work of healing can be integrated into the personal life of the healer. This does not always happen automatically because during so much of the time spent healing, the healer is in an altered state of consciousness. Sometimes it may feel as if someone else is that nice person doing all that good work. I have found that most of the healers I know have had a hard life and need to honor themselves for it, rather than judge themselves for their experiences. I believe it is all part of the training to learn love and sympathy.

Now repeat the above with the patient Mary.

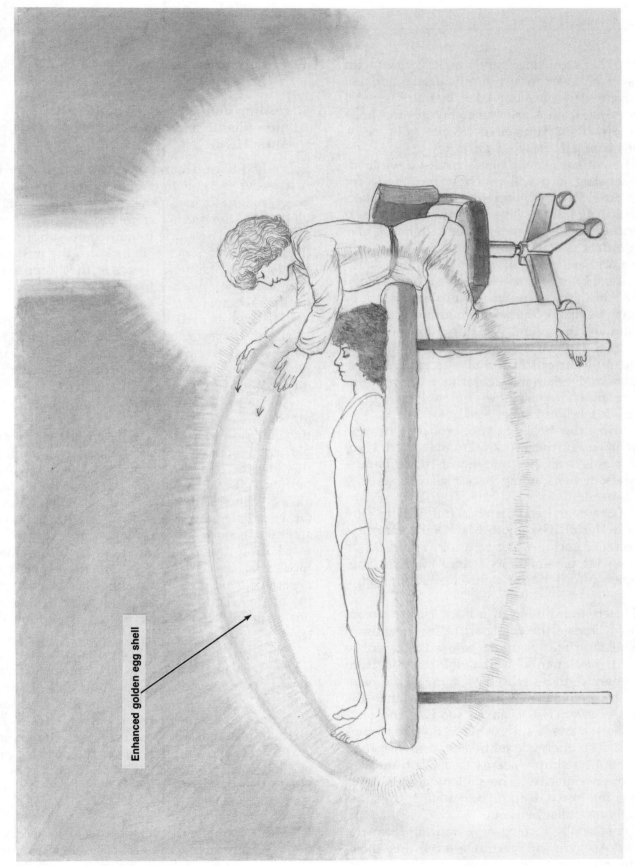

Enhanced golden egg shell

Figure 22-19: Sealing the Ketheric Template Level of the Aura to Complete the Healing

Move to her right side; lightly make contact with her seventh layer from the outside. Honor her, and return her healing back over to her. Sit down away from Mary somewhere in the healing room. Pour yourself back into your body. Honor yourself and your purpose.

The patient usually needs to rest a while after a healing and will probably be groggy for some time. This is a good time for you to make a brief record of the healing for future reference. If etheric template work has been done, I give strict orders not to do any physical exercise and to rest and eat very well for at least three days.

After a brief rest, ask Mary to sit on the edge of the table a few minutes before she gets up, or she may be dizzy. She will be curious as to what you did. At this point, it is important not to go back to the linear mind too much since that would pull her out of the altered state of consciousness. Explain in brief terms what you did, just enough to satisfy her, but not enough to disturb her relaxed state.

During the healing, you probably became aware of any further work Mary may need. If so, discuss this with her and make recommendations about her coming back the next week if that is needed.

You have just completed a full healing. You feel wonderful. Give both Mary and yourself a full glass of spring water to drink. Figure 22–20 shows your patient Mary's aura after healing. Compare it to her aura before healing in Figure 22–4.

That is the outline of a basic full spectrum healing. During the first part of the healing in the chelation and cleaning before the template work, I may channel verbal information from the patient's guides who have come to the healing. The patient may ask questions that the guides answer. However, as soon as the template work starts, I am unable to do both things at once. The energetic template work with high concentration simply seems to take up most of my "brain capacity." The patient also benefits from going into a deep relaxed state at this time and talking pulls them out.

I continually receive new training from the guides. As soon as I learn one level, they move me up to the next. Sometimes a new set of spir-

itual healers come in to work through me.

## 8. Healing on the Cosmic Levels of the Aura (Eighth and Ninth Layers of Auric Field)

Recently, I have begun to see two levels of auric field above the golden template. They appear to be crystalline in nature and of very fine, high vibrations. Everything from the seventh down is, in a sense, a vehicle to guide and support us through this lifetime. This includes the past-life bands in the ketheric, because they represent karmic lessons that we have incarnated to learn in this lifetime.

The eighth and ninth layers on the cosmic level are, however, beyond that. They relate to who we are beyond this lifetime. We are souls reincarnating life after life, slowly progressing in our evolutionary path towards God.

In the lower seven layers of our energy field are stored all the experiences we have had in this lifetime and also all the blueprints for possible experiences we programmed when planning this lifetime. We also constantly create new experiences. Because we have free will, we do not always choose to have all these experiences. Other people have free will also, so that the possibility of experience is a complex affair. In other words, the possible experiences far outnumber those that we actually have. All these possible experiences or probable realities are stacked in the energy field. They are all designed to teach our soul certain lessons we have chosen to learn.

Sometimes these possible experiences are no longer relevant to the growth of the soul and need to be removed from the aura. This is done from the eighth level of the aura. It is as if the healer projects herself beyond the dimensions of this lifetime, then reaches down into the seven lower layers and simply removes the possible experience with what I call the Eighth Level Shield.

### A. The Eighth Level Shield
The Eighth Level Shield is used to remove trauma from this lifetime that is either severely blocking a person's development or is simply no

longer needed. That is, it no longer serves the purpose of teaching whatever soul lesson the individual had intended to be learned.

It is the higher consciousness of the patient that decides when an Eighth Level Shield is appropriate, not the personality level. Most of the time the patient will not be aware of it at all, but sometimes those who have heard of the powerful effect of the Eighth Level Shield will ask for one. This usually does not work. The shield will be given to the healer by her guides only when it is appropriate. To lift a long-term trauma out of someone's field can be very shocking. Sometimes a shield is needed to protect the individual from the greater freedom experienced when a long-term trauma is lifted from the body. Basically, the process consists of the healer putting the shield into a patient's aura, drawing or actually coaxing an old trauma to leave, filling the hole left by the trauma with the rose light of unconditional love and sealing it off. The patient then has time to heal and get used to having lifted the burden he has carried around with him for years. (Not as easy as you might think— freedom is frightening.) Eventually the shield dissolves as the person develops positive experience to remain in its place.

The sequence of setting a shield is quite complicated and usually occurs after the general cleaning and some template work is done. The decision to do so is never made by the healer; it is suggested by the guides. The shield appears to be a flat blue "piece" of light of very impermeable and durable quality. The shield fits along the lower edge of the chakra just above the trauma and is set into the root of the chakra. The left hand makes an opening for setting the shield. To do this, its energy field penetrates deep into the body to the root of the chakra, while the right hand slowly moves it into place. This movement is overseen by the guides. The shield protrudes out of the lower edge of the chakra and extends down over the traumatized area, slightly angularly out from the body. Its lower end is open to provide an exit for the trauma.

The left hand anchors the shield and cannot be moved throughout the entire shielding and trauma-exit process since it separates the upper anatomical part of the auric field from what is being worked on and serves as an entrance for the guides to hold that part of the field separate from the area where the trauma is located. At the same time, the personal guides of the patient usually take him out of his body to protect and teach him.

Once the shield has been set, the healer reaches under it with her right hand and begins to communicate with the energy-consciousness of the trauma to coax it to leave by reminding it of its God connection. This method of healing from such a high level is very different than the way one removes blocks from the field from the lower levels. By connecting directly to the energy-consciousness of the trauma that is ready to leave, the healer provides a way, through shielding, for the trauma to leave. The trauma leaves of its own accord. Any amount of forcing simply disrupts the process and forces the healer to start over. This method allows the entire trauma to leave. In healing from lower auric layers, many times the blocks in the field are energetic signatures of trauma, rather than the entire energy of the trauma itself. In a sense, in the higher level of healing, the trauma is treated as if it has its own being, since it is an integral piece of energy-consciousness. When the trauma leaves, all the effects of that trauma leave with it, and the patient is finished dealing with it. The shield allows for smooth integration of the change into the patient's life and prevents any disturbance in the patient's life which would occur if the patient were not shielded. As the trauma leaves, the guides lovingly take it and fill it with light. Once the entire trauma has left, the area is cauterized with gold or white light, and the cavity is filled with the rose light of unconditional love. The new rose field is then reconnected to the field around it, all of which is still located under the shield. The open exit area at the base of the shield is then covered with a gold seal, which is left in place. The healer then disconnects her left hand from the shield, which is left in. She slowly sinks her right hand energy into where her left hand energy is seated. This releases the left hand, which is then used to integrate the new restructured and shielded area to the rest of the patient's auric field. The healer slowly moves the left hand through the upper part of the auric body, reconnecting the fields.

After setting the shield, the healer then strengthens the main vertical power current of the aura by running pulsating gold light through it. The patient slowly reenters the body. This may be all that is done in a healing. The healer may go down to sixth level healing to enhance the patient's serenity or may simply close the healing with the seventh.

The thing that has been the greatest challenge for me in this type of work is to learn simply to sit and coax the trauma to leave. This is very different from scooping or pulling or knocking it loose with high vibrations. It is difficult to rise above the seventh layer and to stay there in a complete state of peace and alignment with God's will. One must control the breathing with slow, long, in-out breaths and keep the mind focused on surrender to God's will. The Divine spark exists within every cell of a person's being, and that divine spark inexorably follows Divine will. The healer must sit within that Divine spark. In other words, I have to sit with the trauma, make contact with that energy-consciousness while I am in a state of alignment with the Will of God and simply remind each cell of that trauma and every cell of the body that it carries with it a spark of God. I remind it that it is God, light and wisdom and therefore inexorably flows with and is one with the universal will. This is not an easy thing to do. In the beginning, I would tend to start pulling. If I did that, it would mean that my will got in the way, which meant I had dropped to a lower level. That would knock the guides right out of my body and my whole body would shudder. Either they left my body as a signal, or they could not tolerate my low-level "will" vibration. We would then have to start all over.

An Eighth Level Shield is needed when patients are unable to bear the freedom of a life-long trauma being lifted in a healing session; they are likely to fill that space with another negative experience. I was astounded one day when I witnessed such a thing.

After a healing was completed, as the patient was putting on his shoes, suddenly the whole restructured golden field fell apart before my eyes. In my astonishment I thought, "How did you do that so fast?" I wanted to put him right back on the table, but realized that was not right and that something more was involved. Later, Emmanuel, a spiritual teacher channelled through my friend Pat (Rodegast) De Vitalis, said that the patient now knew that he really couldn't accept what he said he wanted, that he was not ready to face certain aspects of his life related to the healing. That would mean confronting himself with issues that were very painful to him, which he simply did not want to do.

It was shortly after this experience that I learned to put the shield in. I also realized that I could not offer to give another healing to this person because that would confront him with his negative decision and possibly make things worse. I can only wait for him to come to the place in himself where he has decided to face those outer issues in his life. Then he may decide to come to a healing, and we can put in the shield so that he can be protected from the uplifting of the burden while he heals internally. After that, the shield will dissolve and he will slowly be able to experience the increased freedom.

An interesting example of a shield healing is shown in Figure 22–21. The patient, whom I shall call Betty, was a businesswoman. Betty was a therapy client. Her mother had died when she was three years old. At the time she began therapy with me several years earlier, she had no idea what her natural mother looked like and could not remember ever seeing a picture of her. During the course of the therapy she was able to obtain pictures of her mother and began reconnecting and relating to her. This helped the woman develop more self-esteem since her natural mother became a reality for her. She had never been able to accept her stepmother. This process also helped her improve her relations with her stepmother. She carried a lot of pain in her chest about the loss of her natural mother.

One day after several years in therapy, she asked me why I never gave her a healing. I said it was because she was so healthy. However, in that moment the guides reminded me of the use of the "new shield I had just learned to put in." The next session was a healing. After going through the normal chelation and cleansing procedure and checking her template level, which did not need work, the guides proceeded to set the shield and remove the trauma of losing her mother while a small child. I was very moved when I saw her mother appear in spirit form, supported by her own guides. Instead of a team of guides receiving and enlightening the energy-consciousness substance of the trauma, I saw her mother receive it with love. (See Figure 22–21.) In the meantime, the guides of my patient had pulled her out of her body to protect and teach her. In the next step of the shield process, the guides filled the cavity emptied of trauma with the rose light of love. The healing then continued with the sealing of the bottom of the shield with gold light as shown in Figure 22–22. Then we reconnected the shielded area to the upper and lower half of the auric field. We then enhanced the main vertical power current in the body. By the time this was completed, the trauma held by the mother had turned to white light.

### B. Healing on the Ninth Level of the Aura

I know very little about this procedure. As I watch the guides working from this level, it appears to me as if they simply remove a whole side of a person's energy bodies (and all the fields with it) and put in a new set. All this appears to my view as crystalline light. This procedure, when done, has the effect of healing the patient very rapidly. My guess is that it has to do with simply reincarnating in the same body without having to go through the birth/childhood experiences to set the life tasks. I have witnessed this a few times.

## Guide Teams

Sometimes it appears to me that different guide teams work on different levels, and at other times it seems to be the same guides at different levels. The guide teams who work on different levels seem to have different characteristics. Those who work on the astral level are concerned primarily with matters of the heart and loving. They are very comforting, loving and caring and speak poetically, teaching us to learn

to love ourselves with all our faults, etc. The guides who do the ketheric and etheric template work look to me to be very serious and quite active and "want to get to work." They are concerned with the perfect template and simply healing efficiently. They do not appear to have a lot of feelings, but at the same time are very supportive and accepting. They are more directive. The Eighth Level Shield guides give a sense of great acceptance and infinite patience with love. The Ninth Level guides are very hard for me to perceive but they seem a bit impersonal.

## HEALING SESSION FORMAT

As a help to the new healer, I will once again list the healing session format in a much shorter form. Following this is a healing session analysis that should help you analyze where you need to practice and where you need to do your own personal growth work.

1. Before the person enters, align yourself with the light. Open your chakras using methods taught in the section called "Channelling for Healing."

2. Listen to why the person has come to you. Why was she guided specifically to you? What do you have to give to her"? Open to your inner repertory.

3. Explain what you do.

4. Analyze the energy flow in her system. What are the main blocks? How does she utilize her energy? How does she misdirect it? What are the results of her long-term misdirecting? What is her major defense? (See Chapters 9, 10 and 12.)

5. Measure chakras with a pendulum. Record. (See Chapter 10.)

6. Attune and align yourself with the light; give an affirmation; align and balance your en-

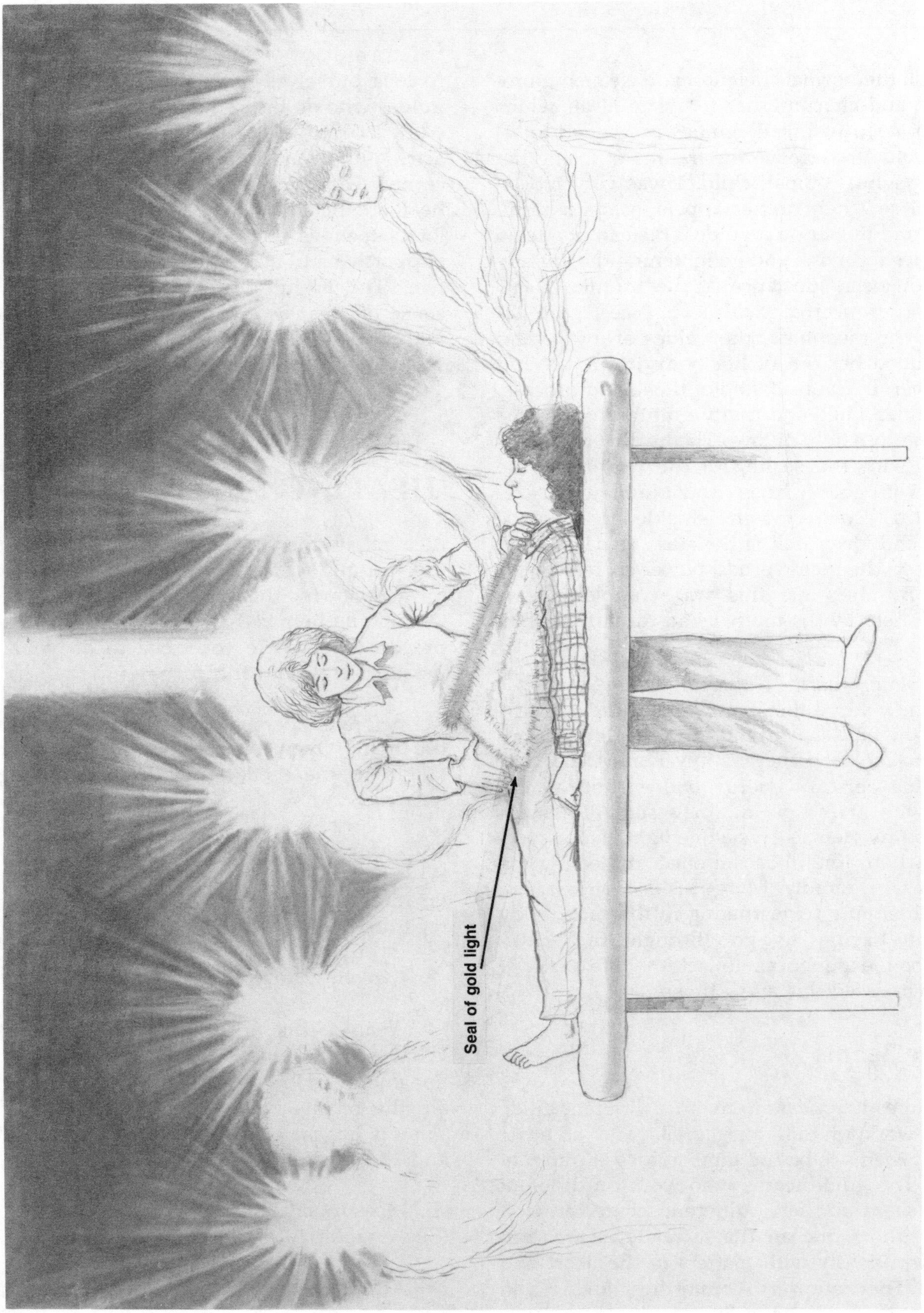

Seal of gold light

Figure 22-22: Sealing an Eighth Level Shield

234

ergy system with the person's. Become aware of your guides, if you have not yet done that. Periodically throughout the session you need to realign and balance your system with the light, your guides and the person's system.

7. Interpret the chakra's readings while running energy through the solar reflex points of the feet: Find the balance of reason, will and emotion; the main closed center(s); the main open center(s) through which the person can work to deal with problems and to open the closed chakras. Find the main issues. Read psychically any information you can pick up. What is the initiating cause of illness? What are the high self qualities you need to appeal to in order to help the person heal herself? (See Chapters 9, 10 and 12.)

8. Chelate the lower auric bodies' chakras while scanning the body systems. If you are a beginner, you should skip to step 16. After more practice, add steps 9 if needed, 10 and 11. After you perceive the fifth, sixth and seventh layers of the field, you can do steps 12, 13, 14 and 15.

9. Do a spine cleaning.

10. Work directly on the places you are drawn to. Choose from various methods you know. As you do so, observe the person's emotional state. Does she take in energy or block emotionally? Be with her. Go through the blocks with her. Allow your guides to help you with specific illness areas. Listen.

11. Clean specific blocks in the lower energy bodies.

12. If you know how, this is the point at which etheric or ketheric template work occurs.

13. Go to the celestial level (sixth); send white light directly into the central brain area. Raise your vibrations by vibrating your pituitary. When the person's vibrations come up to yours, go up to the next level and repeat. Do this until the central brain area lights.

14. At this point, if you have not already done so, you may see the person's guides, angels, visions or get direct messages for the person. Gently break the connection and close the opening.

15. From the position at the head of the table, try to get a nice up-and-down vibrational current from the third ventricle through the spine using the double hand technique.

16. At this point you may want to comb out the celestial and astral body (especially if the person is depressed or suppressed).

17. Enhance and strengthen the eggshell or orb.

18. Move to the patient's right side; recontact the seventh layer; honor your patient and her self-healing power.

19. Gently break the connection, closing all openings, and move away from the person. Give yourself a few minutes to return fully into your body and the earth plane. Allow the healing energy to flow through you. Honor yourself; affirm who you are and your work.

20. If the person has left her body and needs help returning, gently pull her back by grasping the feet and sucking the energy towards you.

21. After each healing, remind the patient to take a large glass of fresh water, and you do the same.

## HEALING SESSION ANALYSIS

1. What happened chronologically? How did each step of the healing go? Which steps were easy? Which did you have trouble with?

2. Answer item 4 of the Healing Session Format.

3. Answer item 7 of the Healing Session Format.

4. What were the internal processes of the healer and the client? Did you lose your centering and perhaps waste energy where it wasn't needed? How? Relate this to the character structures of the healer and the client.

5. What was accomplished in the healing? Did you reach the person's inner light? What was the nature of her high-self qualities? How did you support her and bring her out?

6. On the basis of the above, what personal work do you need to do?

7. Draw a before and an after picture of energy flow.

8. What was the initiating cause of the illness? How did you deal with it?

9. On the basis of the above, what healing work would you concentrate on next time? What is your prognosis? What is your guidance regarding this prognosis?

## Chapter 22 Review

1. What is the first thing a healer does before beginning a healing?
2. What is meant by running energy? By chelating the body?
3. What does chelation do?
4. Does a healer consciously control the color of light when running energy for chelation? Why or why not?
5. If a healer's first chakra is closed on the lower levels of the field, will she be able to use the color red effectively in healing? Why or why not?
6. For a heart patient, describe the direction of chelation. Why is it done this way?
7. Describe the process of spine cleaning.
8. What is the difference between running energy with one hand, two hands separately or two hands together?
9. For fifth level healing, what happens if you do not follow guidance and move your hands before the guides are finished?
10. Name three ways a person can tear the seventh layer. (Also refer to Chapter 15.)
11. If there is a tear in the aura throughout the entire field, which layers need to be sewn up?
12. Will the energy leak stop if you are unable to reach up into and sew the seventh layer if it is torn?
13. Does chelation repair a torn auric field?
14. Why does the patient leave the body for seventh layer work?
15. In healing with white light, how does one focus one's energy and consciousness? Where do you hold your attention? How do you scan?
16. Describe healing on each of the auric levels.
17. What is an Eighth Level Shield? What is it used for? Who decides that it can be used?
18. Describe a procedure to end a healing that allows you to psychically break away from your patient until you wish to make contact again.
19. What is the difference between channelling for healing and channelling for information?

## Food For Thought

20. Who does the healing?

## Chapter 23

# HEALING WITH COLOR AND SOUND

## Healing with Colored Light, Color Modulation

There are many times when a healer will need to hold a certain color that is being channelled through her. Holding a color also means holding your field in a certain frequency range, which you really must do throughout the entire healing. You need to be sensitive enough to keep your energy level at the range that is needed at any given time by the patient. Some examples of holding a certain color have already been given in previous chapters on etheric template healing, ketheric template healing (holding gold), sixth level healing in which you go up into the celestial frequencies, spine cleaning and chakra charging, in which you hold the specific color of a chakra until it is charged. At other times, you may be requested by the guides to pour certain colored light into your patient whenever and wherever it is needed. At these times, you must learn to be in a specific color and hold it.

In the last chapter I stated that it takes practice to learn to produce a color of your choosing to use in healing. For beginning students it is very important to practice color modulation before trying to control the color coming through you. Most chelation is done without color control. However, later in a healing the guides may want you to "sit in" or hold steady a certain color they wish to use. This means that if you do not learn to control color, you may very well interfere with the color being sent through you by changing your field unconsciously. Thus you need to be able to hold your field steady in one particular color.

Dolores Krieger in her book *Therapeutic Touch* gives some very good color modulation exercises. Essentially you must learn what it is like to "be in" a certain color. It is not a matter of thinking the color as in visualization. If you think red, you will make yellow. If you think green, you will make yellow. If you think blue, you will make yellow. Healers call this "doing it in yellow" because when you think you make yellow. Many beginners do it in yellow. Thus to make blue, you must "be" blue, whatever that means to you. So you need to experiment for yourself what it is like to be in a state of blue.

## Exercises to Control the Color You Send

How do you feel when you wear blue clothes or sit in blue light that comes from a cathedral window? What does blue mean to you? Again, you must use the sense that you are most accustomed to using. Do you best access information through seeing, hearing or feeling? What does blue look like, sound like or feel like. Get one of those leaded glass crystals that you can hang in your window. Put your fingers in each of the colors of the rainbow it produces. How does each color feel? Get plates of colored glass, or sheets of colored, clear plastic. Hold them in the sunlight. Explore your relationship to each color. Take colored pieces of paper or material all the same size. Mix them up in a pile. Close your eyes and pick out two of them. Keep your eyes closed. Explore your relationship to that color. What does it feel like? Do you like it? Dislike it? Does it provoke any feelings in you? Does it energize or deenergize you? Does it make you feel calm or uncomfortable? Place it on different parts of your body. Would you like to wear this color? Then after this, with eyes closed, decide which color you like the best. If you like, you can guess what color it is. Then open your eyes. You will be surprised at how much information you now have about your relationship to each color. You will find that you carry prejudice about what each color is "supposed" to do but didn't.

Get a partner, hold hands, and each take a turn at running energy to the other in a certain color. See if your partner can tell what color it is. Practice, practice, practice. Remember that in order to run red, you must have your first chakra clear. To run orange, you must have your second chakra clear, etc. You should clear your chakras before doing these exercises. The exercises to clear your chakras are given in Chapter 21.

## The Meaning of Color in the Aura

Many people come up to me and say, "What color is my aura?" And then they ask, "What does that color mean?" Many people get "Aura Readings" in which the reader will say, "Your aura is such and such a color and that means such and such." As you can see from this book, I don't normally do that. If someone says, "What color is my aura." I usually say, "On which layer?" Or I will simply read the predominant colors on the unstructured levels and say something like, "Primarily blue, with some yellow and purple."

My colleague Pat (Rodegast) de Vitalis, who channels a guide named Emmanuel, reads colors on the "soul" level. Emmanuel simply shows her the "aura" of the person on the soul level as it connects to the task in this lifetime. These colors have a specific meaning to Pat, and

that is how she interprets what she sees. Her color meaning list is given in Figure 23–1. Remember that to use this list to interpret what you are seeing, you must be looking at the same level Pat is.

To read the colors of the soul level, clear your mind through deep meditation, and then ask to be given the colors of the soul level. After some practice, these colors will appear on your mind-screen. You may also see forms or figures with these colors that you can describe to your patients in order to help them understand the meaning of the colors. If you see red, it means passion or strong feelings. When mixed with rose, it means love. Clear red means free or ex-

## Figure 23–1
## COLOR MEANING ON SOUL–TASK LEVEL

| Color | Used for: |
|---|---|
| Red | Passion, strong feelings. Love, when mixed with rose. Clear red: moving anger. Dark red: stagnated anger Red-orange: sexual passion |
| Orange | Ambition |
| Yellow | Intellect |
| Green | Healing, healer, nurturer |
| Blue | Teacher, sensitivity |
| Purple | Deeper connection to spirit |
| Indigo | Moving toward a deeper connection to spirit |
| Lavender | Spirit |
| White | Truth |
| Gold | Connection to God. In the service of humankind, Godlike love. |
| Silver | Communication |
| Black | Absence of light, or profound forgetting, thwarted ambition (cancer) |
| Black Velvet | Like black holes in space, doorways to other realities |
| Maroon | Moving into one's task |

pressed anger; dark red, held anger; red-orange implies sexual passion. When the color is orange, the person has ambition. When it is yellow, it refers to intellect. A person with a lot of green has a lot of healing and nurturing energy. Blue is the color of the teacher and of sensitivity. When purple is seen on the soul level, the person has a deeper connection to spirit, while indigo means moving toward a deeper connection to spirit. Lavender refers to spirit, and white to truth. Gold is connection to God and the service of humankind with godlike love. When a person has silver in her soul level, it means she is connected to or has gifts in communication and is able to communicate well. Velvet black is like holes in space, which are doorways to other realities. Maroon means moving into one's task. Black is the absence of light, or profound forgetting, which leads to cancer, and which is seen on the soul level as thwarted ambition.

## Color in a Healing Session

All the colors of the rainbow are used in healing. Each color has its own effect in the field. Of course each color can be used to charge the chakra that metabolizes that color. Red is used to charge the field, burn out cancer and warm cold areas. Orange charges the field, increases sexual potency and immunity. Yellow is used to clear a foggy head and help the linear mind function well. Green is used as a general balancer and healer for all things. Blue cools and calms. It is also used to restructure the etheric field and in shielding. Purple helps the patient connect to his spirit, while indigo opens the third eye and enhances visualization and clears the head. White is used to charge the field, bring peace and comfort and take away pain. Gold is used to restructure the seventh layer and to strengthen and charge the field. Velvet black brings the patient into a state of grace, silence and peace with God. It is good in restructuring bones that have crumbled from cancer or other trauma. Purple-blue takes away pain when doing deep tissue work and work on bone cells. It also helps expand the patient's field in order to connect to her task.

In general, I do not control the color coming through me when I do healing, but I am able to sustain a color that comes through me. On rare occasions I will send a certain color on purpose. Table 23–2 gives the colors used in healing and what I have seen them used for by the guides. Charging each chakra is done by running the color of that chakra into the field on whichever

### Figure 23–2
### COLOR USED IN HEALING

| Color | Used for: |
| --- | --- |
| Red | Charging the field, burning out cancer, warming cold areas |
| Orange | Charging the field, increasing sexual potency, increasing immunity |
| Yellow | Charging second chakra, clearing a foggy head |
| Green | Charging fourth chakra, balancing, general healing, charging field |
| Blue | Cooling, calming, restructuring etheric level, shielding |
| Purple | Connecting to spirit |
| Indigo | Opening third eye, clearing head |
| Lavender | Purging field |
| White | Charging field, bringing peace and comfort, taking away pain |
| Gold | Restructuring seventh layer, strengthening field, charging field |
| Silver | Strong purging of field (opalescent silver is used to charge sixth level) |
| Velvet Black | Bringing patient into a state of grace, silence and peace with God |
| Purple Blue | Taking away pain when doing deep tissue work and work on bone cells, helping expand patient's field in order to connect to his task |

level you are working on. In general in our society, since we are already so mental, analytical and intellectual, the color yellow is not used a lot in the healing session.

The colors lavender and silver have been used by my guides in a little different fashion from the healing techniques mentioned earlier in this book. When I have observed microorganisms in the field that need to be removed, the guides use first lavender and then silver to blast them out. First they send through lavender light, which makes the microorganisms vibrate at a high rate and apparently knocks them loose. If lavender light doesn't get them all, the guides will increase intensity and frequency and go up to silver. This powerful current seems to disconnect the microorganisms from their space. The guides then reverse the direction of energy flow through my body and suck all the lavender and silver light back out, carrying the microorganism with the light. This procedure is rather like vacuuming with light. In a particular case in which I was cleaning the blood of a leukemia patient, she received her first clear blood test the day after the healing. That is the only time I have had clinical results to check this procedure.

At one point I began experimenting with the effect of purple-blue light with a colleague. We were doing exchange sessions. Daniel Blake of the Structural Bodywork Institute (Santa Barbara, California) did deep-tissue work on me and, in exchange, took my classes. While he worked on me, we experimented with combining color control with deep-tissue work. When he was able to hold a strong purple-blue flame coming out from his fingertips, he could go very deeply into my muscle tissue without causing pain. If he got distracted and "dropped" the color, my muscle would hurt. Controlling the color that came through made his work more effective because he could go much deeper and get a bigger change in muscle and structural alignment. At one point in this work, he was able to get to the bone level. By holding a purple-blue flame mixed with white light, he was able to straighten a slight twist in my femur. As I watched what was happening with HSP, I could see the cells of my femur realigning themselves with each other. The physical sensation was extremely pleasant. Heyoan made the comment that this twisting of the bone is related to how the piezoelectric effect within the bone helps direct bone growth. The piezoelectric effect in bones is the following: When pressure is put on bone tissue, as from walking, the pressure causes a small electrical current to flow through the bone. The bone then grows faster in the direction of the current. If pressure (through walking) is put on a bone in a misaligned fashion, it will cause the bone to grow in a misaligned or twisted way. The original misalignment in my body was the result of a car accident. Daniel's treatment removed the slight twist from my femur permanently.

At a certain point in my healing career, the guides suggested I start using black light. This seemed unusual to me, since the dark colors in the aura usually are associated with illness. This black, however, was not the black of cancer, but a velvet black, like black velvet silk. It is like the life potential held in the womb. It is the black mystery of the unknown feminine within all of us, which teems with undifferentiated life. Sitting within the black velvet void is another way to be one with the creator, but this time without form. To sit within the black velvet void means sitting in silence and peace. It means completely being there, in fullness and without judgment. It means going into a state of Grace and bringing your patient into that Grace with you. It means completely accepting everything that is in that moment. Heyoan and the other healing guides and I often sit in this place with cancer patients or other very serious illnesses for a whole hour at a time. It is very healing. It brings the patient into a state of oneness with the Divine.

## Sounding for Healing

I have found that color in the aura is directly related to sound. Sounding specific pitches into the field not only produces specific colors in the field but is also a powerful agent of healing.

Multiple Sclerosis (M.S.) is known among healers as one of the most difficult diseases to work with. It is very hard to effect a change in the field of someone with M.S. During one of the intensive training weeks I offer, one of the students had M.S. At times during the week, the students and I would work on this student, Liz. Several students were able to perceive a large scar in her field in the sacral area. In the first group healing we did with Liz, she received a normal chelation and went through a lot of feelings. The group healed her, held her and cried with her. At the end of the second hour of healing, however, I and one of the students who had learned to use her HSP could see that the scar was not touched. As the week progressed, each student began to develop the particular form of healing she felt most connected with. Some liked crystals, some concentrated on love, others on spiritual surgery and some on sounding. At the end of the week we worked on Liz again. Each student gave her best in her chosen form of healing. There were several students sounding, two working with crystals, several sitting in love and some running energy. We worked synchronistically as a group. We found that the two of us who were working with crystals were able to lift the scar out of the field if we worked with the sounders. The sound they made would loosen the scar. We used the crystals as scalpels to cut the scar away once it had been loosened with the sound. Then we would direct the sounders to change the pitch just a little, and another part of the scar would loosen. After its removal another change in pitch would loosen more scar. We proceeded in this way until the scar was removed completely. After the healing Liz said that a certain pain that had been in her leg for 15 years was no longer there. Her walking was much improved and still is at the time of writing, which is about four years later. This is only one small part of Liz's self-healing story. She has succeeded in regaining all the use of her body, which was almost completely paralyzed.

Since that time I have used sound regularly in the healings I give. I use it directly on the chakras to charge and strengthen them. I put my mouth about an inch away from the body where the chakra is located. Each chakra has a different pitch, and each person's pitch for a particular chakra is slightly different.

To find the pitch for each chakra, I vary the range a bit until I hit a resonance. This resonance can be heard and felt by the patient. Since I can also see the field, I watch the chakra respond to the sound. When I hit the right pitch, the chakra tenses up and begins to spin rapidly and evenly. Its color brightens up. After holding the sound for some time, the chakra is charged and strengthened enough to hold its new level of energy. Then I move up to the next chakra. I start with the first and move up through all seven.

An interesting effect of this sounding, which is usually very powerfully felt by the patient, is to increase the patient's ability to visualize. If a person has a very undercharged chakra, chances are he will not be able to visualize that color in his head. However, after a few minutes of sounding over the corresponding chakra, the patient is able to visualize the chakra's color.

Whenever I have done a sounding demonstration in a group, everyone in the group can tell when I have hit resonance with a chakra.

The same principles that are used for sounding into the chakras also work with the organs and bones of the body. I sound into the particular organ by holding my mouth about an inch over the body surface where that organ is located. I watch the organ using HSP until I get the appropriate sound that causes the greatest amount of effect on the organ. The effect may be energy flow, cleaning the organ or strengthening it. I simply watch the response and go for it. Over several months of regular healings, I was able to heal ulcerative colitis in this way. The patient was able to avoid a colostomy, which had been recommended by several physicians. Part of this patient's healing was to play a tape recording of that sounding once or twice a day.

This type of sounding also works very well for healing injured disks, enhancing tissue growth, clearing stagnated fluids from the body, tuning up the nervous system, and tuning the organs of the body so that they impedance match or harmonize with each other to function better. I have found that different types of body organs, tissues, bones and fluid all require a different tone and modulation to enhance their healthy functioning. In addition to sounding in the form of tones only, one can make different types of sound. Traditional Indian teachings give a Sanskrit letter and a particular sound for each chakra. I have not yet worked with these, but I can imagine that they are very powerful forms of healing.

Some music groups, like Robbie Gass', perform music to purposefully open the chakras. In a concert I attended, Robbie directed his choir to sing for two hours without stopping. Over that time period, songs were chosen specifically to open the chakras in a progressive series, starting with the first chakra. By the time they finished, most of the people in the audience had most of their chakras opened and charged. Everyone had a wonderful time. Music is very healing.

## Chapter 23 Review

1. List examples of when a healer would consciously control the color of the light being channelled, and explain why.
2. What is so difficult about channelling a chosen color?
3. What does "doing it in yellow" mean?
4. What, in general, do the following colors do in healing: red, red-orange, gold, green, rose, blue, purple and white?
5. What is the main use of the colors lavender and silver? What is the difference between the two?
6. How is black light used?
7. What is the effect of purple-blue light when used with deep-tissue massage?
8. How do you modulate (create) a color to channel? Give several ways.
9. Is there a relationship between color and sound in healing? What is it?
10. By what physical principle does sounding work in the auric field?
11. How can sounding be used for each chakra? What is the effect on the chakra?
12. How can sounding be used on an organ, and what is the effect of the sounding?
13. How do you find the right note to sound? Give two ways by which you can tell it is the right note?
14. Can you passively channel a sound your guide makes? How is that different from the active sounding we have been talking about above?

# Chapter 24

# HEALING TRANSTEMPORAL TRAUMAS

Many people, at a certain point along their spiritual path, begin to have transtemporal experiences that are referred to as past-life experiences. Someone may be meditating and "remember" being another person in another era. Someone else, in doing deep therapy work of reexperiencing traumas from this lifetime, may suddenly find themselves reliving a trauma that was experienced in "another lifetime."

Transtemporal experience probably cannot be completely defined due to our limited sense of time and space. I personally think that the term *past life* is a very limited way to define such an experience. As we have seen in Chapter 4, both physicists and mystics agree that time is not linear nor space only three-dimensional. Many writers have spoken of multi-dimensional and multi-temporal realities existing within each other. Einstein speaks of a time-space continuum where all things of the past and future exist now, somehow interwoven in multi-dimensional reality. Itzhak Bentov says that linear time is only a fabrication of the third dimensional reality (into which I am trying to squeeze this book).

## Exercise to Experience Nonlinear Time

In his book, *Stalking the Wild Pendulum*, he gives an exercise to illustrate this point: Sit quietly in meditation with a watch or clock clearly within visible range so that all you have to do is slightly slit your eyes to see the second hand as it moves around with each minute. When you have reached a high state of consciousness in your meditation, simply slit open your eyes and look at the second hand on the clock. What has happened? Many people have the experience of this hand either completely stopping or drastically slowing down. Of course, as soon as you see this, your emotional reaction will probably pull you back into your normally comfortable reality of linear time, and the second hand will jump forward and resume its normal rate of movement. What has happened here? Bentov says that time is experienced subjectively, not linearly, and that we create a supposed linear time structure for convenience.

Both Edgar Cayce and Jane Roberts speak of multi-dimensional reality where all our past and future are being lived now, each in its own dimension, and say that each personality in each dimension is a part of an expression of a greater soul or greater being. According to Roberts, we can penetrate into these other dimensions or "lives" to bring knowledge and understanding for transformation. By doing this, this dimension or our present lives can transform our other lives and dimensions. Or, said in more popular terms, how we live now in what we call this life affects both our past and future lives.

All of these things are quite hard to understand, but they serve to help point out and challenge the limitations in our thinking about the nature of reality.

On the therapeutic and healing levels, I have found working with past lives very effective when handled in a manner in which the transformation process is kept as the main objective. It is not something to play with or to use to boost the ego. We all would rather think of ourselves as having been a great queen or leader of some sort, rather than a peasant, beggar, murderer, etc. That is not at all the point. The usefulness of reexperiencing past lives is clearly to free the personality from problems that now hold us back from attaining our greatest potentials and from completing our life's work (or life task). Problems related to past-life experiences always relate to what the personality is dealing with in this present life, when the past-life memory is unearthed in a natural and nonforcing way. This is a very important fact that must be kept in mind by the healer or therapist whose job it is to make sure that the interlife connection is made. Past-life memory may then be applied to this life circumstances to help heal this life's problems.

Some therapists will spontaneously see a past-life of a client when they are making body contact with the client, for example, in a mothering type therapy where the therapist holds the client the way a mother would hold a child. The therapist can then utilize this information by weaving it into a session in a sensitive manner.

## "Seeing" and Healing Past-Life Trauma

There are three major ways that I "see" and heal past-life trauma, each related to what level or levels of the aura on which the healing is done. All levels, from the ketheric on down, are affected by past-life trauma. In the first four auric levels, a past-life trauma looks like a normal energy block in the field. On the etheric and ketheric template levels, it shows up as a structural problem and, in addition, on the ketheric, the past life shows up as a ring or band in the eggshell level of the field.

To "see" a past life, I may just be "given" the past-life scene relevant to the present healing situation or illness as the client is speaking with me. Or I may hold my hands on a particular block and then see the past life. To read the

past lives related to the bands in the eggshell level, I simply put my hands in the band and see the pictures of the past life. I will now describe these three methods of healing in more detail.

## Healing Past-Life Blocks in the Lower Four Levels of the Aura

A method of clearing past-life blocks, which I learned from Petey Peterson at the Healing Light Center in Glendale, California, is very effective in removing past-life trauma that has been blocking a person's freedom in this life.

This kind of work really addresses the blocks from this lifetime, first. The healer focuses energy into the block. This starts energy moving out of the block and usually the trauma is released. The first layers will be blocks that occurred in this lifetime; then after they are cleared, the traumas from other lifetimes are uncovered and worked with in the same manner. The healer must be experienced with and be able to handle very strong, painful, fearful or angry feelings in the client in order to do this work. The healer must be there for the client through all types of feelings that are experienced and gone through. The healer must not withdraw her energy if affected by these strong feelings, but must continue to be there, steadily running a supportive foundation energy that sustains the client through the experience so that he can complete and clear it.

To do this, one begins a healing in the normal manner with alignment (Chapter 22) and balancing the three energy systems of client, healer and UEF guides. Then, during the chelation, the healer will become aware of the blocks in the system. The healer is lead through intuition or guidance to the block which is appropriate to concentrate on in that particular session. The healer then lays hands on that area of the body and runs energy into that area. Many times the left hand is on the back of the body and the right hand on the front.

After a good amount of energy is flowing, the healer will ask the client to allow his memory to open and go back to the first time the client put that block there. The healer continues to run energy into the block while the client goes backward in time. The healer usually gets pictures of the event in question as the client is trying to remember. The client will also either see pictures or go into a feeling state (or both) that relates to the experience. The client may then reexperience that trauma fully as if living through it again or he may just see the experience as an observer. The healer may or may not tell the client what the healer sees, depending on whether or not it is appropriate to do so. It is not always appropriate, especially if the client does not see it. The healer must always respect the client's energy system, which is what determines how much information the client can tolerate about any given trauma. If, however, the client reexperiences the trauma, it is always good for the healer to verify the information through the healer's gift of "seeing."

The timing of discovery is very important in these things. When past-life information is uncovered in the right moment, it will help the person understand himself and learn to love themselves better. If it is done with the wrong timing, it can enhance a person's negativity either toward self or others. For example, if the person has done something very violent to another person in a past life, he may not be able to handle knowing about it in this lifetime without placing great guilt upon himself. If he knows the victim in this lifetime, the present life situation may be made worse because of guilt. Or if the situation is reversed and the patient is a past-life victim of someone he knows in this lifetime, he may find himself increasing and justifying a grudge he may already be holding against that person.

After the trauma is experienced at whatever level was appropriate, the healer asks the client if he is ready to give it up and let it go. If the answer is yes, the healer removes it from the field by scooping it out. The process of experiencing the trauma has loosened it from the field, so it is easy to remove. Both the healer and the client fill the open clear area where the trauma was with unconditional love, which is a rose colored light, working through the heart chakra, as discussed in Chapter 23.

The client may say "no" to the question of letting the trauma go. This means there is more to be experienced, and he is not finished with it, or the healer may see more work to be done. The healer begins the process of running energy again and helping the client to experience more of the trauma. The healer increases both intensity and frequency of the energy s/he runs into the block. This is repeated until the area has cleared and the client is ready to let it go and allow the area to be filled with the rose light of unconditional love.

If the area has not cleared, there is usually another trauma sitting under the first that was experienced. I have seen as many as five traumas from different lifetimes layered upon each other in the same area of the body. These five layers were left after the client had cleared the layers of trauma from this lifetime. In other words the traumas that are experienced by a person are laid down in the field on top of each other, probably chronologically. When you clear one trauma, the next is left uncovered to be dealt with and cleared.

Many times when a client reexperiences a past life, there is a very strong field effect called a direct current (DC) field shift by Rev. Rosalyn Bruyere. In the shift, Rev. Bruyere says that the whole auric field expands to a much greater size than normal but still maintains its high vibration rate. Almost twice as much energy stays in the field for about 24 hours, and the client is very vulnerable and impressionable. A great deal of the unconscious memory is opened during this time, so memories continue to flow into the consciousness of the individual. It is very important for him to stay in a quiet, safe and nourishing environment to allow the healing to continue and complete itself. Unpleasant experiences from external sources during this time will affect the individual very deeply and should be avoided. It is time for the field to reestablish healthy flow patterns that, if allowed to stabilize over 24 hours will, become part of the normal flow of the system, thus making the healing permanent. It is important for the healer to explain to the patient what is happening and to emphasize the importance of the healing period and encourage him to take good care of himself during that time. The power in this time must be respected. This time period is similar to one when someone goes into shock.

As the client goes backward in time, clearing trauma after trauma, usually starting with this lifetime and going to previous lifetimes, the blocked area becomes clearer and clearer. Each layer is filled with the rose light of unconditional love before going onto the next layer to be cleared. Thus, one can see that any natural purification process that clears away body blocks (and most spiritual paths do) will eventually lead to past-life clearing. It is very important that the past-life clearing be done at an appropriate point in a person's path. That point is reached when a good deal of clearing has already taken place concerning this lifetime, when a lot of the person's personal life is in order and when he would not be so tempted to use past-life experiences to avoid issues that need to be dealt with in this lifetime, here and now.

At the appropriate time, past-life clearing can release certain places in a person's life that cannot seem to change, even though a lot of spiritual work has been done to clear them. Then past-life clearing can sometimes initiate dramatic changes in a person's present life.

For example, one client who was in a very destructive marriage where her husband would hurt her physically was unable to leave the marriage until she reexperienced about 15 past lifetimes where she had been physically abused by men in some form or another. She saw the continuation of her pattern of dependency in which she thought that men have all the power (and also all the responsibility). She saw that she lived out her belief in situations that proved men did have more power than she on the physical level. When she saw her pattern and knew she had to face her dependency, stand on her own two feet and face her fear of being alone, she was ready to leave the marriage and rebuild her life. Her life has dramatically changed in the year since this occurrence, and she is free, happy and healthy. She is letting go of her fear of being alone and through this is regaining her independence and taking responsibility for her life.

## Healing Past-life Traumas on the Etheric and Ketheric Template Levels of the Aura

To heal a structural problem in the aura caused by a past life, you follow the same procedure as healing any structural problem on the template level as described in Chapter 22. The important difference here is that as soon as the healer knows the trauma is from a past life, the healer must help the client connect present life issues to the past-life experience. The structural problems on this level of the aura from past lifetimes usually result in congenital problems in the physical body. These issues are very important to deal with as they are held very tightly and deeply within the soul substance of the individual. It is clear that part of the main task of the individual with birth-related problems is to deal with that problem both on the physical level and the psychodynamic level. This work will then lead to the spiritual issue that the soul has incarnated to resolve in the first place. It is important for the healer to keep in mind the scope of the work that is being done. The object is not only to heal the physical body, although that is what usually brings the client to the healer in the first place. The object is to heal the soul. On the template level, it is to straighten the auric field and realign it with its natural flow—the universal flow of all life.

In the case of a young man named John that follows, I first saw the structural problems in the aura. I also "saw" a picture of the past-life scene that was related to the auric wound. Figures 24–1 to 24–5 are drawings of the healing work that followed.

This young man didn't tell me ahead of time what the problem was. Figure 24–1 shows what his field on the ketheric template looked like when he arrived. Compare it to Figure 7–13 in Chapter 7, which shows what the normal field on the ketheric template level looks like. Instead of beautiful golden fibers forming the spinning petals of the chakras at his solar plexus, John had a formation that looked rather like a sunspot. A large mass of tangled red, yellow and

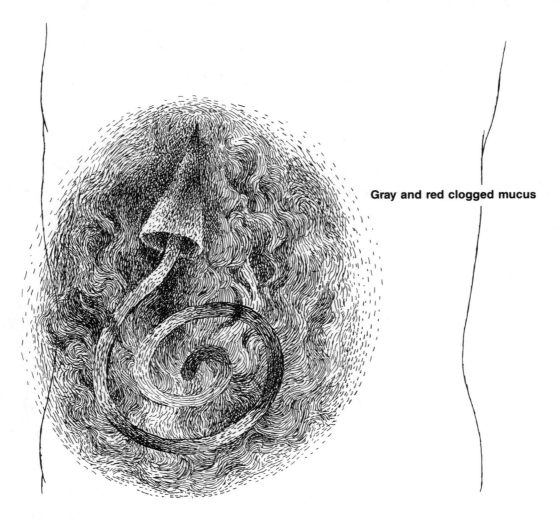

**Gray and red clogged mucus**

Figure 24–3:  Past-Life Lance Revealed as Aura Clears

black energy created little whirlpools flowing off from it that appeared mostly in gray. Most of the other chakras were intact (and are not shown here). The main vertical golden power current that runs up and down the spine had a large deviation to the right towards the sunspot area and was very dark in that area. Small gray secondary whirlpools formed on the rear part of the aura too. As John talked about his life, I suddenly saw him in a past life sometime around the era of Genghis Khan. The scene was in a battle where he was lustfully killing a soldier from the "other army" with a hand weapon. He had a rod with a chain, and on the end of the chain was a metal ball with spikes with which he impaled his enemy's head. At the same time this happened, the enemy was plunging a lance into John's solar plexus. Both were killed in this interaction. This experience left him with the belief that any lusty, powerful expression of the life-force energy leads to injury and death.

In this lifetime, John tended to hold back any strong integrated expression of the life force from within him. Instead, he divided his power into separate parts for expression. His profession of directing plays served as a tool to help integrate the parts of himself. By expressing different aspects of strong life force in the different characters in the different plays, he could experience the results of what a particular expression

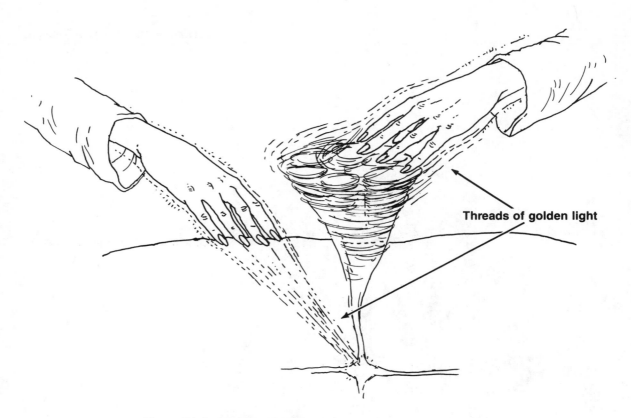

**Threads of golden light**

Figure 24–4:   Golden Threads of Ketheric Template Healing

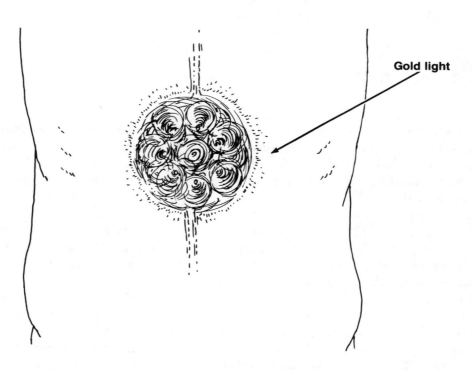

**Gold light**

Figure 24–5:   Ketheric Level of the Healed Third Chakra

248

caused. Thus, his plays gave him many mini-life-like experiences to help him learn how to express his power.

When he came into the office, I was unaware that John had scoliosis until he turned around and I could see it with regular sight. He had been born with it and had never had an operation to straighten his spine. Thus, my interpretation was that this congenital disease was a direct outcome of that past life.

In the healing sequence, after chelation, I used a crystal to scoop out the stagnated energy in the wound near the solar plexus (Figure 24–2). This stagnated energy was from the auric bodies two and four. The crystal works very well for this purpose and speeds up the process of cleansing. It also protects the healer from absorbing any of this stagnated energy.

Figure 24–3 shows what could be seen once a lot of the stagnated energy from the second and fourth auric levels had been cleared. I found the lance embedded in his solar plexus on the fifth energy level, or etheric template level. The handle of the lance was completely embedded within the auric field and curled into a spiral. To remove it, first I had to straighten the handle and then yank out the lance by the handle, cleaned the wound more and revitalized the area.

In the next few healings that followed, I worked with the guides to restructure the aura on the ketheric template (or seventh auric level). First, I restructured the template of the organs in that area and then the chakra. Figure 24–4 shows what I see while doing the chakra restructuring. Tiny lines of gold-white light come out of my fingertips which move very rapidly to weave a golden structure of vortices that constitute the structure of that chakra. The blue etheric level (first auric layer) is then filled in and rests upon the golden level, just as the cells of the body rest upon the blue (lower) etheric level. After restructuring, the chakra then looks like Figure 24–5, a beautiful lotus of golden spinning vortices.

After the chakra was restructured, I and the guides restructured the main power current that was darkened and out of alignment and reconnected the chakra to it. Thus, when the set of healings was completed, my client again looked like Figure 7–13 in Chapter 7 with a complete set of functioning chakras and main power current.

During the five or so sessions that it took to do this work, the client progressively felt more freedom of movement in that area of his body. He felt less tension in the muscles of the back that he used to compensate for his imbalanced field. He also said that he felt more freedom in his personal life.

I saw him a month later for a check up to make sure everything held and then referred him to someone who works primarily on the body level for further physical restructuring now that the energy restructuring was completed. Just how much straighter his spine will become is questionable. This would take a lot of very deep healing. (See the section on purple-blue light in Chapter 23.)

## Healing Past-life Bands in the Ketheric Template Layer

As noted earlier, another way to read past lives is simply to put your hands into the bands of color that appear at the ketheric or eggshell level of the aura. By doing this and tuning into the energy there, you can see the past lives flow before your eyes.

The past-life band that is relevant to what is happening right now in the person's present life is found around the face and neck area of the client and in the aura about two and one half to three feet out. By putting your hands above the face and following the band to the right with the right hand and to the left with the left hand, you can see the past life pass by in linear time. Just what you do with this information is very important. Again, it is not good to expose the client to something he is not ready for. If the client has done a lot of purification work on himself, then it may be okay to let him know what is there. It may be very related to his present life. I would never give this information out unless I was very familiar with the client's process and knew that he was ready for it.

I have done very little to change these past-life bands and think that very little should be done with them. I sometimes run my hands through them to make them clearer or "lighten" them when they appear to be burdened. At times I have seen the energy in such a band all bunched up, in which case I usually spread it out along the band. The person usually feels some relief and a lightening of his load when I do this.

It is my impression that these bands are related to the task the person has undertaken in this lifetime and needs to do in order to grow. Many times I get the sense that I am invading a very private personal space when I reach into these areas, so I withdraw from them. It is very important for the healer to respect the power of the work that the client is doing in these high levels of the field and only do what the healer and client are ready for. This is actually a general rule for working on all levels of the aura: Respect the work and humility of your position in the great scheme of the universe while always focusing on unconditional love, the greatest healer of all.

## Chapter 24 Review

1. How are blocks sometimes related to past-life experiences seen on the psychological level?
2. Describe the relationship between blocks in the HEF from this lifetime and those from other lifetimes.
3. How can one do past-life therapy with the use of laying-on of hands?
4. What is a very important thing to do in healing after a past-life trauma has been removed from the HEF?
5. When is past-life healing appropriate? When is it not? Is it necessary?
6. How are past-life blocks laid down in the auric field?
7. What is a direct current (DC) shift? Describe how it is related to past-life experience.

## Food For Thought

8. What is a past life anyway, if time is not linear?

# PART VI

# SELF HEALING AND THE
# SPIRITUAL HEALER

"Physician, heal thyself."

Jesus

*Introduction*

# TRANSFORMATION AND SELF RESPONSIBILITY

You and only you are responsible for your health. If you have a physical problem you must make the final decision to follow a particular curative program. Only with the greatest of care should you make these decisions. To start with, you choose from a vast array of help available to you. Whom do you trust? How long do you follow a cure when you cannot tell whether or not it is working? These questions can only be answered from your deep searching for what is right for you.

If you don't trust a diagnosis, there is nothing wrong with a second or third opinion, or another technique altogether. If you are confused about what has been said to you about your particular ailment, ask the doctor more questions, find some books, learn about what you are involved with. Take charge of your health. Most of all, do not let yourself be limited by a negative prognosis. Rather take it as a message to look deeper into yourself and wider into the available alternative methods. Standard western medicine has many answers, but not all. If it is not efficient in curing a certain disease, then look elsewhere. Cover all bases. You will be surprised about how much there is to learn about yourself and your health. The search will change your life in ways you would never expect. I have met many people whose illness has eventually brought them great joy, a deep understanding and appreciation of life and the fulfillment they were not able to achieve before becoming ill.

If we can only change our attitude toward illness to one of acceptance and understanding that it is a message to be learned from, we would alleviate a great deal of fear that we have about illness, not only on a personal level but perhaps on a national or global scale as well.

In this section, I will present my suggestions on how to maintain your health. This includes daily practices from which to choose as well as comments on diet, space and clothing. But most of all, you need love to maintain your health. Self-love is the greatest healer, and self-love also requires daily practice.

# Chapter 25

# THE FACE OF THE NEW MEDICINE: PATIENT BECOMES HEALER

As our view of illness changes, so does our way of treating it. As we become more efficient in diagnosis and treating illness, we can individualize our curative programs more. Each individual is unique and requires a slightly different combination of agents used in the healing process. Each healing session is different. The healer must be prepared with a wide background of information, lots of love and good contact with her spirit guides in healing and in channelling. As we move into a more refined way of doing healing, the practice becomes an art. Here is a detailed case study of a patient I worked with for over two years that demonstrates what I think is a small peek at what is ahead for us. I have chosen David because his work illustrates all levels and phases of healing. It shows how deep healing can go into the structure of personality when it is done over a long period of time. Heyoan has said that "the precise substance taken in the precise amount at the precise time acts as a transformative substance." In this case study I use a combination of laying-on of hands, direct accessing of information and psychodynamic analysis. These combined with the patient's own initiative and self-responsibility effected not only a cure of the illness, but also very deep life changes. These profound changes were only possible because the patient took full responsibility for his own healing.

Finding the initiating cause of an illness is always a key part of a healing. Direct accessing of information is always an invaluable tool for this. In the case presented, the cause of the illness is discussed from the point of view of the physical life circumstance, the psychodynamics involved, the patient's belief systems and the patient's spiritual life plan.

## The Healing of David

David grew up in California. His parents were psychologists. He loved the ocean, surfing and the sun. David received a Ph.D. in Kinesiology from the University of California and then began to teach. Later he spent some time in India, where he fell in love with another American, Anne, and also became quite ill. He and Anne returned to the U.S. For the next four years, his search for healing took him over the U.S., where he received various diagnoses from possible mononucleosis, chronic persistent hepatitis and unknown viruses to "it's all in your head, there is nothing wrong with you." Meanwhile his energy was decreasing rapidly, and it was getting more and more difficult for him to work. By the time he got to my office, his energy would be good for a day or two, then it would disappear, and he would spend a day or two in bed.

David walked into my office with the energy field shown in Figure 25–1. The most obvious and serious problem was in the solar plexus chakra, which was torn open and needed to be

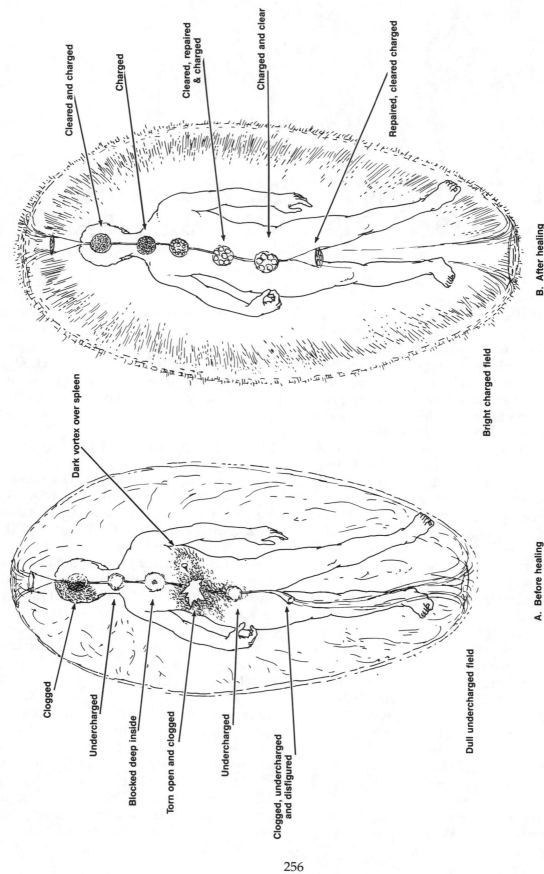

Cleared and charged

Charged

Cleared, repaired & charged

Charged and clear

Repaired, cleared charged

B. After healing

Bright charged field

Dark vortex over spleen

Clogged

Undercharged

Blocked deep inside

Torn open and clogged

Undercharged

Clogged, undercharged and disfigured

Dull undercharged field

A. Before healing

Figure 25-1: Case Study of David (Diagnostic View)

256

sewn back into form on all the structured layers of the field, including the seventh. The second most important problem was the distortion of the first chakra. It was bent to the left and was clogged. This caused a lack of ability to take energy into the energy system through the base chakra. The combination of a torn third chakra that leaked energy and a clogged first chakra caused a very depleted energy system. This depletion would be strongly felt physically because the first chakra metabolizes the majority of energy associated with physical strength, as discussed in Chapter 11. In addition to these problems, the aura also showed a depletion and weakness in the second chakra, which is associated not only with sexual function (which was down), but also with the immune system. There is a lymphatic center located there. The heart center showed a block deep inside its vortex. It is also associated with the immune system through the thymus gland. This block was located two-thirds of the way down into the spiral of the heart chakra. Whenever I have seen this configuration in people, it has been associated with an issue regarding the individual's relationship to God and his belief about what God's Will is. (More about that later.) The throat center was undercharged. This center is associated with communication, self-responsibility and also giving and receiving. The third eye was clogged and blocked all the way deep into the head and into the pineal gland. The crown chakra was weak and undercharged. The whole aura was deflated and dull.

Upon examining the organs, I could see a great deal of clogging and dark energy in the liver. There were layers of discoloration in the liver. One was dark slimy green, one was an ugly yellow, and deeper inside near the spine there were areas that were almost black. The etheric matrix of the liver itself was torn and deformed. Upon closer inspection, I saw multiple infectious organisms, some bacterial and some viral in size and appearance. These organisms spread throughout the middle abdominal area, including the pancreas, spleen and digestive tract. Over the pancreas there was a small, swiftly spinning vortex making a high-pitched screeching sound. This configuration is usually associated with sugar metabolism problems like diabetes or hypoglycemia. The overall field was undercharged and weak. Instead of nice, bright streamers coming from the sixth layer, they were limp and dull. This was a very sick man.

For the student of healing, I suggest that at this point you stop reading, analyze the field and make out the healing plan that you would follow. Where would you start first? Would you use as much energy as you could possibly run into this system to charge it? Why or why not? When would you repair the seventh layer tear, and why? What would you imagine could be the initiating cause of this illness, and how does it show in the auric field? Will this be a rapid recovery or a slow one? Why? All these questions will be answered in the following description on the healing process that occurred.

## The Healing Sequence: First Phase: Clearing, Charging and Restructuring the Field

For the first several weeks, healings were centered on first chelating the field, straightening the first chakra and then slowly but surely repairing the problem in the third chakra area. I would sit sometimes for a half to three quarters of an hour with my hands on David's liver and third chakra area. It was impossible to charge the aura very strongly because of the weakness in the third chakra area. A strong energy charge would have the possibility of ripping that chakra more. It was relatively easy during these weeks to straighten and clear the first chakra. This was done systematically, whereas most of the focus of each healing would center on the mid-abdominal area. Repairing the tears in the auric field took a long time because the changes needed were so great. The aura couldn't be charged fully because the tear in the third chakra would either tear more or certainly leak more energy if a strong charge were sent through it. Each time David came in we would chelate, charge and repair part of the area of the third chakra, put a temporary "seal" or "bandage" over the tear and let it heal for a week. The next week a little more was done. Each week I would go deeper into the field to repair the structure of the aura, first cleansing, then restructuring, in a step-by-step process. It was necessary to repair the structure of the etheric level first, then the etheric template level of the liver and other anatomical structures in that area as well as the chakra. As the weeks wore on, David's energy began to level out. Rather than the rapid up-and-down phases, he stayed at an even low. This did not seem like progress to him, but it did to me. I could see the field slowly readjusting itself. Rather than the strong energy flip-flops caused by his body's trying to compensate for the weakness, and then not being able to maintain the compensation, his energy leveled out to the actual level his body could maintain in his condition. For David this was very discouraging.

David's first chakra began to hold its straightened position, and the second chakra began to charge up. Finally, he began to regain his energy and sexuality. He also started to feel less vulnerable emotionally.

During most of David's first three months of healing, Heyoan would not make comments to him. Heyoan would simply say to me that David had had quite enough psychological or spiritual lectures, and it would be rather like "cosmic law jammed down his throat." So I refrained from doing much psychodynamics in this phase of the work. It was not the most important thing at this phase. Charging and repair were much more important. The healer can only move as fast as the patient is able to move. Finally, David's field was strong enough to run enough energy through it at a high vibration to repair the seventh layer.

Then David began to want more information. He started asking questions about the meaning of his illness in order to understand it in terms of his personal life situation.

## The Healing Sequence:
## Second Phase: Psychodynamics and Some Initiating Causes

David's inquiry came as his third chakra (the linear mind) began to function more smoothly. Slowly a picture formed of the human level of causative factors of his illness.

Every child has strong connections with the mother, as discussed in Chapter 8. This connection is made when the child is in the womb and after birth that connection can be seen through the auric umbilical cord that remains between mother and child. This cord connects their third chakras. After birth there is also a strong heart connection formed between child and mother through their heart chakras.

The original tear in David's third chakra happened at a time near puberty when he rebelled from a very domineering and controlling mother. Before this time, David had done all he could to please her. Both his psychologist parents had unwittingly misused their knowledge of psychology to exert control over their son.

David's solution to gain autonomy was like that of many teenagers. He broke ties with his parents. Unfortunately, the only way he knew how to do this was literally to break the tie that bound him to his mother. He was left with loose auric umbilical cords and a hole in the solar plexus area. Of course the most natural thing to do is to find someone else with whom to connect and thereby to replace mother. (At this stage everyone thinks the problem is mother's, not one's self.) Unfortunately, he discovered that he kept connecting with women who were controlling. His energy system would automatically attract someone who was controlling, simply because that is the kind of energy David was used to being connected to. That is what felt like "normal" to him. (Like attracts like.) These unsatisfactory relationships led him on a search for himself, and eventually to an ashram in India. He began to see that the problem was inside himself.

On the heart level, David's fourth chakra never really connected strongly to his mother's. She had, from the beginning, not accepted who he was. When he did connect to her with his heart, he found it necessary to become the person she wanted him to be. That meant self-betrayal. David felt betrayal in his heart. Every young man has a plight of the heart. Although he strongly connects through his heart to his mother, he must eventually learn to transfer that to his mate, so that he can become a full man with sexual potency—an experience he can never have with his first love, his mother. If he does not connect to the heart of his mother, then he has no model for doing so when it is time to find a mate and will have a difficult time loving.

David's problem in relationship was also one of not knowing how to connect with love through the heart. This brought him to India, to a guru who, in David's words, had "One Big Heart." Through this ashram experience, David learned how to make the heart connection. First with his guru, and then with Anne, who he met there. However, he found that when connecting through the heart to his guru, he also little by little gave up his will. He was trying to learn unconditional love, but conditions set in. As David gave up his will, he began again to feel betrayed, but this time the issue was not just loving another human being, but loving humanity and loving God. The issue was now revealed in the form of David's will versus God's will. This showed in the heart configuration in the auric field. David had found that now that he was no longer a "good boy" for Mom, he was being a "good boy" for the guru and God. He and Anne decided to leave, and another tear in the third chakra was experienced when breaking away from the guru. But he had gained the use of his heart. For the first time in his life he was deeply connected to a woman from the heart, as well as through the solar plexus chakras.

The search for acceptance and perfect love is very strong in the human soul and will lead it through many lessons. I have found that people who spent years living in a spiritual community in the 70s learned to open up their hearts, but slowly gave up a lot of autonomy—just as they did in childhood. Many found it helpful to experience profound love within the confines of a structured community before they could bring it out into the world on their own. This is especially true if it was not experienced in the childhood home. After having experienced love in a community, and having unfortunately given up some of their free will to do so, they need now to hold that love in the heart and to surrender to God's will as manifested within their own heart—not to someone else's definition of God's will.

As David's healing progressed, problems in his relationship with his girlfriend that were chronic became intolerable to David. He was changing in ways that were not compatible to his mate's vibrations because she did not change in the same way. Their fields no longer pulsed in harmony.

Anyone in a long-term relationship knows this phenomenon. If you change and your mate does not change at the same rate, there is a time period when the two wonder who it is they are living with. Will the other change and be compatible? This is usually possible if both live with patience and love. If not, eventually one will move on. David and Anne began to work together to solve their problems. With a great deal of love and sincerity, they focused primarily on the psychodynamics of the situation. David's main interest had turned to his work, his freedom and gaining his own personal power. Anne, however, wanted to continue following her guru and to build a different kind of life.

In addition to the cords that grow between mother and child, people in relationships grow cords of energy between each other. These are connected through the chakras. In a healthy relationship these cords are clear bright gold, balanced and connected through most of the chakras. In a lot of relationships, these cords simply repeat the unhealthy connections that were there from childhood between parent and child. Many of these cords connect in the solar plexus and are dark in color. During the process of transforming a relationship from unhealthy to healthy, the unhealthy cords must be disconnected, energized and reconnected deep into the individual's own core. They are cords of dependency that must be rooted back into the individual so that he can rely upon himself. David and his friend slowly disconnected their dependent cords. This is a very scary process. The personal feeling sometimes is as if one is floating in space, not connected to anything. In doing this one leaves the "illusory safety" of rigidity and replaces it with a flexible self-reliance.

If you have ever gone through a divorce or the death of a mate, you will understand this phenomenon. Many people refer to their spouses as their "better half." I have heard be-reaved people speak of feeling torn apart or of losing their better half. In such a serious trauma, one feels as if one's whole front has been torn off. This is literally true. Many times I see those threads from the solar plexus dangling about in space after such a painful separation.

## The Healing Sequence:
## Third Phase: Transformative Substances

As David took his power back, he took more of an active role in the healings. He began to ask Heyoan very specific questions. He asked Heyoan what physical treatment he should be taking. (I could still see the microorganisms in David's mid-abdominal area. He needed something.) David had heard of a serum from Canada that helped people with debilitating diseases. Should he take that? "No," Heyoan answered. "Well, it might help a little, but there is another drug that would be powerful." Heyoan told me it was related to what is used in the treatment of malaria, like quinine. Then Heyoan showed me a picture of a swimming pool and said the first part of the word was *chlorine,* as in a swimming pool. The drug's name was like chlorine-quinine. Chloroquine. Heyoan said that if David took that drug it would act to wash the liver clean. He showed me a picture of David's liver being washed clear with a silvery liquid. Heyoan then added that David could get this drug from a doctor in the New York area where we lived. Heyoan also stated that David should not take a standard dosage, but should vary the dosage according to his needs, checking every day to see what he needed by using his High Sense Perception and a pendulum.

David began his search. I was stunned when he came back to my office the next week with some chloroquine. I had never heard of it. David had asked a doctor if he had ever heard of a drug like the one Heyoan had described. The doctor immediately took a book down from the shelf describing the uses of chloroquine. It was used in some cases of chronic persistent hepati-tis like David had. Since the doctor's diagnosis agreed with Heyoan's, he prescribed chloroquine in the normal dosages.

David began taking the drug and checking the dosage with his pendulum on a daily basis. The first five days on the drug affected David strongly, not only physically but also emotionally. He went into the depths of emotional agony. He experienced his problems (described earlier) very strongly. He described one day's experience as having spent the day "burrowing into his girlfriend's belly." He knew it was a cleansing. He wanted to reexperience the feelings in order to heal himself. After five days he stopped the chloroquine as his pendulum reading suggested.

Heyoan told David to take cleansing teas and vitamins for a week or two after the first bout with the chloroquine. I could see from the auric field that after taking the drug for five days David's colon (slimy, yellow-brown) was clogging up from the discharge of toxins as he cleared his infections. Cleansing teas were needed. After several days off the chloroquine, David "read" with the pendulum that it was time to go back on it again. He did. He would be on it for several days, then off for several. Each time he took it, he would sink into another layer of his personality that needed clearing. Each time he did so, he would come out stronger, more alive and more powerful. Each time he took it, more of the microorganism cleared from his body, and his aura grew brighter and fuller. He was truly transforming himself. At times, Heyoan would suggest another vitamin or cell salt (like ferrum phosphate, iron phosphate) to help the healing along.

I asked Heyoan why he had not mentioned the chloroquine earlier? He said that David's field was so damaged that he would not have been able to stand the strong effects of the chloroquine until the repair was completed.

During the second phase of healing, when David began dealing with psychodynamics, he and Anne broke up several times. They had been together over a decade and had a lot to clear up between them. Slowly they got further and further apart and finally separated. From the auric point of view, since David's solar plexus chakra was no longer torn and his auric field was so brightly charged, he was no longer compatible in vibrations with his old mate. Her choice was to change in another way, to walk her own path and to create her own new life.

As David regained his power, he started dealing with his relationship to God and God's will. He began to meditate to find God's will within himself. As he did this, he began to clear the deep holding within his heart chakra. He began to surrender to his own heart. Emmanuel (1985) has said,

> Willing a release makes the
> release tighter
> because it does not yield to will.
> It yields to yielding.
>
> The final lesson for each soul
> is the total surrender to
> God's will
> manifest in your own heart.

Sometime soon after David met a woman and started a relationship. This relationship was very supportive and nurturing to him. As I read the relationship for David, I could see him being soothed by the field of his new partner. It was as if the effect of her company alone expanded his auric field, whereas previously he had always contracted his field in the presence of the person he was in a relationship with.

## The Healing Sequence: Fourth Phase: Transmutation and Rebirth

During the last month that I worked with David, I began to see a configuration within his field that I had never seen before. It appeared to be uncovered by the work we had done. It looked like a cocoon surrounding the spine. It is difficult for me to say which level of the field it was on. But it appeared that this cocoon held a lot of dormant energy waiting to be tapped. I didn't speak to David about this cocoon, but quietly watched it as I worked primarily on clearing the

sixth chakra. All the rest of the aura was clear and bright (Fig. 26–1B).

David came to his last session looking very different. His aura was twice as bright and much larger than usual. The cocoon had opened. I asked what had happened to him? He said that he had taken a drug popularily called ecstasy or MDMA, a synthetic drug of the phenylethylamine class synthesized from meth-amphetamine and safrole, over the weekend. Upon closer inspection, I could see that the MDMA had opened the left side of the pineal gland. The mucus from the third eye that had been placed there partially from doing pot and LSD was cleared away on the right side. There was still work to be done, but the overall change in David's field was amazing.

Since my observations had always shown psychotrophic drugs to have a negative effect on the aura, I asked Heyoan about it. He said, "That depends on who takes it, and what their field configuration is at the time of taking it. Since David's sixth chakra was clogged, and it was time for him to work on opening it, the drug had a strong effect. But if the individual involved needed to focus on a different chakra, the effect would most likely be negative."

When a different patient asked if she could take MDMA, Heyoan said, "No, I would not recommend it for you. Rather take ovatrophine to strengthen your second chakra, where you need to work." (Ovatrophine is made of freeze-dried beef ovaries.) She took ovatrophine and had experiences similar to those David had when he took chloroquine. Heyoan wishes to emphasize that the new medicine deals on all levels to heal the whole person. It focuses on the soul's destiny as the main issue. What lesson is being learned, and how can the individual best learn that lesson? Ultimately the lesson is that you are a spark of the Divine. The more you remember that, the closer to home you get. Drugs can be used as transformative substances. That is their purpose. They do not cure the disease; they assist the individual to cure himself. "The precise substance in the precise amount at the precise times assists the individual to transform himself," says Heyoan.

David asked Heyoan a lot of questions during our last meeting. What was revealed about his changing and the meaning of the cocoon was encouraging for all of us to hear. David asked what had happened to him about a month earlier when he began to feel a deep profound change within himself that seemed permanent. That's when I had started to see the cocoon. At that time he began to feel he had control over his life that was beginning to turn out the way he wanted it. He had a beautiful relationship, and he decided to move to the west coast. Heyoan said that one month ago David had actually completed his incarnation. David had started the last round of completion six years previously when he went to India. That was the last cycle of this lifetime, in which he had chosen to incarnate, to open his heart. One month ago he had actually completed that task. He, at that time, was free to leave, but had chosen not to do so, but to reincarnate in the same body. Heyoan said that future lifetimes were laid down into the field before birth and could be taken on at the completion of a life if the individual so chose. This could be done without leaving the body. "Think of how much more efficient it is," Heyoan said. The cocoon energy manifest around David's spine was the energy consciousness of the life he was about to begin. Heyoan said that the next three years would be spent integrating two levels of his being into one, and that would take some getting used to. He would have much more energy and much more knowledge available to him as he integrated this energy into his reality. Heyoan suggested that if David wished, he could change his name. Heyoan added that the future did not have to be like the past. Here is part of one of their dialogues:

David: "What does it mean to reincarnate within the same body?"

Heyoan: "In a sense, and here we must use metaphor, you sit down with your spirit guides before birth and choose your parents; choose a set of probable realities; choose work to do; and choose a set of energies that will then build a body. You in a sense separate a portion of your Greater Being, take that consciousness and cre-

ate a body with it. You choose your parents and the physical inherited qualities gained from them.

"You sit down and you choose all that for a specific purpose. If in a particular lifetime, you complete that purpose and reach a certain goal, then it is always very easy to add another lifetime. You simply interweave the new consciousness that would be used in the next body into the old body and consciousness.

"So you have done your work well and, as you fuse your new consciousness within the 'old body,' you will find many changes occurring, for you are now integrating the two."

David: "They already are."

Heyoan: "Absolutely. Isn't it a wonderful thing? When you die, or we prefer to say leave or drop the body, and no longer need the body as a tool for transformation, transmutation and transcendence, you will no longer create one. The body is a tool, a vehicle that you have created to focus on certain points within the self that you wish to transform in a most efficient way. All of the systems in your body are built precisely for that transformation. You will see that in your work, in the nervous system, in the automatic functioning of the body, down to the very cells of the bones. You will find each portion of the body a delicate and beautiful tool for the use of transformation. It is not a burden. It is a gift. It is unfortunate that most human beings do not understand that.

"If again we use the metaphor of sitting down at the conference table with us to choose your life, then you, the greater portion of you, that is not completely incarnated (and we must say that you couldn't possibly do that anyway), that greater portion of you decides whether or not the best place for you for the next transformative work is in a body or not. And when you have made full use of these physical vehicles, whichever one it may be, that is when you end the round of life and death, as it is called, or the wheel of incarnations on the physical plane. It simply is that you no longer need this tool to separate out a linear time, and a three-dimensional space that makes it easier for you to see the particular points that you wish to transform. It is at that point where you decide—you, the greater you, and you are a great soul, much greater than that small portion that is incarnated. You then decide whether or not it is, shall we say, profitable to utilize the physical body. It is more or less like picking up a hoe or a rake. Does the garden still need to be raked? If so, why not do it with a rake, rather than the hand, say?"

David: "And after one finishes his rounds of incarnation on the physical plane?"

Heyoan: "Then enlightenment goes on in another way. We also are clearing ourselves and moving toward God. There are an infinite number of stages. For if you were to be carried from one level of reality to the next to the next, you would go into an infinite space. At this point you can only go to a certain height because your perception ability is not that broad. The more enlightened one gets, the broader the perception. There is really no end to it. Healing on the higher levels becomes creativity.

"Your physical reality is now in transition into the next phase, where transformation will no longer focus on pain. Future transformation and healing will encompass movement, music and art in a creative way. Healing turns into creativity as one moves into the light and holds it within. As the darkness fades, the transformation process becomes one of creativity rather than of healing."

# Chapter 26

# HEALTH, A CHALLENGE
# TO BE YOURSELF

This chapter focuses on specifics of self-care and self-healing. The most important thing to learn about your health is how to maintain it. In my opinion, the most important principles to maintain your health are the following:

1. Maintaining a deep connection to yourself and your purpose in this life, both on the personal level and the world level. This means self-love and self-respect. (Chapters 3 and 26)

2. Understanding what health and healing means to you and for you. (Chapters 14, 15 and 16)

3. Attending to yourself and taking care of yourself. This means listening to inner guidance that tells you as soon as there is an imbalance somewhere and following through on that guidance. (Chapters 1, 3, 17 and 19)

## Taking Care of Yourself

To take good care of yourself, you need a daily routine that includes meditation, exercise, good food, good hygiene, the right amount of rest for you when it is needed, the right clothes, home, pleasure, personal challenge, intimacy and friends. Mix these with a good amount of love, and you will reap great rewards. Your personal needs will vary over the weeks and years. Be flexible. What is right in one period may not be in another. Rather than being told what regimen you in particular need, it is most important for you to determine that for yourself. That is what the essence of healing and good health is all about: Self-responsibility and bringing the power back home to the self. Here is a list of self-care tips and healing exercises found in this book. Remember, variety is the spice of life, and personal growth thrives on change.

1. Meditation (Chapters 3, 17, 19 and 20). My favorite meditation is one that was given by Emmanuel in a workshop that Pat, Emmanuel, Heyoan and I gave. I call it the future/past meditation.

Sit comfortably, preferably with your back straight. Pay attention to your breathing. Breathe in and breathe out. With each inbreath, breathe in the future, and all its potent possibilities. As you breathe out, breathe out the past and all that went with it. Simply breathe in the future and breathe out the past. For what you breathe in is the future and what you breathe out is the past. Let the past go. Breathe in the future, and all that you wish to create. Breathe out the past, and all those false limitations you place upon yourself. The future does not have to have anything to do with the past. Let the past go. Continue to breathe in the future and breathe out the past. See all of your past going out behind you, and the future coming to you. See your past lifetimes flowing out behind you, and your future lifetimes flowing toward you. Breathe in the future and out the past. Watch the flow of time and see yourself as the central point of consciousness. You are the central point of consciousness, and experience moves by you. You sit in the center of reality. That you is unchanging. You exist outside the boundaries of time. Now, in that moment between the in-breath of the future and the outbreath of the past there is a pause. It is in that moment of pause between breaths when you will slip into the eternal now.

2. Physical exercises (Chapter 21). In addition to these exercises there are lots of fitness centers around the country now that offer aerobics, nautilus, yoga and martial arts like t'ai chi. Do you like to swim or jog? What gives you the most pleasure? Do it.

3. Good food. This is not mentioned much in this book. There are good diets listed in the many diet books to be found in bookstores. I recommend a diet that follows many of the rules of the macrobiotic schools. Very little meat, organic if you want it. I especially do not recommend red meat. Plenty of balanced grains, vegetables, salads and some fruit. Eat what is in season. According to season, the winter diet leans more toward root vegetables and the summer more toward fresh salads, vegetables and fruits. Grains are needed all year round.

Be careful of the vitamins you take. Many people have strong negative reactions to some of the vitamins they take regularly, but don't know it. If you are doing healing work, you will need to supplement your diet with a good multi-mineral/multi-vitamin product and take extra amounts of calcium, potassium, magnesium and vitamin C. You may need some extra B vitamins too. I am being purposely vague about this, because each person's body needs vary. You will want to find what you need to take, the amount you need, when to take it and for how long.

Pay attention to your food when you eat it. Make it look appealing on the plate. Be aware that the food is going into your body to nourish you, give you energy and grow your cells. Chew it, taste it and, most of all, enjoy it since food is from the abundant earth.

For an experiment some time, follow the food through your body once you swallow it.

Pay attention to your apestat, which is the mechanism through which your body tells the taste buds what it needs. That is different from craving. What do you crave? Usually what you crave is what you are allergic to. Don't eat it. In three to ten days the craving will go away. Give your body what it needs. Listen to its messages. Of course if you crave one thing all the time, then something is wrong. If you always want sweet things, then find out why. You probably haven't been feeding yourself properly, and your body is making up for it by craving fast energy.

Of course you know that many of the additives used in food to preserve them are very bad for you. Most of our foods also contain small amounts of poisons from the pesticides, herbicides, fertilizers and chemicals found in the environment. The best way to deal with this is to eat only organically grown foods. Do not buy processed foods with preservatives. Yes, organic foods take longer to cook and cost more, but in the long run you will save the money in medical bills. Eat only fertile eggs.

If you cannot get organic vegetables and eggs where you live, you can remove some of the poisonous effect by soaking them in Clorox. When you come home from the grocery store, simply fill the sink with water, add one quarter cup Clorox, and soak all your fresh produce and eggs in it for twenty minutes. Rinse thoroughly, wash off the dirt and put the food away. Also use extra rinses, especially with dishes, to ensure no detergent residues are being ingested which can cause breakdowns of our defenses in the digestive system.

Just remember, the fresher your food, the healthier it is and the more life energy it has to give you.

4. Good hygiene. Cleansing your body and caring for your skin, teeth and hair are important. In cleansing your body use soaps or other skin

cleansers that are pH-balanced acid/alkali balanced for your skin. The skin has a natural acid mantle that prevents infection. If you work against that protection by using soaps and creams that are alkaline, you will be working against your body, rather than with it. Use a shower brush on your skin when you shower. This will help remove the old dead layer of skin which your body sloughs off regularly to leave room for the new cells to grow. Use a pH-balanced skin lotion if you are in a dry climate. It helps maintain the moisture in your skin. Use natural, hypoallergenic and nontoxic soaps and cosmetics whenever possible.

The same holds true for your hair. Don't use rinses that leave heavy residue on the hair. Make sure your shampoo is pH-balanced and is nontoxic for you.

Be sure to floss your teeth once a day. Brush your teeth at least twice a day. If you have gum problems, use a mixture of 1 part salt to 8 parts baking soda to brush with once a day.

5. Rest. The amount of rest you need is again a personal thing. Are you a night or day person? Listen to your body. When does your body need rest? Does it like a full six to nine hours or would it prefer less sleep time at night and naps during the day? When you are tired, rest, no matter what time of day it is. You will find that if you lie down immediately, it will take only half an hour or so to regain your energy again. Listen to your body's needs. If you can't get a half hour, try fifteen minutes. I bet you can find that in your busy day.

6. Clothing. I have found that many synthetic fabrics interfere with the natural energy flow of the aura. These are acrylics, many polyesters and nylon. Nylon stockings strongly interfere with the energy flow up and down the legs and are, in my opinion, related to many of the female illnesses we have in our modern societies now. I recommend that you only wear them when you really must. Find substitutes. It is best to avoid fabrics with aldehyde/formaldehyde in them and made from petroleum by-products—especially if you think you might be hypersensitive.

Natural fibers have a strong positive effect on the aura. They enhance and sustain it. Cottons, silks and wools are best. Fabrics that are mixtures are also fine. 50% cotton fabrics are great. Some synthetics seem to be fine also. My body and energy field like rayon and some things made of orlon, like socks.

When you look in the closet in the morning, and there is "nothing to wear," it may be because the color you need is not there. What color do you need today? Your aura may be low in a color, and you need to energize yourself with that color by wearing it.

Stock your closet. Stock it with different textures of clothes too. Have a variety of textures to choose from, depending on how you feel that day.

Does your style of clothes suit you, or do you dress for others? Make sure what you wear expresses who you are.

7. Home. Do you have the space and amount of light you need? Is your home comfortable for you? If you have time to care for them, plants lend a nice healing energy to your space. Does your home have the colors you need? Is the air that you breathe fresh? If not, get an air ionizer/precipitator. If you have fluorescent lights in your home or workspace, get rid of them. Turn them off. Use incandescent lights.

8. Pleasure. If you do not give yourself enough time for pleasure, budget that time just as you do your work time. Pleasure is just as important as work. Do those things you always wanted to do to have fun. Now is the time. Laugh regularly, discover the child in you and enjoy every moment.

9. Personal challenge. Everyone has things they have always wanted to do but put it off to next year or assume they never can. Wrong assumption. This is the year. Whether it is a pleasure trip, a creative challenge or a change in profession, you really need to give yourself the chance to at least try it. Is there a certain kind of work you have always wanted to do? Check it out. See what it would take and make a plan to deal with this inner longing. Remember that *your*

*deepest inner longing, that which you want to do more than anything, is precisely what you have come into this life to do. Your best assurance of health is to do it.* Start now, explore what it would take and begin. Even if it takes a long time to get there, if you don't start out on the journey, you won't reach the goal. If you do and continue to walk toward it, you will. Your inner guidance will guarantee it.

10. Intimacy and friends. We all need intimacy and friends. Find what that means for you and create it in your life. Make your own rules about this. If there is someone you have always liked, but haven't done anything about it because you are too shy, take a chance. Tell that person you like him or her and would like to be a friend. You will be surprised how well that works. If it doesn't, try another person.

11. Self-care in accident and illness. Before you need one, find a local health care professional of your choice. There are many available now, and it is better to know what to do and where you will go before you have to do it. Pick a physician with whom you have a good rapport and whom you really trust. There are healers, homeopaths, naturopaths, acupuncturists, chiropractors, masseuses, people that do kinesiology, nutritionists, etc.

For yourself, I suggest some courses on home care or care of the family. Homeopathy is a wonderful way for a woman or man to nurse her or his own family back to health. I have been using it for years and have found that in practically every case I have encountered with my children the right homeopathic remedy combined with a simple laying-on of hands did the trick. I have treated all the typical child's problems from strep throat to crunched fingers successfully with homeopathy.

12. The simple healing techniques I recommend that you use for your family are the following: Start with the chelation (Chapter 22). Everyone can learn it. Then, after going through all the chakras, put your hand directly on the place that hurts. Sit in a state of love for the person involved. It will make both of you feel wonderful.

If the area seems to be clogging up with energy, you may want to pull some clogged stuff out. Simply imagine your fingers growing three inches longer and becoming filled with blue light. Now reach into the place that is clogged and scoop up handfuls of it and hold it up into the air. Let it turn to white light. Since your fingers are now three inches longer than normal, you can reach right through the skin and three inches into the body. Go ahead, try it. It works, and it is very easy.

Complete the healing by holding your hands on your wife's/husband's/daughter's/son's head. Then after a few minutes, comb their whole auric field with your long fingers. Make long strokes from the head down to the toes holding your hand about six inches away from the body. Cover the whole body on all sides.

End by holding your hands in running water for a while. Use a pleasant temperature.

If you are the one who is sick or has had an injury, do as much of this for yourself as you can. Get a friend to do it for you. If you have an illness, each night when you go to bed put your hands on that area. Send it love and energy. Visualize yourself well and balanced. Ask what the message is that is coming to you from your body. Where and how have you not been listening to yourself? What is the meaning of this injury or illness to you both on the personal level and on the life task level? And most important, love yourself, accept yourself. If you have a serious illness, don't judge yourself for it. Love yourself. You have the courage to make the message strong enough to hear. You have decided to face whatever it is that you need to face in order to learn what it is you want to know. That is a very courageous act. Respect yourself for it. Love yourself. Love yourself. Love yourself. You are a part of the Divine. You are one with God. Here are two of Heyoan's self-healing meditations. They will help you:

## Heyoan's Meditation on Self-healing

1. "Scan your body in any way that you wish: inner sight, intuition, feeling sense.

"Find the area of your body, with help of your guide if you wish, that you are most concerned about.

"If you do not find a problem area, you can focus on something that is happening in your life right now that you are concerned about. Find the area in the body or life.

2. "If you wish, give it a form, color, substance, shape, density. Is it sharp, dull? If it is a particular pain, does it last a long time? Does it ache? Is it sharp? Does it come and go?

"Is the situation in your life new? Old? How do you feel when you are confronted with it and what has your chronic or habitual response been? Consider any particular situation that we are speaking of.

"Example: If there is a pain in your body, what happens in your mind when you feel it?

"Does your mind read and put terrible labels on it?

"In the circumstances in your life, do you feel anger or fear? Do you feel fear about what is happening in your body? And what do you do then with the response? What is the habitual response that has (in a sense) gotten you nowhere. You know the habitual response doesn't work, because the pain is still there. Especially if the pain is a chronic one, the habitual response has not worked. The message (the lesson, if you will) has not gotten through. So, I would venture to say, my dear, that whatever that response is, it is completely wrong because it does not solve the situation.

"Look at your life and your body—you have fashioned it as a schoolroom in which to learn, and any illness, any pain or any disease is a message, a message to you to teach you a lesson.

3. "So the next question I ask you is why would you create such a pain in your body?

Why would you create such a situation in your life? What is it that you can learn from this? What is the situation or the pain saying to you over and over again until you understand it? Or get it? For until you learn that lesson you will continue to create the situation, for you are your best teacher and you have designed your lessons well and you will not pass yourself into another lesson until you have learned this one.

"If you have found that place in your body, I would recommend that you put your hand or hands there. Allow your greater consciousness to begin merging into that place in your body. And as you do it, if you have not already discovered it, find the nature of the fear. When you have sensed the essence of the nature of that fear, I recommend that you feel it with love. What kind of love is most suitable for this fear? Do this for any area of your life or area of your body. Any illness you have is a direct result and any negative experience in your life is a direct result of the fact that you have not fully loved yourself—you have not fully followed what you wish to do. How have you not harkened to that inner voice? How have you not let yourself be fully who you are? *Any illness is a direct message to you that tells you how you have not been loving who you are, cherishing yourself in order to be who you are.* **This is the basis of all healing.**

4. "Another clue: The lesson is never ever about something you have done wrong or something bad about you.

5. "And so, having found the answer, you will immediately find, most likely, **pain** and **fear** when you have blocked yourself from doing what you have really desired to do. And at that point the choice is to face the fear and allow yourself to feel it and to work with it in your life. For whenever there is **fear**, there has been then the absence of love, for fear is the opposite of love. So wherever there is fear, you can be sure you are not in truth, and most likely what you fear is not real, but illusion. For you are not centered, you are

not within the wholeness of your being when you are afraid. When you take courage to step into that fear you begin the healing process on a new level.

"Homework before going to bed:

1. List your fears.
   What do you fear?
   Perhaps it will focus on your body.
   Perhaps it will focus on your life situation.
   Perhaps they are general fears.

2. "Connect that fear with circumstances in your life. Fear is always directly related to something you are not doing that you want to do. It blocks you from your greatness and is also the doorway to it.

Make a list that says:

| Fears | Life Situations | How You Have Not Loved Yourself— What/How You Wish To Be |
|-------|-----------------|---------------------------------------------------------|
| ——— | ——— | ——————————— |
| ——— | ——— | ——————————— |
| ——— | ——— | ——————————— |
| ——— | ——— | ——————————— |

"What does this all have to do with the aura? It can be seen in the aura. There is form and substance to these things. When you open your perceptions wider you will be able to look at people and see how they have not loved themselves. And then you as a healer will be the link to help them remember who they are and help them love themselves. You as a healer become love."

## Meditation to Dissolve Self-Limitations

"This is a good meditation for those who find themselves confined in areas of their life in which they do not wish to be confined. It is good for self-exploration, good for practice of healership, because illness is nothing but a result of confining oneself within limited definitions of self. As a healer, you must be able to first understand that process in yourself to sense it in others—to help them define it and to help them release those boundaries.

"All of these things have their form in the auric field. They are energy and consciousness that limits you. And thus while working with the aura and healing, you can directly work on the energetic form that is the substance of the limitation.

1. Lift yourself to an expanded state.

2. Drop in the question: Who am I?

3. When you find an answer, search for a limitation that you have placed upon yourself by the simple definition of who you are. When you find that limitation, know that it is a boundary you have placed upon yourself.

4. Throw that limitation outside the boundary, and thus the boundary grows.

5. Again drop in the question, Who am I? Whatever the answer will be, it will give you another definition of self.

6. Separate out the Essence from the limited definition.

7. Throw the limitation outside the boundary, expand again.

8. Ask the question again, etc.

"Practice this meditation regularly during the next coming week. No, I will not define Essence. It is something that you will define in the exercise."

If you wish to become a healer, you can. Your first challenge is to heal yourself. Focus on that, then focus on finding ways to help others heal themselves. This will lead you to your development as a healer. In the next chapter I will talk about what that road may be like.

# Chapter 26 Review

## Food For Thought

1. Grade yourself on a scale of 1–10 on the eleven self-care points listed in this chapter, starting with (1) Meditation.
2. For the points where you gave yourself a low score, find your lower self or shadow self reaction that blocks you. What is the belief and limited conclusion that this reaction is based on?
3. Relate this to an imbalanced chakra or chakras.
4. Do Heyoan's meditation for self-healing.
5. Do Heyoan's meditation to dissolve self-limitations.

*Chapter 27*

# THE DEVELOPMENT OF A HEALER

Becoming a healer is a very individual and personal process. There are no set rules on how that should happen. Everyone's life is unique. No one can bestow healership upon another. It is something that grows from the inside. There are many courses to take, a lot of technical material to study and different schools of thought as to what is really happening in the healing process. Some do not call their practices spiritual at all.

My path to healership was guided along the spiritual way, which was most natural for me. What is most natural for you? Walk your own path, not the well-formed trail. You can take what you choose from the well-formed trail and use it to support and help you create your new ideas. My guide Heyoan has made the following comment about becoming a healer.

## Dedication

"To become a healer means dedication. Not to any specific spiritual practice, religion, or set of rigid rules, but dedication to your particular path of truth and love. This means that your practice of that truth and love will probably change as you travel through your life. There are many roads to 'Heaven,' I dare say, as many as there are souls returning home. If we were to search throughout the history of the human being, we would find many who have traveled before us and found enlightenment. Many of those particular ways that were traveled are no

longer known by the human race at this time in history. Some are being recovered; others are still lost. But no matter, for new ways are continually being formed from the depths of the human soul, from wherever each soul is at any moment, to provide a way home. You see, my dear, this is the process. It is the ever renewing process of the creative force welling up inside of you and everyone else. It is what coming home is all about. When you learn to flow completely, without resistance, with that inner creative movement, then you are home. This is what being home is."

## Tests

As soon as you decided to dedicate yourself to your true path and make that the central priority of your life, you become aware of an overall process taking place in your life. This life process carries you through inner landscapes that change the nature of your personal reality. You begin to see cause and effect relationships between your inner personal reality and the "outer" world.

I was carefully led (by my higher self and guides) through a step-by-step process which was designed to help me learn spiritual law. I spent fairly long periods of time concentrating on and learning about the nature of truth, Divine will and love. After a period of time concentrating on one of these principles, I felt as if I was being tested. I continually found myself in situations where it was very difficult to stay with the truth, love, or to even have much of an idea as to what Divine will might be. At times it appeared that my guides, the angels or God was testing me, and I couldn't do much about it. Eventually, I could see that these tests are designed (with my full agreement) by a consciousness much greater than mine. I am part of that greater consciousness. Ultimately then, in a sense, I design the tests. The small "ego-me" usually wants no part of it. The wiser part of me knows better.

The first thing you will face after committing yourself to your path is your fear.

## Dealing with Fear

Fear is the emotion that is associated with being disconnected from the greater reality. Fear is the emotion of separation. Fear is the opposite of love, which is being connected to the unity of all things.

## Exercise to Find Your Fears

Ask yourself: What is my worst fear at this time in my life? What assumptions about reality is that fear based on? What really is so terrible about that happening? Whatever you try to avoid is related to your fear of feeling the emotions involved. What are they? Deep inside you is a place where you know you can face and go through anything.

If you look within, you will feel your demand that you do not have to experience whatever it is you fear. However, if you let go and surrender to your Divine Spark, you will see that you probably need to face it. As you go through the feared experience, your fear will transform into loving compassion. This includes the experience of dying. For, as Emmanuel says:

> It is not a matter of
>     destroying fear,
> but of knowing its nature
> and of seeing it as a less
>     powerful force
> than the power of love.

> It is illusion.

> Fear
> is only looking in the mirror
> and making faces
> at oneself.

When looking back at my path, I can see clear patterns of development. I was not so aware of the greater pattern when it was happening. I spent most of the time being aware of the issues at hand in each moment.

## Truth

When I first moved to the Phoenicia Pathwork Center and began to practice "the Pathwork" in the form of private sessions, groups and participation as a member of a spiritual community, I found myself immediately faced with the issue of the truth. Was I speaking the truth, or was I convincing myself of a certain reality for my convenience? I was stunned at how I rationalized myself into believing things to validate my behavior and explain unpleasant experiences in my life. My major defense was to blame someone else. How much do you do this? Look for the subtle ways, not the obvious ones.

Slowly, after examining your behavior you will see that cause and effect works in much clearer ways then you thought, and that you, in fact, are creating those negative experiences in some way or another. This is a tough one to face. Buried under these painful creations, you will find an intent to actually live your life that way. This is called "negative intent." My negative intent was based on two things. One was a belief system that life is basically hard, a lot of work and painful. This belief system is not just general, but it is very specific for each person.

## Exercise to Find Your
## Negative Beliefs

For example, fill in the following sentences for yourself. "All men are _____. All women are _____. In a relationship I will be hurt the following ways _____. Maybe I will get sick and die of _____. I will be ripped-off in the following ways _____. I will lose _____ if I don't _____." The other thing my negative intent was based on was negative pleasure; that is, I actually enjoyed negative experiences.

Warning, don't fool yourself, no matter how many workshops you have attended and how much you have worked on yourself, you will benefit from answering the questions. We all have these patterns, though they may not be as overt as they were before.

Everyone does this on some level of her personality. For example, by blaming someone else for your problems (mother, father, wife or husband), you have the pleasure of being the "good one," while they are the "bad ones." Negative pleasure has many variations and forms. You can actually feel the pleasure in being hurt, in being sick or in being a loser. Most of us repeat patterns of being victimized because as the victim we always receive a secondary gain. To explain why we haven't succeeded, we pretend we are the good ones that could have made it in life if only someone else had not messed it up. Hear your pleasure in why you can't do something. Statements like, "I wanted to do it, but my mother/father/wife/husband wouldn't let me, or my back was too sore, or I didn't have time because I have to work so much." These are all excuses that contain a lot of negative pleasure. Listen to yourself the next time you explain why you haven't done something. Are you in truth?

Why would we, as humans, behave this way? Let us look at the etiology of negative pleasure.

Negative pleasure is distorted natural or positive pleasure. Negative pleasure is based on separation. Positive pleasure is based on unity. It does not in any way separate you from others. Positive pleasure comes from your center or core. It flows from deep within and seeks to create. It flows with movement and energy which are pleasurable. Negative pleasure is created when the original creative impulse flowing with movement and energy from the core gets distorted or twisted and partially blocked in some

way. This happens primarily through early childhood experiences which are crystallized into our personalities. For example, a child reaches for the pretty bright red burner on the kitchen stove. The mother slaps away the hand before it is burned. The pleasure impulse is stopped. The child cries. The union of pain and pleasure begins in a way as simple as this.

There are many other much more complicated experiences in childhood that link the negative experience with pleasure. We are constantly being told we cannot be who we are, we cannot let our life force flow. Our choice is to opt for negative pleasure, because it is connected to the original life impulse. We still feel the life impulse. Even if the pleasure is negative, it is still life; it is better than no movement and no energy, which is death. Our distorted pleasure impulse becomes habitual as we grow up.

In a sense, each time we distort our pleasure impulse and do not allow ourselves to be who we are, we die a small death. The purification process is then to resurrect ourselves from each of those small deaths and to regain the full flowing pleasure of energy, movement and consciousness which enhances our creative force.

I spent the first two years of living at the Phoenicia Pathwork Center being meticulously honest with myself, finding and separating out the negative pleasure from the positive, finding just how I created the negative experiences in my life, and why. I looked for the faulty beliefs or misconceptions on which my actions were based.

Doing this will completely change your perspective of reality as it did for me. If you are, after all, responsible for creating negative experiences in your life, then you can change and create positive ones. It will work. It did for me, and old problems began to clear away.

## Divine Will

After two years of concentrating mostly on living by the truth as much as possible, I realized I was having trouble with my will. The way I used my will was creating problems in my life. It was unsteady. I would change my decisions about things. I found many levels of "wanting" or will issues inside. All of us have these. They are from the defended self and are often found in the will of the inner child, the teenager, or the young adult. Most of these wills are rather demanding. Our wills need to grow up. Deep inside of us there exists a spark of the Divine will, God's will. Many people experience Divine will as outside of themselves. This means they must always find someone else to tell them what to do. This leads to a feeling of worthlessness. I have found that a spark of Divine will exists within every human being. It is essential that you allow yourself time to search for it inside yourself until you find it. It is there, you are not the exception. What does it mean to follow God's will anyway? It certainly doesn't mean to follow God's will as defined by an outer authority. I decided to find out. I realized that I needed to align all the little wills inside with the spark of Divine will inside. I decided the best way to do this (for me) was to develop a positive use of my will by committing it to a daily practice.

I found a beautiful commitment from the Guide Lectures (lectures coming through the channel of Eva Pierrakos (1957–80), upon which the Pathwork is based). It stated:

> I commit myself to the will
>     of God.
> I give my heart and soul to God.
> I deserve the best in Life.
> I serve the best cause in Life.
> I am a divine manifestation
>     of God.

Each day, several times a day, I made this commitment. I did this every day for two years, until it became apparent to me that I was pretty good at finding the Divine will inside.

Emmanuel said, "Your will and God's will are the same . . . when something brings you joy and fulfillment, it is the will of God speaking through your own heart."

Examine your use of will. How much do you "should" yourself according to an external set of morals? How often do you listen and follow your heart's desire? As you align yourself with your Divine will, you may find it is time to concentrate on loving as I did.

## Love

Many of us have a very narrow view of what love is. As I spent the next two years concentrating on giving love in whatever way I could in whatever way it was needed, I found many forms of love, all of them saying: "I care for your well-being in any way I can"; "I honor your soul and respect your light"; "I support and trust your integrity and light as a fellow traveler along the way of life." You begin to learn that giving is receiving, is giving, is receiving.

The hardest is to learn self-love. If you do not infuse yourself with love, how can you give it to others? Self-love takes practice. We all need it. Self-love comes from living in ways that do not betray yourself. It comes by living by your truth.

Self-love needs to be practiced. Here are a couple of simple exercises that will challenge you.

Find the thing that is easiest for you to love, like a small flower, a tree, an animal or a work of art. Then simply sit with it and give it your precious love. After doing so a number of times, see if you can extend a bit of that precious love of yours to yourself. Anyone having such a precious gift as that love of yours is certainly worth loving.

Another exercise is to sit in front of the mirror for ten minutes and love that person that you see there. Do not be critical of her. We are all so good at looking in the mirror and finding every little flaw. That is not allowed here; only positive compliments are allowed in this exercise. If you want a real challenge, every time you criticize yourself, start all over. See if you can make it to ten minutes without one criticism.

## Faith

As I look back on it, after the completion of that six-year period, great changes had taken place within me. A great deal of the time, I was aligned with a strong faith in the benign abundance of the universe. You can do this too. By constantly trying to let go of your demanding will, align it with Divine will, to find the truth in any situation and to respond with love in that situation, you will develop faith—faith in yourself, faith in spiritual law, faith in the unity of the universe, faith that whatever happens in your life could be a stepping stone to greater understanding, love and growth, and ultimately self-purification toward the light of God.

Faith means carrying on with your truth when all the outer signs that come to you tell you that it couldn't possibly be true, but deep inside, you know it is. This does not mean blind belief. It means to keep aligned with your intent to become aware of and follow through with the truth and love as best you can, even though you feel terrible.

When he was on the cross, Christ had the faith to acknowledge that he no longer felt his faith. He exclaimed, "Father, why hast thou forsaken me?" He was being meticulously honest with himself. In that moment, he had lost his faith. He did not hide this fact or try to change it into something else. He loved himself by honestly expressing his dilemma. Later, he regained his faith when he stated, "Father, into your hands I commit my soul."

I have seen that people of a spiritual path go through stages of faith. At first they begin to learn the connections of cause and effect. They find that a positive belief and positive actions bring positive rewards. Their dreams begin to be fulfilled. They begin establishing faith within themselves. "It works!" They exclaim with delight. However, after a while, they are ready to test their faith from a deeper level. They are probably not aware of this inner decision to test themselves because that would change the nature of the test. What happens? All outer verification of the process of positive cause and effect seem to disappear from life for awhile. Things start going wrong. The positive feedback wanes, and the person begins to waver. The old pessimism rears its ugly head. Where is spiritual law? "Perhaps it was a Pollyannaish view of the universe after all." This will probably happen to you, too.

When this happens in your life, it is a sign of greater growth. You begin to deal with much longer-term cause and effect, both in your own life and ultimately in your own life as part of the evolution of the human race. The reward for living in truth becomes the pleasure of life in each moment you live it. No waiting for the spiritual goody. You are receiving it right now. Being in the here and now means accepting the slow process of human evolution, accepting your immediate limitations as perfection.

## Dealing with Time

Faith helped me deal with something I have always had trouble with: doing things in time. I once asked my Mom what was the thing she remembered me having the most trouble with when I was growing up. She said, "Whenever you wanted something, you had to have it right away."

In these past few years, I have been learning patience, and I am finally beginning to understand what it is about for me. Here is a thought that may work for you too. *Having patience is a direct statement of faith in the Divine plan.* It is the acceptance that everything is right for you as it is now, for you have created it this way. It means also that you can change what exists now through your own efforts of transformation. *Impatience ultimately means that you do not believe that you can create what you want. It means lack of faith in the self and the Divine plan.* It takes time to manifest what you wish on the physical plane. To help me accept that reality, I developed the following affirmation: "I want to honor my commitment to being on the physical plane by honoring the time that it takes to accomplish things here." The apparent slowness between cause and effect that is built into this plane is here for a reason. We need to be able to see clearly the cause and effect connections in relationships that we do not understand. These relationships are ultimately between parts of ourselves that are not yet unified.

## Power

At one point in my training in healing, I had a sudden increase in the power flowing through my hands. It came with what appeared to me to be a new set of guides. I was working on a person's infected toe. I would hold my hands a certain way, which would send very strong blue-silver light streaking through the toe. My hands were about one inch away from the toe. The patient would cry out in pain when I did this because of the increased energy flow. When I moved my hands differently, I could make a soft white cloudy energy come out of my hands. This would take all the pain away. The guides kept directing me to switch between the two. I was tired, and every fifteen minutes or so the guides directed me to go to work on this woman. There seemed to be an urgency about it. The results of the little healings were powerful. No infection, and no need to operate. I was ecstatic, and told my healing teacher. I said, "C., there was so much power flowing through me!" Her answer was, "Well, that is it; do you want to heal with love or with power?" I decided I was not ready to have that much power flowing through me. I enjoyed it too much in a "Wow! Look at me!" kind of way. I sent the guides away. I didn't work with them until two years later. Then I was ready. I had learned a great deal more about love. Later I understood that it was the spiritual surgeons from the fifth level who were working with me.

Faith based on truth, Divine will, and love brings power. Power that stems from deep within the individual, from the Divine spark within. Power is the result of aligning with, connecting to, and allowing the Divine spark of life within to flow. It comes from the core of the individual, or what my guide Heyoan calls the Holy of Holies. Having power means to be seated within the center of one's being.

Power brings you the ability to be in and to practice unconditional love. This means returning all that comes to you with love, without betraying the self. You can only do this by loving yourself first and being in truth. That means being honest with yourself as to what you feel, and committing yourself to move through that place to another place of loving. You see, if you deny the negative reactions you have by pushing them down, you are not loving yourself or others. If you feel and acknowledge them in some way, you then make room for your love to flow. You release yourself to move to a loving place inside. Unconditional love allows the action of grace in our lives.

## Grace

With the practices of Truth, Divine will and Love leading to Faith which leads to power, we make room for the action of Grace to come into our life. Grace is received by letting go to Divine Wisdom and is experienced as Bliss. It is experiencing the unity in all things and our complete safety no matter what happens. It is the state of knowing that every experience we have, including pleasurable and painful experiences like illness and death are simply lessons we create for ourselves along the pathway back home to God. It is living in synchronicity. Emmanuel said,

> The state of Grace
> needs the recipient
> in order to be complete.
>
> You are held in the hand of God
> and totally loved.
> And when that love can
>     be received
> the circuit is completed.

## Who Is Healed?

The healer must remember that it is the healing of the soul that we are working for. It is important for healers to understand death in this way and to treat the whole person, not just this incarnation of the person. The healer must not give up healing someone simply because he may be physically dying.

It is important to keep two things in mind when we are trying to understand just what we are doing as healers. One is that there is deep meaning in each person's experience of his illness, and two is that death does not imply failure, but probably healing. In order to remember this, the healer must live in two worlds, the spiritual and the physical. It is only by being centered within herself and the universe that she can go through the experiences of continually witnessing the deep pain that is so widespread in humanity. I asked my friend Emmanuel about this with the following question: "If we create our illness, isn't going to a healer a way to distract us from working on ourselves, working on the source of the disease?"

Emmanual said, "That all depends on why you go to the healer, and which healer you go to. That is an excellent question, and one, may I dare say, that our healer has asked herself a lot. What is the responsibility and, therefore, what is to be given and what is to be received, and if something is envisioned, is it to be said? The questions never end, and yet there is a basic fundamental reality that should give you comfort. When there is the moment of realization that perhaps there is another mode of healing, then already a door has been opened, already the consciousness has reached beyond the physically manifested available medical care. Now, I am not in any way degrading the medical profession. Doctors do excellent work; some are most guided and would be free to admit it to you behind closed doors. There are others who, whether they be in the medical profession or another form of making a living, simply are not aware and are not at this point able to be aware. This does not mean that they are mean, cruel, vicious or evil; it simply means that they have yet to come into the area of knowing. It behooves you to be willing to bless them and go on your way and find someone who feels more compatible with your consciousness, and you all know how to do that. When you find the calling to move into the area of spiritual healing (I do not say psychic healing; I say spiritual healing), then there is the awareness of spirit, and you are welcomed by the healer and the spirits who are there to work with that healer. Now often there is not the healing that is expected. Often there is, perhaps, identification and easing of discomfort, but no miracle. Well, what does that mean? It means that is as far as your consciousness will go at that point. It means that there is something else to learn; there is something else to know. For every physical body is a schoolroom, and every disease is a lesson. Not in a punitive way, for you have written your own text; you

have chosen your own bodies that carry with them all of the weaknesses that, yes, may be said are genetic because your grandmother or grandfather had something. But remember you chose them as well. So you need to trust your body not only in illness, but especially in illness, for what is it saying to you? There are many ways of hearing this, and a qualified spiritual healer can be most effective there, to help you hear what it is that your body is saying to you. Certainly you are the one who is able best to understand it for it is within your language that your body has been formed, and it is to you, directly, that it is speaking. But a spiritual healer can alter that consciousness to the oneness again and can bring you into alignment with the truth. Whether you are able to sustain that truth or whether you are able to heal an ailing body at that moment depends on so many factors that I could not even begin to enumerate them now. But you, yourselves, are perfectly capable of doing that. If there is, ultimately, what in your human terms is a failure—if someone would, heaven forbid, die—then you must see it all as a blessed event. That soul has completed its task, and there is a great and joyous welcoming committee greeting it in the primary reality. After all, your physical being was not meant to be infinite. You are not here to sit in these clothes forever. I hope that pleases you. Therefore, there are no failures in spiritual healing; there are only steps. Never be afraid to put your hand on another with love and compassion. Never hesitate to pray for someone. Do not demand results, for there is no way of knowing for sure what a particular soul requires. I understand that this demands, or seems to demand, an incredible amount of faith. Yes, it does."

As the body and mind become more purified through the transformative processes described in this book, the amount of power flowing through the healer increases and so does the range of vibrations. The higher the power, the more effective the healing, and the more sensitive the healer.

Each time I have been given new insight and power, this insight came after a self-initiated test.

To go through such tests, one must be meticulously honest with the self. It is in the little self-delusions where we tend to avoid looking at our own lower self's intent or actions that we betray our integrity and decrease our power from within. Each test is related to whatever issues we are dealing with in our lives at the present time; we design our tests well, so that when we have learned, there is no question about graduation.

## Exercises to Find Your Readiness to Be a Healer

How truthful am I? How well do I use my will in alignment with the universal will? How do I use power? How well do I love? Can I give unconditional love? Do I respect the authority of those to whom I have chosen to give authority in order to learn from them? Can I do this without selling out my own inner authority? How do I betray my integrity? What is it that I long for? What do I wish to create in my life? What are my limitations as a woman, as a man, as a human being, as a healer? Do I respect the integrity, the personal power, the will and the choices of my patients? Do I see myself as a channel that evokes the power from within the patient so that they are healing themselves ultimately? What is my personal stake in having someone get well? Do I see death as a failure?

## Exercise to Consider the Nature of Healing

> What is a healer?
> What is a healing?
> What is the main purpose of
>   a healing?
> What is giving a healing?
> Who heals?
> Who is healed?

Heyoan has recently said, "Now, dear reader, do not set judgment upon yourself from the above questions. We are all walking a path of purification, and love is the most healing agent of all. Do not reject yourself, saying you can never do all of this. You can and you will. It is simply a matter of accepting where and who you are now as perfect in your imperfections. We of the spirit world hold you in great honor and respect. You have chosen to become physical beings as a great gift not only to yourselves, but to the physically manifest universe as well. Your personal changes toward health and wholeness affect those around you, not only those within your immediacy but all those sentient beings upon the face of the earth; indeed the earth herself. You are all children of the earth. You are of her; she is of you. Never forget that, for as we move more and more into planetary consciousness in the near future, you will become leaders of this great adventure into the light. Above all, love and honor yourselves as we honor you. After all we are in the presence of the Divine when we are with you. You are fully held in the arms of God and loved. Know this, and you shall be home free."

When you understand that life is experienced as a pulsation, you expand and feel joyous, you move into the silence of peace, and then you contract. Many people experience that contraction as negative. Many of you will experience wonderous joy, like being in the company of angels during a workshop, or a healing. So will the patient. But remember, by the very nature of the expanded high energy state, you will later contract, and feel more of the separated consciousness that is inside of you. The sheer force and intensity of the spiritual energy knocks loose and begins to enlighten the stagnated dark soul substance. As it comes back to life again, you experience it as real. All of its pain, anger, and agony. You may say to yourself. "Why now I'm worse than I was before I started." Let me assure you that this not true. You are more sensitive. After experiencing these ups and downs, these expansions and contractions many times for each personal issue, you will find that they do clear away. Months later you will say, "Wow! I don't do that any more." And you will weep with joy, just as you did the first several times you came back into and experienced the light. Remember, patience is the word of faith.

# Chapter 27 Review

1. What are the main personal attributes a healer must develop to remain clear?
2. What are life tests all about?

## Food For Thought

3. What has your personal process of purification been to bring you to where you are now on your path?
4. Are you ready to be a healer? On what levels?
5. In what area of your being would you be most likely to misuse the power you have as a healer? What is your lower self or shadow self intent there? Upon what erroneous belief is that intent based? How can you heal that part of yourself, and realign yourself with your inner Divine will?
6. Answer the questions under the heading "Exercise to Find Your Fears."
7. Answer the questions under the heading "Exercise to Find Your Negative Beliefs."
8. Do the self love exercise under the heading "Love."
9. Answer the questions under the heading "Exercise to Find Your Readiness to Be a Healer."

# Bibliography

Allen R., "Studies into Human Energy Fields Promises Better Drug Diagnosis," **Electronic Design News**, April 1974, Vol. 17, pp.

Anderson, Lynn, **The Medicine Woman**. New York, Harper & Row, 1982.

Anonymous, **Etheric Vision and What It Reveals**. Oceanside, Calif., The Rosicrucian Fellowship, 1965.

Anonymous, **Some Unrecognized Factors in Medicine**. London, Theosophical Publishing House, 1939.

Bagnall, O., **The Origins and Properties of the Human Aura**. New York, University Books, Inc., 1970.

Bailey, A. A., **Esoteric Healing**. London, Lucis Press, Ltd., 1972.

Becker, R. O., Bachman, C., and Friedman, H., "The Direct Current Control System," **New York State Journal of Medicine**, April 15, 1962, pp.

Beesely, R. P., **The Robe of Many Colours**. Kent, The College of Psycho-therapeutics, 1969.

Bendit, P. D., and Bendit, L. J., **Man Incarnate**. London, Theosophical Publishing House, 1957.

Bentov, I., **Stalking the Wild Pendulum**. New York, Bantam Books, 1977.

Besant, A., and Leadbeater, C. W., **Thought-Forms**. Weaton, Ill., Theosophical Publishing House, 1971.

Blavatsky, H. P., **The Secret Doctrine**. Wheaton, Ill., Theosophical Publishing House, 1888.

Bohm, David, **The Implicate Order**. London, Routledge & Kegan Paul, 1981.

Brennan, B., **Function of the Human Energy Field in the Dynamic Process of Health, Health and Disease**. New York, Institute for the New Age, 1980.

Bruyere, Rosalyn, Personal Communication. Glendale, Calif. Healing Light Center, 1983.

Bruyere, Rosalyn, **Wheels of Light**. Glendale, Calif., Healing Light Center, 1987.

Burks, A. J., **The Aura**. Lakemont, Georgia, CSA Printers & Publishers, 1962.

Burr, H. S., Musselman, L. K., Barton, D. S., and Kelly, N. B., "Bioelectric Correlates of Human Ovulation". **Yale Journal of Biology and Medicine**, 1937, Vol. 10, pp. 155-160.

Burr, H. S., and Lane, C. T., "Electrical Characteristics of Living Systems." **Yale Journal of Biology and Medicine**, 1935, Vol. 8, pp. 31-35.

Burr, H. S., "Electrometrics of Atypical Growth." **Yale Journal of Biology and Medicine**, 1952, Vol. 25, pp. 67-75.

Burr, H. S., and Northrop, F. S. G., "The Electro-Dynamic Theory of Life." **Quarterly Review of Biology**, 1935, Vol. 10, pp. 322-333.

Burr. H. S., and Northrop, F. S. G., "Evidence for the Existence of an Electrodynamic Field in the Living Organisms." **Proceedings of the National Academy of Sciences of the United States of America**, 1939, Vol. 24, pp. 284-288.

Burr, H. S., **The Fields of Life: Our Links with the Universe**. New York, Ballantine Books, 1972.

Burr, H. S., "The Meaning of Bio-Electric Potentials." **Yale Journal of Biology and Medicine**, 1944, Vol. 16, pp. 353-360.

Butler, W. E., **How to Read the Aura**, New York, Samuel Weiser, Inc., 1971.

Capra, Fritjof, **The Tao of Physics**. Berkeley, Shambhala, 1975.

Cayce, Edgar, **Auras**. Virginia Beach, Virginia, ARE Press, 1945.

Cohen, Dr. David, Interview with **The New York Times**, April 20, 1980.

De La Warr, G., **Matter in the Making**. London, Vincent Stuart Ltd., 1966.

Dobrin, R., Conaway (Brennan), B., and Pierrakos, J., "Instrumental Measurements of the Human Energy Field." New York, Institute for the New Age, 1978. Presented at "Electro '78, IEEE Annual Conference, Boston, May 23-25, 1978.

Dobrin, R., and Conaway (Brennan) B., "New Electronic Methods for Medical Diagnosis and Treatment Using the Human Energy Field." Presented at Electro '78, IEEE Conference, Boston, May 23-25, 1978.

Dumitrescu, I., "Electronography." Electronography Lab, Romania. Presented at Electro '78, IEEE Annual Conference, Boston, May 23-25, 1978.

Eddington, Arthur, **The Philosophy of Physical Science**. Ann Arbor, University of Michigan Press, 1958.

Emmanuel, Quote from a guide coming through my friend, Pat Rodegast, during a workshop we were running at the Phoenicia Pathwork Center, Phoenicia, New York, July 1983.

"Experimental Measurements of the Human Energy Field." Energy Research Group, New York, 1973.

"High Frequency Model for Kirlian Photography." Energy Research Group, New York, 1973.

Gerber, J., **Communication with the Spirit World of God**. Teaneck, New Jersey, Johannes Gerber Memorial Foundation, 1979.

Hodson, G., **Music Forms**. London, The Theosophical Publishing House, 1976.

Hunt, Dr. Valorie, Massey, W., Weinberg, R., Bruyere, R., and Hahn, P., "Project Report, A Study of Structural Integration from Neuromuscular, Energy Field, and Emotional Approaches." U.C.L.A., 1977.

Inyushin, V. M., and Chekorov, P. R., "Biostimulation Through Laser Radiation of Bioplasma." Kazakh State University, USSR. Translated by Hill and Ghosak, University of Copenhagen, 1975.

Inyushin, V. M., "On the Problem of Recording the Human Biofield." **Parapsychology in the USSR, Part II**, San Francisco, Calif., Washington Research Center, 1981.

Inyushin, V. M., Seminar paper, Alma-Ata, USSR, 1969.

Jaffe, Dr. Lionel, Interview with **The New York Times**, April 20, 1980.

Karagulla, Schafica, **Breakthrough to Creativity**. Los Angeles, De Vorss, 1967.

Kilner, Walter J., M.D., **The Human Aura**. (retitled and new edition of **The Human Atmosphere**) New Hyde Park, New York, University Books, 1965.

Krieger, D., **The Therapeutic Touch**. Englewood Cliffs, N.J., Prentice-Hall, 1979.

Krippner, S., and Ruhin, D., (eds.), **The Energies of Consciousness**. New York, Gordon and Breach, 1975.

Kunz, Dora, and Peper, Erik, "Fields and Their Clinical Implications." **The American Theosophist**, December 1982, pp.   .

Leadbeater, C. W., **The Chakras**. London, Theosophical Publishing House, 1974.

Leadbeater, C. W., **The Science of the Sacraments**. London, Theosophical Publishing House, 1975.

Leibnitz, Gottfreid, **Monadology and Other Philosophical Essays**. trans. by Paul Schrecker and Ann Schrecker. Indianapolis, Bobbs-Merrill, 1965.

Le Shan, L., **The Medium, the Mystic, and the Physicist**. New York, Ballantine Books, 1966.

Lowen, A., **Physical Dynamics of Character Structure**. New York, Grune & Stratton, 1958.

Mann, W. E., **Orgone, Reich and Eros**. New York, Simon & Schuster, 1973.

Meek, G., **Healers and the Healing Process**. London, Theosophical Publishing House, 1977.

Mesmer, F. A., **Mesmerism**. trans. by V. R. Myers. London, Macdonald, 1948.

Moss, T., **Probability of the Impossible: Scientific Discoveries and Explorations in the Psychic World**. Los Angeles, J. P. Tarcher, 1974.

Motoyama, Dr. Hiroshi, **The Functional Relationship Between Yoga Asanas and Acupuncture Meridians**. Tokyo, Japan, I.A.R.P., 1979.

Murphy, Pat and Jim, "Murphy's Theories, The Practical and the Psychic." Healing Light Center, Glendale, Calif., 1980.

Mylonas, Elizabeth, **A Basic Working Manual and Workbook for Helpers and Workers**. Phoenicia Pathwork Center, Phoenicia, New York, 1981.

Niel, A., **Magic and Mystery in Tibet**. Dover, New York, 1971.

Ostrander, S., and Schroeder, L., **Psychic Discoveries Behind the Iron Curtain**. Englewood Cliffs, N.J., Prentice-Hall, 1970.

Pachter, Henry M., **Paracelsus: Magic Into Science**. New York, Henry Schuman, 1951.

Pierrakos, Eva, **Guide Lectures, 1–258**. New York, Center for the Living Force, 1956–1979.

Pierrakos, John C., **The Case of the Broken Heart**. New York, Institute for the New Age, 1975. (Monograph).

Pierrakos, John C., **The Core Energetic Process**. New York, Institute for the New Age, 1977. (Monograph).

Pierrakos, John C., **The Core Energetic Process in Group Therapy**. New York, Institute for the New Age, 1975. (Monograph).

Pierrakos, John C., **The Energy Field in Man and Nature**. New York, Institute for the New Age, 1975. (Monograph).

Pierrakos, John C., **Human Energy Systems Theory**. New York, Institute for the New Age, 1975. (Monograph).

Pierrakos, John C., **Life Functions of the Energy Centers of Man**. New York, Institute for the New Age, 1975. (Monograph).

Pierrakos, John C., and Brennan, B., Personal Communication, 1980.

Powell, A. E., **The Astral Body**. London, Theosophical Publishing House, 1972.

Powell, A. E., **The Causal Body**. London, Theosophical Publishing House, 1972.

Powell, A. E., **The Etheric Double**. London, Theosophical Publishing House, 1973.

Ravitz, L. J., "Application of the Electrodynamic Field Theory in Biology, Psychiatry, Medicine and Hypnosis, I. General Survey." **Am. Journal of Clin. Hypnosis**, 1959, Vol. 1, pp. 135–150.

Ravitz, L. J., "Bioelectric Correlates of Emotional States." **Conn. State Medical Journal**, 1952, Vol. 16, pp. 499–505.

Ravitz, L. J., "Daily Variations of Standing Potential Differences in Human Subjects." **Yale Journal of Biology and Medicine**, 1951, Vol. 24, pp. 22–25.

Ravitz, L. J., **The Use of DC Measurements in Psychiatric Neuropsychiatry**, Fall 1951, Vol. 1, pp. 3–12.

Reich, Wilhelm, **Character Analysis**. London, Vision Press, 1950.

Reich, Wilhelm, **The Cancer Biopathy**. New York, Farrar, Straus, and Giroux, 1973.

Reich, Wilhelm, **The Discovery of the Orgone, Vol. I, The Function of the Orgasm**. trans. by Theodore P. Wolfe, New York, Orgone Institute Press, 1942. 2nd ed., New York, Farrar, Straus, and Giroux, 1961.

Reich, Wilhelm, **The Discovery of the Orgone, Vol. II, The Cancer Biopathy**. trans. by Theodore P. Wolfe, New York, Orgone Institute Press, 1948.

Roberts, J., **The Nature of Personal Reality**. New York, Bantam, 1974.

Rodegast, Pat, and Stanton, Judith, "Emmanuel's Book," Some Friends of Emmanuel, New York, 1985.

Rongliang, Dr. Zheng, "Scientific Research of Qigong." Lanzhou University, People's Republic of China, 1982.

Sarfatti, J., "Reply to Bohm-Hiley," **Psychoenergetic Systems**. London, Gordon & Breach, Vol. 2, 1976, pp. 1–8.

Schwarz, Jack, **The Human Energy Systems**. New York, Dutton, 1980.

Schwarz, Jack, **Voluntary Controls**. New York, Dutton, 1978.

Steiner, Rudolf, **The Philosophy of Spiritual Activity**. Blauvelt, New York, Steiner Books, 1980.

Surgue, T., **There is a River. The Story of Edgar Cayce**. Virginia Beach, Virginia, ARE Press, 1957.

Tansely, D. V., **Radionics and the Subtle Anatomy of Man**. Devon, England, Health Science Press, 1972.

Tansely, D. V., **Radionics Interface with the Ether-Fields**. Devon, England, Health Science Press, 1975.

Targ, Russell, and Harary, Keith, **The Mind Race**. New York, Ballantine, 1984.

Vithoulkas, G., **Homeopathy, Medicine of the New Man**. New York, Avon Books, 1971.

Vladimirov, Y. A., **Ultraweak Luminescence Accompanying Biochemical Reactions**. USSR Academy of Biological Sciences, Izdatelstvo "Nauka," Moscow.

Von Reichenbach, C., **Physico-physiological Researches on the Dynamics of Magnetism, Electricity, Heat, Light, Crystallization, and Chemism, In Their Relation to Vital Force**. New York, Clinton-Hall, 1851.

Westlake, A., **The Pattern of Health**. Berkeley, Shambhala, 1973.

White, John, and Krippner, S., **Future Science**. New York, Anchor Books, 1977.

White, John, **Kundalini, Evolution and Enlightenment**. New York, Anchor Books, 1979.

Wilhelm, Richard., **The Secret of the Golden Flower**. New York, Harcourt, Brace & World, Inc., 1962.

Williamson, Dr. Samuel, Personal Communication. New York, 1982.

Zukav, Gary, **The Dancing Wu Li Masters**. New York, William Morrow & Co., 1979.